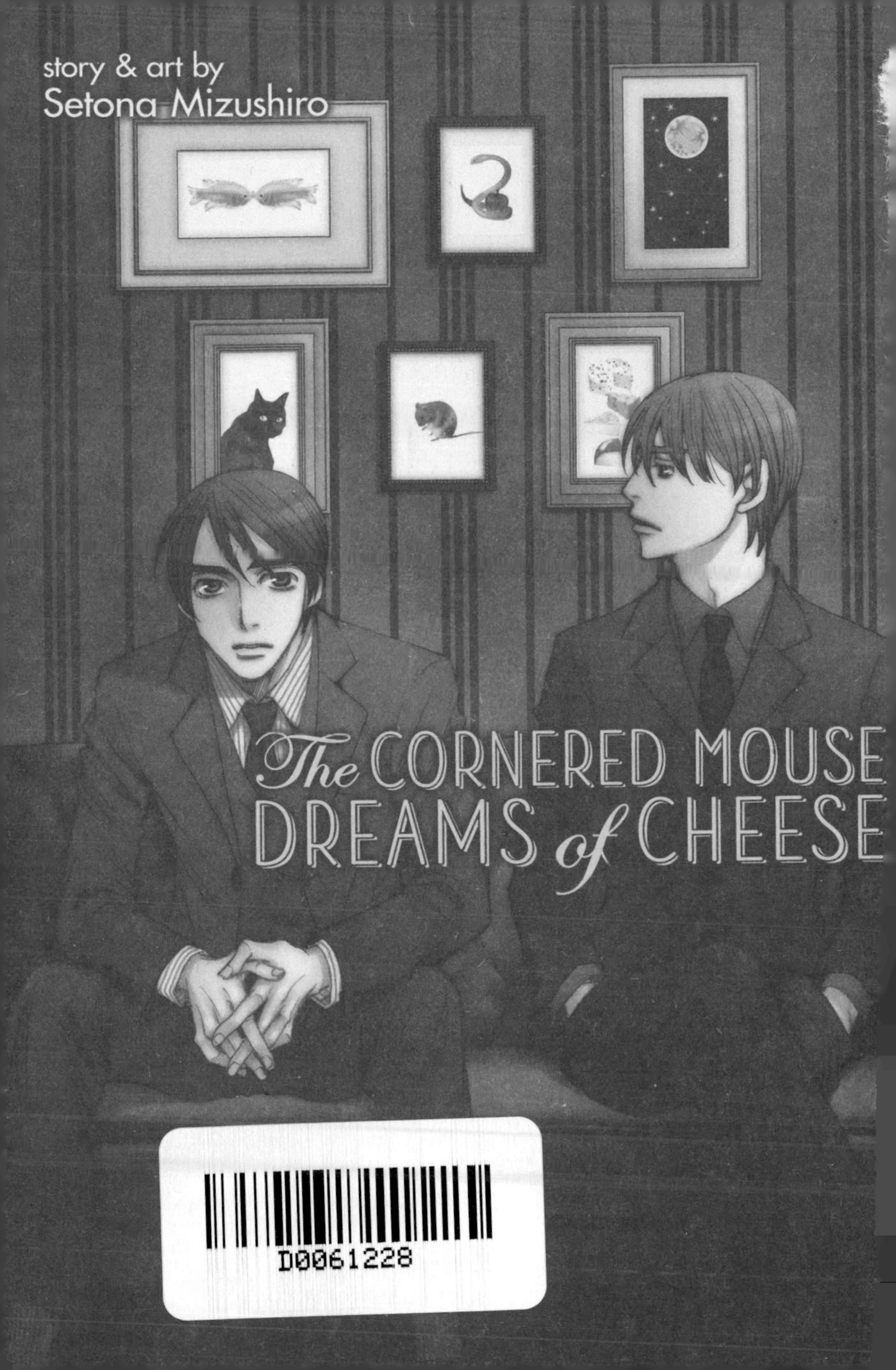
story & art by
Setona Mizushiro
The CORNERED MOUSE
DREAMS of CHEESE

The CORNERED MOUSE DREAMS of CHEESE

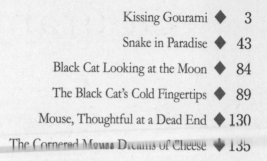

CONTENTS

Kissing Gourami

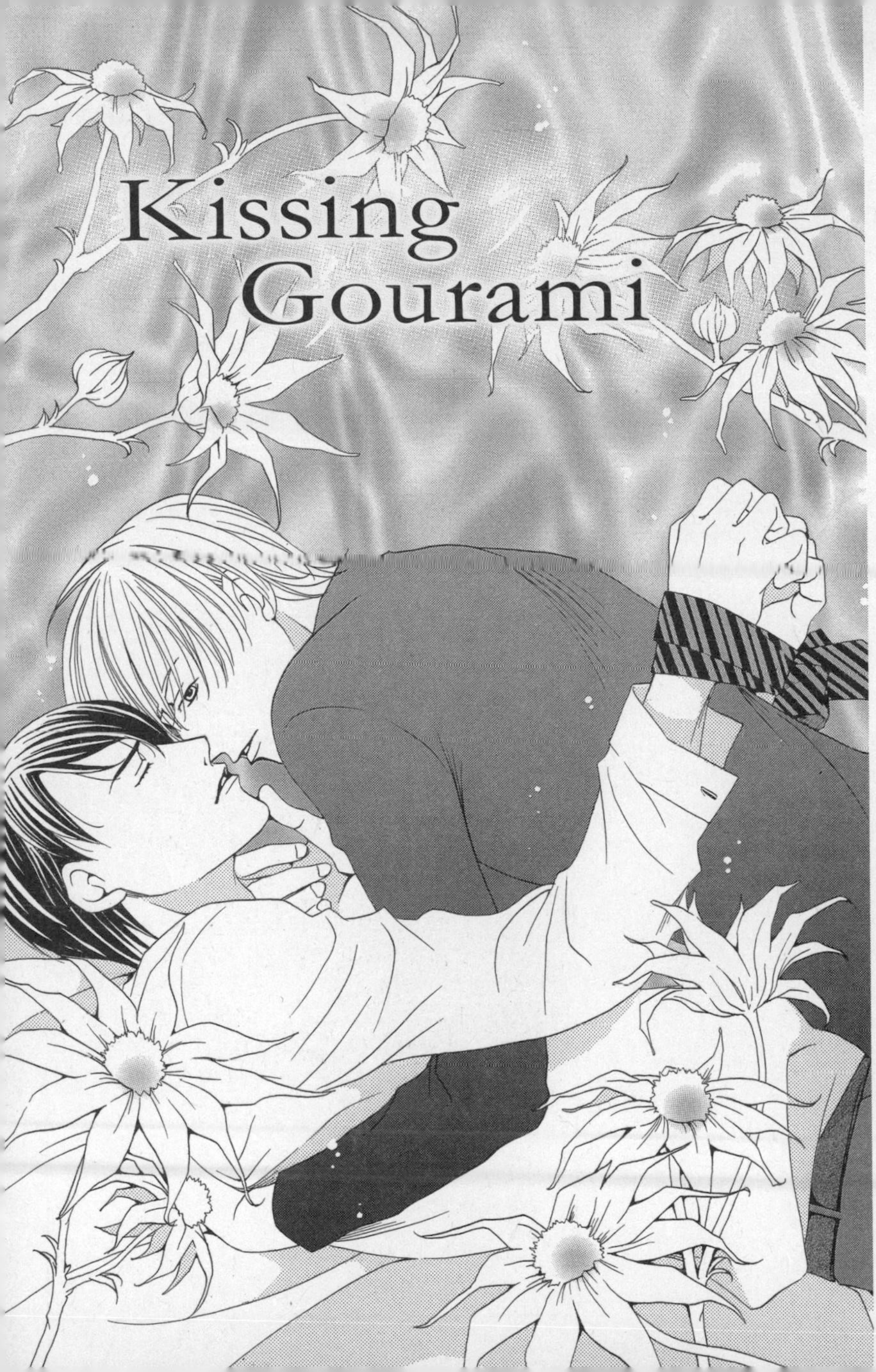

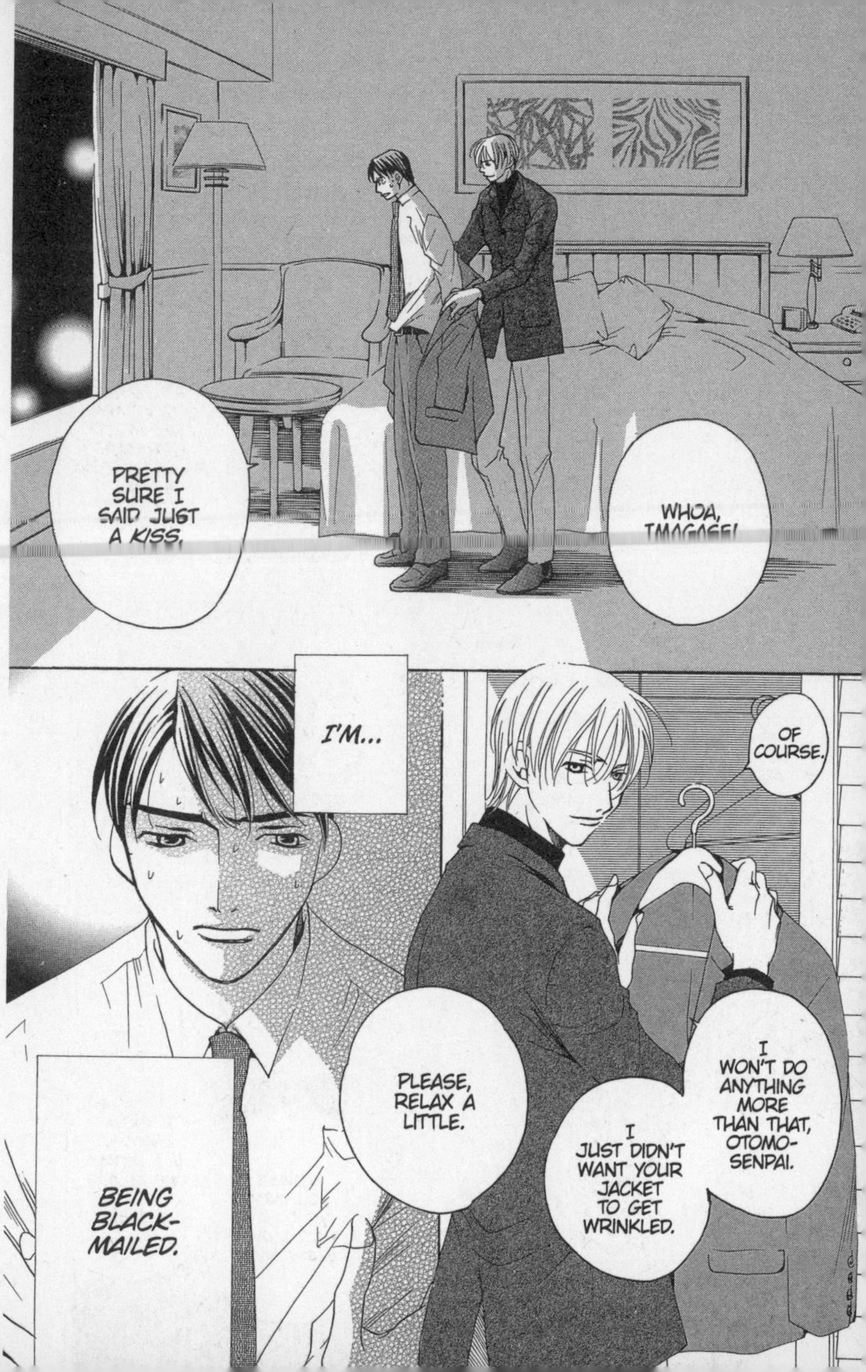
WHOA, IMAGASE!
PRETTY SURE I SAID JUST A *KISS*.
OF COURSE.
I WON'T DO ANYTHING MORE THAN THAT, OTOMO-SENPAI.
I JUST DIDN'T WANT YOUR JACKET TO GET WRINKLED.
PLEASE, RELAX A LITTLE.
I'M...
BEING BLACK-MAILED.

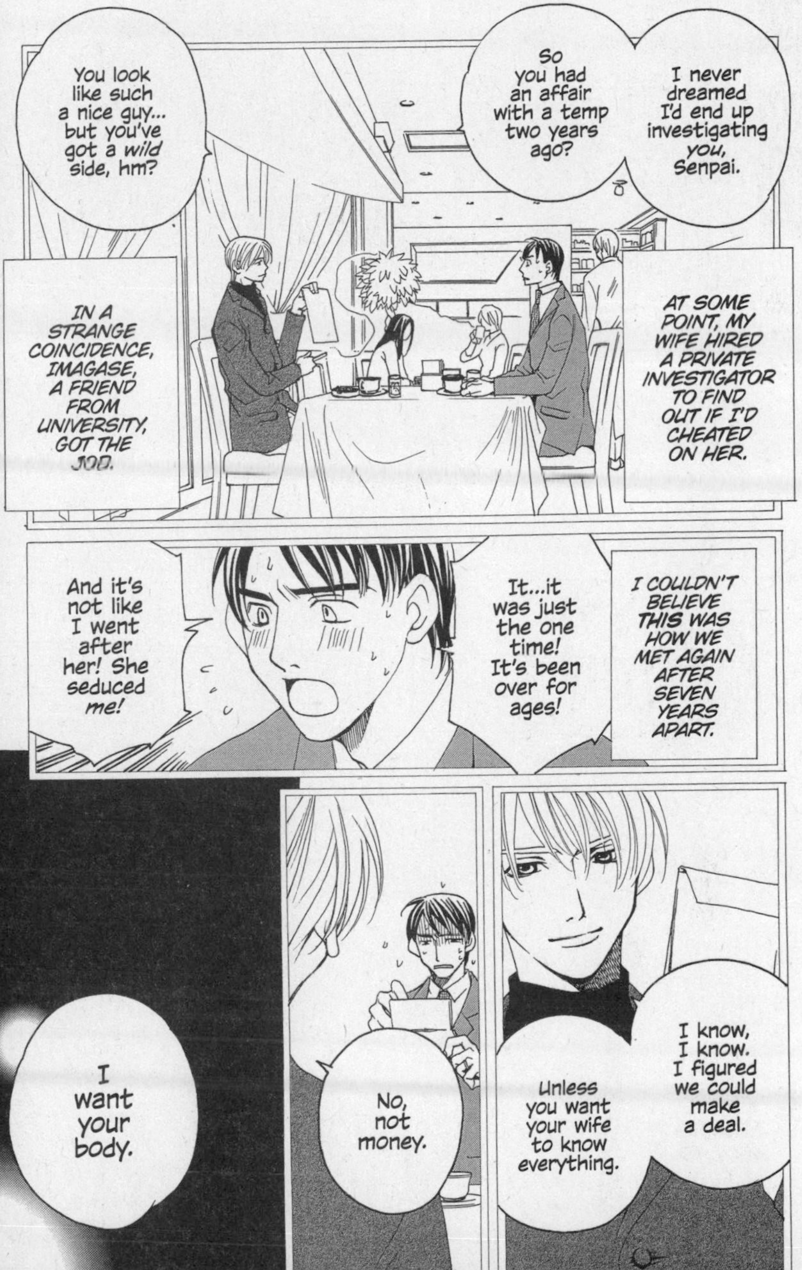
I never dreamed I'd end up investigating you, Senpai.
So you had an affair with a temp two years ago?
AT SOME POINT, MY WIFE HIRED A PRIVATE INVESTIGATOR TO FIND OUT IF I'D CHEATED ON HER.
You look like such a nice guy... but you've got a *wild* side, hm?
IN A STRANGE COINCIDENCE, IMAGASE, A FRIEND FROM UNIVERSITY, GOT THE JOB.
I COULDN'T BELIEVE THIS WAS HOW WE MET AGAIN AFTER SEVEN YEARS APART.
It...it was just the one time! It's been over for ages!
And it's not like I went after her! She seduced me!
I know, I know. I figured we could make a deal.
Unless you want your wife to know everything.
No, not money.
I want your body.

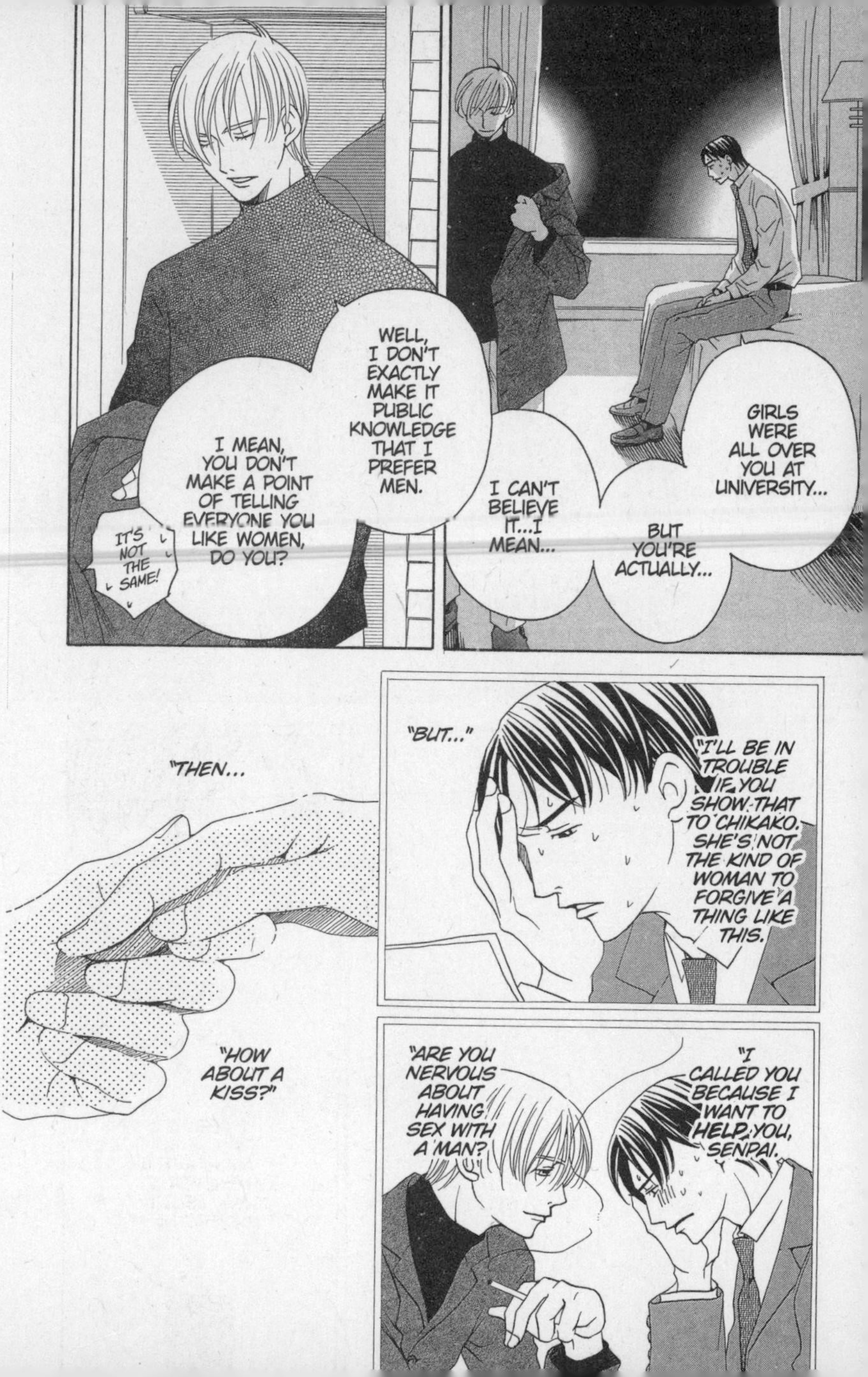
GIRLS WERE ALL OVER YOU AT UNIVERSITY...
BUT YOU'RE ACTUALLY...
I CAN'T BELIEVE IT...I MEAN...
WELL, I DON'T EXACTLY MAKE IT PUBLIC KNOWLEDGE THAT I PREFER MEN.
I MEAN, YOU DON'T MAKE A POINT OF TELLING EVERYONE YOU LIKE WOMEN, DO YOU?
IT'S NOT THE SAME!
"BUT..."
"I'LL BE IN TROUBLE IF YOU SHOW THAT TO CHIKAKO. SHE'S NOT THE KIND OF WOMAN TO FORGIVE A THING LIKE THIS.
"I CALLED YOU BECAUSE I WANT TO HELP YOU, SENPAI.
"ARE YOU NERVOUS ABOUT HAVING SEX WITH A MAN?
"THEN...
"HOW ABOUT A KISS?"

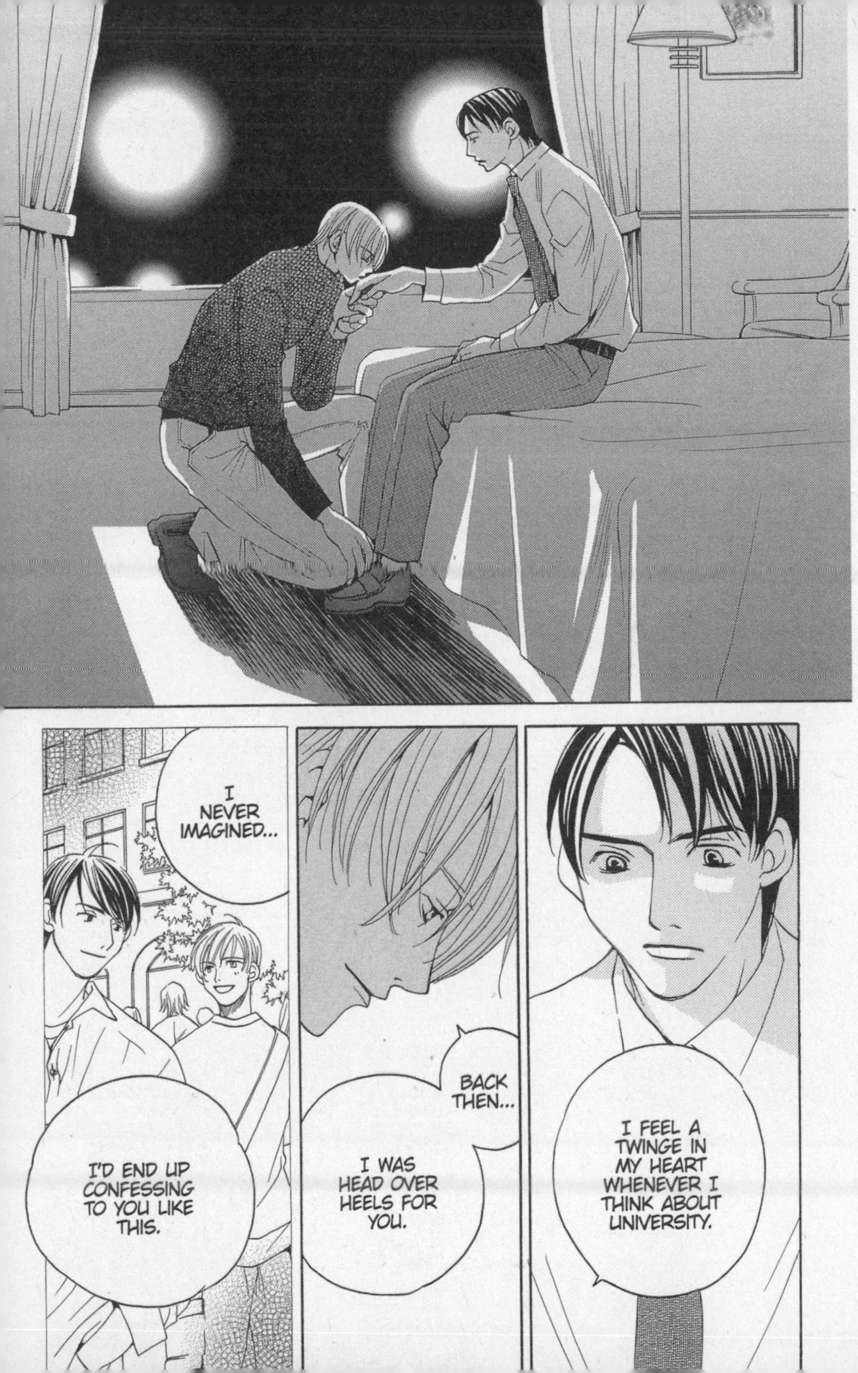
I FEEL A TWINGE IN MY HEART WHENEVER I THINK ABOUT UNIVERSITY.
BACK THEN...
I WAS HEAD OVER HEELS FOR YOU.
I NEVER IMAGINED...
I'D END UP CONFESSING TO YOU LIKE THIS.

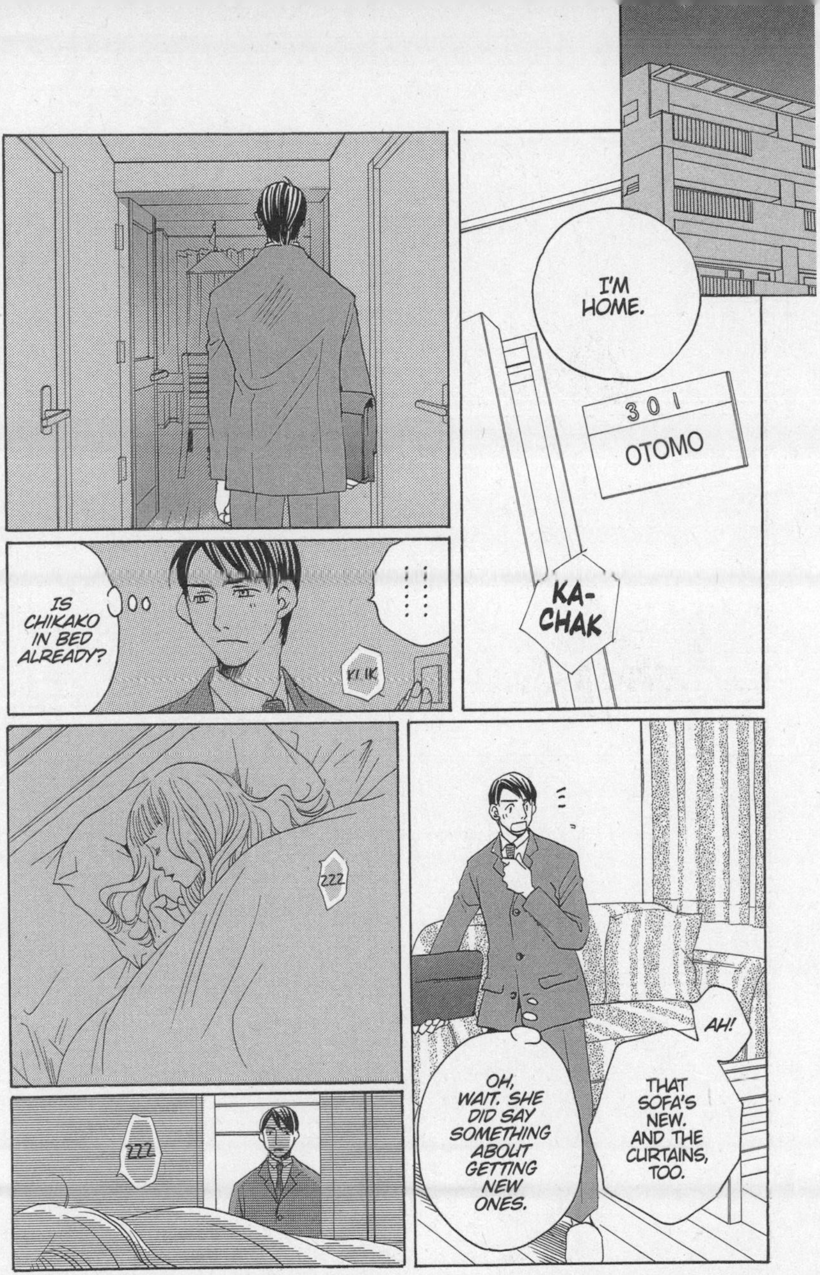

I'M HOME.
301
OTOMO
KA-CHAK
......
IS CHIKAKO IN BED ALREADY?
KLIK
AH!
THAT SOFA'S NEW. AND THE CURTAINS, TOO.
OH, WAIT. SHE DID SAY SOMETHING ABOUT GETTING NEW ONES.
ZZZ
ZZZ

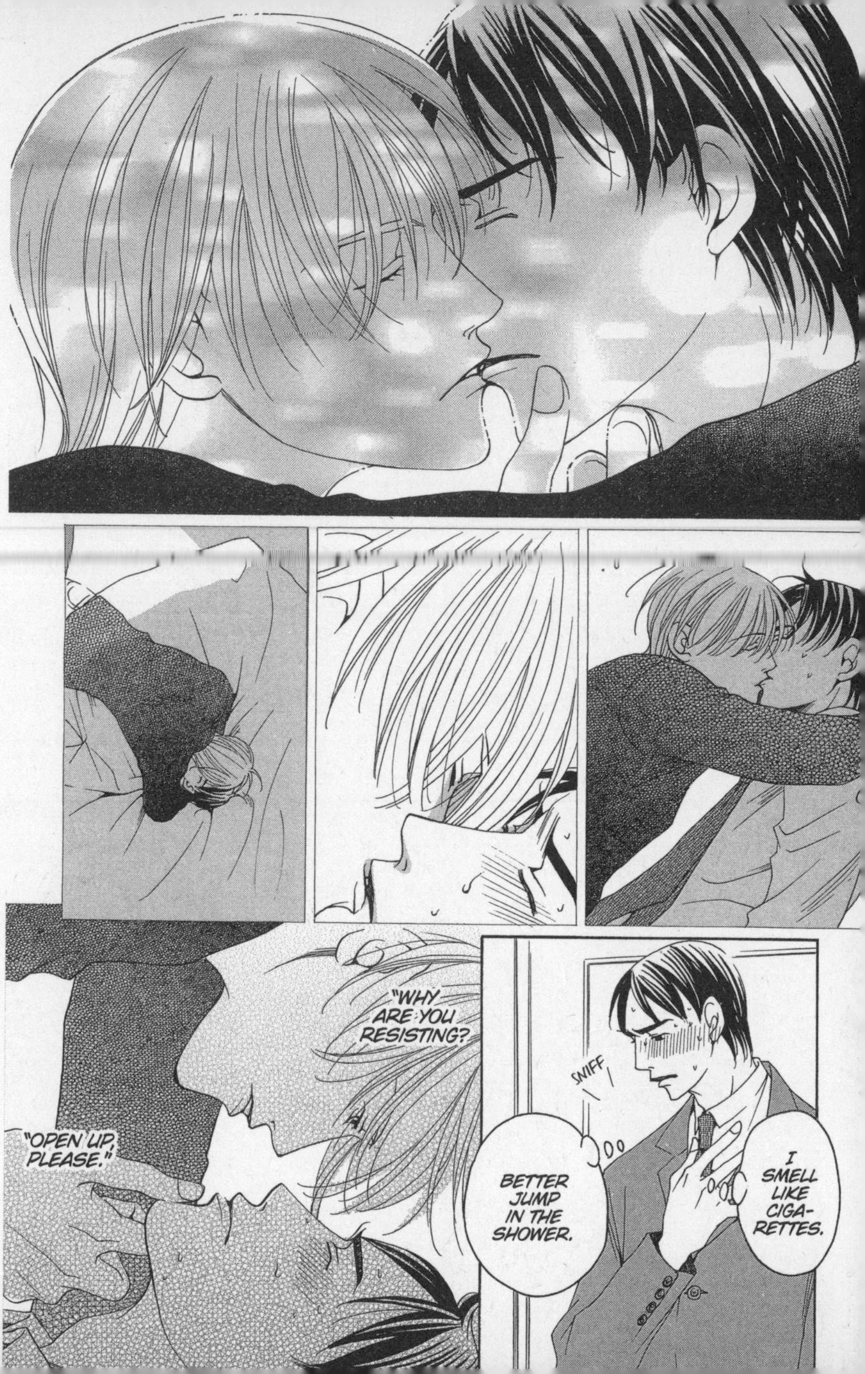
SNIFF
I SMELL LIKE CIGA-RETTES.
BETTER JUMP IN THE SHOWER.
"WHY ARE YOU RESISTING?
"OPEN UP, PLEASE."

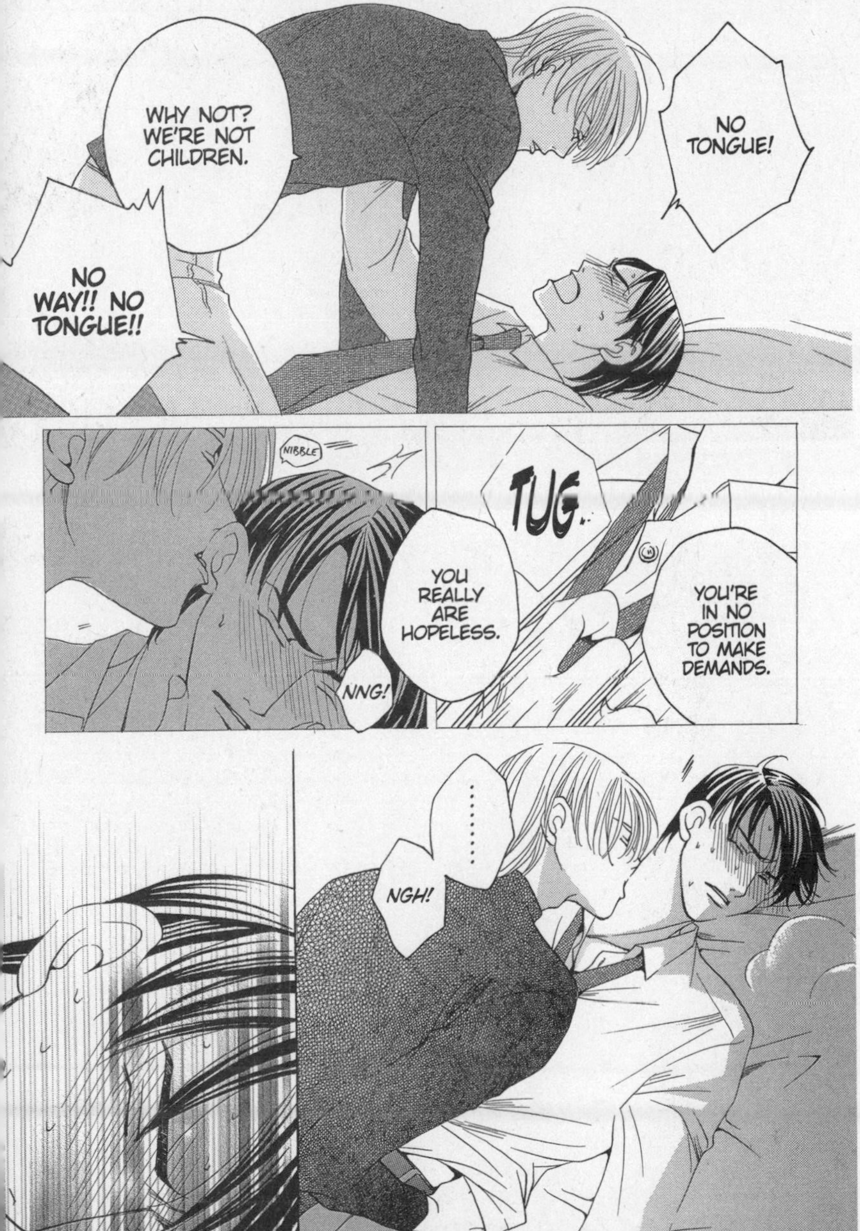
NO TONGUE!
WHY NOT? WE'RE NOT CHILDREN.
NO WAY!! NO TONGUE!!
TUG...
YOU'RE IN NO POSITION TO MAKE DEMANDS.
NIBBLE
YOU REALLY ARE HOPELESS.
NNG!
......
NGH!

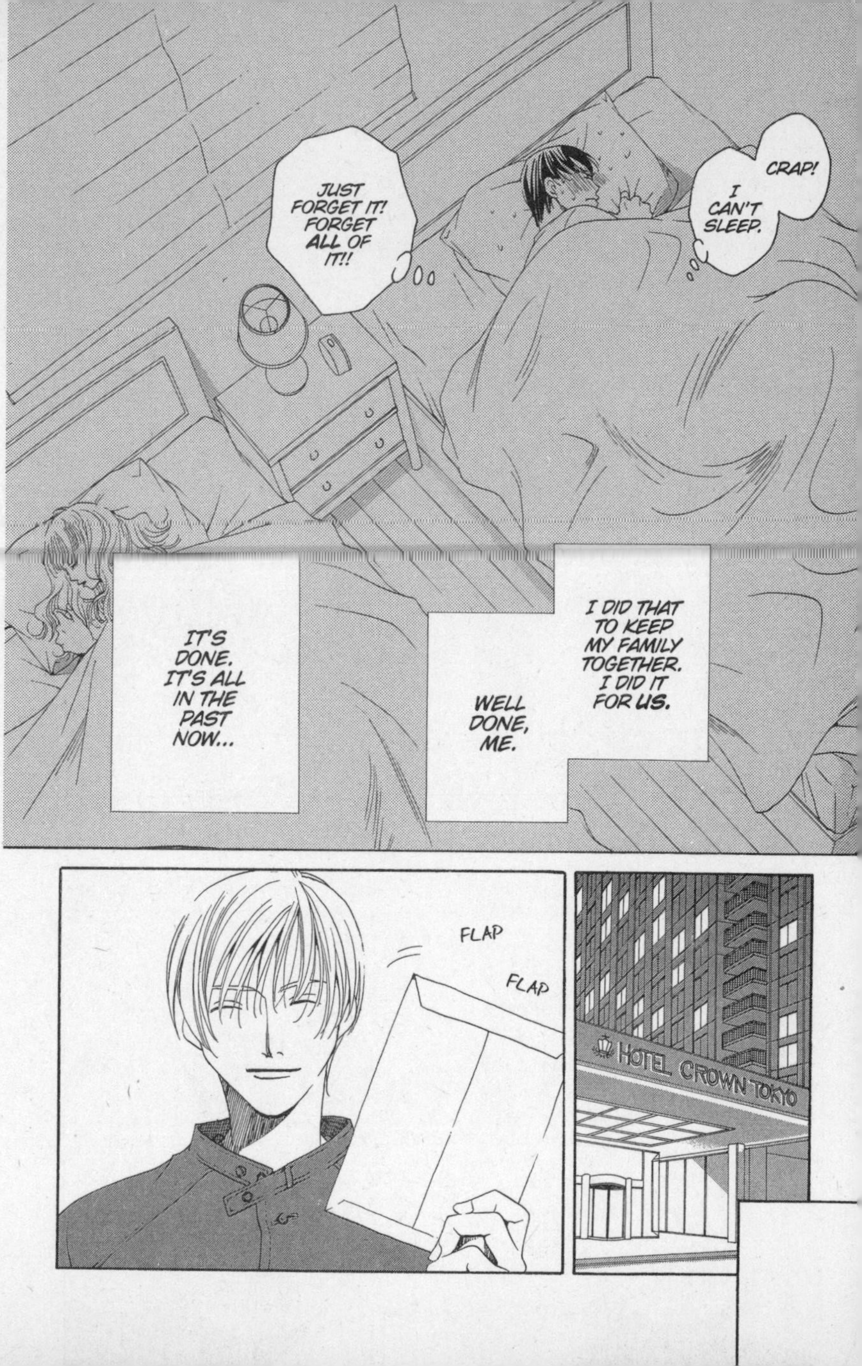
CRAP! I CAN'T SLEEP.
JUST FORGET IT! FORGET ALL OF IT!!
I DID THAT TO KEEP MY FAMILY TOGETHER. I DID IT FOR US.
WELL DONE, ME.
IT'S DONE. IT'S ALL IN THE PAST NOW...
HOTEL CROWN TOKYO
FLAP
FLAP

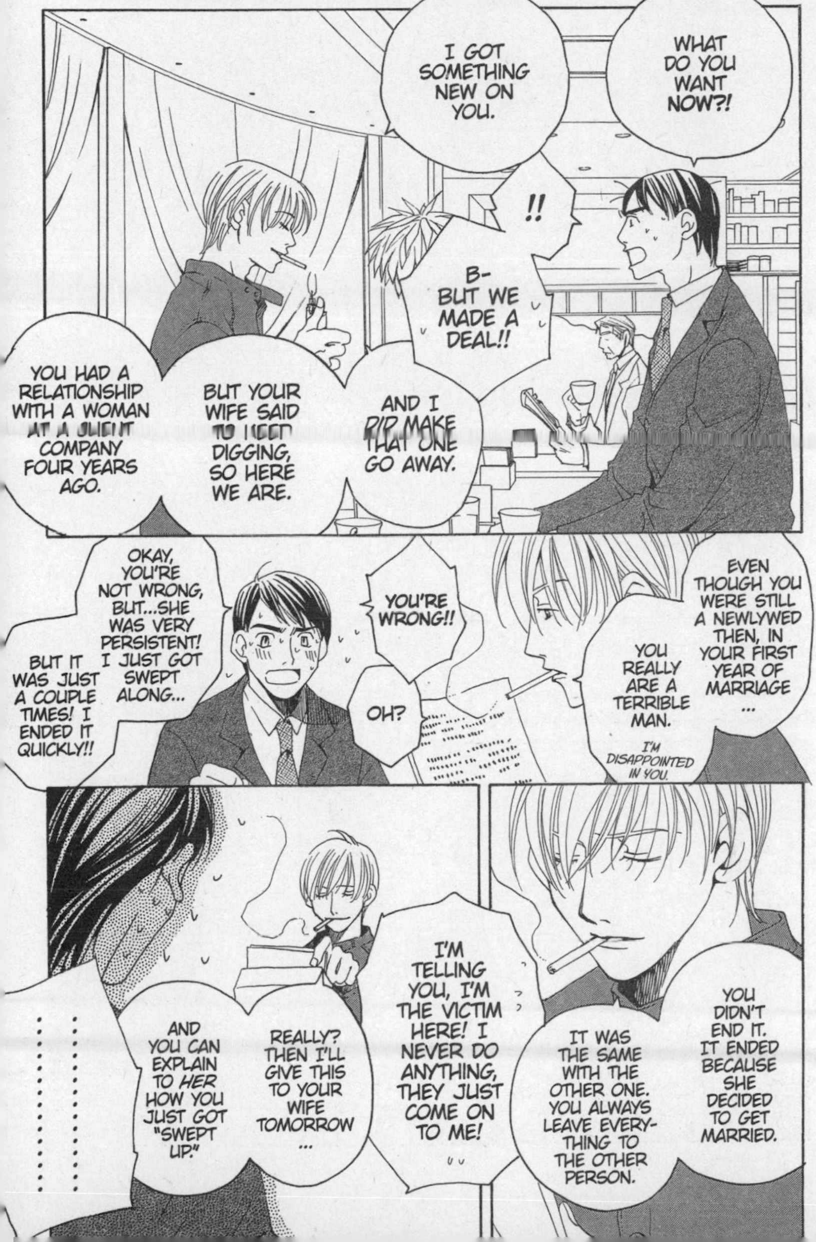
WHAT DO YOU WANT NOW?!
I GOT SOMETHING NEW ON YOU.
!!
B-BUT WE MADE A DEAL!!
AND I *DID* MAKE THAT ONE GO AWAY.
BUT YOUR WIFE SAID TO KEEP DIGGING, SO HERE WE ARE.
YOU HAD A RELATIONSHIP WITH A WOMAN AT A CLIENT COMPANY FOUR YEARS AGO.
EVEN THOUGH YOU WERE STILL A NEWLYWED THEN, IN YOUR FIRST YEAR OF MARRIAGE ...
YOU REALLY ARE A TERRIBLE MAN.
I'M DISAPPOINTED IN YOU.
OH?
YOU'RE WRONG!!
OKAY, YOU'RE NOT WRONG, BUT...SHE WAS VERY PERSISTENT! I JUST GOT SWEPT ALONG...
BUT IT WAS JUST A COUPLE TIMES! I ENDED IT QUICKLY!!
YOU DIDN'T END IT. IT ENDED BECAUSE SHE DECIDED TO GET MARRIED.
IT WAS THE SAME WITH THE OTHER ONE. YOU ALWAYS LEAVE EVERY-THING TO THE OTHER PERSON.
I'M TELLING YOU, I'M THE VICTIM HERE! I NEVER DO ANYTHING, THEY JUST COME ON TO ME!
REALLY? THEN I'LL GIVE THIS TO YOUR WIFE TOMORROW ...
AND YOU CAN EXPLAIN TO *HER* HOW YOU JUST GOT "SWEPT UP."

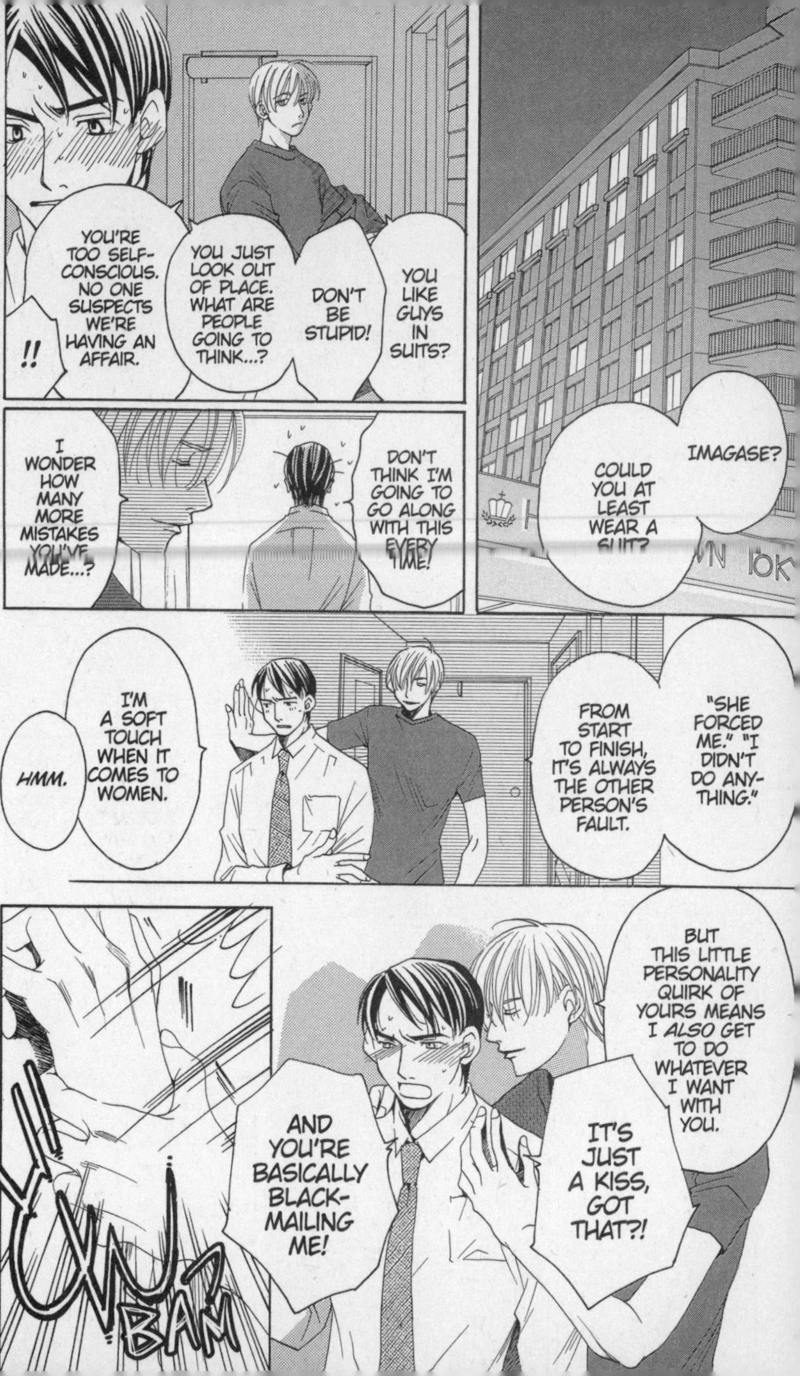
IMAGASE?
COULD YOU AT LEAST WEAR A SUIT?
YOU LIKE GUYS IN SUITS?
DON'T BE STUPID!
YOU JUST LOOK OUT OF PLACE. WHAT ARE PEOPLE GOING TO THINK...?
YOU'RE TOO SELF-CONSCIOUS. NO ONE SUSPECTS WE'RE HAVING AN AFFAIR.
!!
DON'T THINK I'M GOING TO GO ALONG WITH THIS EVERY TIME!
I WONDER HOW MANY MORE MISTAKES YOU'VE MADE...?
"SHE FORCED ME." "I DIDN'T DO ANYTHING."
FROM START TO FINISH, IT'S ALWAYS THE OTHER PERSON'S FAULT.
I'M A SOFT TOUCH WHEN IT COMES TO WOMEN.
HMM.
BUT THIS LITTLE PERSONALITY QUIRK OF YOURS MEANS I *ALSO* GET TO DO WHATEVER I WANT WITH YOU.
IT'S JUST A KISS, GOT THAT?!
AND YOU'RE BASICALLY BLACK-MAILING ME!
BAM

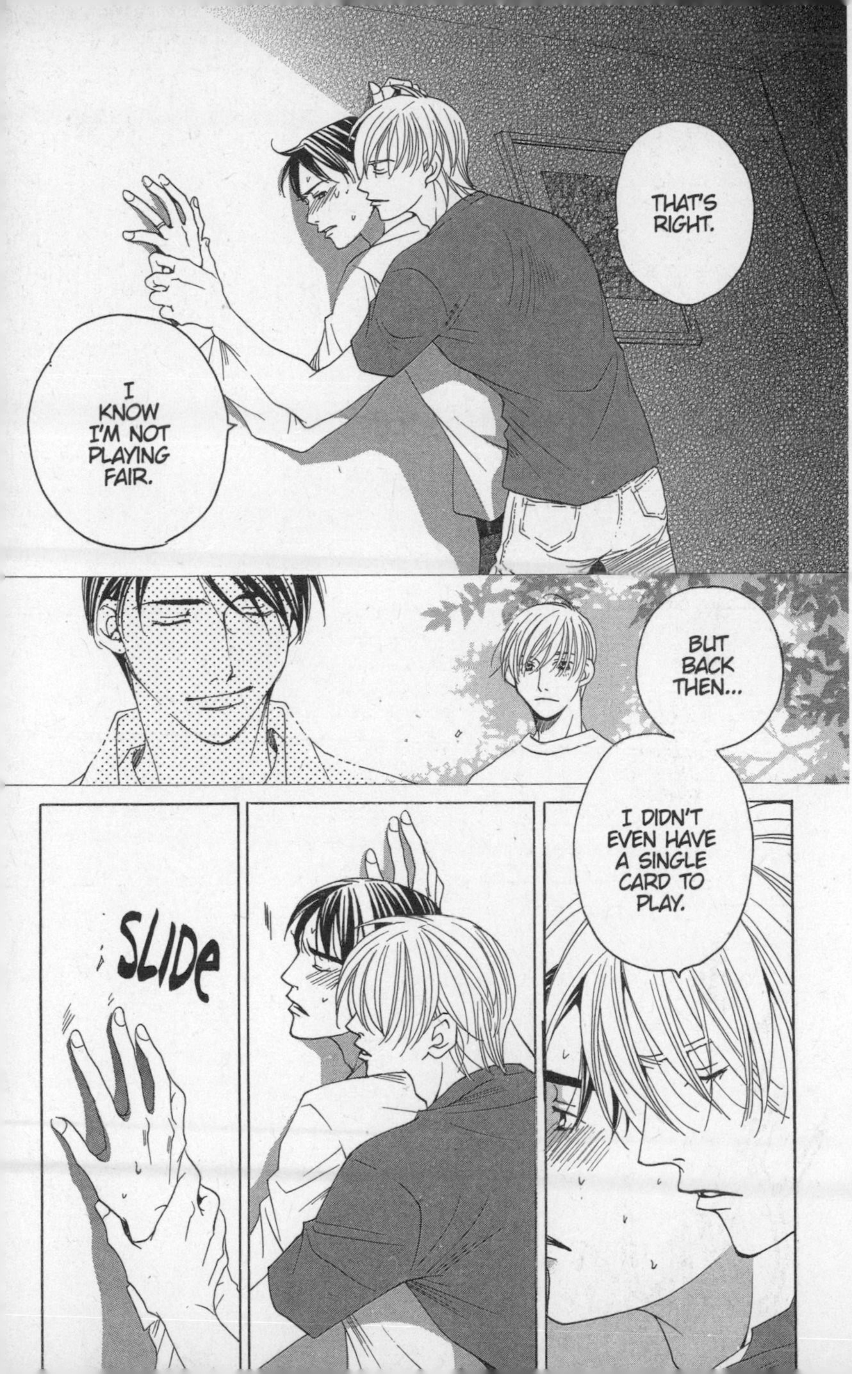
THAT'S RIGHT.
I KNOW I'M NOT PLAYING FAIR.
BUT BACK THEN...
I DIDN'T EVEN HAVE A SINGLE CARD TO PLAY.
SLIDE

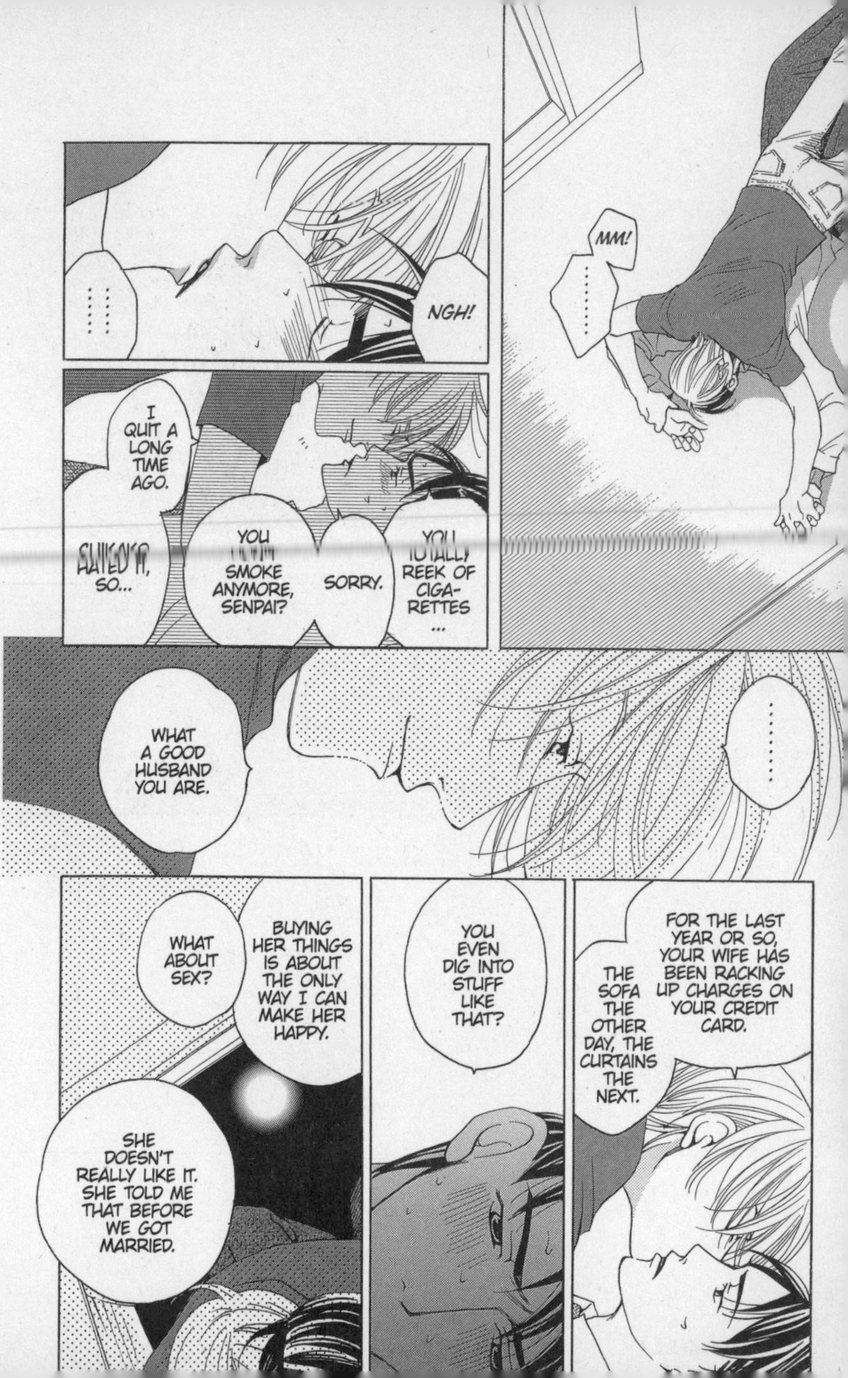
MM!
......
......
NGH!
YOU TOTALLY REEK OF CIGARETTES ...
SORRY.
YOU SMOKE ANYMORE, SENPAI?
I QUIT A LONG TIME AGO.
HATED IT, SO...
......
WHAT A GOOD HUSBAND YOU ARE.
FOR THE LAST YEAR OR SO, YOUR WIFE HAS BEEN RACKING UP CHARGES ON YOUR CREDIT CARD.
THE SOFA THE OTHER DAY, THE CURTAINS THE NEXT.
YOU EVEN DIG INTO STUFF LIKE THAT?
BUYING HER THINGS IS ABOUT THE ONLY WAY I CAN MAKE HER HAPPY.
WHAT ABOUT SEX?
SHE DOESN'T REALLY LIKE IT. SHE TOLD ME THAT BEFORE WE GOT MARRIED.

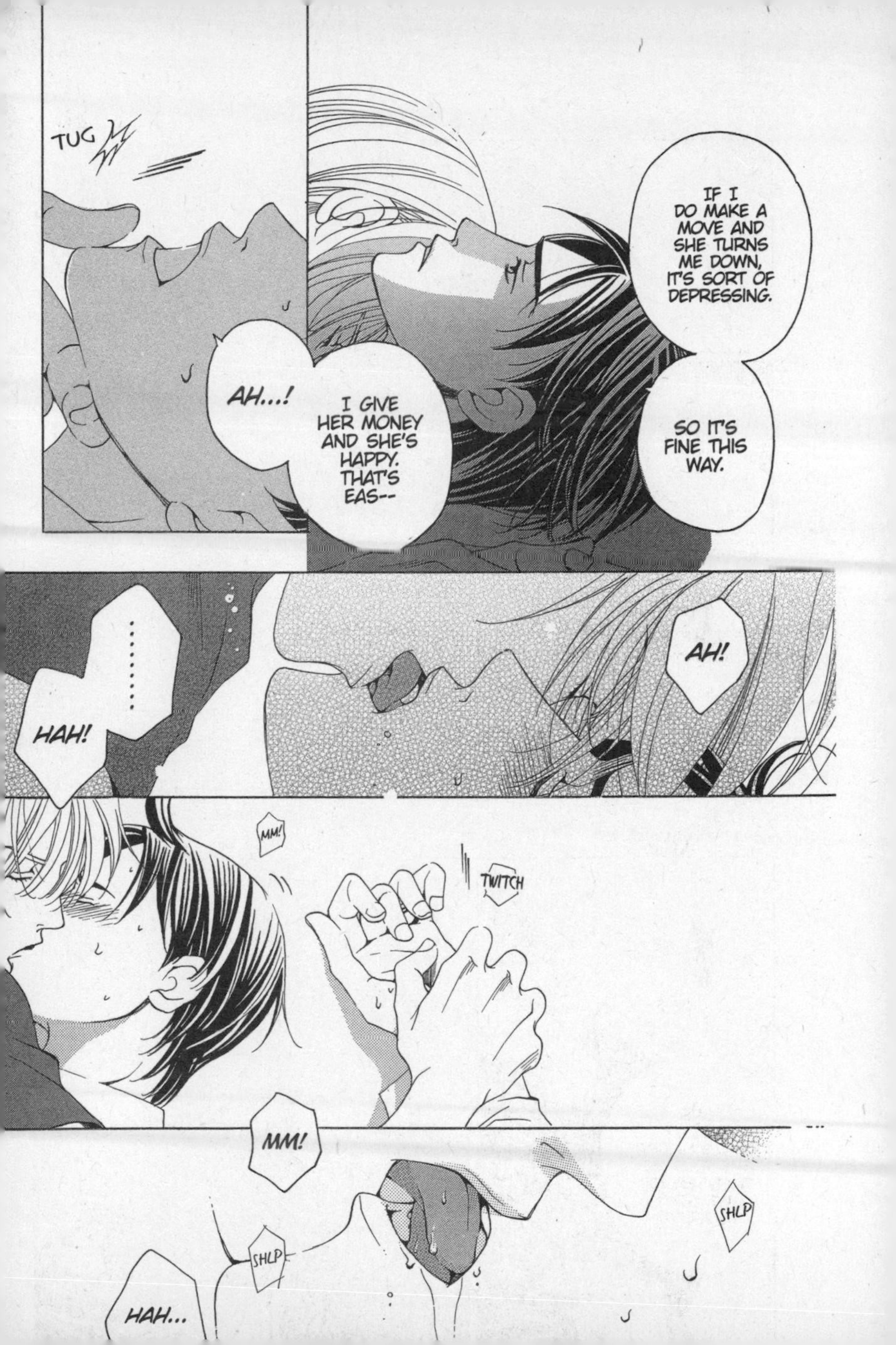

IF I DO MAKE A MOVE AND SHE TURNS ME DOWN, IT'S SORT OF DEPRESSING.
SO IT'S FINE THIS WAY.
I GIVE HER MONEY AND SHE'S HAPPY. THAT'S EAS--
TUG
AH...!
AH!
......
HAH!
TWITCH
MM!
SHLP
MM!
SHLP
HAH...

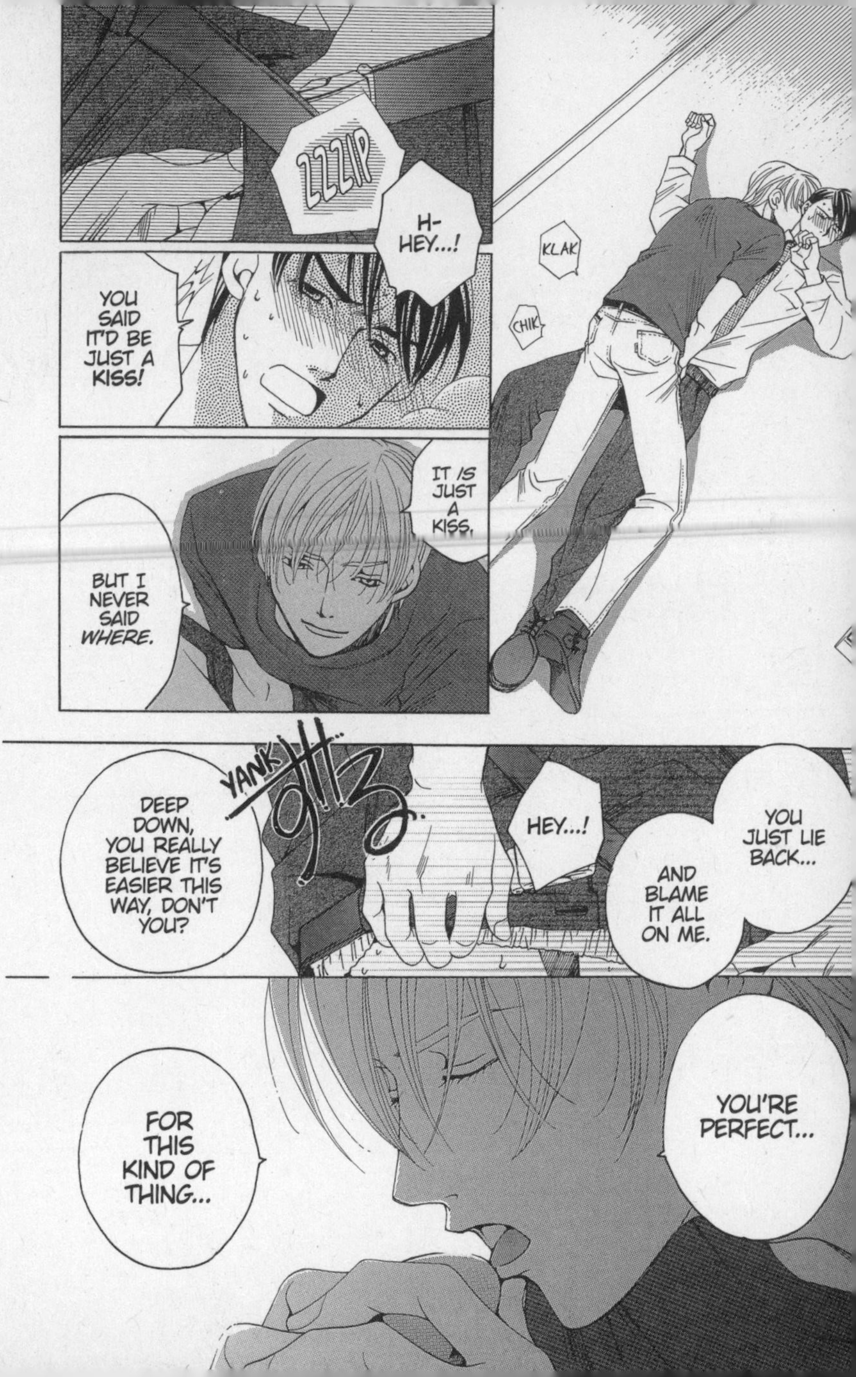
KLAK
CHIK
ZZZIP
H-HEY...!
YOU SAID IT'D BE JUST A KISS!
IT *IS* JUST A KISS.
BUT I NEVER SAID *WHERE.*
YOU JUST LIE BACK...
AND BLAME IT ALL ON ME.
HEY...!
YANK
DEEP DOWN, YOU REALLY BELIEVE IT'S EASIER THIS WAY, DON'T YOU?
YOU'RE PERFECT...
FOR THIS KIND OF THING...

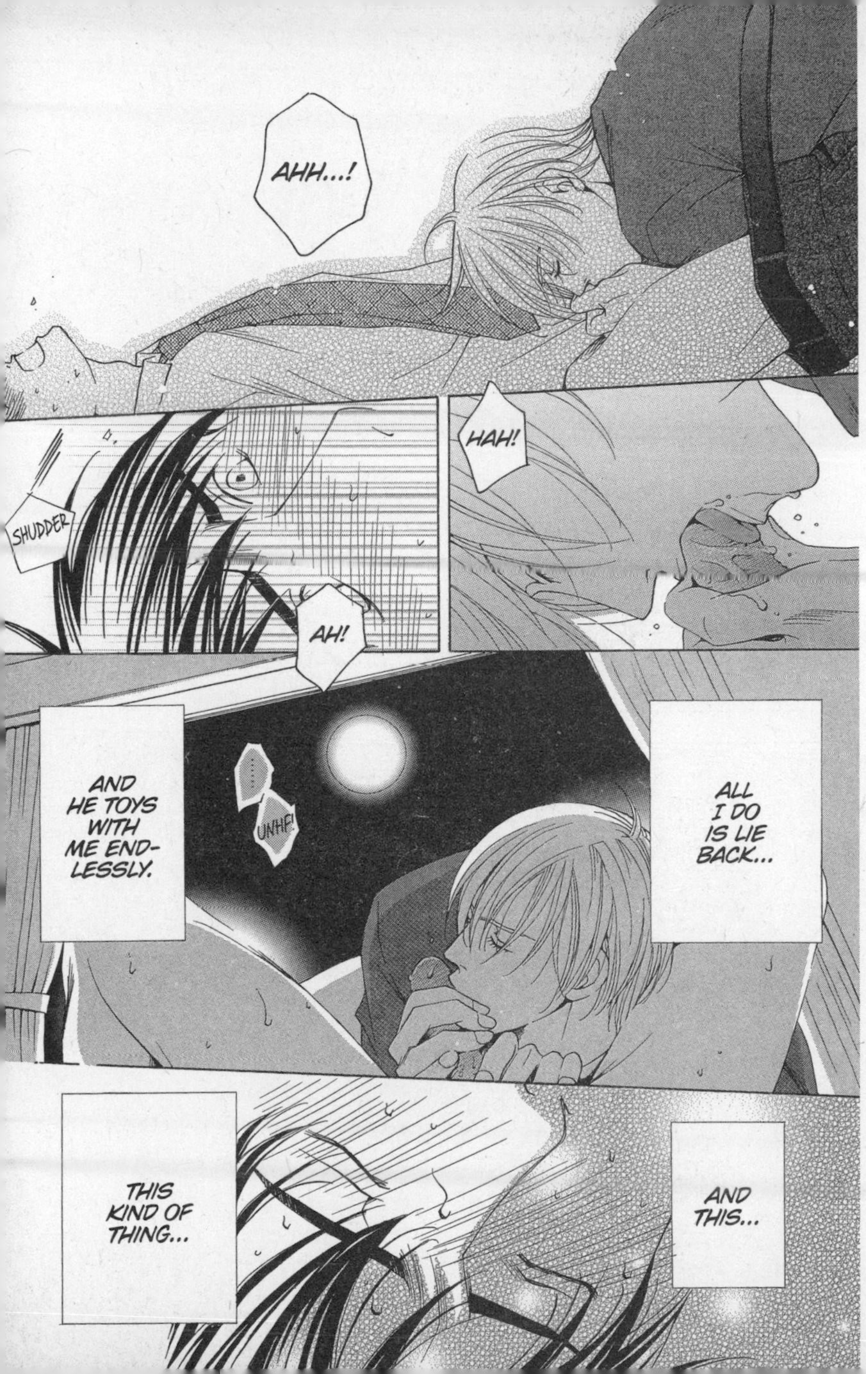
AHH...!
HAH!
SHUDDER
AH!
ALL I DO IS LIE BACK...
......
UNHF!
AND HE TOYS WITH ME END-LESSLY.
AND THIS...
THIS KIND OF THING...

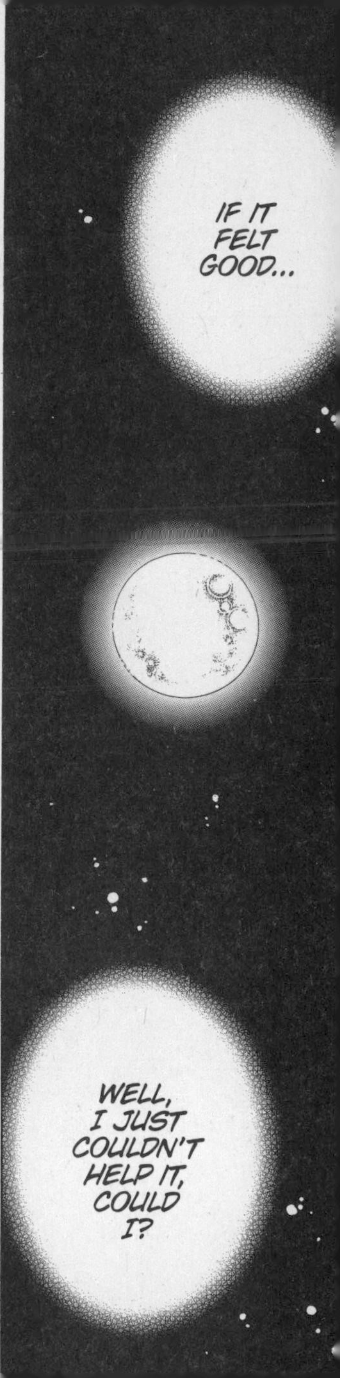
IF IT FELT GOOD...
WELL, I JUST COULDN'T HELP IT, COULD I?

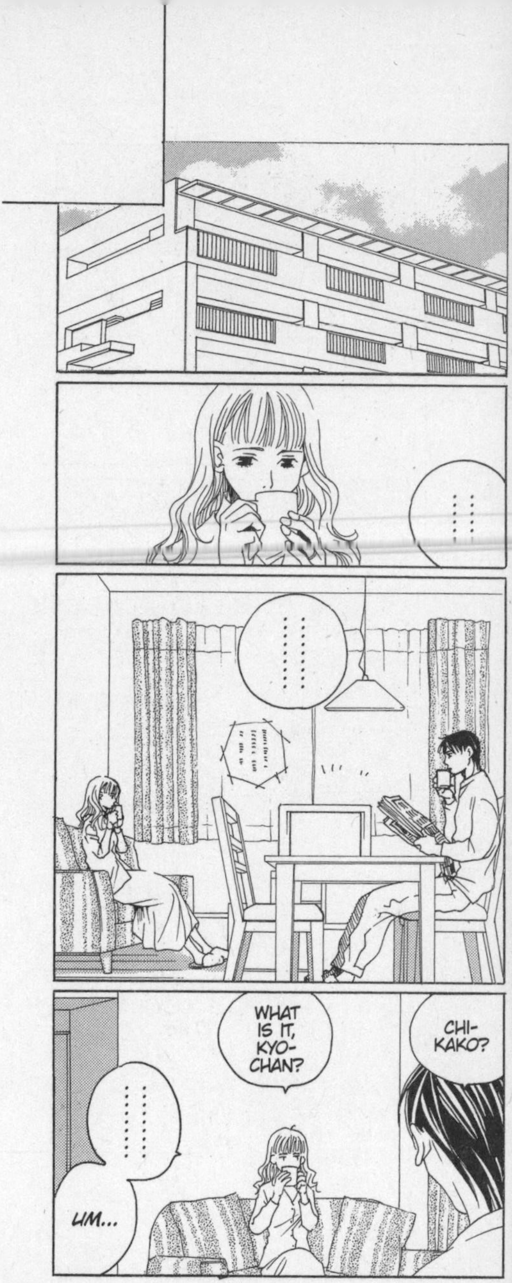
......
......
CHI-KAKO?
WHAT IS IT, KYO-CHAN?
......
UM...

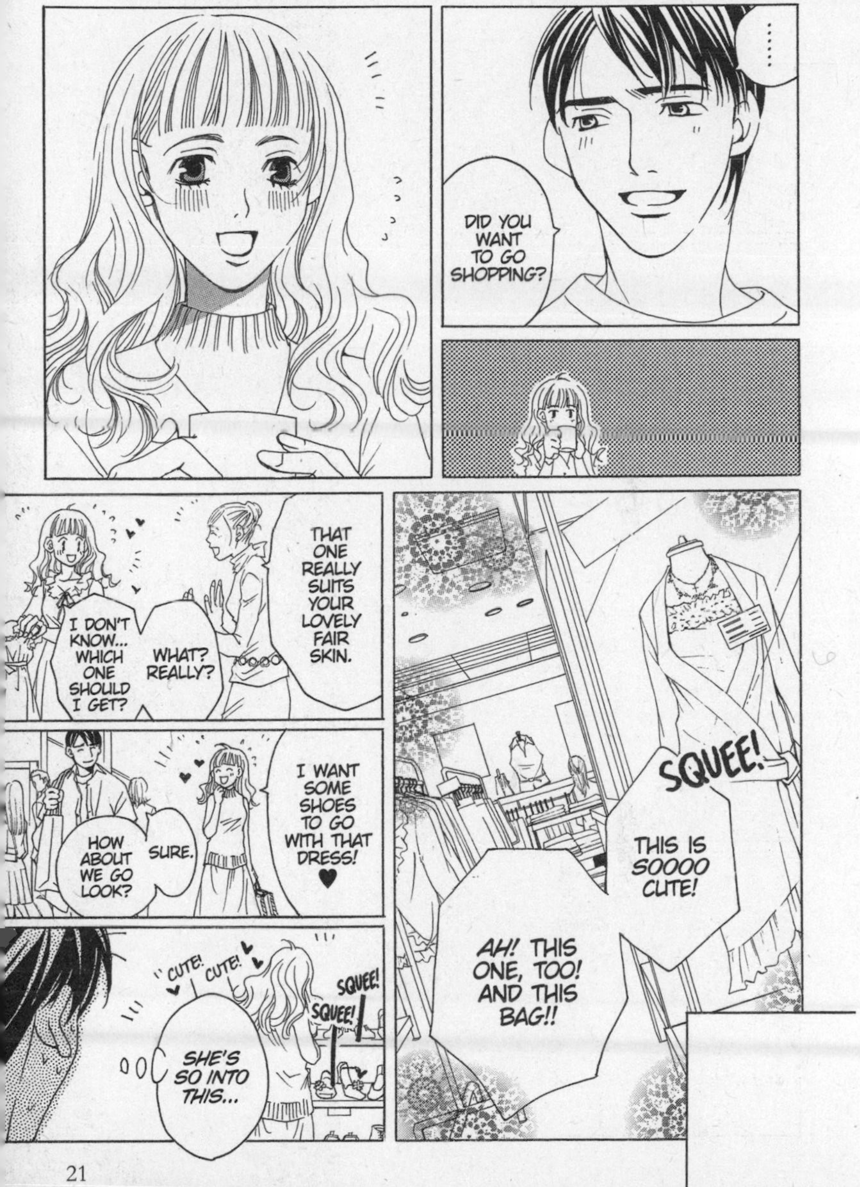
......
DID YOU WANT TO GO SHOPPING?
SQUEE!
THIS IS SOOOO CUTE!
AH! THIS ONE, TOO! AND THIS BAG!!
THAT ONE REALLY SUITS YOUR LOVELY FAIR SKIN.
WHAT? REALLY?
I DON'T KNOW... WHICH ONE SHOULD I GET?
I WANT SOME SHOES TO GO WITH THAT DRESS! ♥
SURE.
HOW ABOUT WE GO LOOK?
SQUEE!
SQUEE!
CUTE!
CUTE!
SHE'S SO INTO THIS...

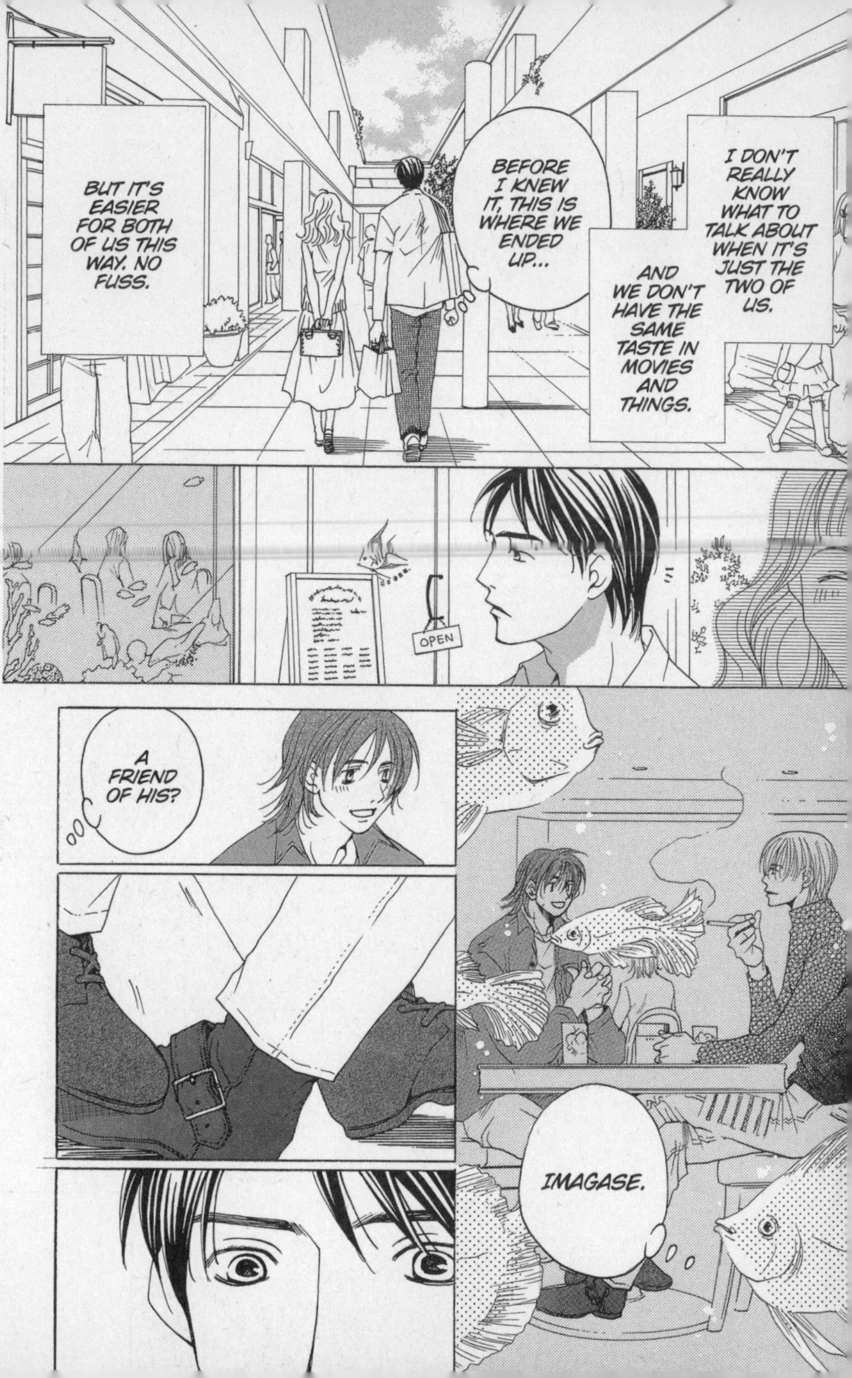
I DON'T REALLY KNOW WHAT TO TALK ABOUT WHEN IT'S JUST THE TWO OF US.
AND WE DON'T HAVE THE SAME TASTE IN MOVIES AND THINGS.
BEFORE I KNEW IT, THIS IS WHERE WE ENDED UP...
BUT IT'S EASIER FOR BOTH OF US THIS WAY. NO FUSS.
OPEN
IMAGASE.
A FRIEND OF HIS?

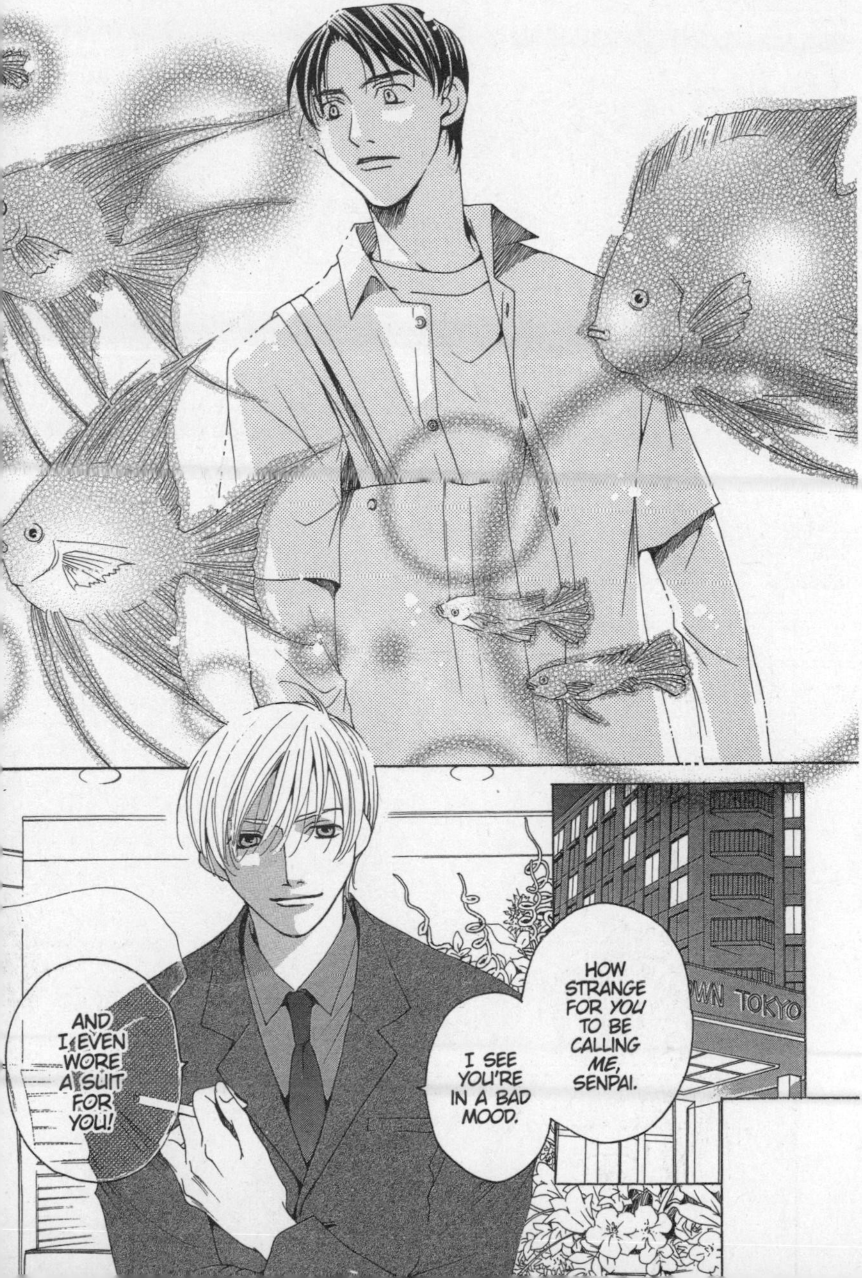
WN TOKYO
HOW STRANGE FOR YOU TO BE CALLING ME, SENPAI.
I SEE YOU'RE IN A BAD MOOD.
AND I EVEN WORE A SUIT FOR YOU!

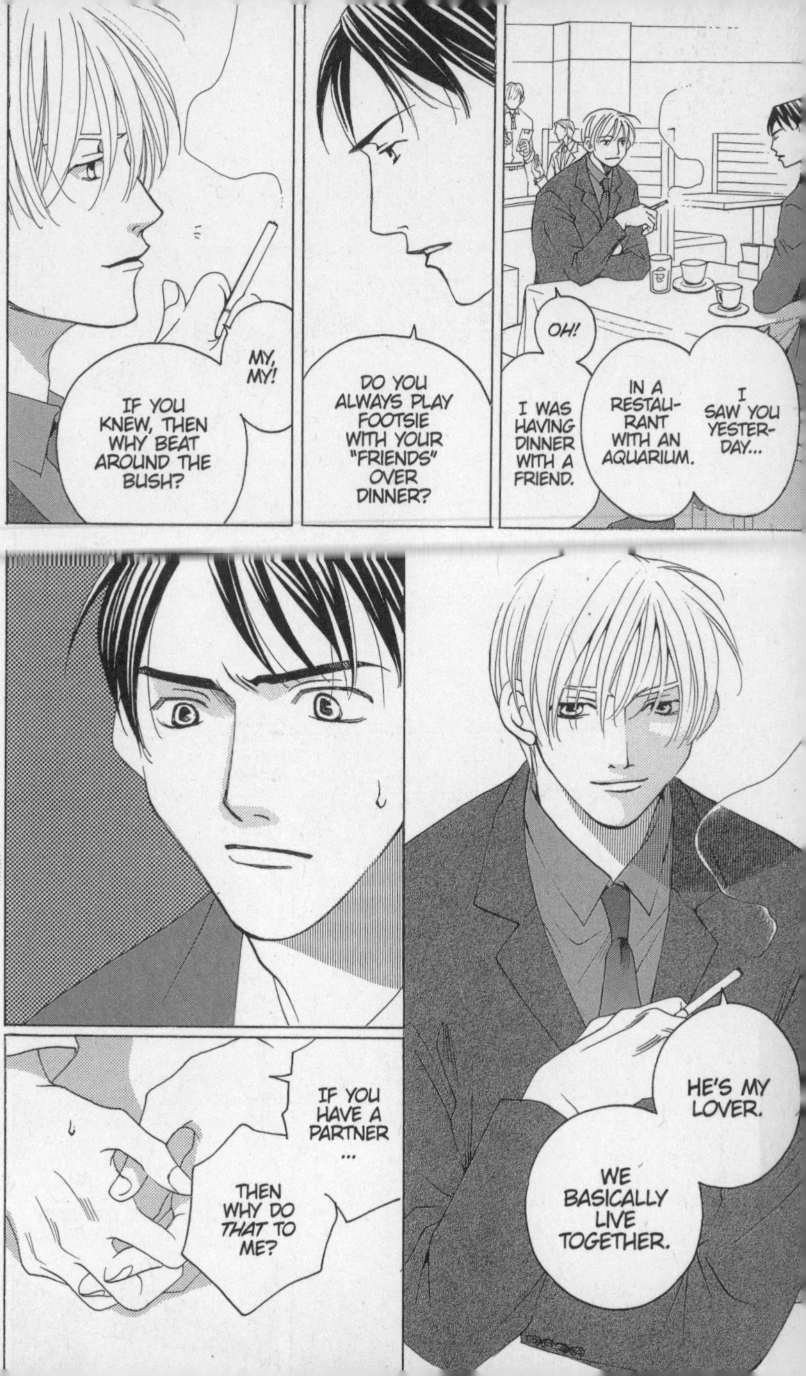
I SAW YOU YESTERDAY...
IN A RESTAURANT WITH AN AQUARIUM.
OH!
I WAS HAVING DINNER WITH A FRIEND.
DO YOU ALWAYS PLAY FOOTSIE WITH YOUR "FRIENDS" OVER DINNER?
MY, MY!
IF YOU KNEW, THEN WHY BEAT AROUND THE BUSH?
HE'S MY LOVER.
WE BASICALLY LIVE TOGETHER.
IF YOU HAVE A PARTNER ...
THEN WHY DO *THAT* TO ME?

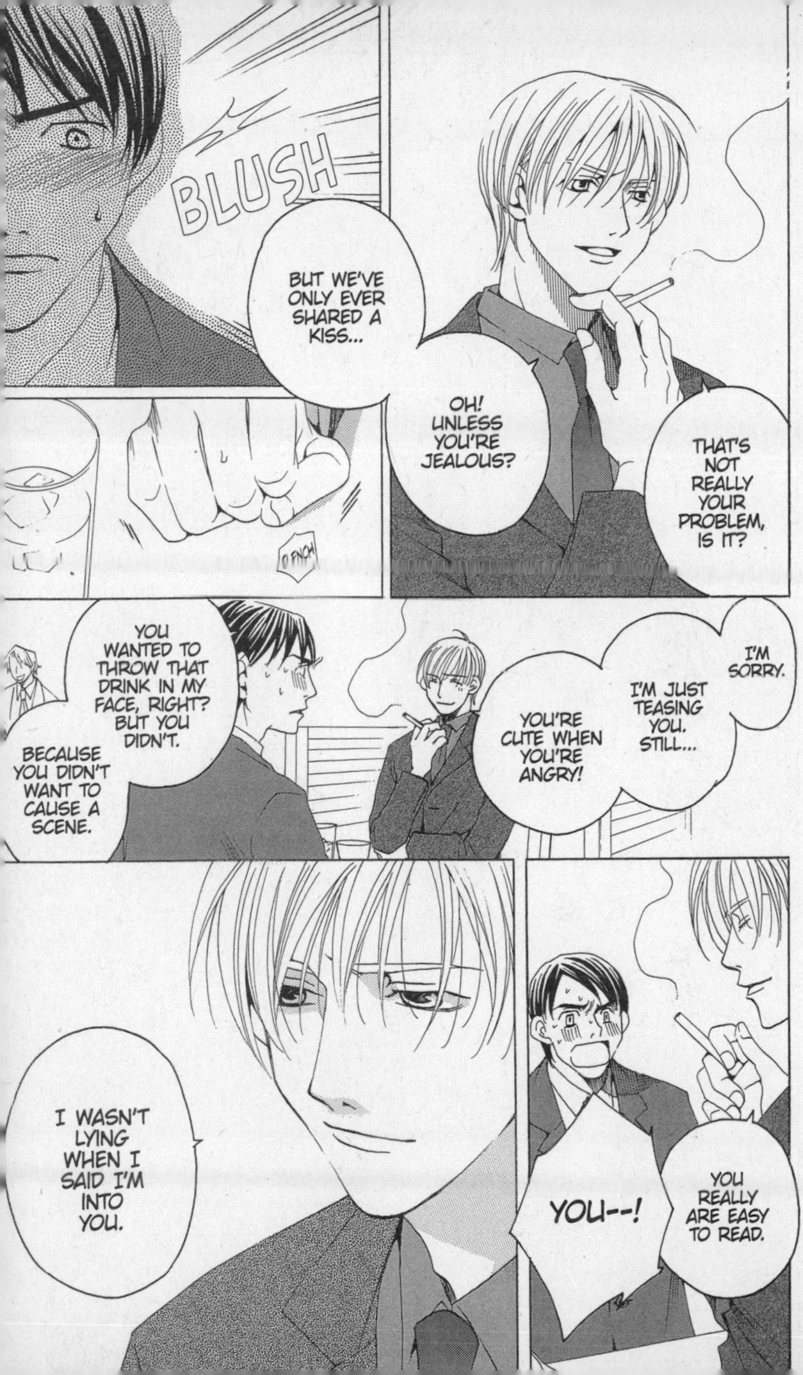
THAT'S NOT REALLY YOUR PROBLEM, IS IT?
OH! UNLESS YOU'RE JEALOUS?
BUT WE'VE ONLY EVER SHARED A KISS...
BLUSH
I'M SORRY.
I'M JUST TEASING YOU. STILL...
YOU'RE CUTE WHEN YOU'RE ANGRY!
YOU WANTED TO THROW THAT DRINK IN MY FACE, RIGHT? BUT YOU DIDN'T.
BECAUSE YOU DIDN'T WANT TO CAUSE A SCENE.
YOU REALLY ARE EASY TO READ.
YOU--!
I WASN'T LYING WHEN I SAID I'M INTO YOU.

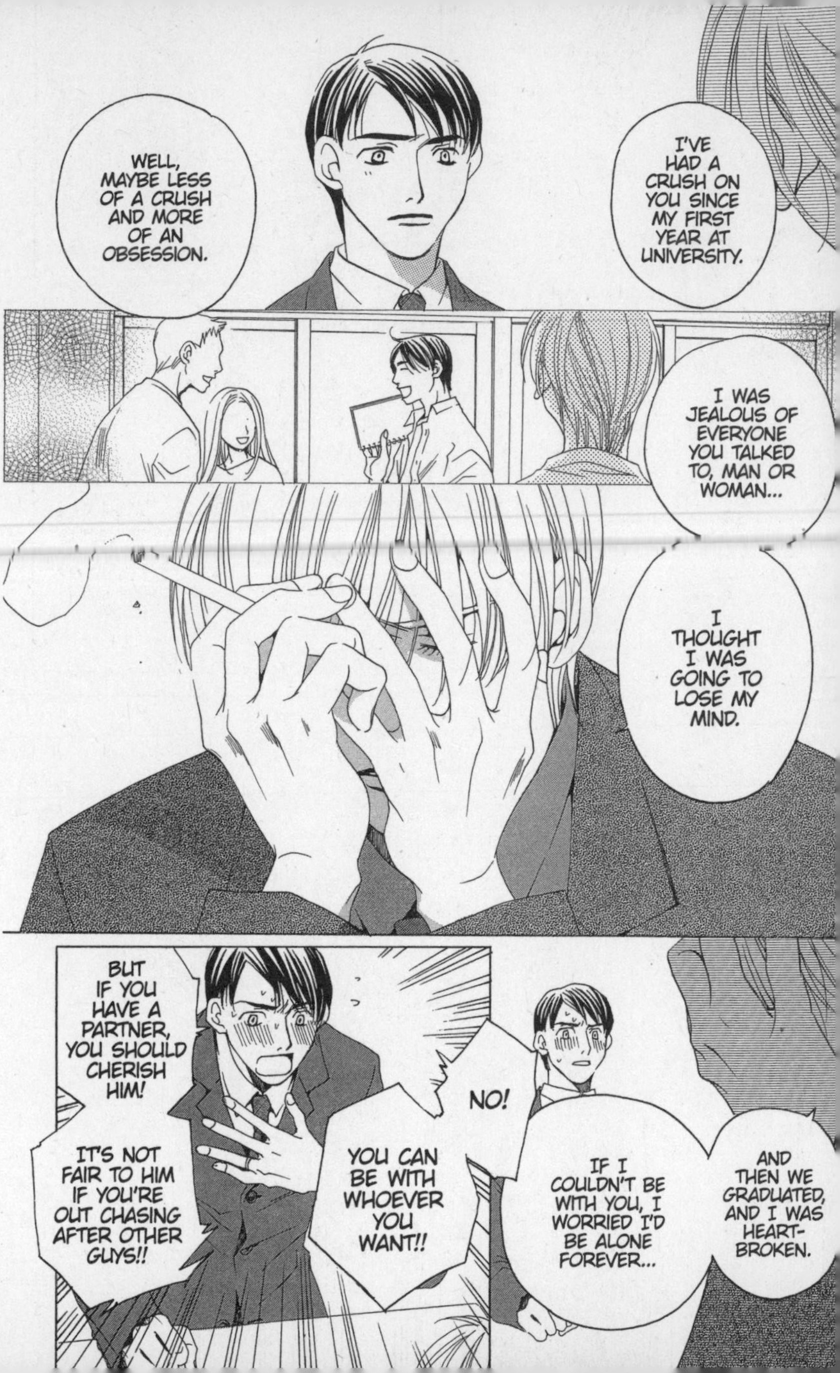
I'VE HAD A CRUSH ON YOU SINCE MY FIRST YEAR AT UNIVERSITY.
WELL, MAYBE LESS OF A CRUSH AND MORE OF AN OBSESSION.
I WAS JEALOUS OF EVERYONE YOU TALKED TO, MAN OR WOMAN...
I THOUGHT I WAS GOING TO LOSE MY MIND.
AND THEN WE GRADUATED, AND I WAS HEART-BROKEN.
IF I COULDN'T BE WITH YOU, I WORRIED I'D BE ALONE FOREVER...
NO!
YOU CAN BE WITH WHOEVER YOU WANT!!
BUT IF YOU HAVE A PARTNER, YOU SHOULD CHERISH HIM!
IT'S NOT FAIR TO HIM IF YOU'RE OUT CHASING AFTER OTHER GUYS!!

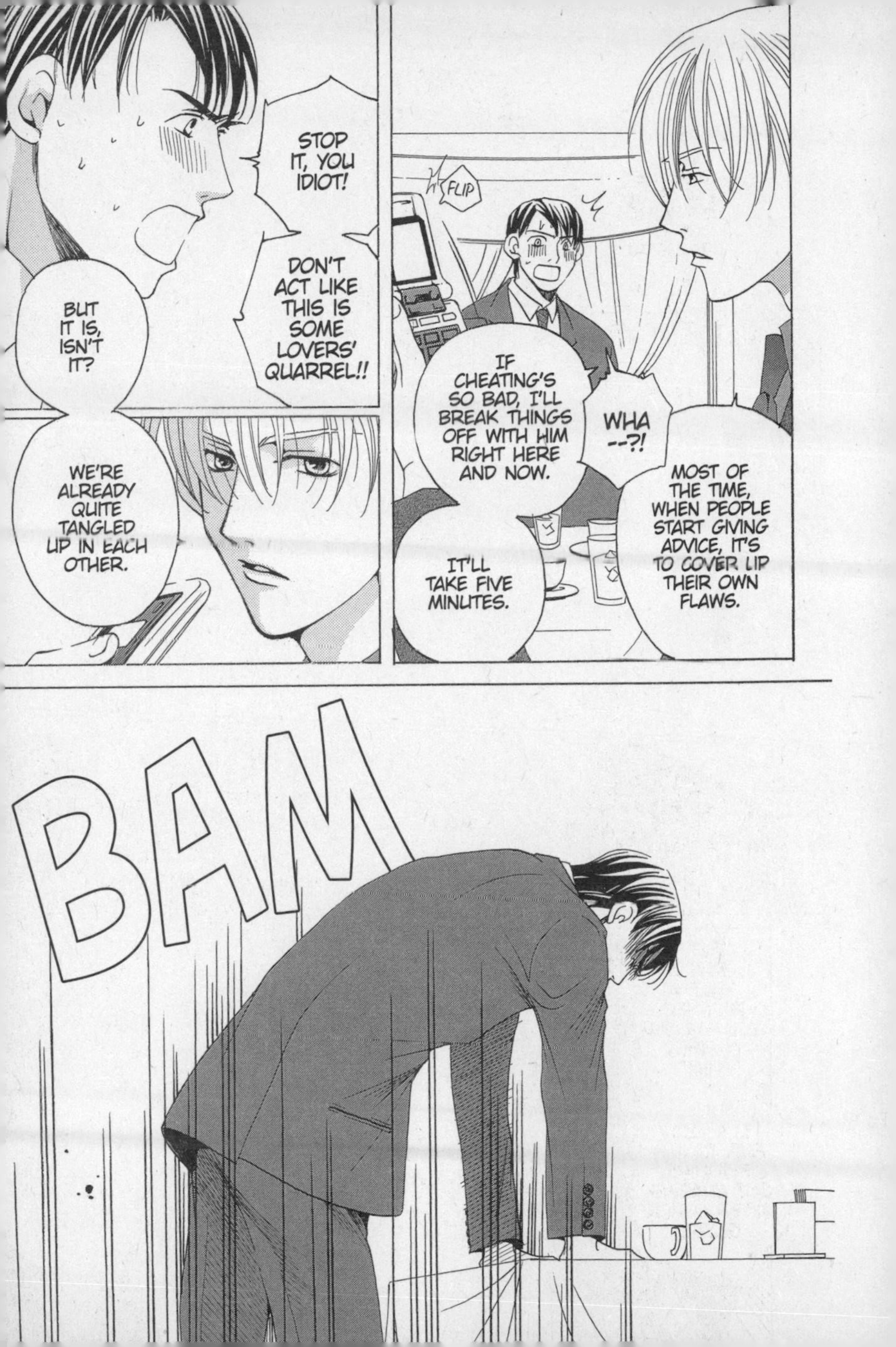
FLIP
WHA--?!
IF CHEATING'S SO BAD, I'LL BREAK THINGS OFF WITH HIM RIGHT HERE AND NOW.
MOST OF THE TIME, WHEN PEOPLE START GIVING ADVICE, IT'S TO COVER UP THEIR OWN FLAWS.
IT'LL TAKE FIVE MINUTES.
STOP IT, YOU IDIOT!
DON'T ACT LIKE THIS IS SOME LOVERS' QUARREL!!
BUT IT IS, ISN'T IT?
WE'RE ALREADY QUITE TANGLED UP IN EACH OTHER.
BAM

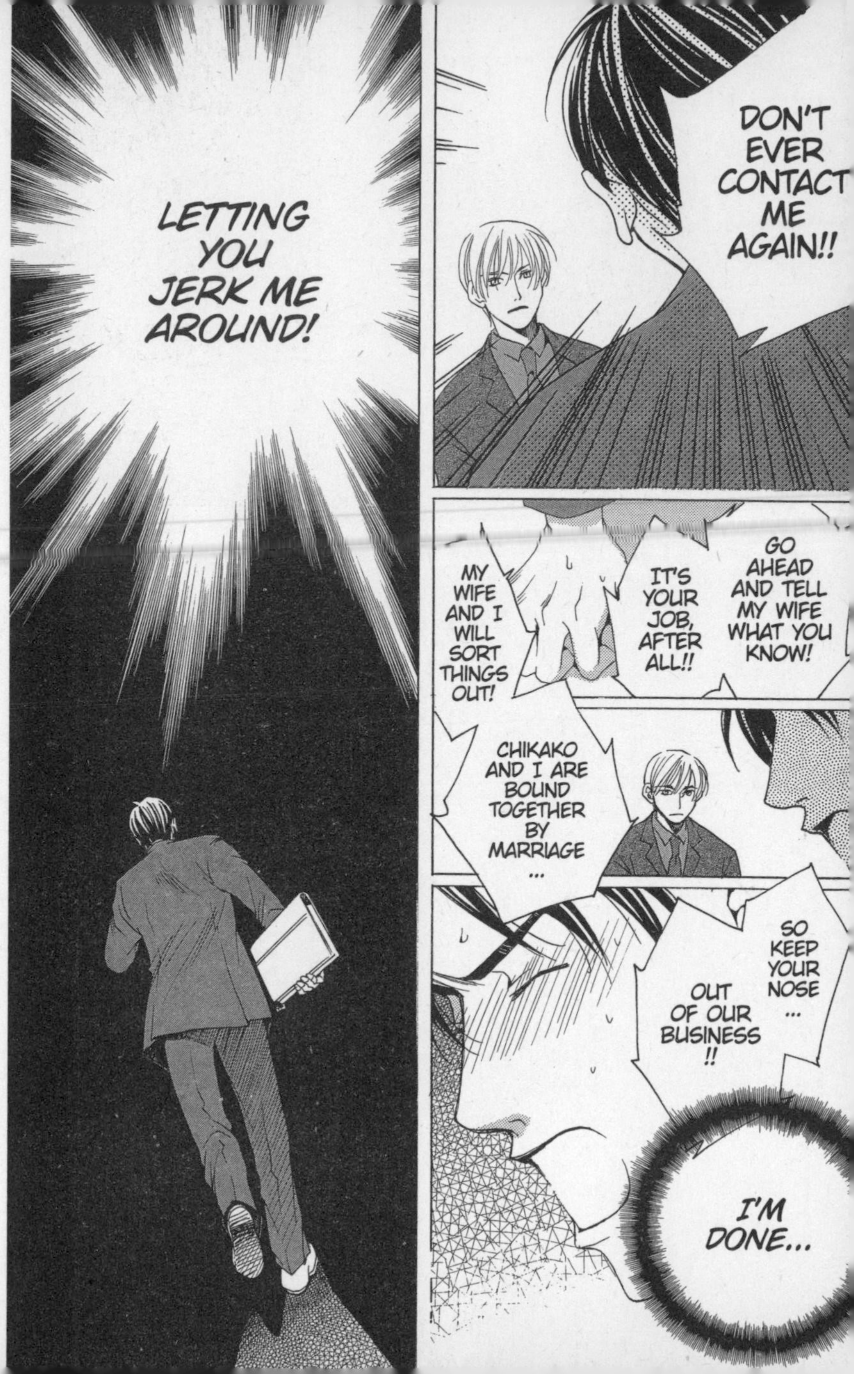
DON'T EVER CONTACT ME AGAIN!!
GO AHEAD AND TELL MY WIFE WHAT YOU KNOW!
IT'S YOUR JOB, AFTER ALL!!
MY WIFE AND I WILL SORT THINGS OUT!
CHIKAKO AND I ARE BOUND TOGETHER BY MARRIAGE ...
SO KEEP YOUR NOSE ...
OUT OF OUR BUSINESS !!
I'M DONE...
LETTING YOU JERK ME AROUND!

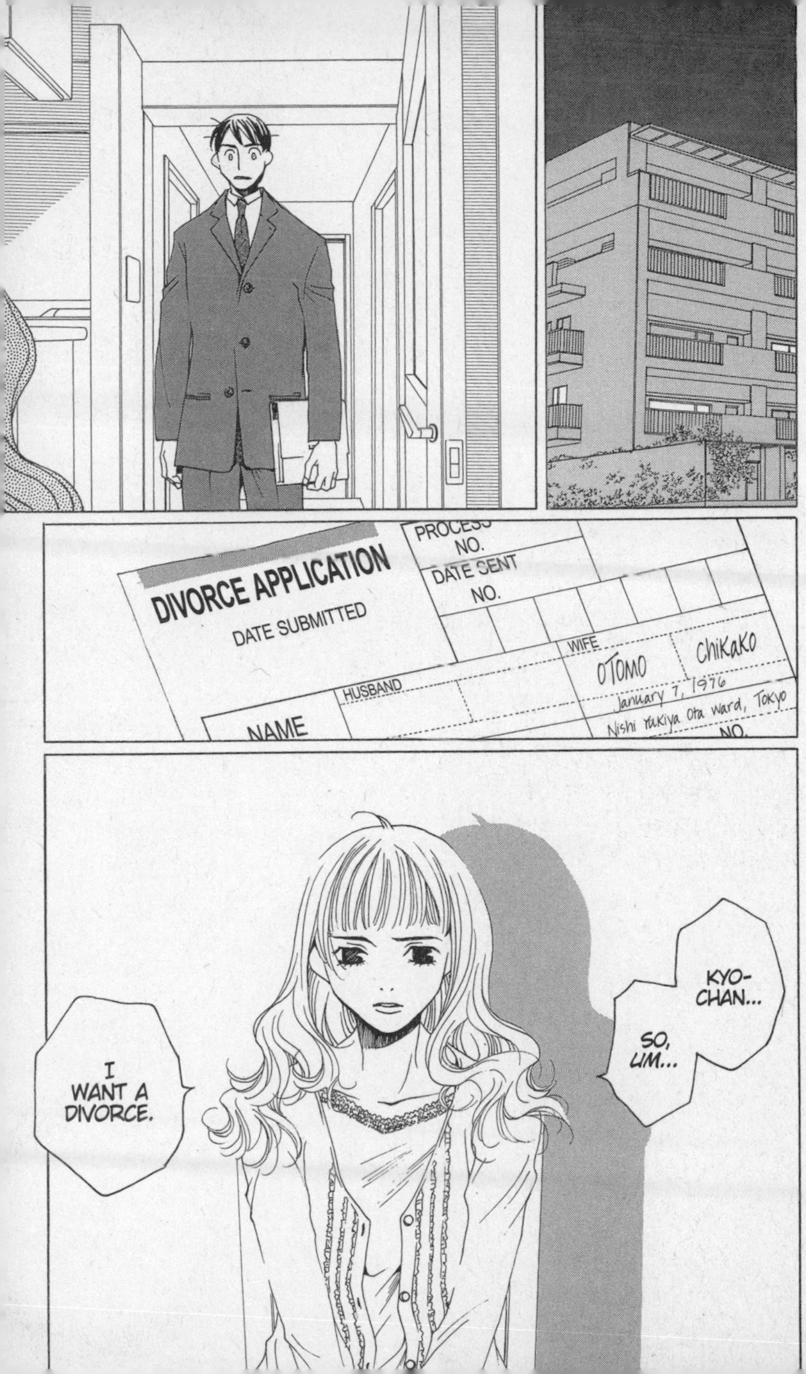
DIVORCE APPLICATION
DATE SUBMITTED
PROCESS NO.
DATE SENT NO.
WIFE
OTOMO CHIKAKO
January 7, 1976
Nishi Yukiya Ota Ward, Tokyo
NO.
HUSBAND
NAME
KYO-CHAN...
SO, UM...
I WANT A DIVORCE.

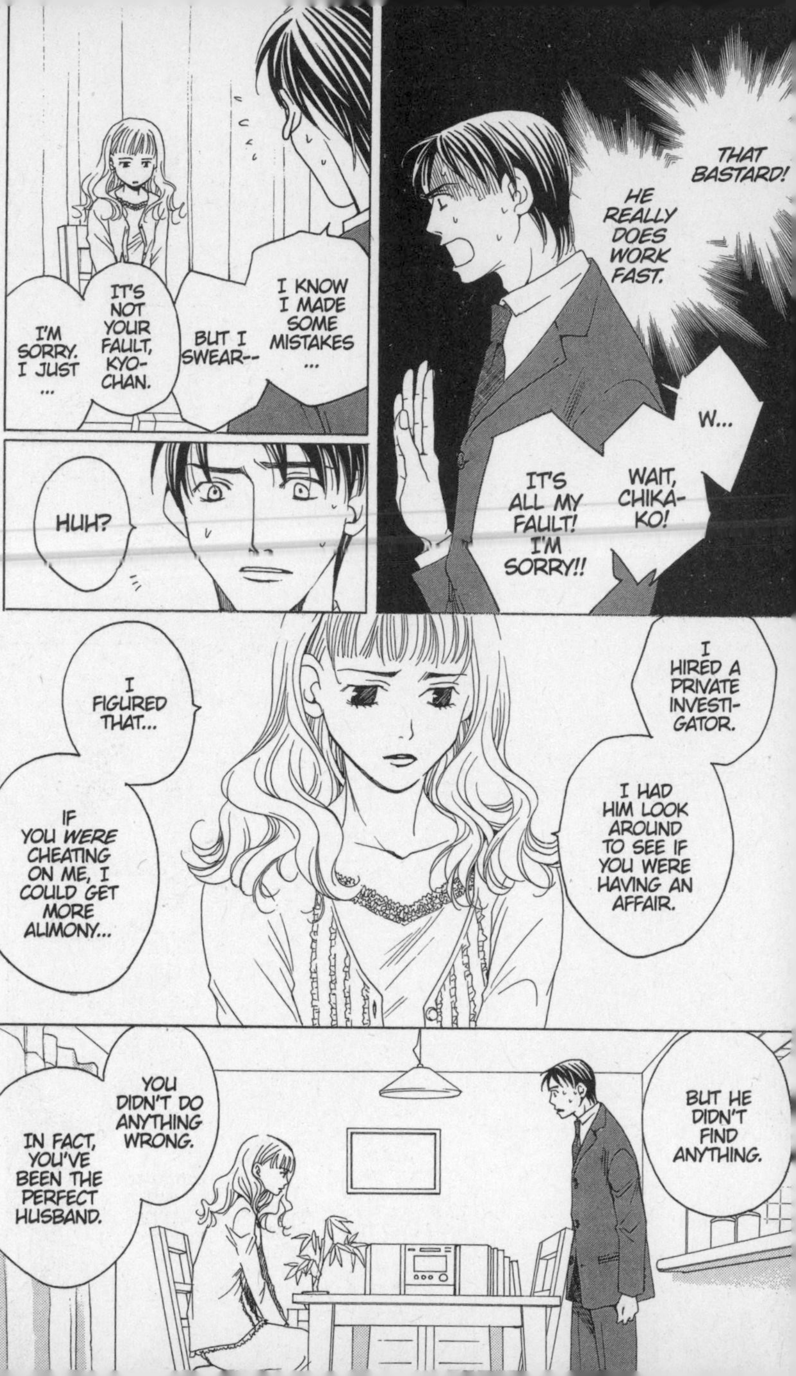
THAT BASTARD!
HE REALLY DOES WORK FAST.
W...
WAIT, CHIKAKO!
IT'S ALL MY FAULT! I'M SORRY!!
I KNOW I MADE SOME MISTAKES...
BUT I SWEAR--
IT'S NOT YOUR FAULT, KYO-CHAN.
I'M SORRY. I JUST...
HUH?
I HIRED A PRIVATE INVESTIGATOR.
I HAD HIM LOOK AROUND TO SEE IF YOU WERE HAVING AN AFFAIR.
I FIGURED THAT...
IF YOU *WERE* CHEATING ON ME, I COULD GET MORE ALIMONY...
BUT HE DIDN'T FIND ANYTHING.
YOU DIDN'T DO ANYTHING WRONG.
IN FACT, YOU'VE BEEN THE PERFECT HUSBAND.

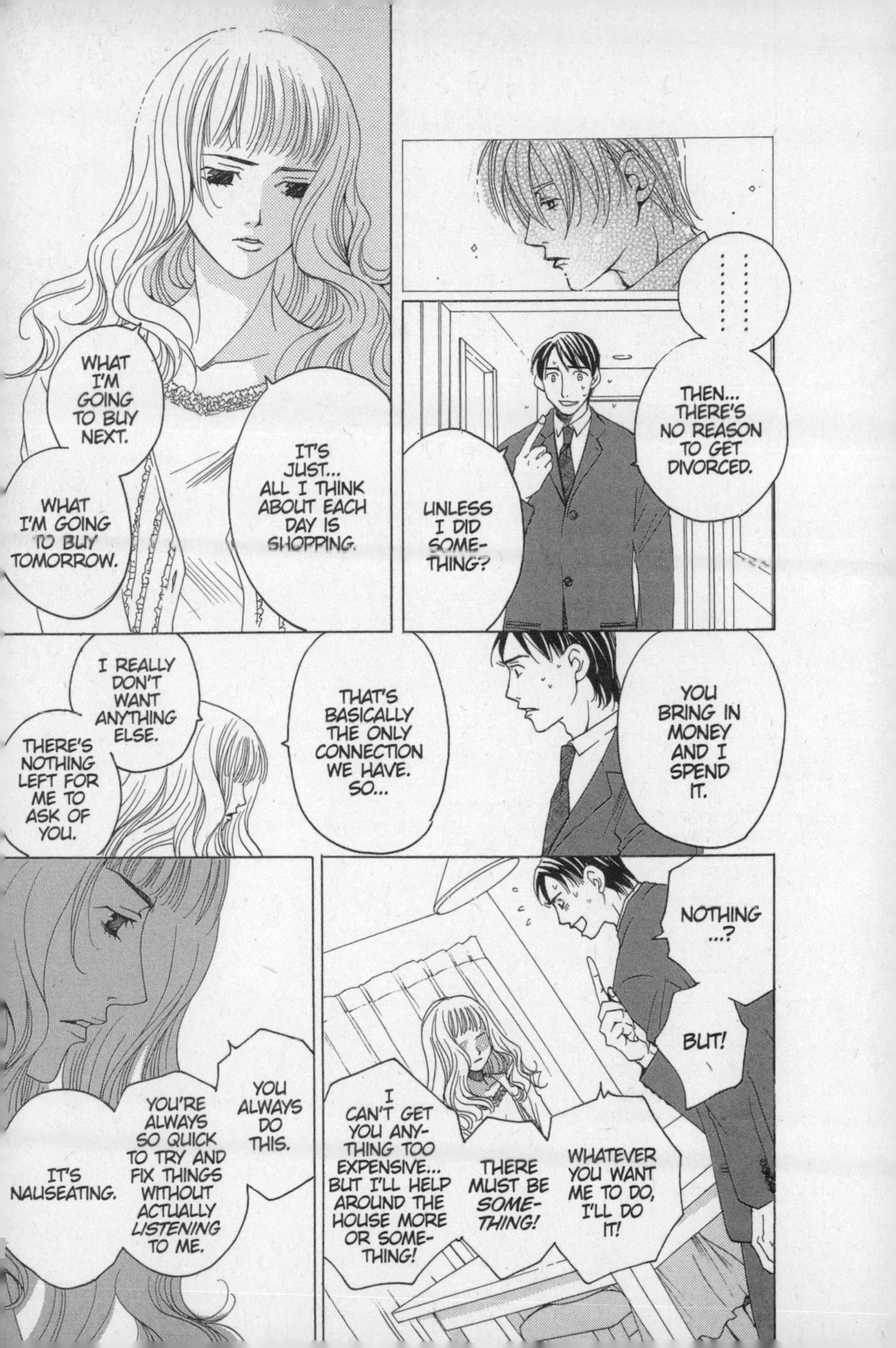
......
THEN... THERE'S NO REASON TO GET DIVORCED.
UNLESS I DID SOMETHING?
IT'S JUST... ALL I THINK ABOUT EACH DAY IS SHOPPING.
WHAT I'M GOING TO BUY NEXT.
WHAT I'M GOING TO BUY TOMORROW.
YOU BRING IN MONEY AND I SPEND IT.
THAT'S BASICALLY THE ONLY CONNECTION WE HAVE. SO...
I REALLY DON'T WANT ANYTHING ELSE.
THERE'S NOTHING LEFT FOR ME TO ASK OF YOU.
NOTHING ...?
BUT!
WHATEVER YOU WANT ME TO DO, I'LL DO IT!
THERE MUST BE *SOMETHING*!
I CAN'T GET YOU ANYTHING TOO EXPENSIVE... BUT I'LL HELP AROUND THE HOUSE MORE OR SOMETHING!
YOU ALWAYS DO THIS.
YOU'RE ALWAYS SO QUICK TO TRY AND FIX THINGS WITHOUT ACTUALLY *LISTENING* TO ME.
IT'S NAUSEATING.

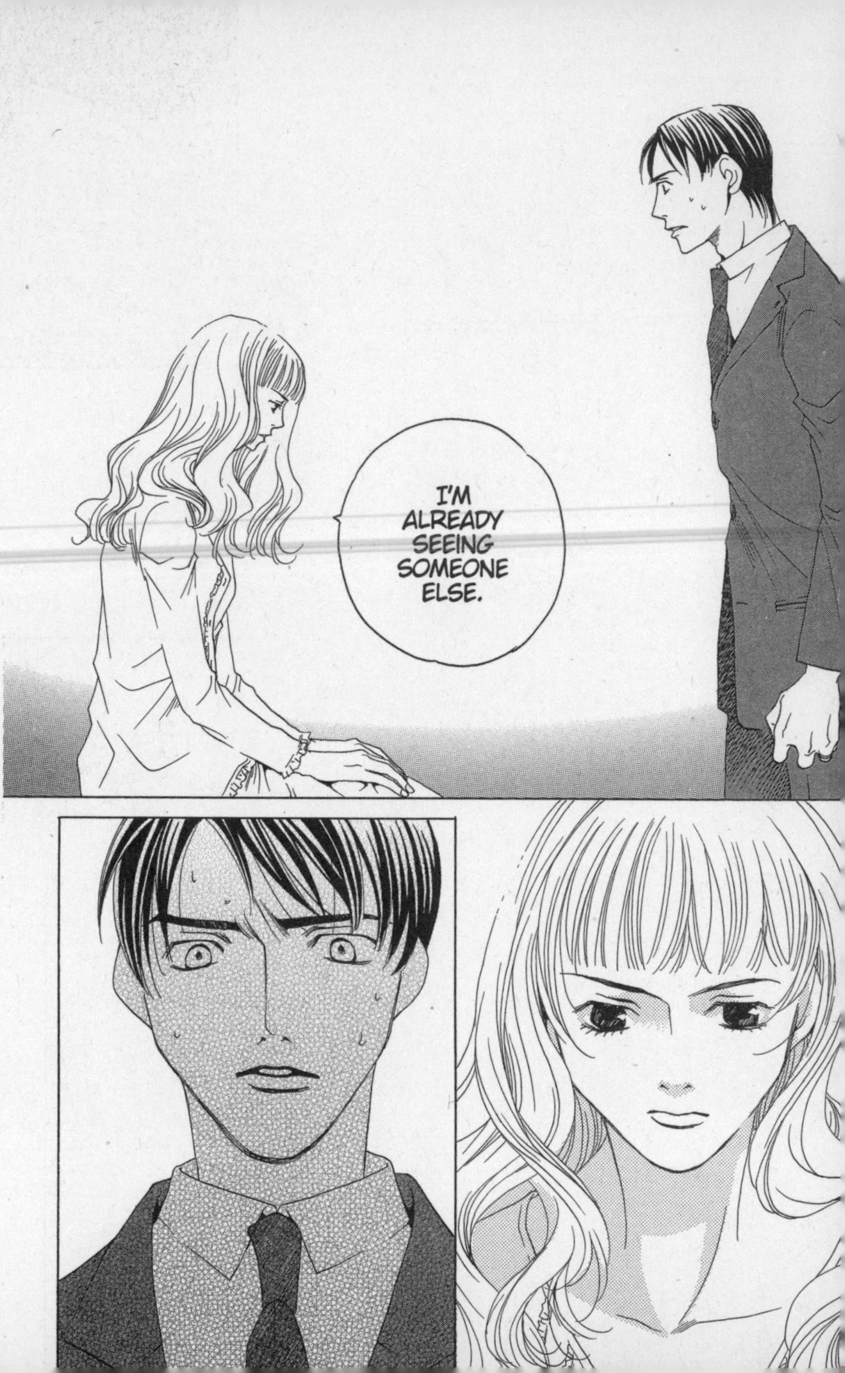
I'M ALREADY SEEING SOMEONE ELSE.

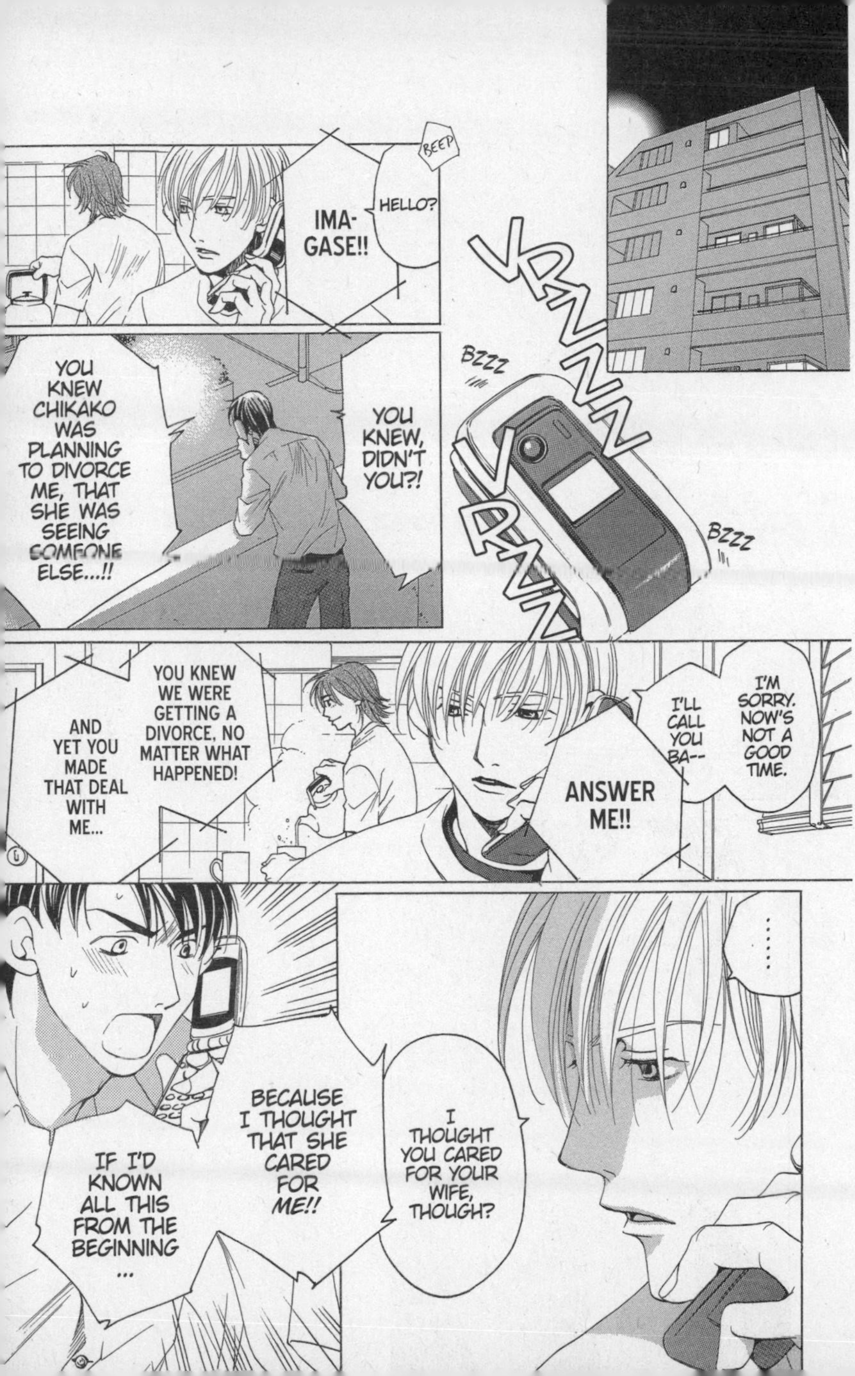
VRNNN
VRNN
BZZZ
BZZZ
BEEP
HELLO?
IMA-GASE!!
YOU KNEW, DIDN'T YOU?!
YOU KNEW CHIKAKO WAS PLANNING TO DIVORCE ME, THAT SHE WAS SEEING SOMEONE ELSE...!!
I'M SORRY. NOW'S NOT A GOOD TIME.
I'LL CALL YOU BA--
ANSWER ME!!
YOU KNEW WE WERE GETTING A DIVORCE, NO MATTER WHAT HAPPENED!
AND YET YOU MADE THAT DEAL WITH ME...
......
I THOUGHT YOU CARED FOR YOUR WIFE, THOUGH?
BECAUSE I THOUGHT THAT SHE CARED FOR *ME!!*
IF I'D KNOWN ALL THIS FROM THE BEGINNING...

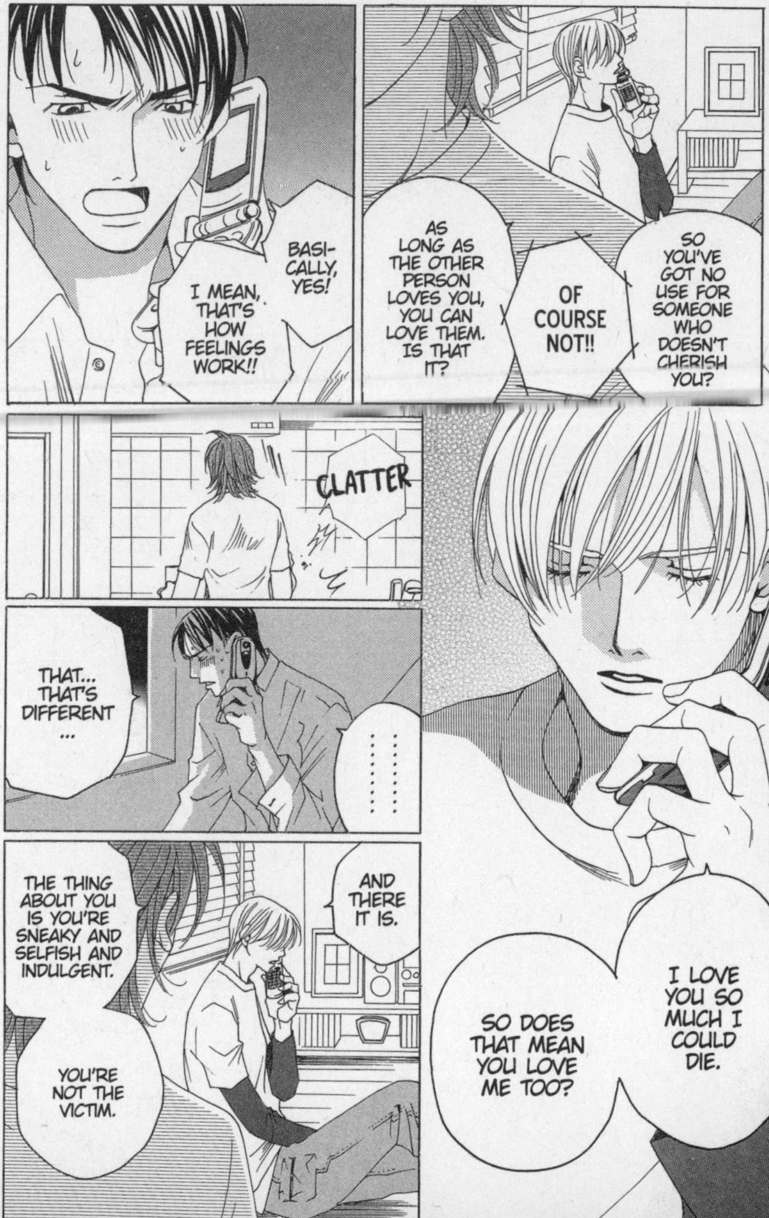
SO YOU'VE GOT NO USE FOR SOMEONE WHO DOESN'T CHERISH YOU?
OF COURSE NOT!!
AS LONG AS THE OTHER PERSON LOVES YOU, YOU CAN LOVE THEM. IS THAT IT?
BASI-CALLY, YES!
I MEAN, THAT'S HOW FEELINGS WORK!!
I LOVE YOU SO MUCH I COULD DIE.
SO DOES THAT MEAN YOU LOVE ME TOO?
CLATTER
......
THAT... THAT'S DIFFERENT ...
AND THERE IT IS.
THE THING ABOUT YOU IS YOU'RE SNEAKY AND SELFISH AND INDULGENT.
YOU'RE NOT THE VICTIM.

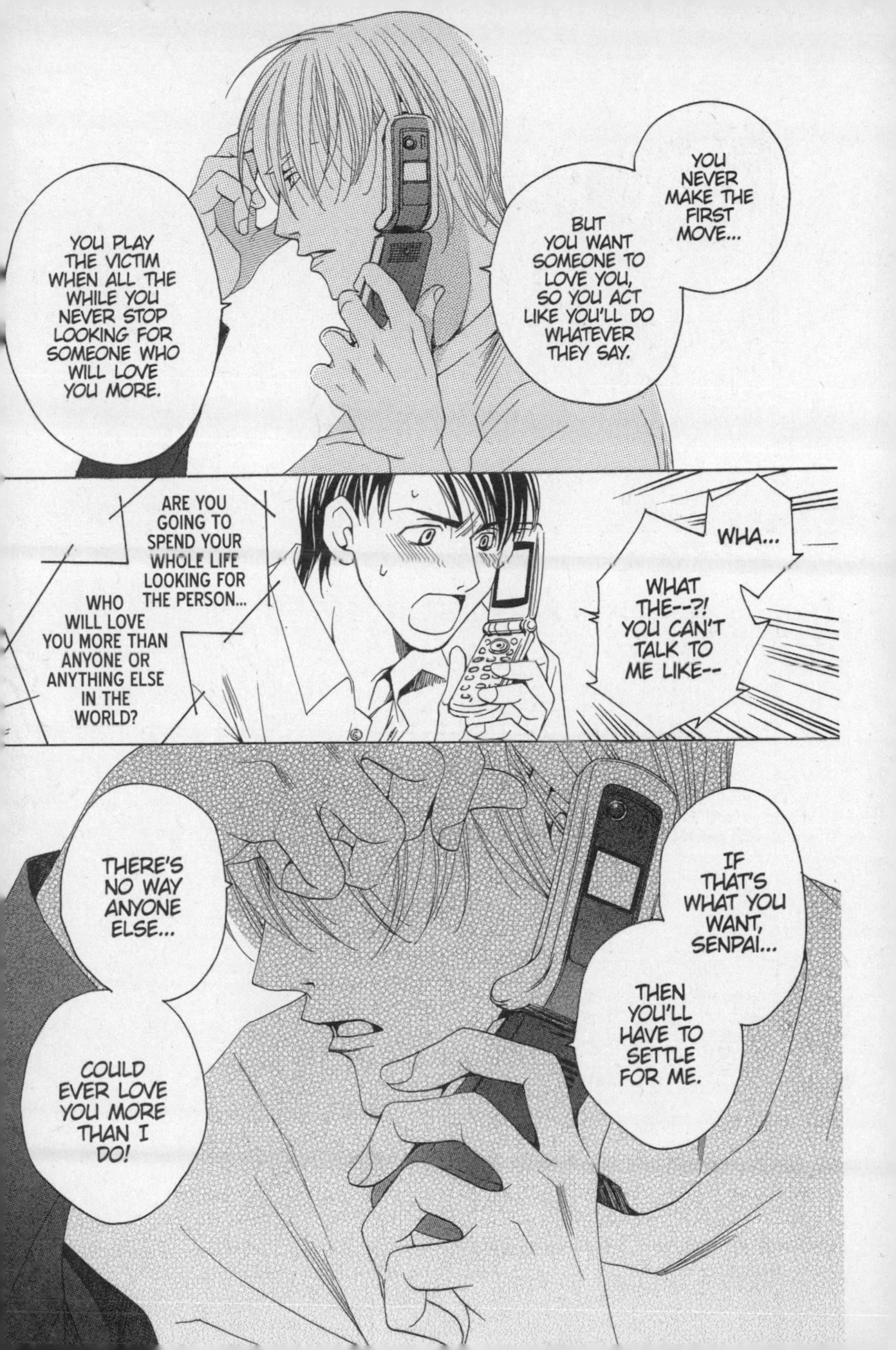
YOU NEVER MAKE THE FIRST MOVE...
BUT YOU WANT SOMEONE TO LOVE YOU, SO YOU ACT LIKE YOU'LL DO WHATEVER THEY SAY.
YOU PLAY THE VICTIM WHEN ALL THE WHILE YOU NEVER STOP LOOKING FOR SOMEONE WHO WILL LOVE YOU MORE.
WHA...
WHAT THE--?! YOU CAN'T TALK TO ME LIKE--
ARE YOU GOING TO SPEND YOUR WHOLE LIFE LOOKING FOR THE PERSON...
WHO WILL LOVE YOU MORE THAN ANYONE OR ANYTHING ELSE IN THE WORLD?
IF THAT'S WHAT YOU WANT, SENPAI...
THEN YOU'LL HAVE TO SETTLE FOR ME.
THERE'S NO WAY ANYONE ELSE...
COULD EVER LOVE YOU MORE THAN I DO!

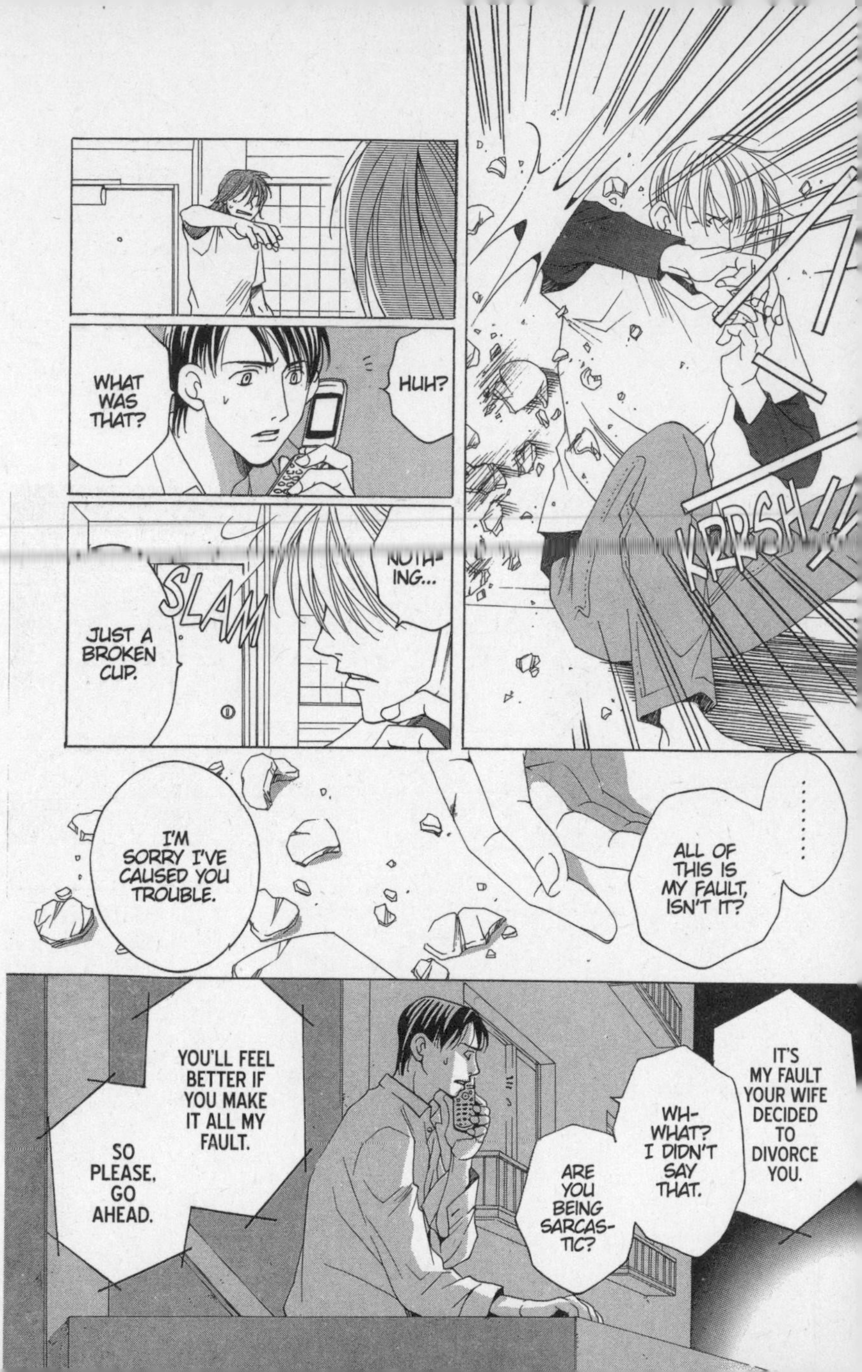
KRRSH
HUH?
WHAT WAS THAT?
NOTHING...
SLAM
JUST A BROKEN CUP.
......
ALL OF THIS IS MY FAULT, ISN'T IT?
I'M SORRY I'VE CAUSED YOU TROUBLE.
IT'S MY FAULT YOUR WIFE DECIDED TO DIVORCE YOU.
WH-WHAT? I DIDN'T SAY THAT.
ARE YOU BEING SARCASTIC?
YOU'LL FEEL BETTER IF YOU MAKE IT ALL MY FAULT.
SO PLEASE, GO AHEAD.

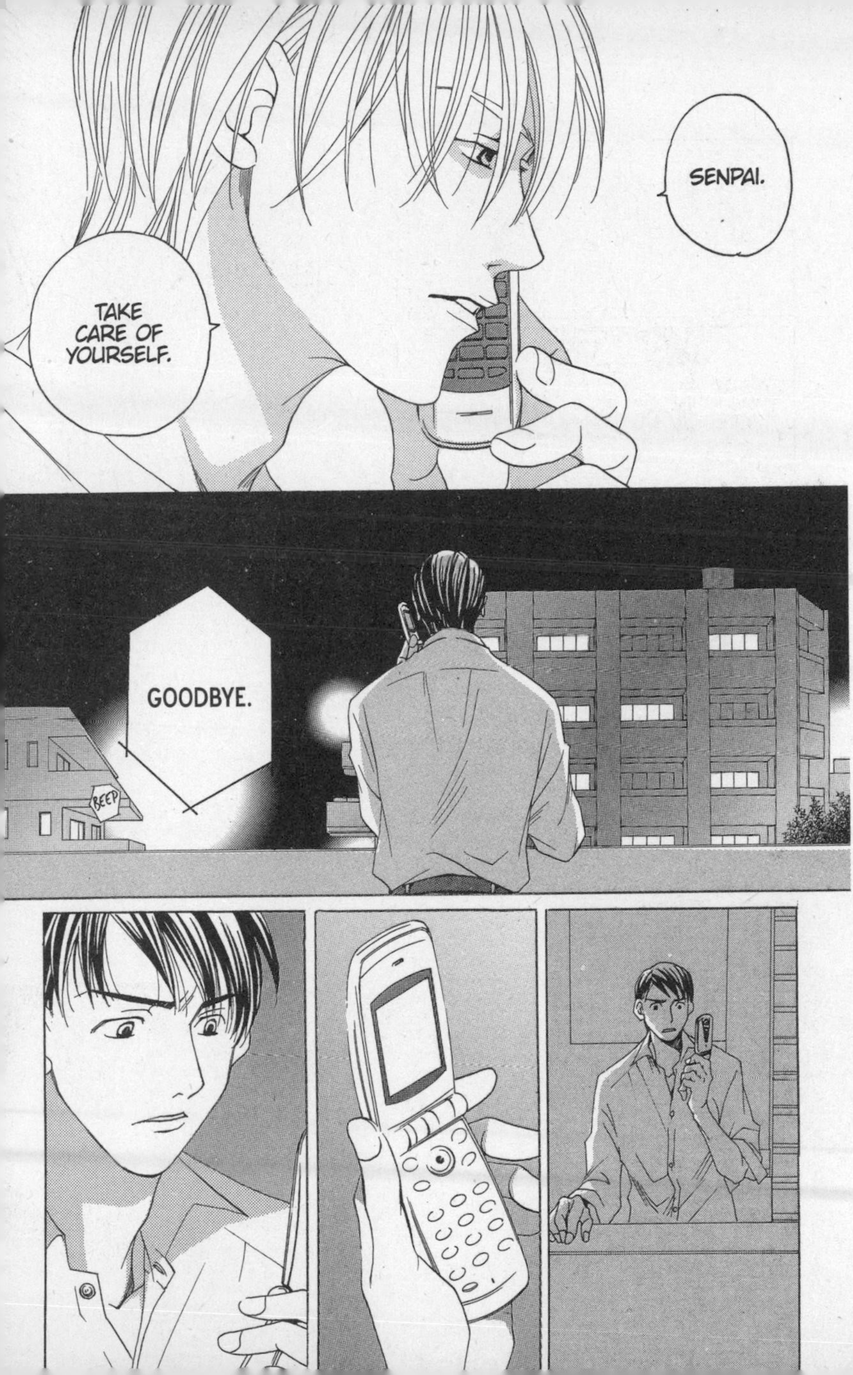
SENPAI.
TAKE CARE OF YOURSELF.
GOODBYE.
BEEP

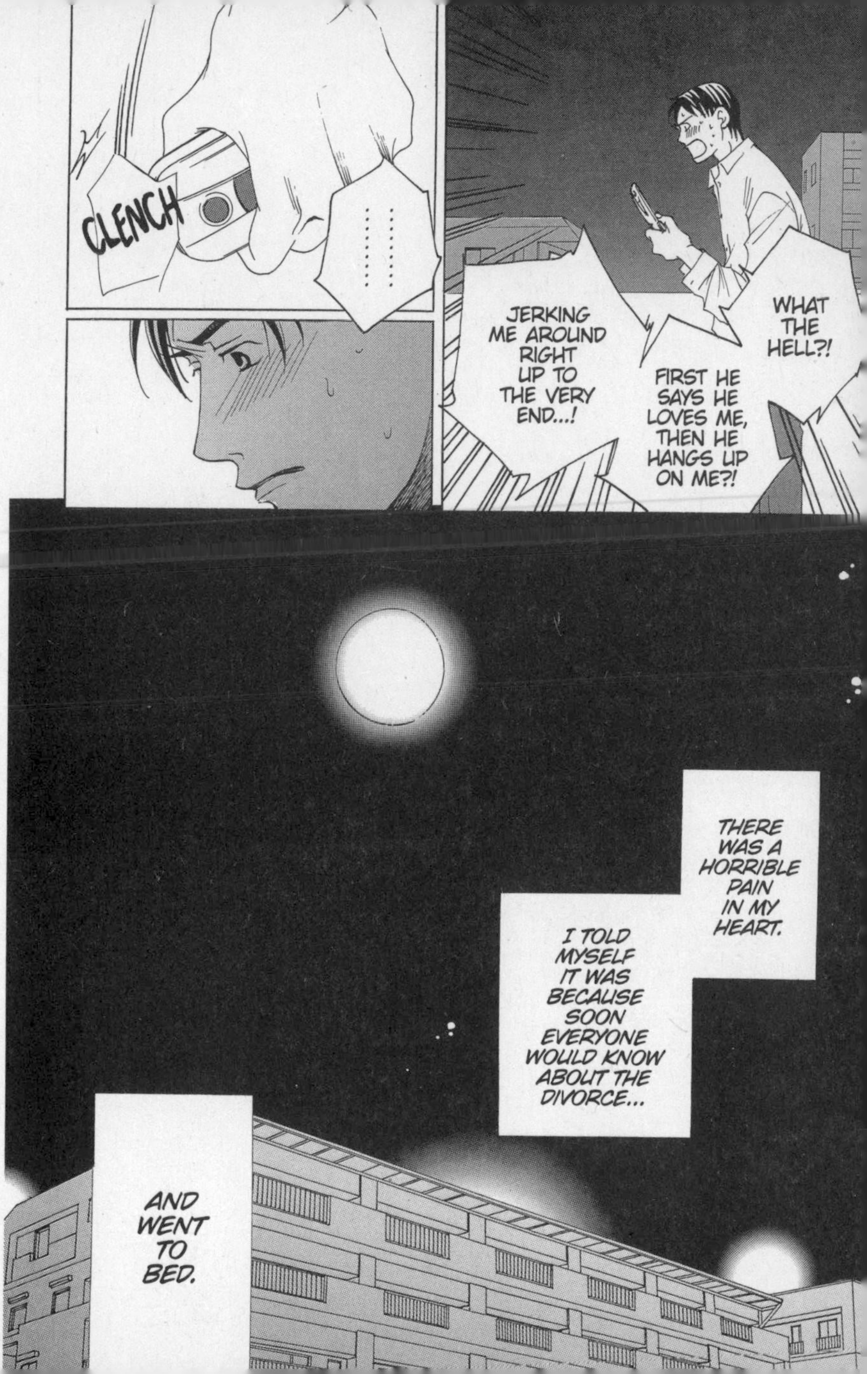
WHAT THE HELL?!
FIRST HE SAYS HE LOVES ME, THEN HE HANGS UP ON ME?!
JERKING ME AROUND RIGHT UP TO THE VERY END...!
CLENCH
THERE WAS A HORRIBLE PAIN IN MY HEART.
I TOLD MYSELF IT WAS BECAUSE SOON EVERYONE WOULD KNOW ABOUT THE DIVORCE...
AND WENT TO BED.

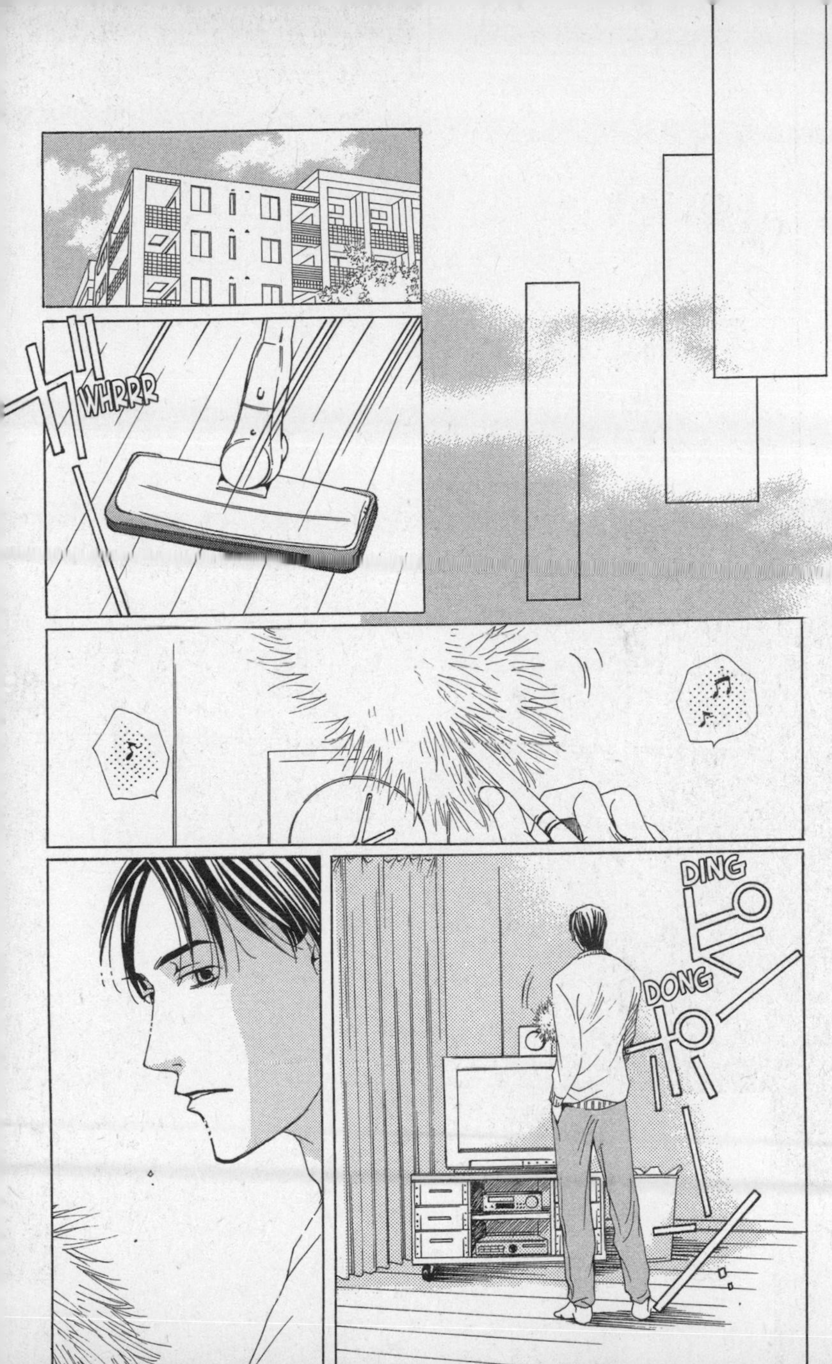
WHRRR
DING
DONG

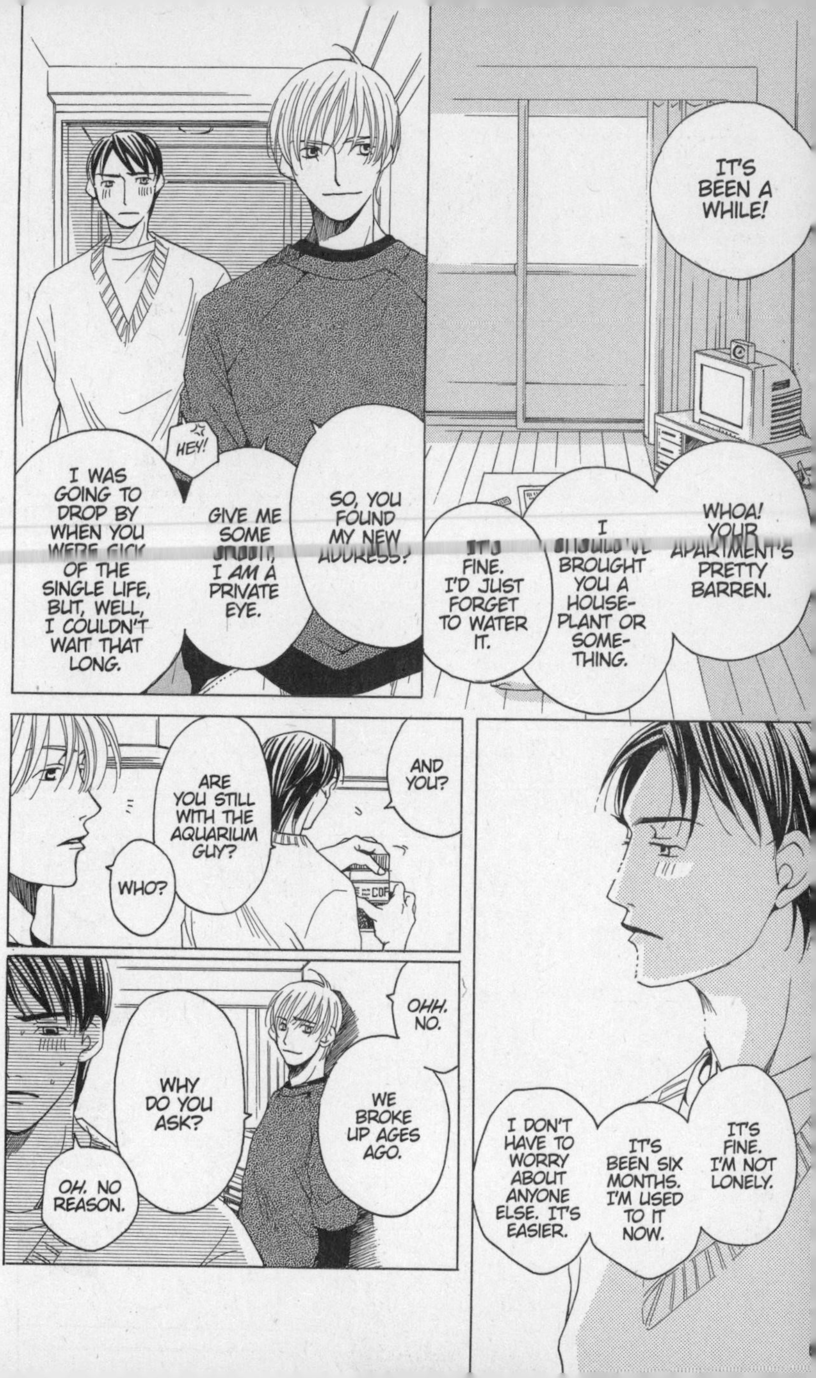
IT'S BEEN A WHILE!
WHOA! YOUR APARTMENT'S PRETTY BARREN.
I SHOULD'VE BROUGHT YOU A HOUSE-PLANT OR SOME-THING.
IT'S FINE. I'D JUST FORGET TO WATER IT.
SO, YOU FOUND MY NEW ADDRESS?
GIVE ME SOME CREDIT, I AM A PRIVATE EYE.
HEY!
I WAS GOING TO DROP BY WHEN YOU WERE SICK OF THE SINGLE LIFE, BUT, WELL, I COULDN'T WAIT THAT LONG.
IT'S FINE. I'M NOT LONELY.
IT'S BEEN SIX MONTHS. I'M USED TO IT NOW.
I DON'T HAVE TO WORRY ABOUT ANYONE ELSE. IT'S EASIER.
AND YOU?
ARE YOU STILL WITH THE AQUARIUM GUY?
WHO?
OHH. NO.
WE BROKE UP AGES AGO.
WHY DO YOU ASK?
OH. NO REASON.

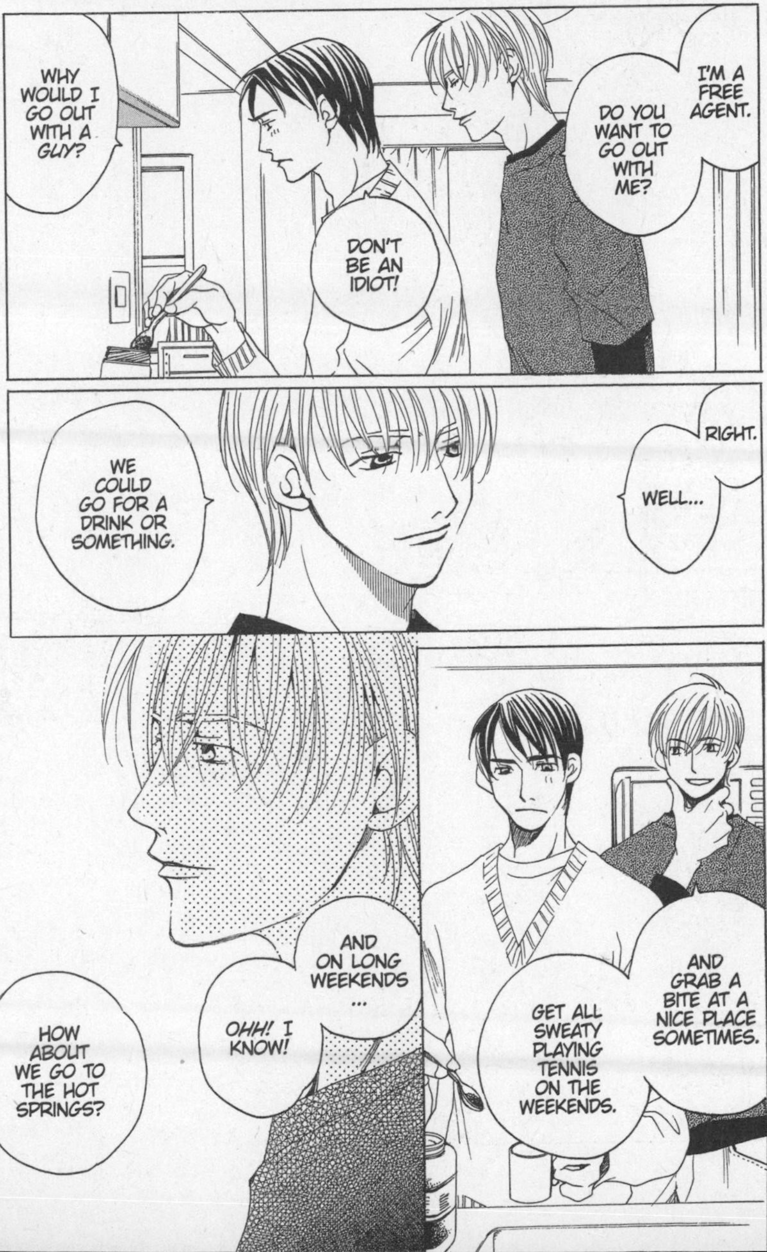
I'M A FREE AGENT.
DO YOU WANT TO GO OUT WITH ME?
WHY WOULD I GO OUT WITH A GUY?
DON'T BE AN IDIOT!
RIGHT.
WELL...
WE COULD GO FOR A DRINK OR SOMETHING.
AND GRAB A BITE AT A NICE PLACE SOMETIMES.
GET ALL SWEATY PLAYING TENNIS ON THE WEEKENDS.
AND ON LONG WEEKENDS ...
OHH! I KNOW!
HOW ABOUT WE GO TO THE HOT SPRINGS?

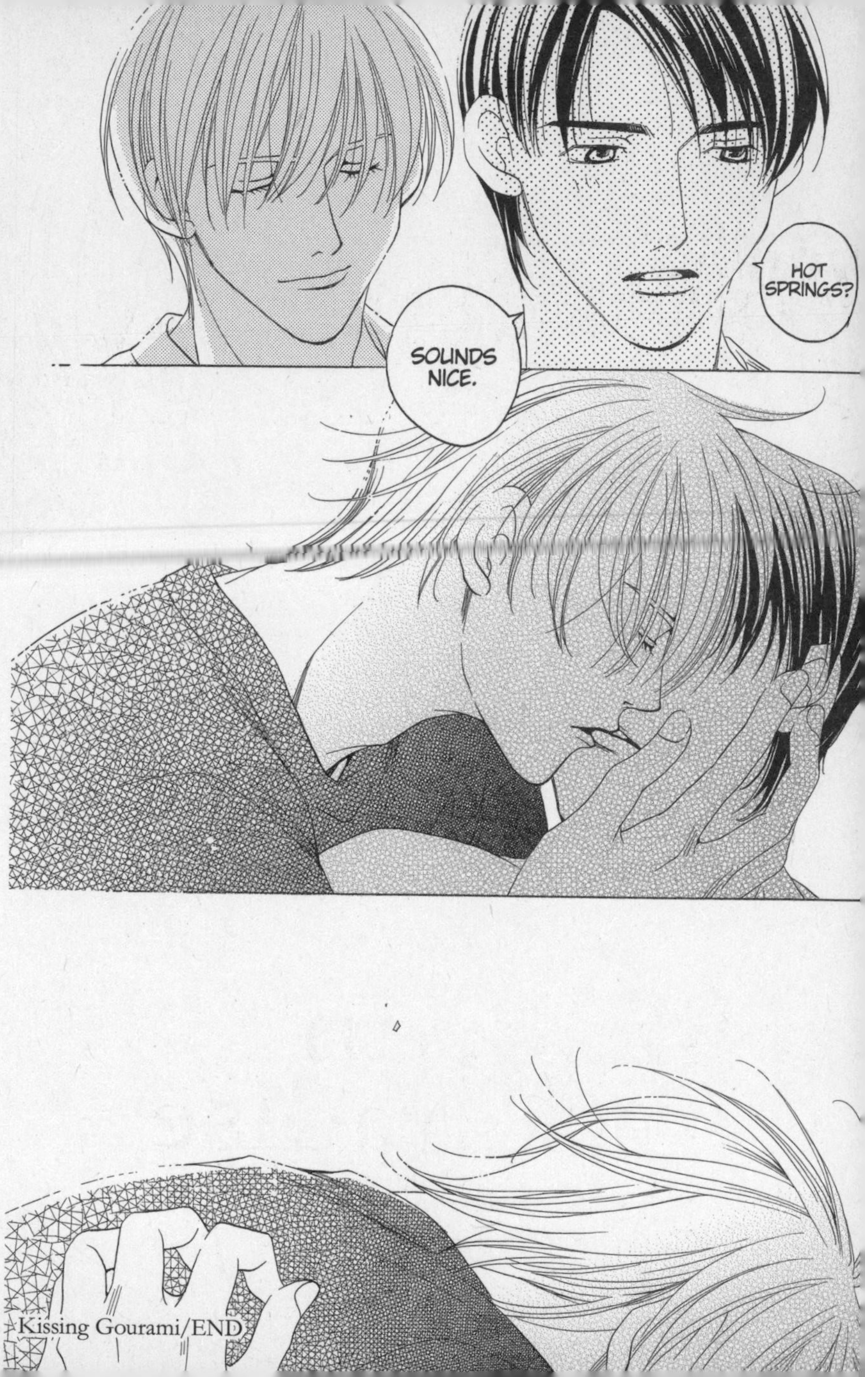
HOT SPRINGS?
SOUNDS NICE.
Kissing Gourami/END

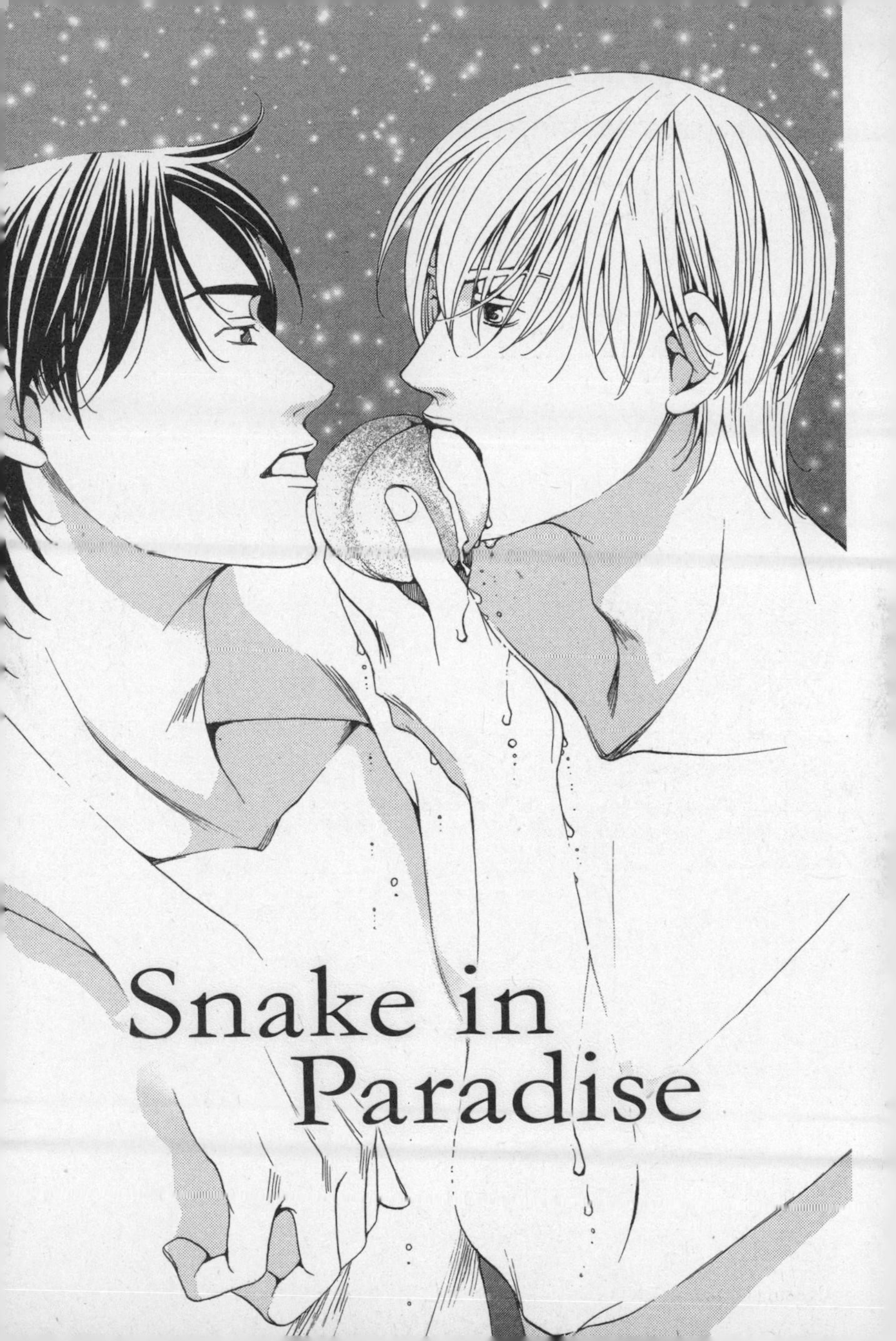
Snake in
Paradise

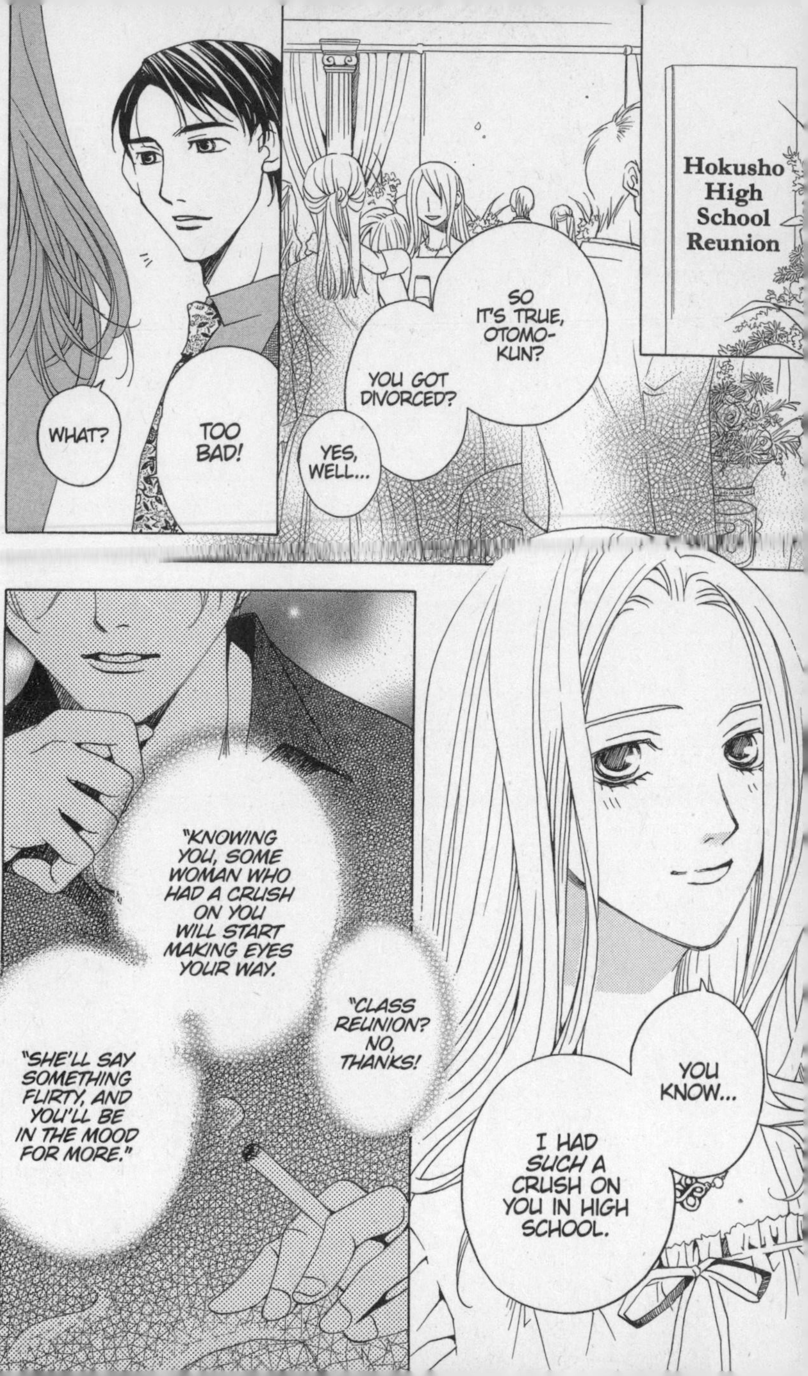
Hokusho High School Reunion
SO IT'S TRUE, OTOMO-KUN?
YOU GOT DIVORCED?
YES, WELL...
TOO BAD!
WHAT?
YOU KNOW...
I HAD SUCH A CRUSH ON YOU IN HIGH SCHOOL.
"CLASS REUNION? NO, THANKS!
"KNOWING YOU, SOME WOMAN WHO HAD A CRUSH ON YOU WILL START MAKING EYES YOUR WAY.
"SHE'LL SAY SOMETHING FLIRTY, AND YOU'LL BE IN THE MOOD FOR MORE."

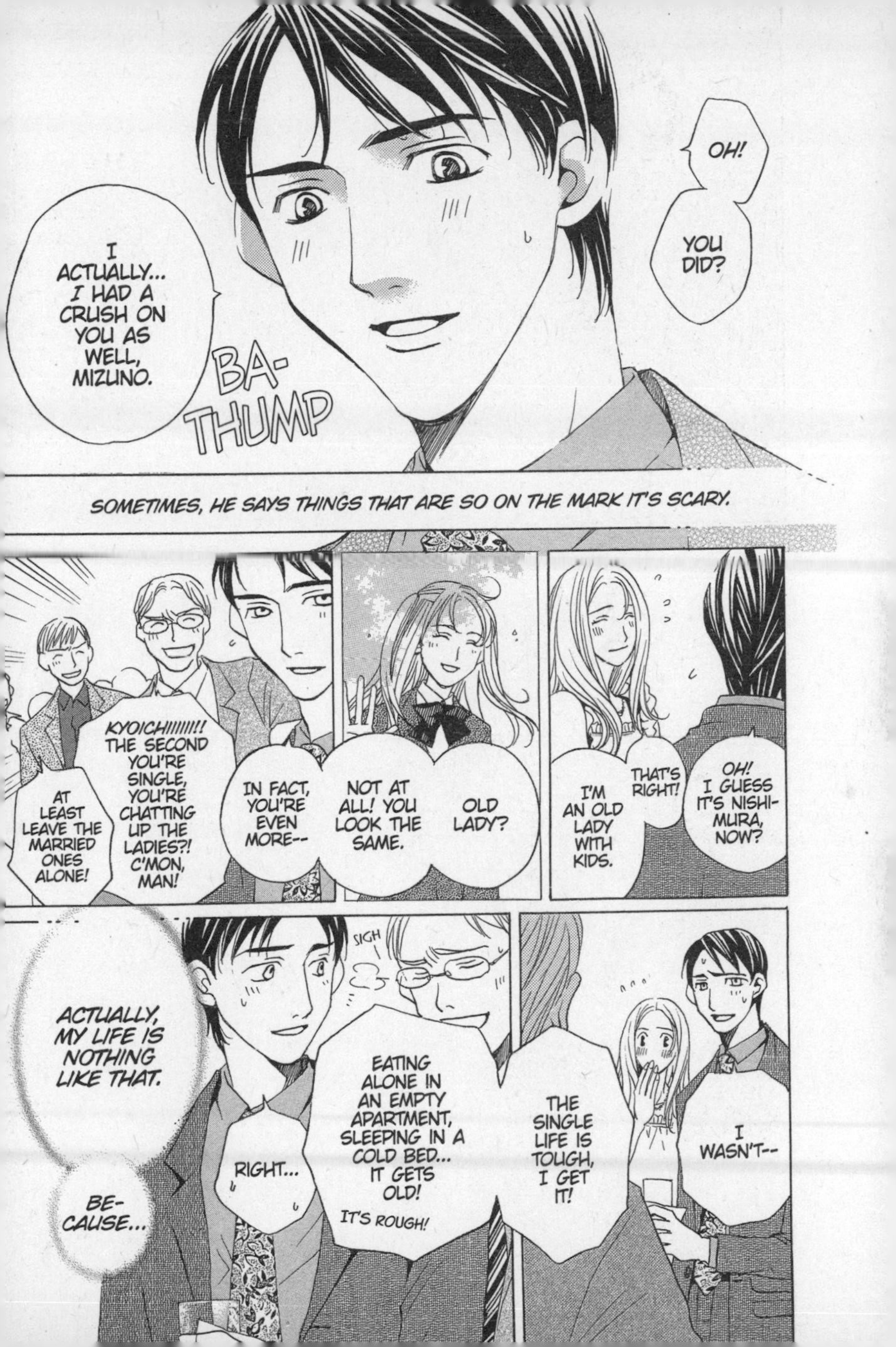
OH!
YOU DID?
I ACTUALLY... I HAD A CRUSH ON YOU AS WELL, MIZUNO.
BA-THUMP
SOMETIMES, HE SAYS THINGS THAT ARE SO ON THE MARK IT'S SCARY.
OH! I GUESS IT'S NISHI-MURA, NOW?
THAT'S RIGHT!
I'M AN OLD LADY WITH KIDS.
OLD LADY?
NOT AT ALL! YOU LOOK THE SAME.
IN FACT, YOU'RE EVEN MORE--
KYOICHI!!!!!!! THE SECOND YOU'RE SINGLE, YOU'RE CHATTING UP THE LADIES?! C'MON, MAN!
AT LEAST LEAVE THE MARRIED ONES ALONE!
I WASN'T--
THE SINGLE LIFE IS TOUGH, I GET IT!
EATING ALONE IN AN EMPTY APARTMENT, SLEEPING IN A COLD BED... IT GETS OLD!
IT'S ROUGH!
SIGH
RIGHT...
ACTUALLY, MY LIFE IS NOTHING LIKE THAT.
BE-CAUSE...

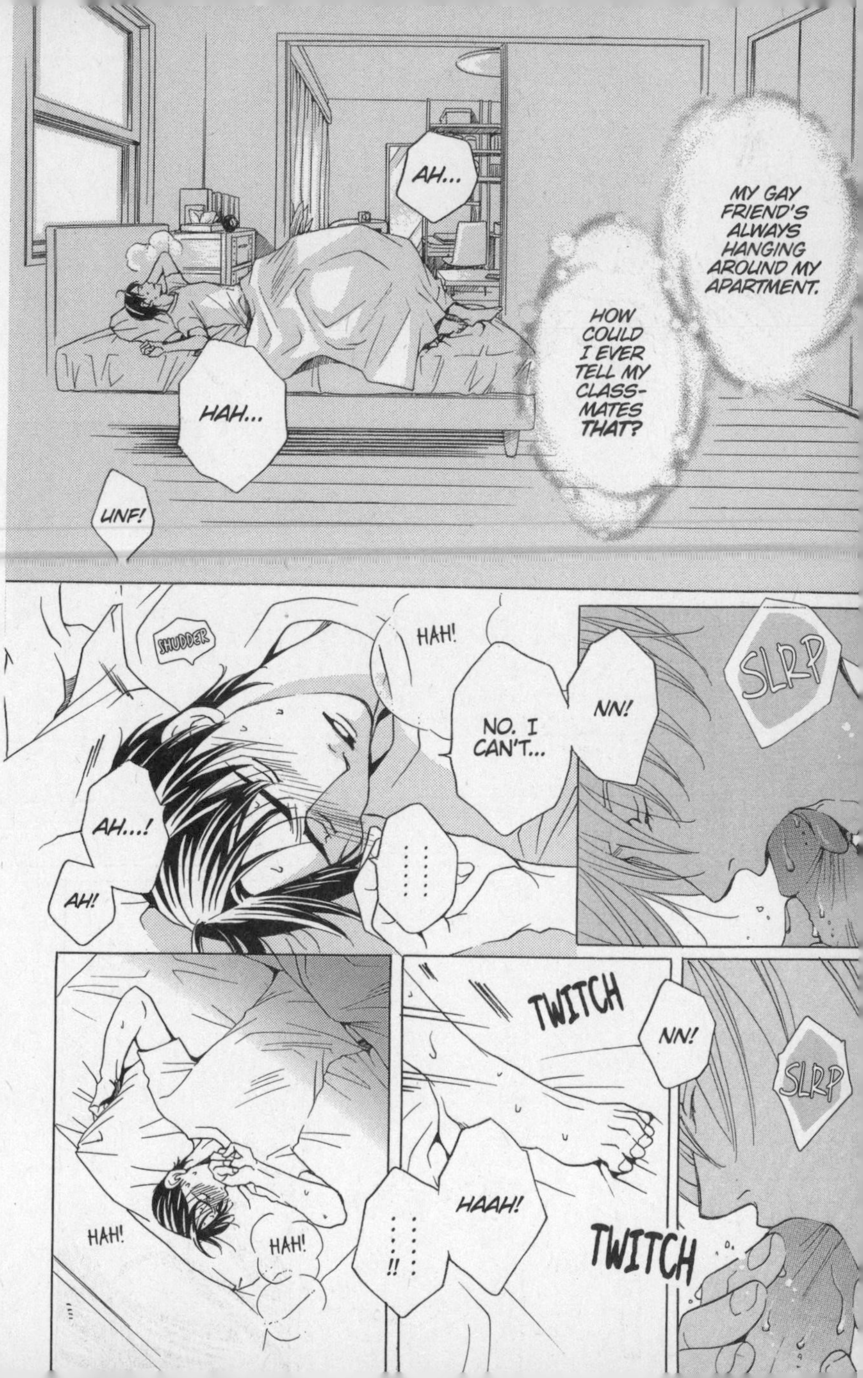
MY GAY FRIEND'S ALWAYS HANGING AROUND MY APARTMENT.
HOW COULD I EVER TELL MY CLASSMATES THAT?
AH...
HAH...
UNF!
SLRP
NN!
HAH!
NO. I CAN'T...
SHUDDER
......
AH...!
AH!
SLRP
TWITCH
NN!
TWITCH
HAAH!
......!!
HAH!
HAH!

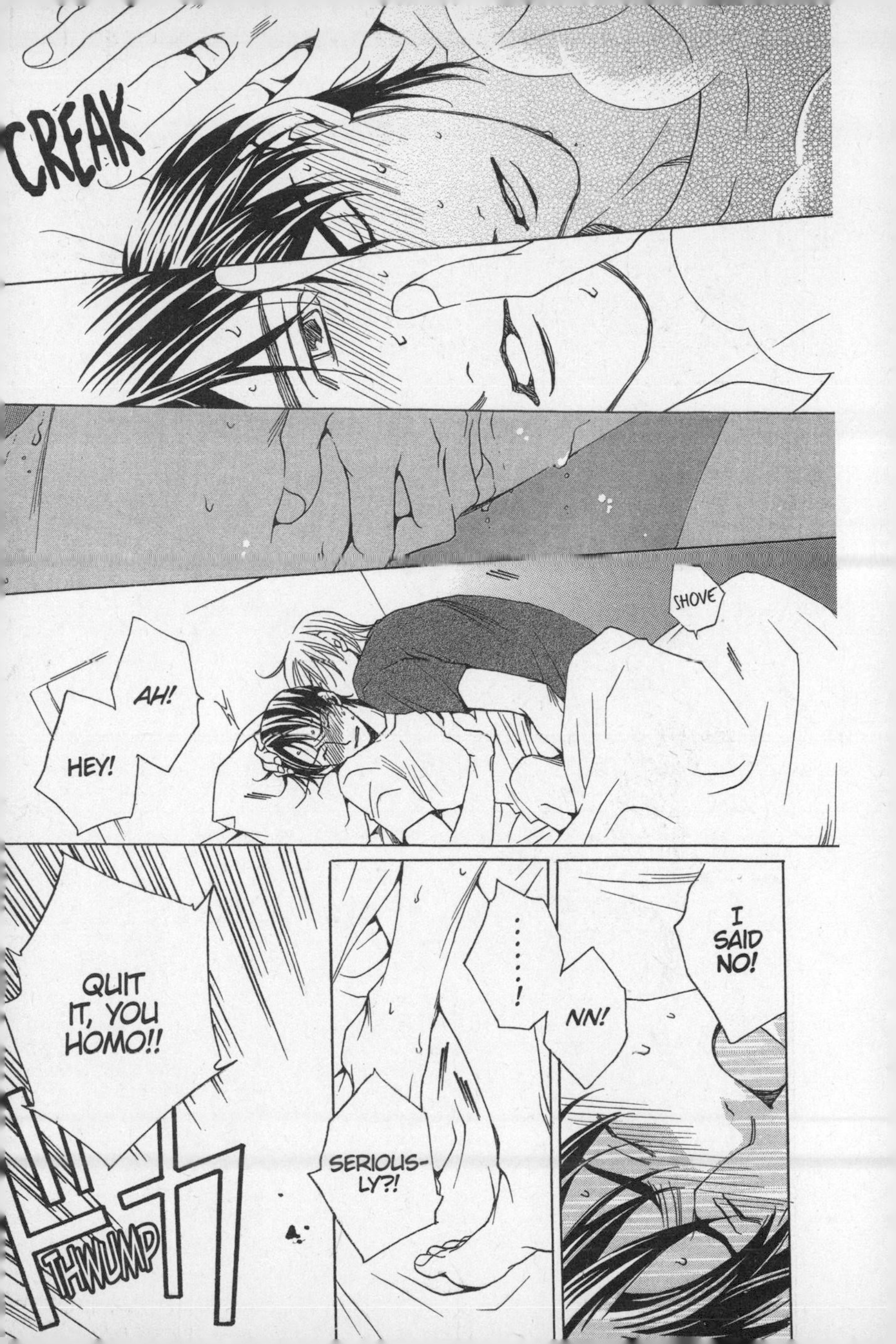
CREAK
SHOVE
AH!
HEY!
I SAID NO!
NN!
......!
SERIOUS-LY?!
QUIT IT, YOU HOMO!!
THWUMP

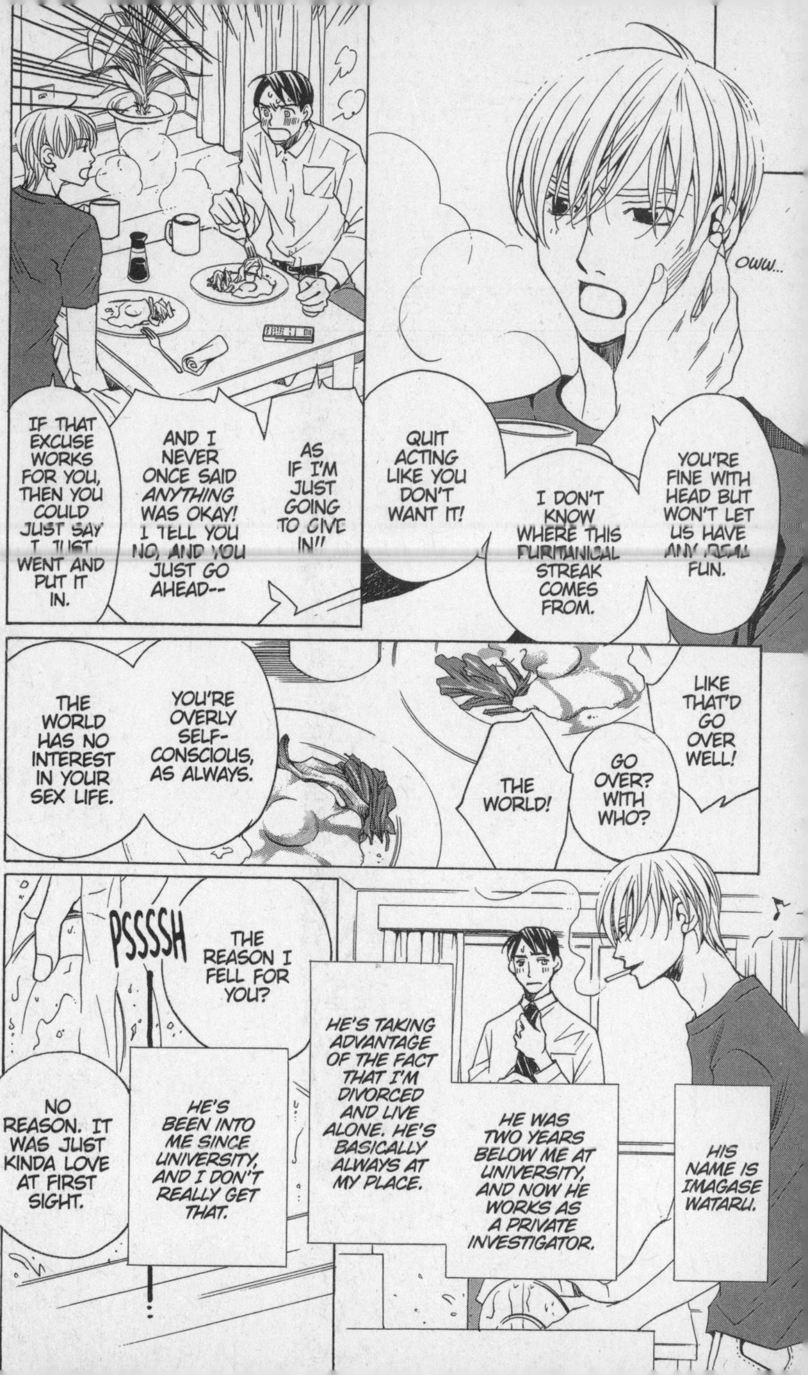
OWW...
YOU'RE FINE WITH HEAD BUT WON'T LET US HAVE ANY REAL FUN.
I DON'T KNOW WHERE THIS PURITANICAL STREAK COMES FROM.
QUIT ACTING LIKE YOU DON'T WANT IT!
AS IF I'M JUST GOING TO GIVE IN!!
AND I NEVER ONCE SAID ANYTHING WAS OKAY! I TELL YOU NO, AND YOU JUST GO AHEAD--
IF THAT EXCUSE WORKS FOR YOU, THEN YOU COULD JUST SAY I JUST WENT AND PUT IT IN.
LIKE THAT'D GO OVER WELL!
GO OVER? WITH WHO?
THE WORLD!
YOU'RE OVERLY SELF-CONSCIOUS, AS ALWAYS.
THE WORLD HAS NO INTEREST IN YOUR SEX LIFE.
HIS NAME IS IMAGASE WATARU.
HE WAS TWO YEARS BELOW ME AT UNIVERSITY, AND NOW HE WORKS AS A PRIVATE INVESTIGATOR.
HE'S TAKING ADVANTAGE OF THE FACT THAT I'M DIVORCED AND LIVE ALONE. HE'S BASICALLY ALWAYS AT MY PLACE.
THE REASON I FELL FOR YOU?
PSSSSH
HE'S BEEN INTO ME SINCE UNIVERSITY, AND I DON'T REALLY GET THAT.
NO REASON. IT WAS JUST KINDA LOVE AT FIRST SIGHT.

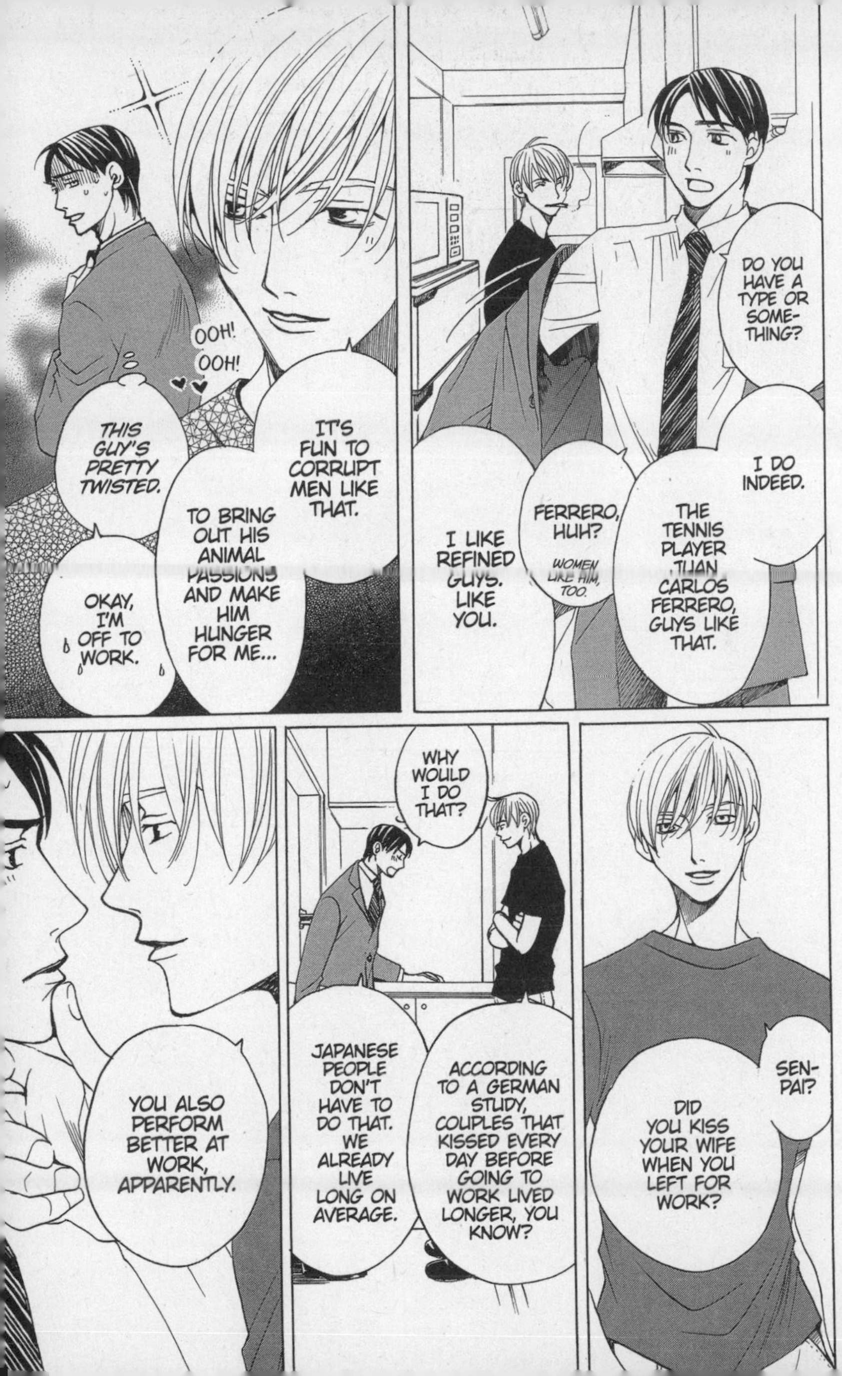
DO YOU HAVE A TYPE OR SOME-THING?
I DO INDEED.
THE TENNIS PLAYER JUAN CARLOS FERRERO, GUYS LIKE THAT.
FERRERO, HUH?
WOMEN LIKE HIM, TOO.
I LIKE REFINED GUYS. LIKE YOU.
IT'S FUN TO CORRUPT MEN LIKE THAT.
OOH! OOH!
TO BRING OUT HIS ANIMAL PASSIONS AND MAKE HIM HUNGER FOR ME...
THIS GUY'S PRETTY TWISTED.
OKAY, I'M OFF TO WORK.
SEN-PAI?
DID YOU KISS YOUR WIFE WHEN YOU LEFT FOR WORK?
WHY WOULD I DO THAT?
ACCORDING TO A GERMAN STUDY, COUPLES THAT KISSED EVERY DAY BEFORE GOING TO WORK LIVED LONGER, YOU KNOW?
JAPANESE PEOPLE DON'T HAVE TO DO THAT. WE ALREADY LIVE LONG ON AVERAGE.
YOU ALSO PERFORM BETTER AT WORK, APPARENTLY.

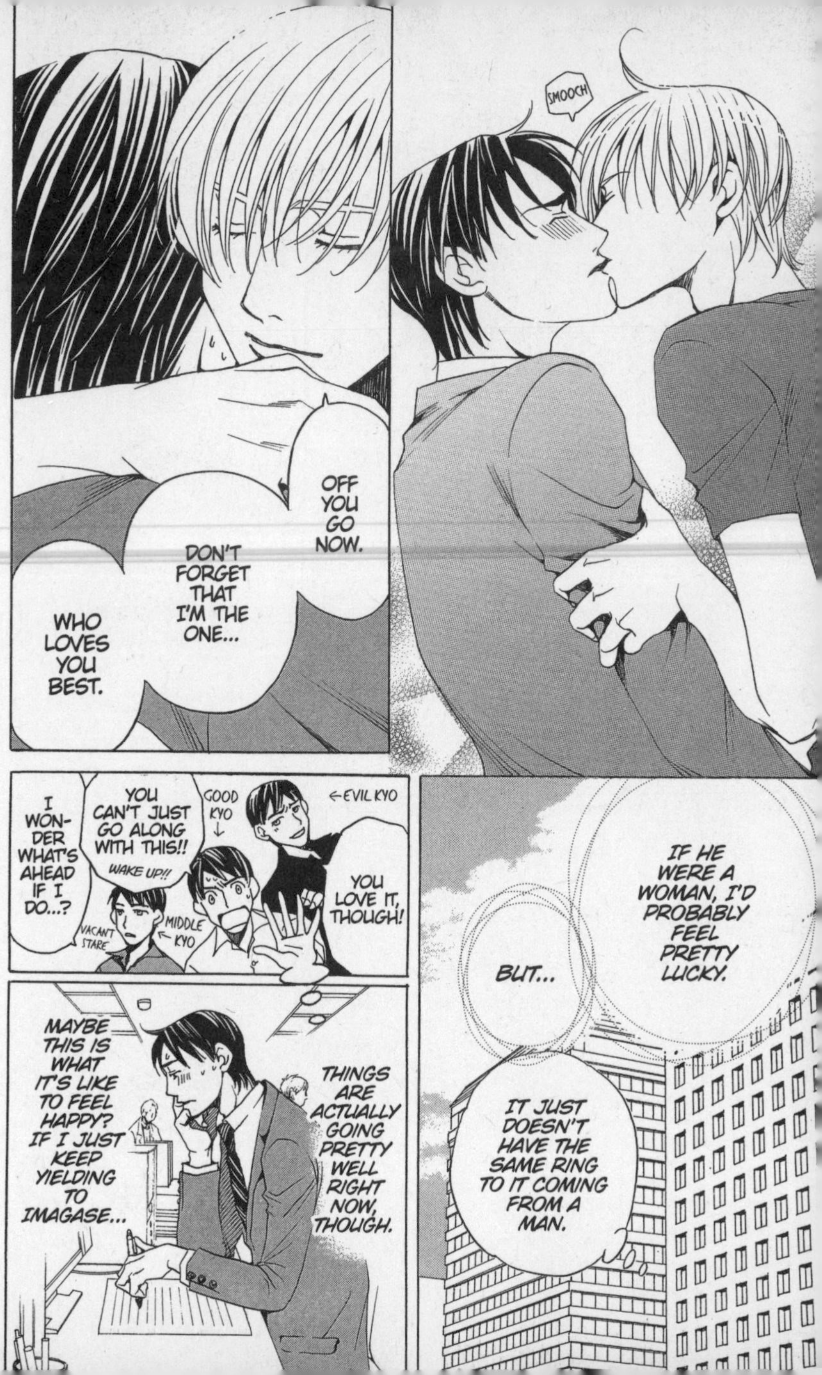
SMOOCH
OFF YOU GO NOW.
DON'T FORGET THAT I'M THE ONE...
WHO LOVES YOU BEST.
IF HE WERE A WOMAN, I'D PROBABLY FEEL PRETTY LUCKY.
BUT...
IT JUST DOESN'T HAVE THE SAME RING TO IT COMING FROM A MAN.
←EVIL KYO
YOU LOVE IT, THOUGH!
GOOD KYO ↓
YOU CAN'T JUST GO ALONG WITH THIS!!
WAKE UP!!
MIDDLE KYO
I WONDER WHAT'S AHEAD IF I DO...?
VACANT STARE
THINGS ARE ACTUALLY GOING PRETTY WELL RIGHT NOW, THOUGH.
MAYBE THIS IS WHAT IT'S LIKE TO FEEL HAPPY? IF I JUST KEEP YIELDING TO IMAGASE...

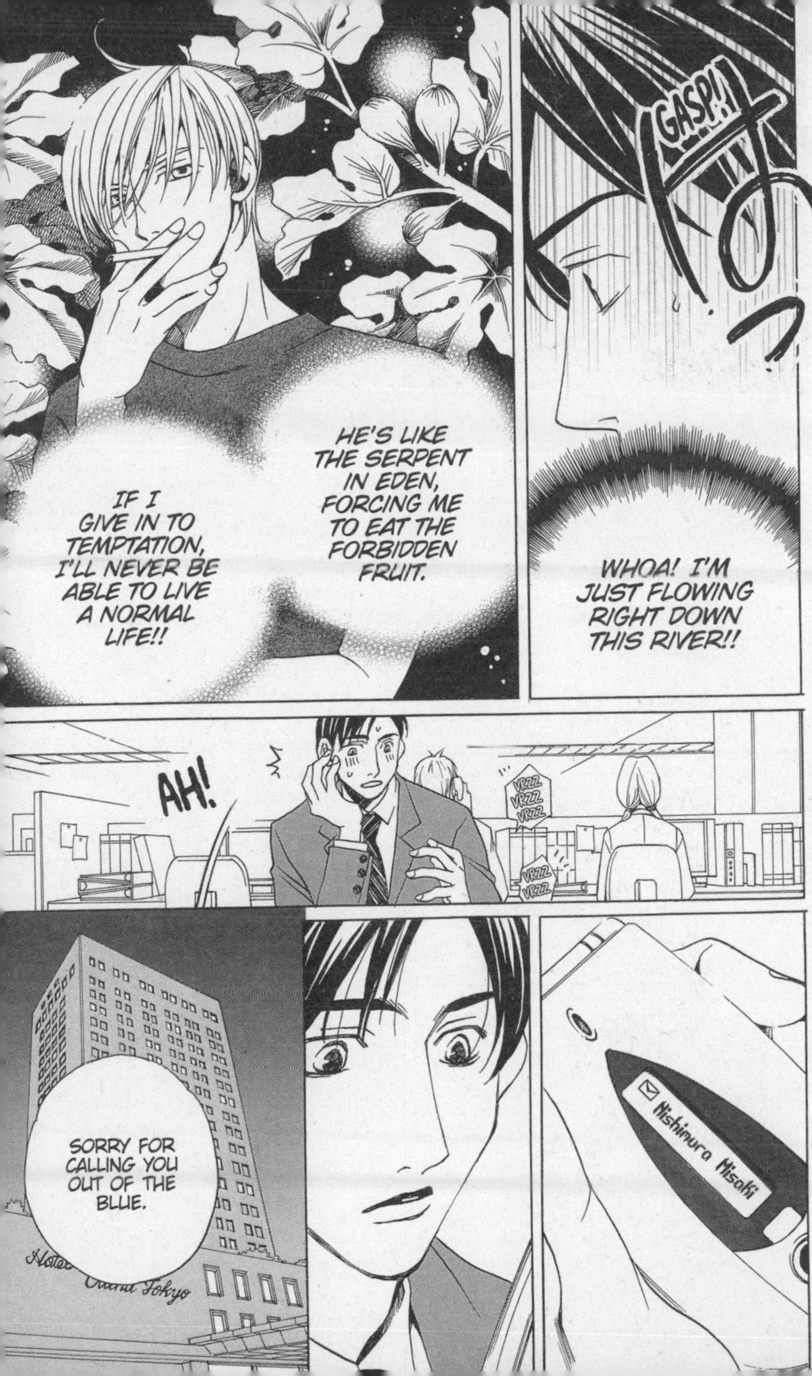
GASP!!
WHOA! I'M JUST FLOWING RIGHT DOWN THIS RIVER!!
HE'S LIKE THE SERPENT IN EDEN, FORCING ME TO EAT THE FORBIDDEN FRUIT.
IF I GIVE IN TO TEMPTATION, I'LL NEVER BE ABLE TO LIVE A NORMAL LIFE!!
VRZZZ VRZZZ VRZZZ
VRZZZ VRZZZ
AH!
Nishimura Misaki
SORRY FOR CALLING YOU OUT OF THE BLUE.

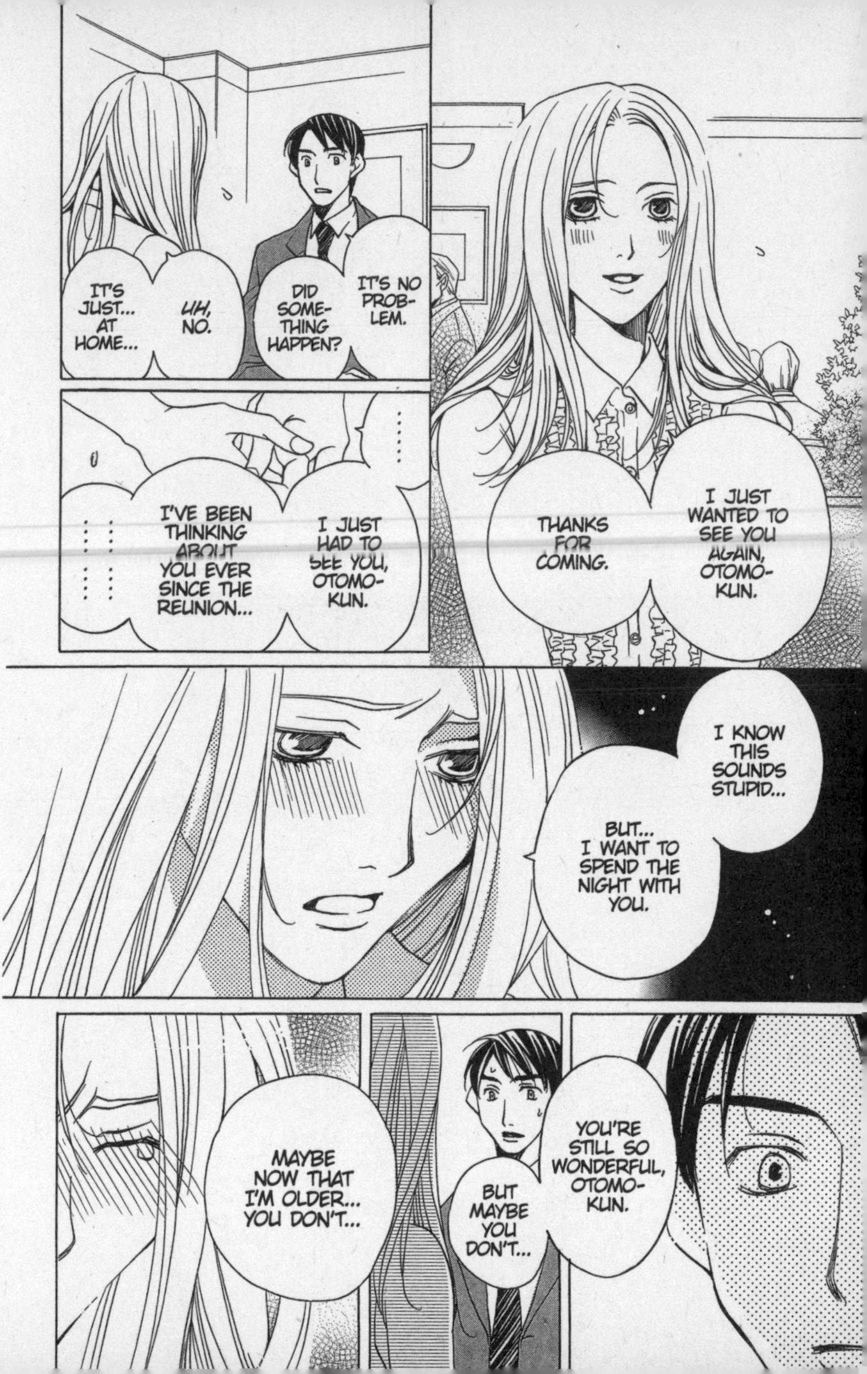
I JUST WANTED TO SEE YOU AGAIN, OTOMO-KUN.
THANKS FOR COMING.
IT'S NO PROB-LEM.
DID SOME-THING HAPPEN?
UH, NO.
IT'S JUST... AT HOME...
......
I JUST HAD TO SEE YOU, OTOMO-KUN.
I'VE BEEN THINKING ABOUT YOU EVER SINCE THE REUNION...
......
I KNOW THIS SOUNDS STUPID...
BUT... I WANT TO SPEND THE NIGHT WITH YOU.
YOU'RE STILL SO WONDERFUL, OTOMO-KUN.
BUT MAYBE YOU DON'T...
MAYBE NOW THAT I'M OLDER... YOU DON'T...

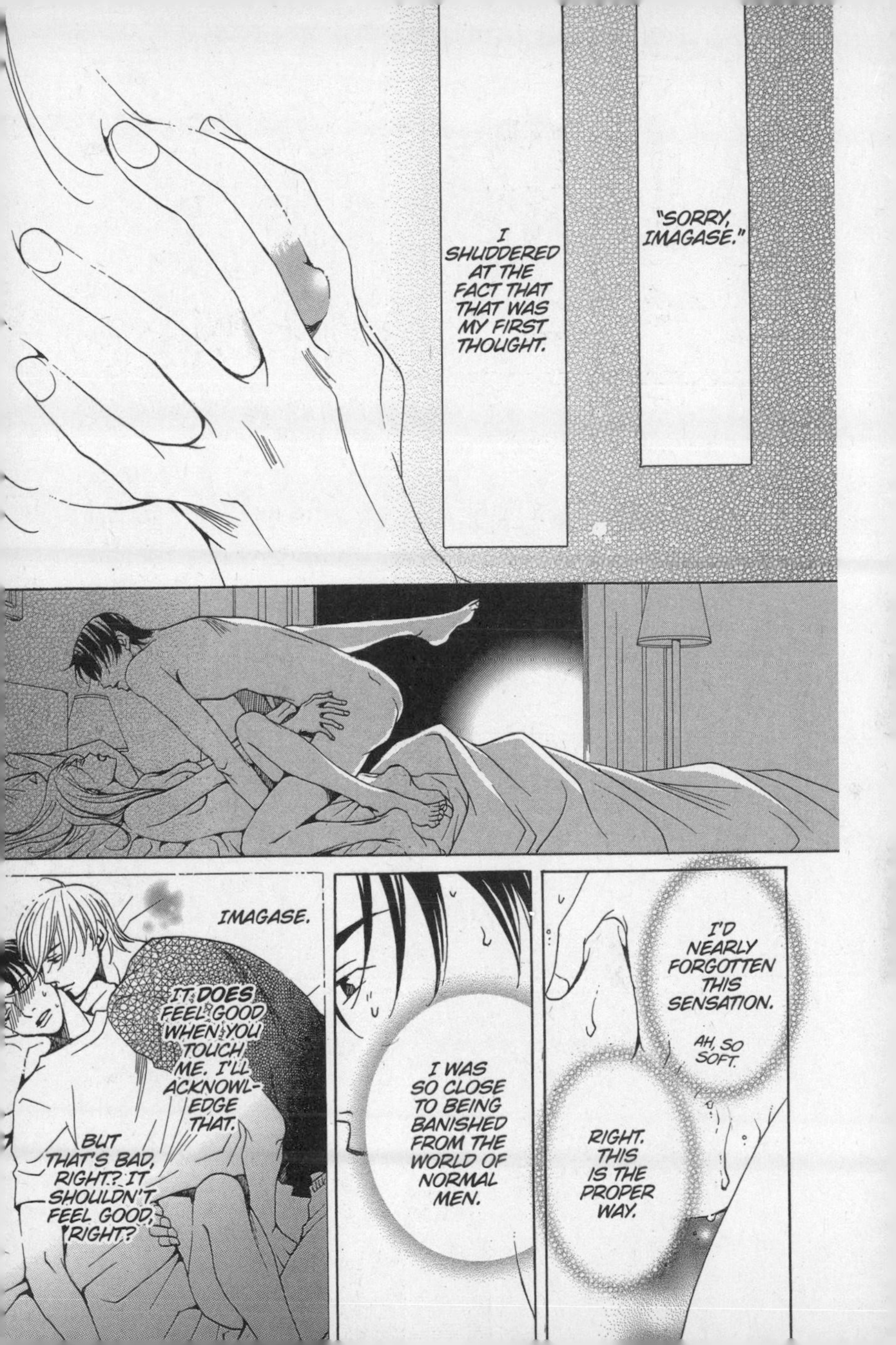
"SORRY, IMAGASE."
I SHUDDERED AT THE FACT THAT THAT WAS MY FIRST THOUGHT.
I'D NEARLY FORGOTTEN THIS SENSATION.
AH, SO SOFT.
RIGHT. THIS IS THE PROPER WAY.
I WAS SO CLOSE TO BEING BANISHED FROM THE WORLD OF NORMAL MEN.
IMAGASE.
IT DOES FEEL GOOD WHEN YOU TOUCH ME. I'LL ACKNOWL-EDGE THAT.
BUT THAT'S BAD, RIGHT? IT SHOULDN'T FEEL GOOD, RIGHT?

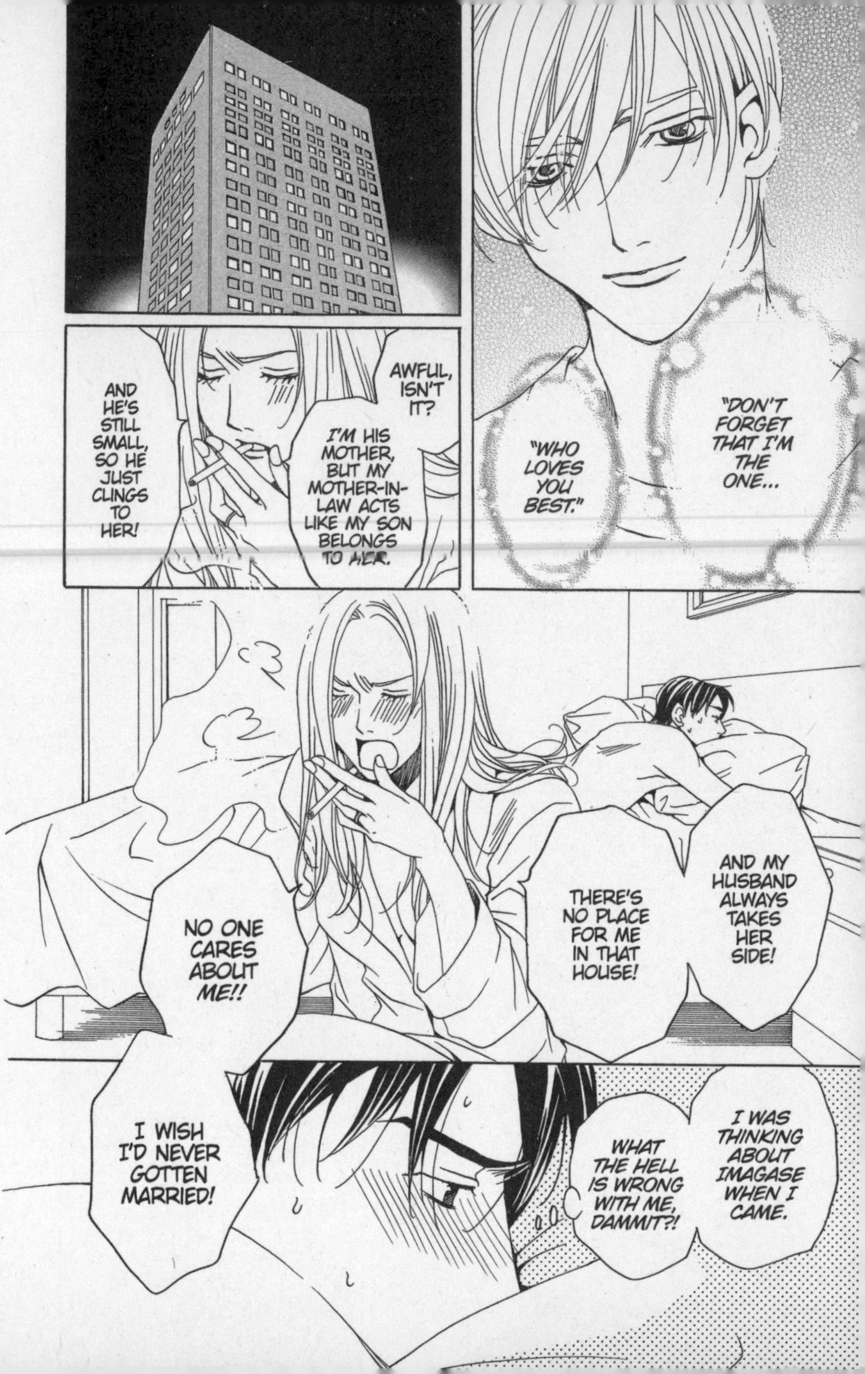
"DON'T FORGET THAT I'M THE ONE...
"WHO LOVES YOU BEST."
AWFUL, ISN'T IT?
I'M HIS MOTHER, BUT MY MOTHER-IN-LAW ACTS LIKE MY SON BELONGS TO HER.
AND HE'S STILL SMALL, SO HE JUST CLINGS TO HER!
AND MY HUSBAND ALWAYS TAKES HER SIDE!
THERE'S NO PLACE FOR ME IN THAT HOUSE!
NO ONE CARES ABOUT ME!!
I WAS THINKING ABOUT IMAGASE WHEN I CAME.
WHAT THE HELL IS WRONG WITH ME, DAMMIT?!
I WISH I'D NEVER GOTTEN MARRIED!

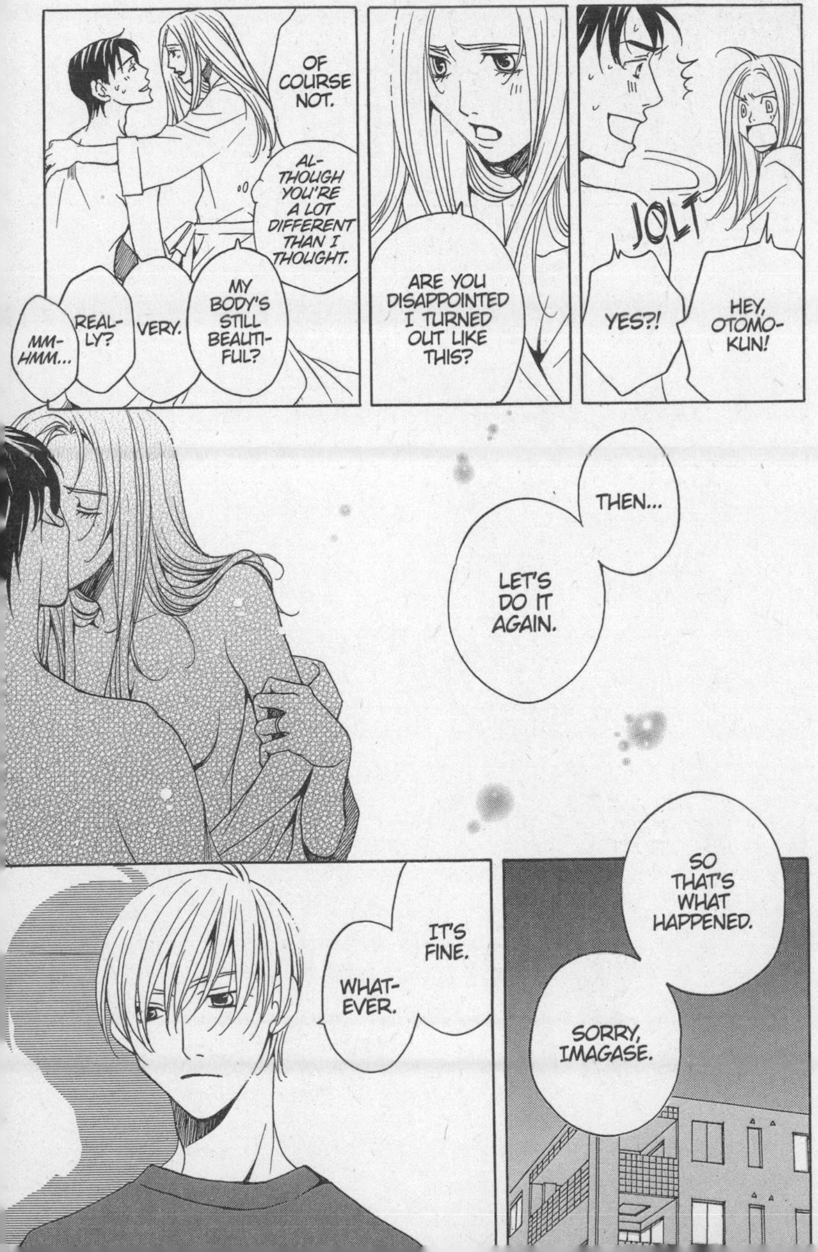
HEY, OTOMO-KUN!
JOLT
YES?!
ARE YOU DISAPPOINTED I TURNED OUT LIKE THIS?
OF COURSE NOT.
ALTHOUGH YOU'RE A LOT DIFFERENT THAN I THOUGHT.
MY BODY'S STILL BEAUTIFUL?
VERY.
REALLY?
MM-HMM...
THEN...
LET'S DO IT AGAIN.
SO THAT'S WHAT HAPPENED.
SORRY, IMAGASE.
IT'S FINE.
WHATEVER.

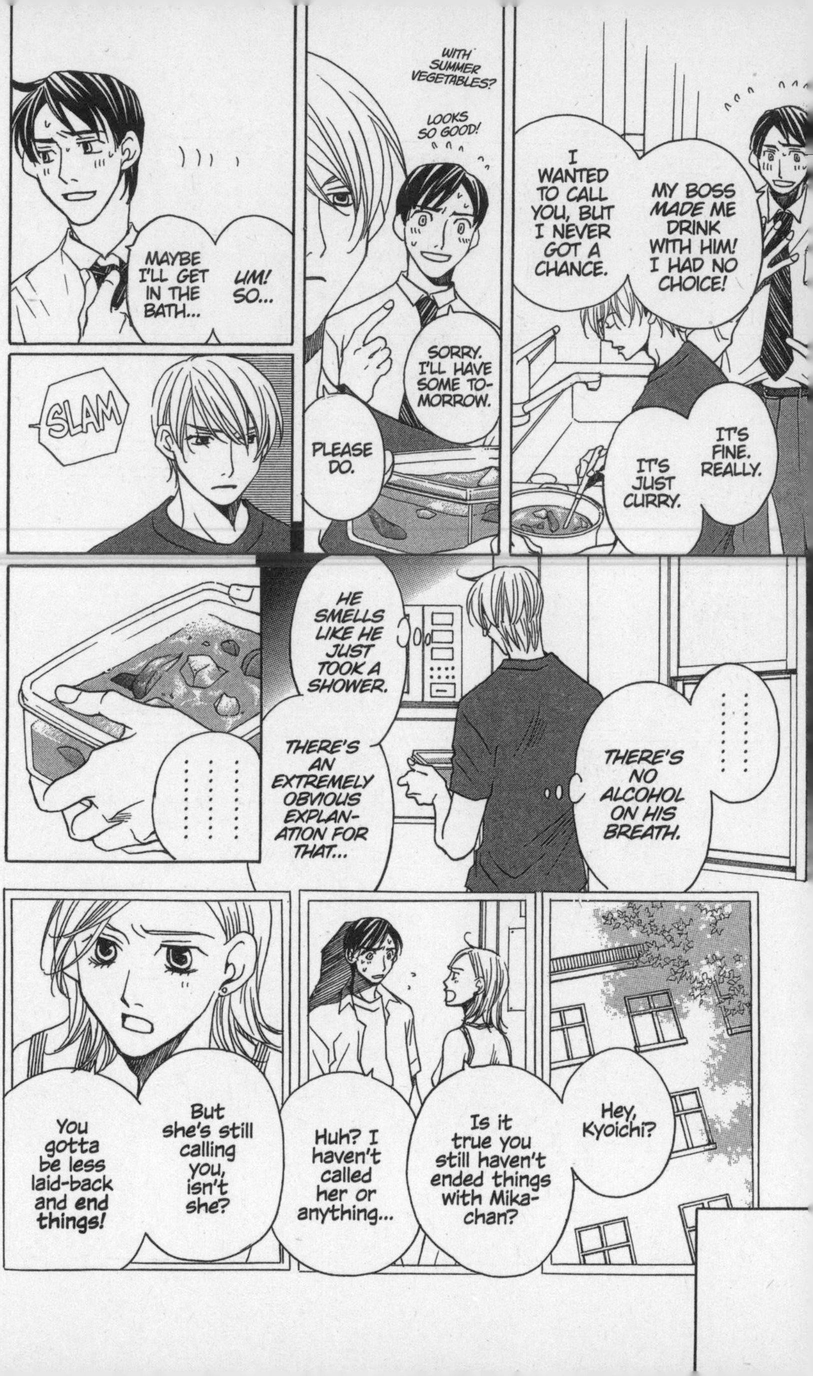
MY BOSS MADE ME DRINK WITH HIM! I HAD NO CHOICE!
I WANTED TO CALL YOU, BUT I NEVER GOT A CHANCE.
IT'S FINE. REALLY.
IT'S JUST CURRY.
WITH SUMMER VEGETABLES?
LOOKS SO GOOD!
SORRY. I'LL HAVE SOME TO-MORROW.
PLEASE DO.
UM! SO...
MAYBE I'LL GET IN THE BATH...
SLAM
......
THERE'S NO ALCOHOL ON HIS BREATH.
HE SMELLS LIKE HE JUST TOOK A SHOWER.
THERE'S AN EXTREMELY OBVIOUS EXPLAN-ATION FOR THAT...
......
Hey, Kyoichi?
Is it true you still haven't ended things with Mika-chan?
Huh? I haven't called her or anything...
But she's still calling you, isn't she?
You gotta be less laid-back and end things!

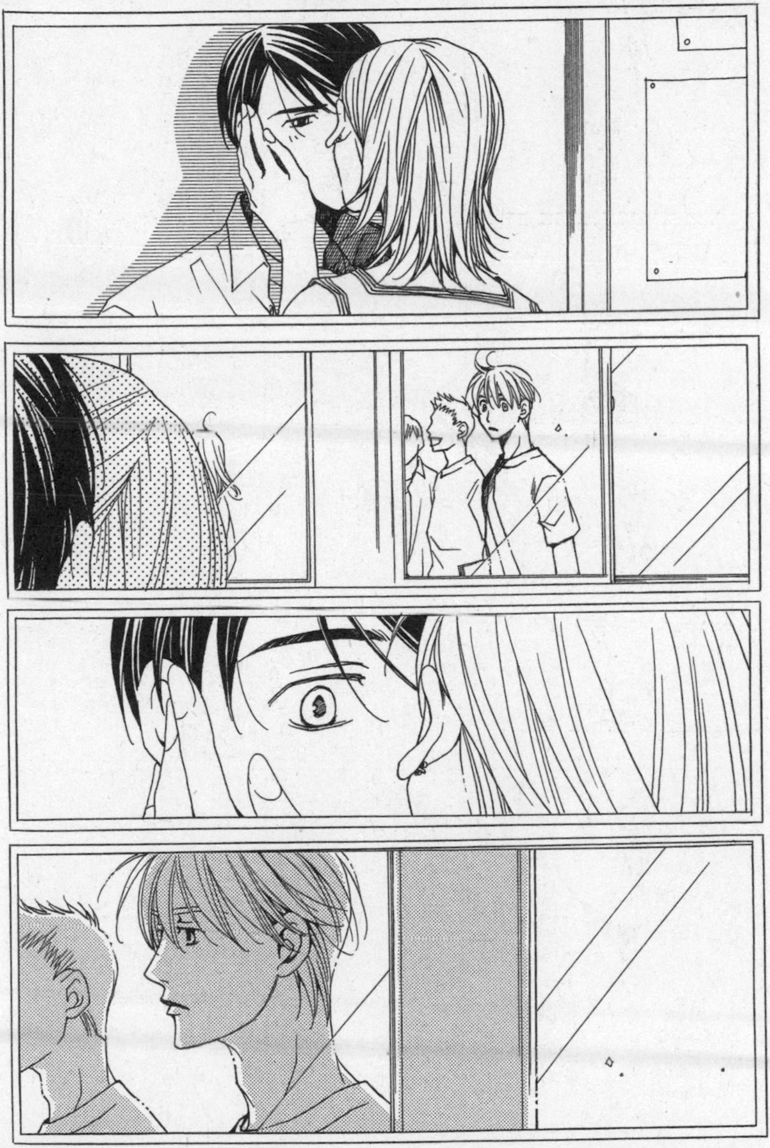

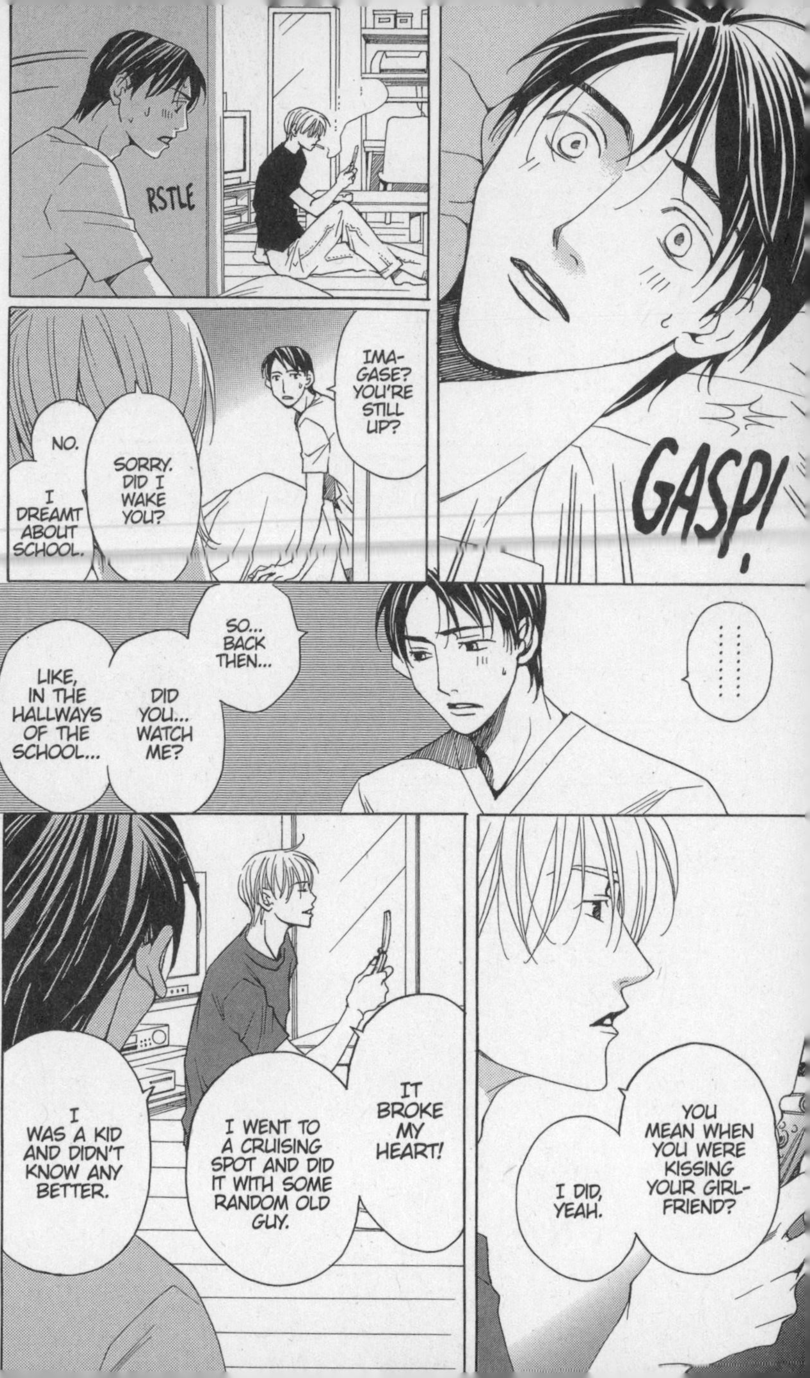
GASP!
RSTLE
IMAGASE? YOU'RE STILL UP?
SORRY. DID I WAKE YOU?
NO.
I DREAMT ABOUT SCHOOL.
......
SO... BACK THEN...
DID YOU... WATCH ME?
LIKE, IN THE HALLWAYS OF THE SCHOOL...
YOU MEAN WHEN YOU WERE KISSING YOUR GIRLFRIEND?
I DID, YEAH.
IT BROKE MY HEART!
I WENT TO A CRUISING SPOT AND DID IT WITH SOME RANDOM OLD GUY.
I WAS A KID AND DIDN'T KNOW ANY BETTER.

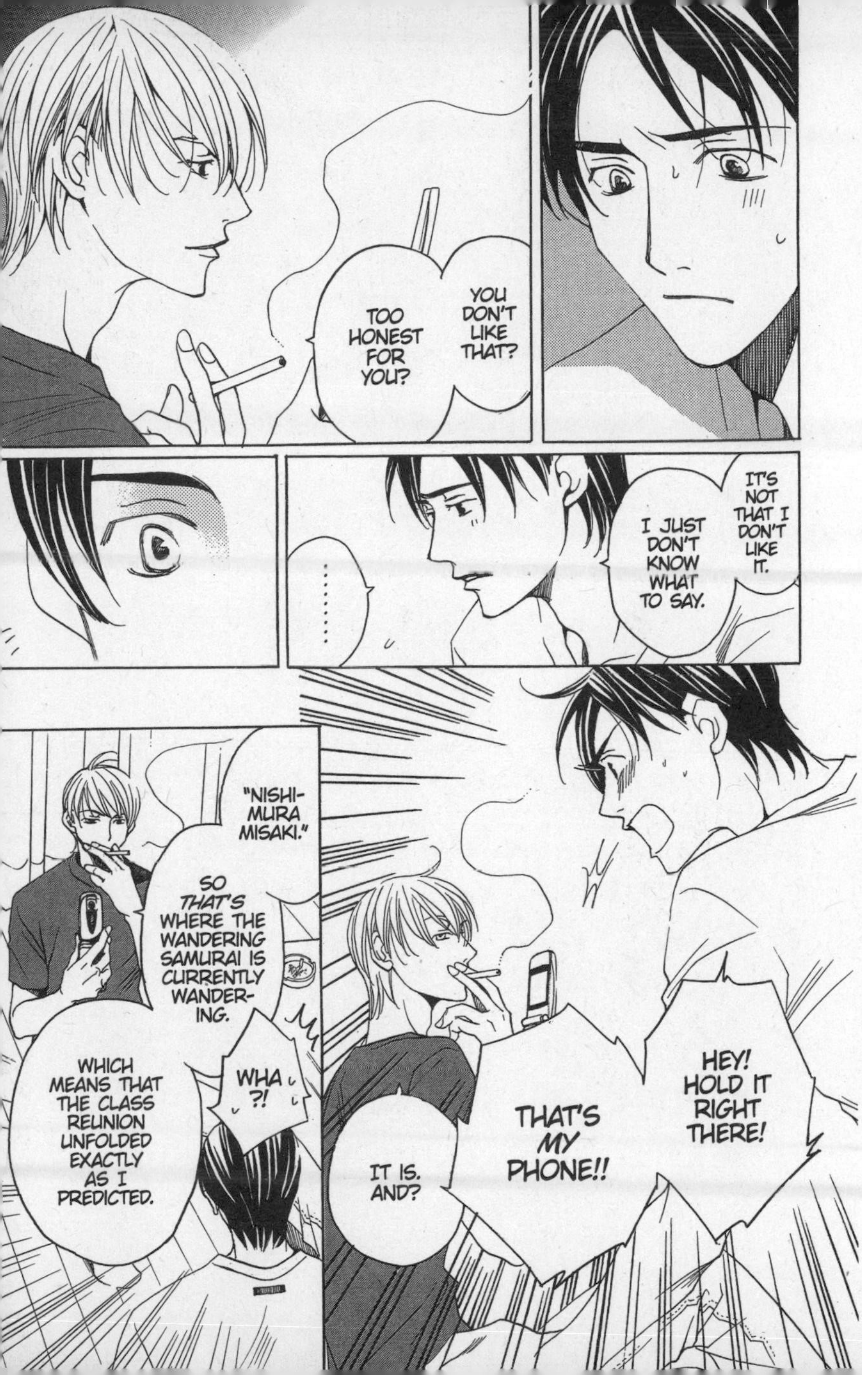
YOU DON'T LIKE THAT?
TOO HONEST FOR YOU?
IT'S NOT THAT I DON'T LIKE IT.
I JUST DON'T KNOW WHAT TO SAY.
......
HEY! HOLD IT RIGHT THERE!
THAT'S *MY* PHONE!!
IT IS. AND?
"NISHI-MURA MISAKI."
SO *THAT'S* WHERE THE WANDERING SAMURAI IS CURRENTLY WANDER-ING.
WHA ?!
WHICH MEANS THAT THE CLASS REUNION UNFOLDED EXACTLY AS I PREDICTED.

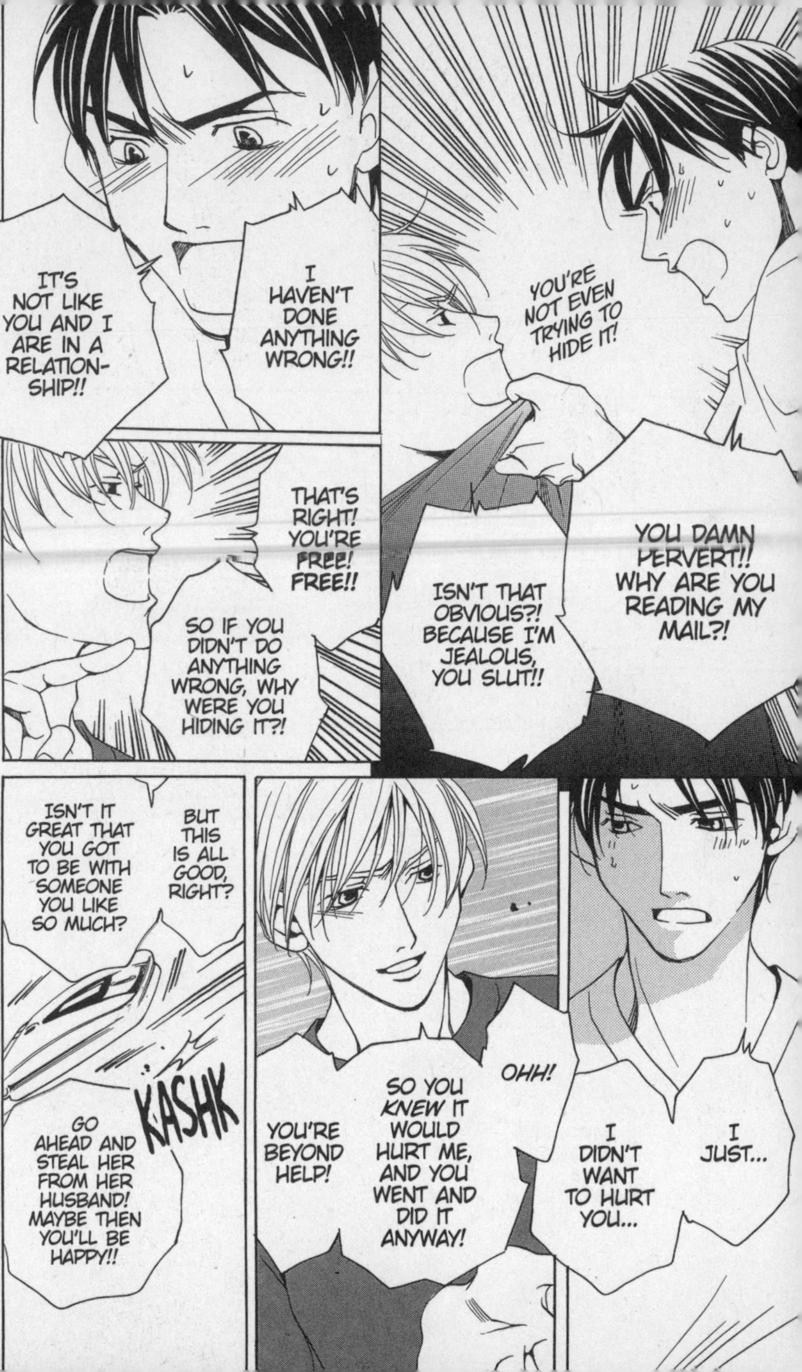
YOU'RE NOT EVEN TRYING TO HIDE IT!
YOU DAMN PERVERT!! WHY ARE YOU READING MY MAIL?!
ISN'T THAT OBVIOUS?! BECAUSE I'M JEALOUS, YOU SLUT!!
I HAVEN'T DONE ANYTHING WRONG!!
IT'S NOT LIKE YOU AND I ARE IN A RELATION-SHIP!!
THAT'S RIGHT! YOU'RE FREE! FREE!!
SO IF YOU DIDN'T DO ANYTHING WRONG, WHY WERE YOU HIDING IT?!
I JUST...
I DIDN'T WANT TO HURT YOU...
OHH!
SO YOU KNEW IT WOULD HURT ME, AND YOU WENT AND DID IT ANYWAY!
YOU'RE BEYOND HELP!
BUT THIS IS ALL GOOD, RIGHT?
ISN'T IT GREAT THAT YOU GOT TO BE WITH SOMEONE YOU LIKE SO MUCH?
KASHK
GO AHEAD AND STEAL HER FROM HER HUSBAND! MAYBE THEN YOU'LL BE HAPPY!!

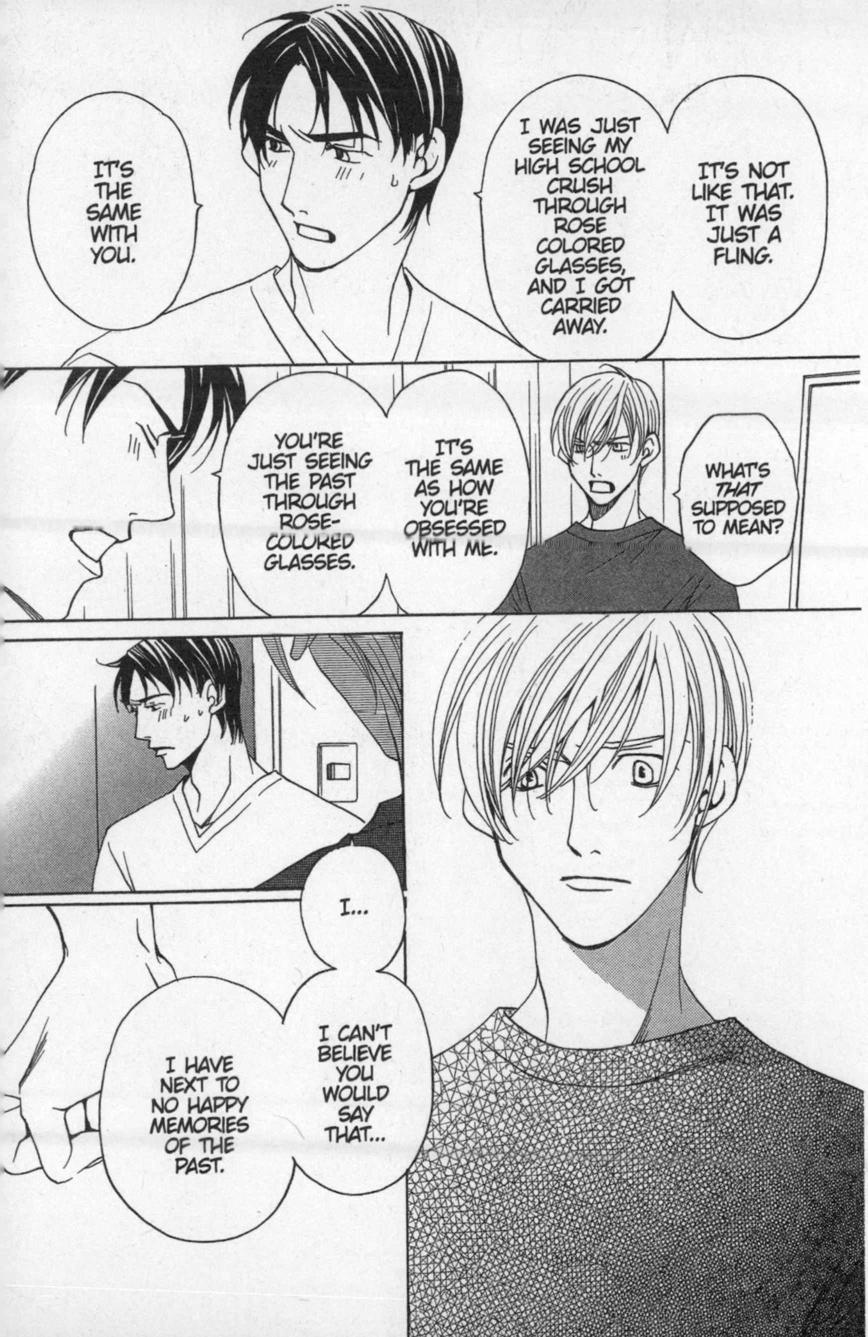
IT'S NOT LIKE THAT. IT WAS JUST A FLING.
I WAS JUST SEEING MY HIGH SCHOOL CRUSH THROUGH ROSE COLORED GLASSES, AND I GOT CARRIED AWAY.
IT'S THE SAME WITH YOU.
WHAT'S *THAT* SUPPOSED TO MEAN?
IT'S THE SAME AS HOW YOU'RE OBSESSED WITH ME.
YOU'RE JUST SEEING THE PAST THROUGH ROSE-COLORED GLASSES.
I...
I CAN'T BELIEVE YOU WOULD SAY THAT...
I HAVE NEXT TO NO HAPPY MEMORIES OF THE PAST.

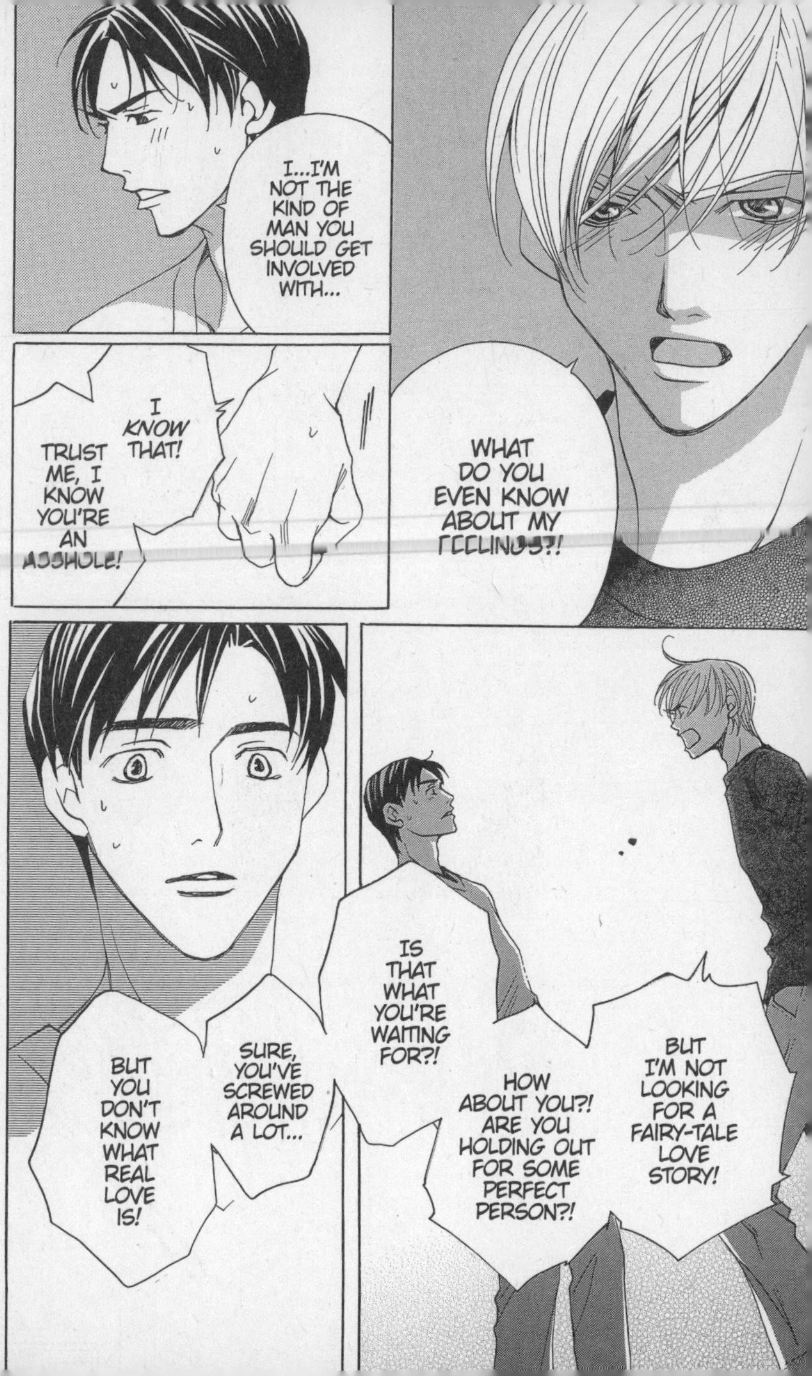
WHAT DO YOU EVEN KNOW ABOUT MY FEELINGS?!
I...I'M NOT THE KIND OF MAN YOU SHOULD GET INVOLVED WITH...
I KNOW THAT!
TRUST ME, I KNOW YOU'RE AN ASSHOLE!
BUT I'M NOT LOOKING FOR A FAIRY-TALE LOVE STORY!
HOW ABOUT YOU?! ARE YOU HOLDING OUT FOR SOME PERFECT PERSON?!
IS THAT WHAT YOU'RE WAITING FOR?!
SURE, YOU'VE SCREWED AROUND A LOT...
BUT YOU DON'T KNOW WHAT REAL LOVE IS!

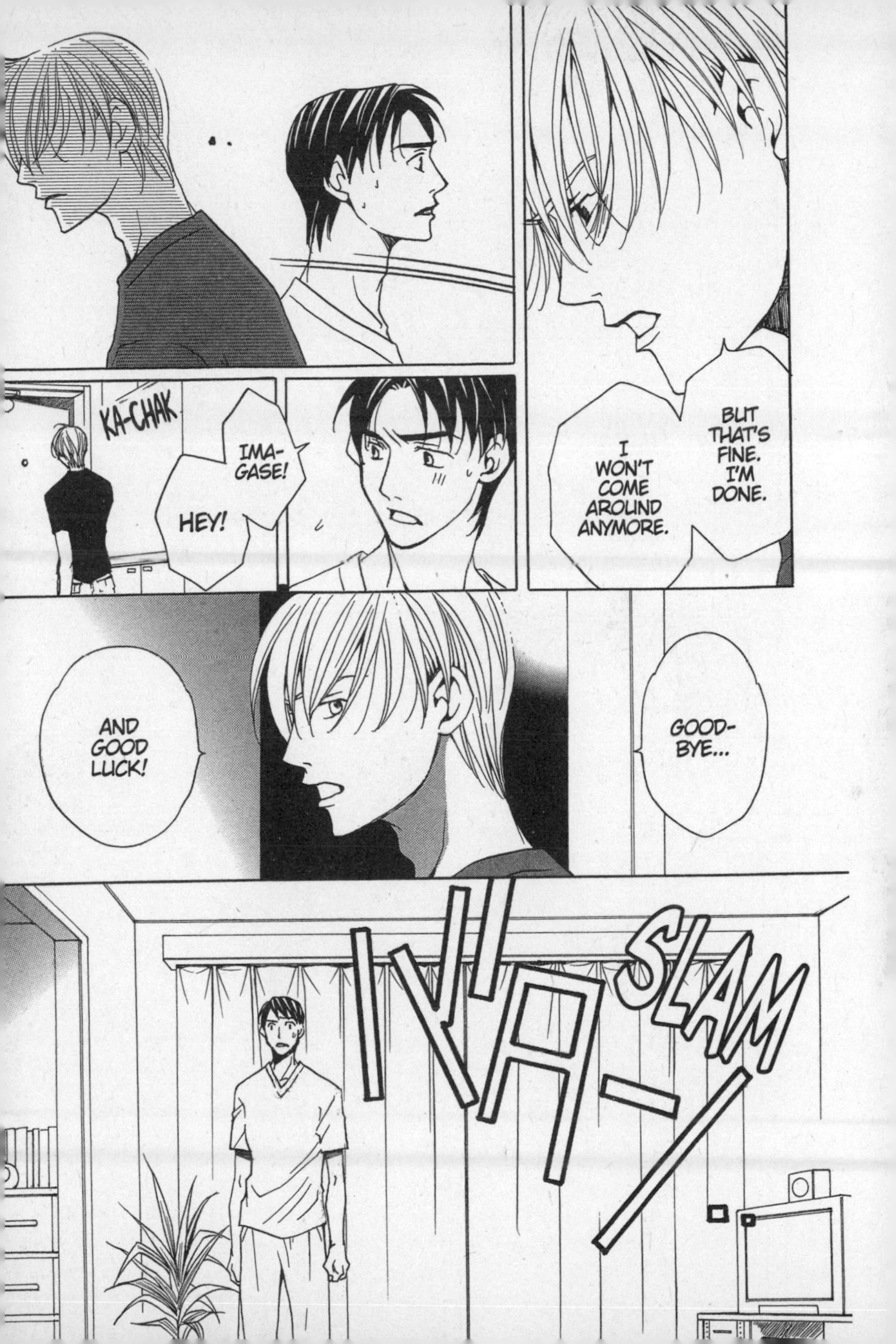
BUT THAT'S FINE. I'M DONE.
I WON'T COME AROUND ANYMORE.
IMA-GASE!
HEY!
KA-CHAK
GOOD-BYE...
AND GOOD LUCK!
SLAM

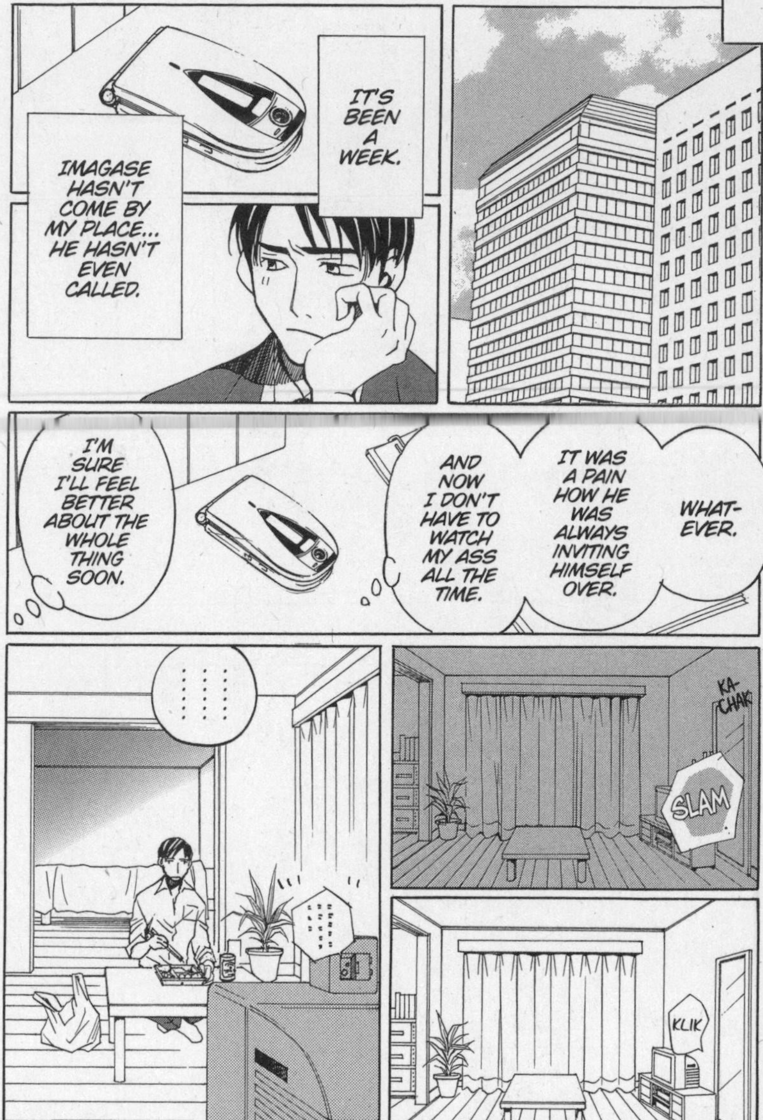
IT'S BEEN A WEEK.
IMAGASE HASN'T COME BY MY PLACE... HE HASN'T EVEN CALLED.
WHAT-EVER.
IT WAS A PAIN HOW HE WAS ALWAYS INVITING HIMSELF OVER.
AND NOW I DON'T HAVE TO WATCH MY ASS ALL THE TIME.
I'M SURE I'LL FEEL BETTER ABOUT THE WHOLE THING SOON.
KA-CHAK
SLAM
KLIK

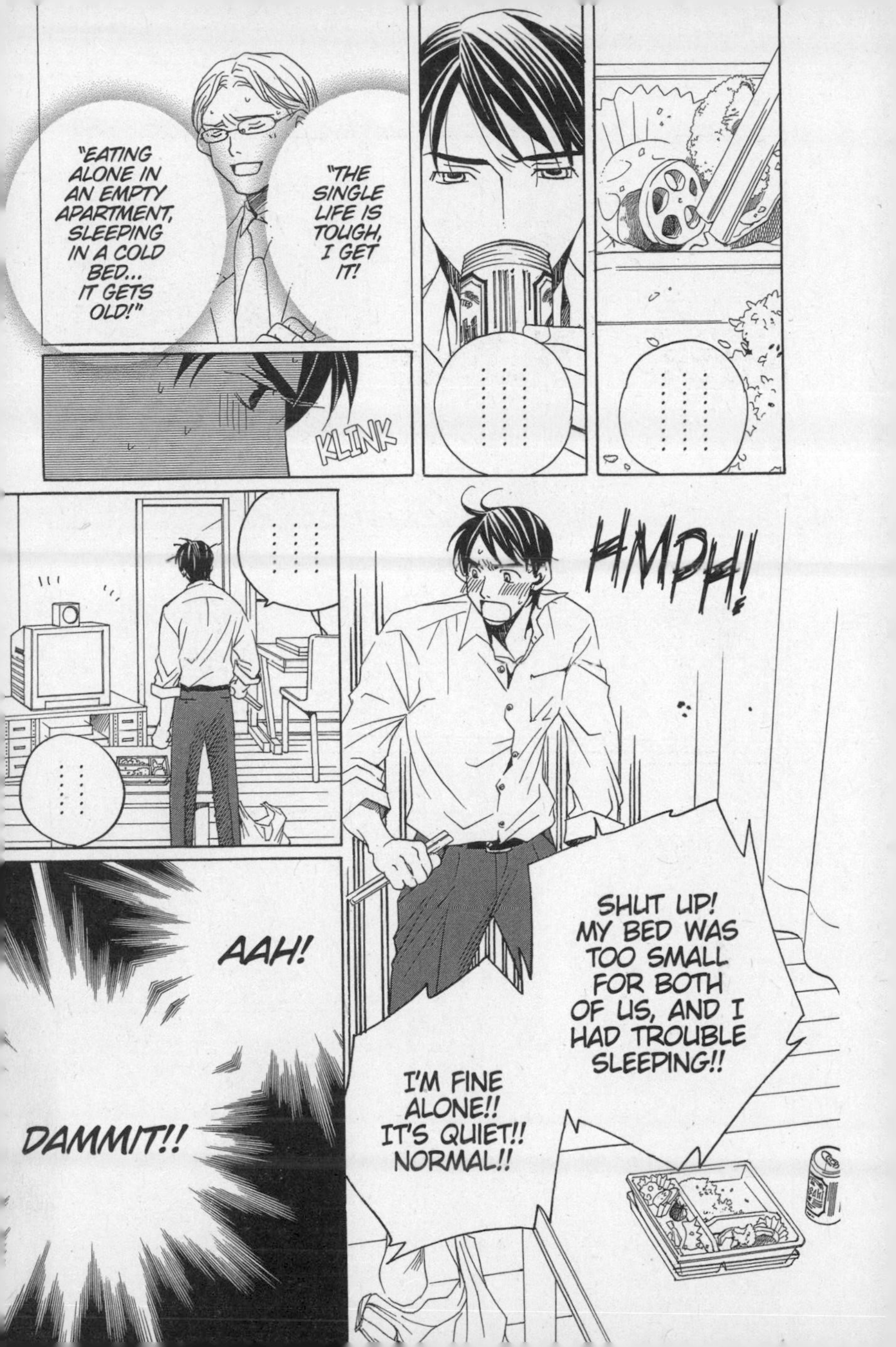
......
......
"THE SINGLE LIFE IS TOUGH, I GET IT!
"EATING ALONE IN AN EMPTY APARTMENT, SLEEPING IN A COLD BED... IT GETS OLD!"
KLINK
HMPH!
SHUT UP! MY BED WAS TOO SMALL FOR BOTH OF US, AND I HAD TROUBLE SLEEPING!!
I'M FINE ALONE!! IT'S QUIET!! NORMAL!!
......
......
AAH!
DAMMIT!!

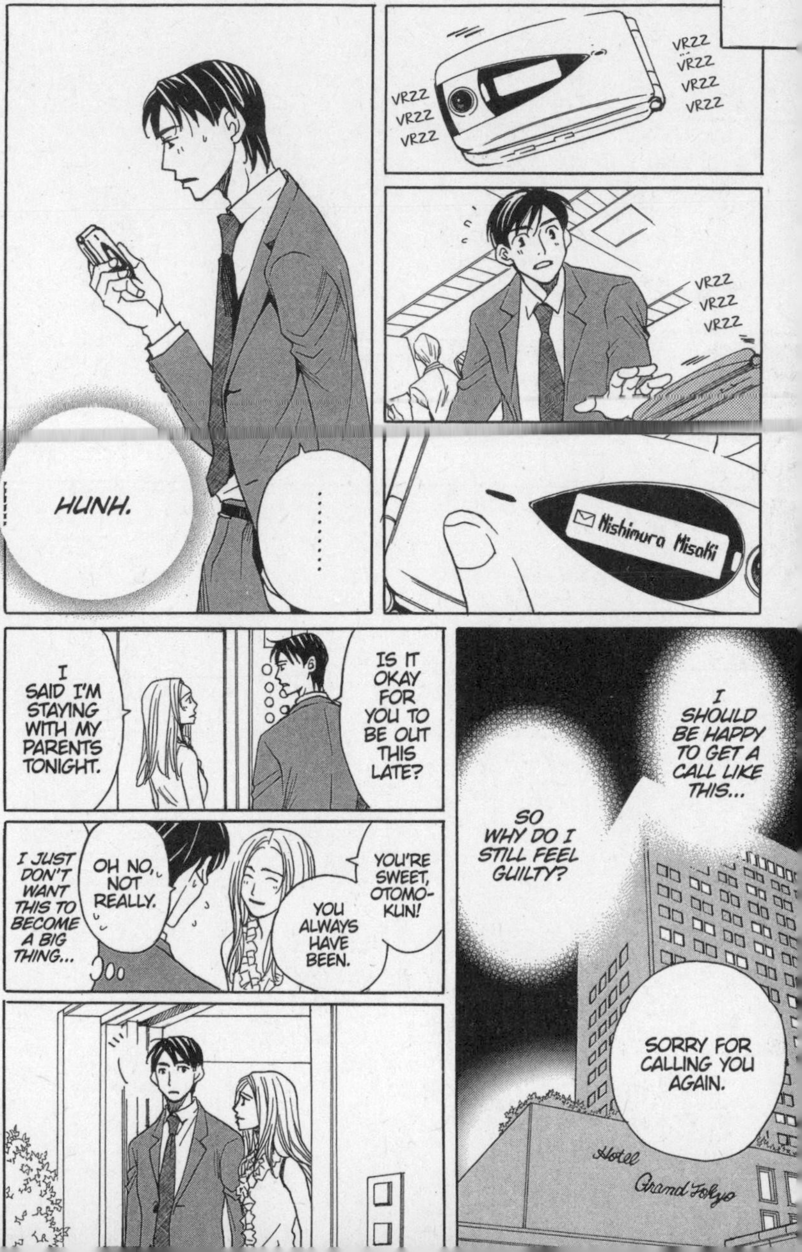
VRZZ VRZZ VRZZ VRZZ
VRZZ VRZZ VRZZ
VRZZ VRZZ VRZZ
Nishimura Misaki
......
HUNH.
I SHOULD BE HAPPY TO GET A CALL LIKE THIS...
SO WHY DO I STILL FEEL GUILTY?
SORRY FOR CALLING YOU AGAIN.
Hotel Grand Tokyo
IS IT OKAY FOR YOU TO BE OUT THIS LATE?
I SAID I'M STAYING WITH MY PARENTS TONIGHT.
YOU'RE SWEET, OTOMO-KUN!
YOU ALWAYS HAVE BEEN.
OH NO, NOT REALLY.
I JUST DON'T WANT THIS TO BECOME A BIG THING...

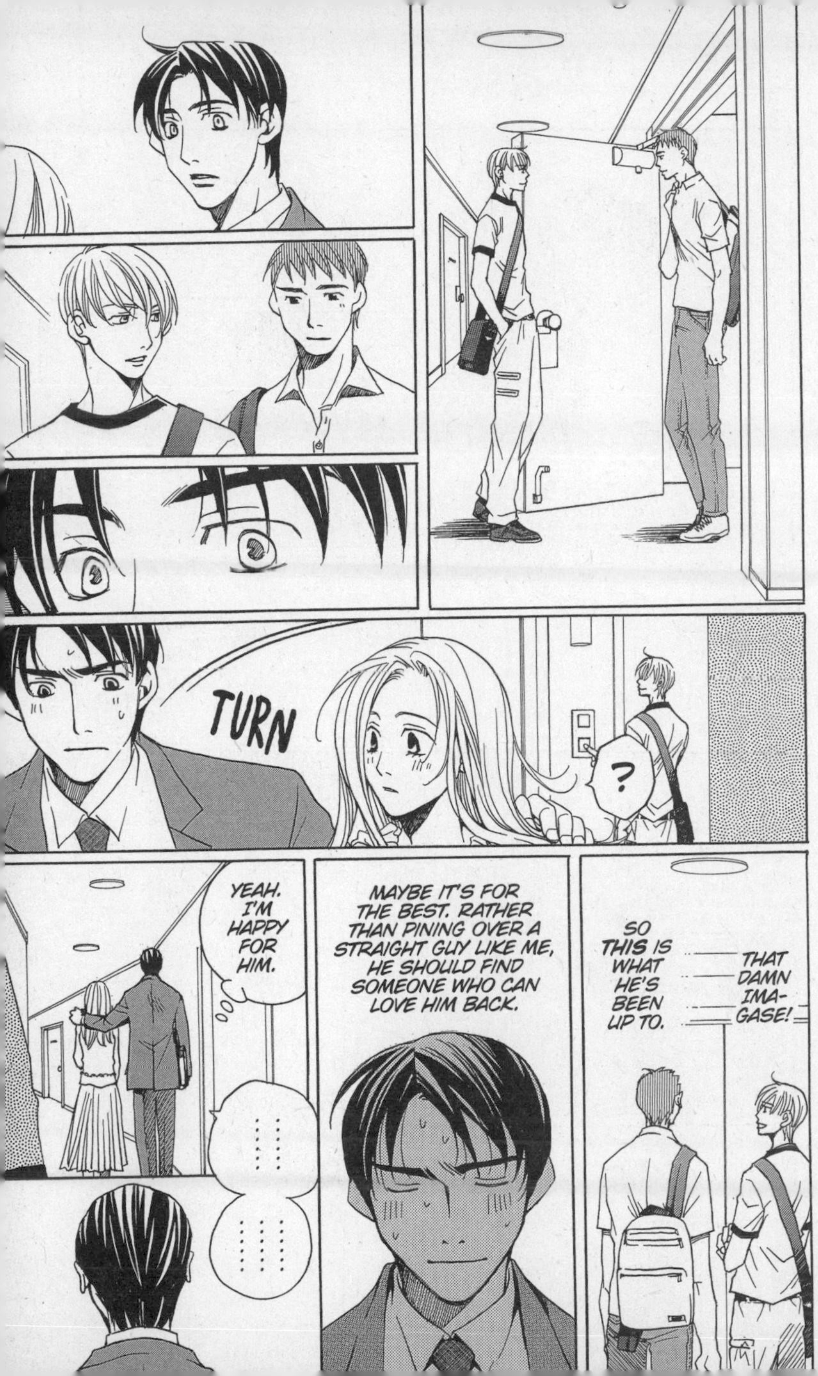
?
TURN
THAT DAMN IMA-GASE!
SO THIS IS WHAT HE'S BEEN UP TO.
MAYBE IT'S FOR THE BEST. RATHER THAN PINING OVER A STRAIGHT GUY LIKE ME, HE SHOULD FIND SOMEONE WHO CAN LOVE HIM BACK.
YEAH. I'M HAPPY FOR HIM.
......
......

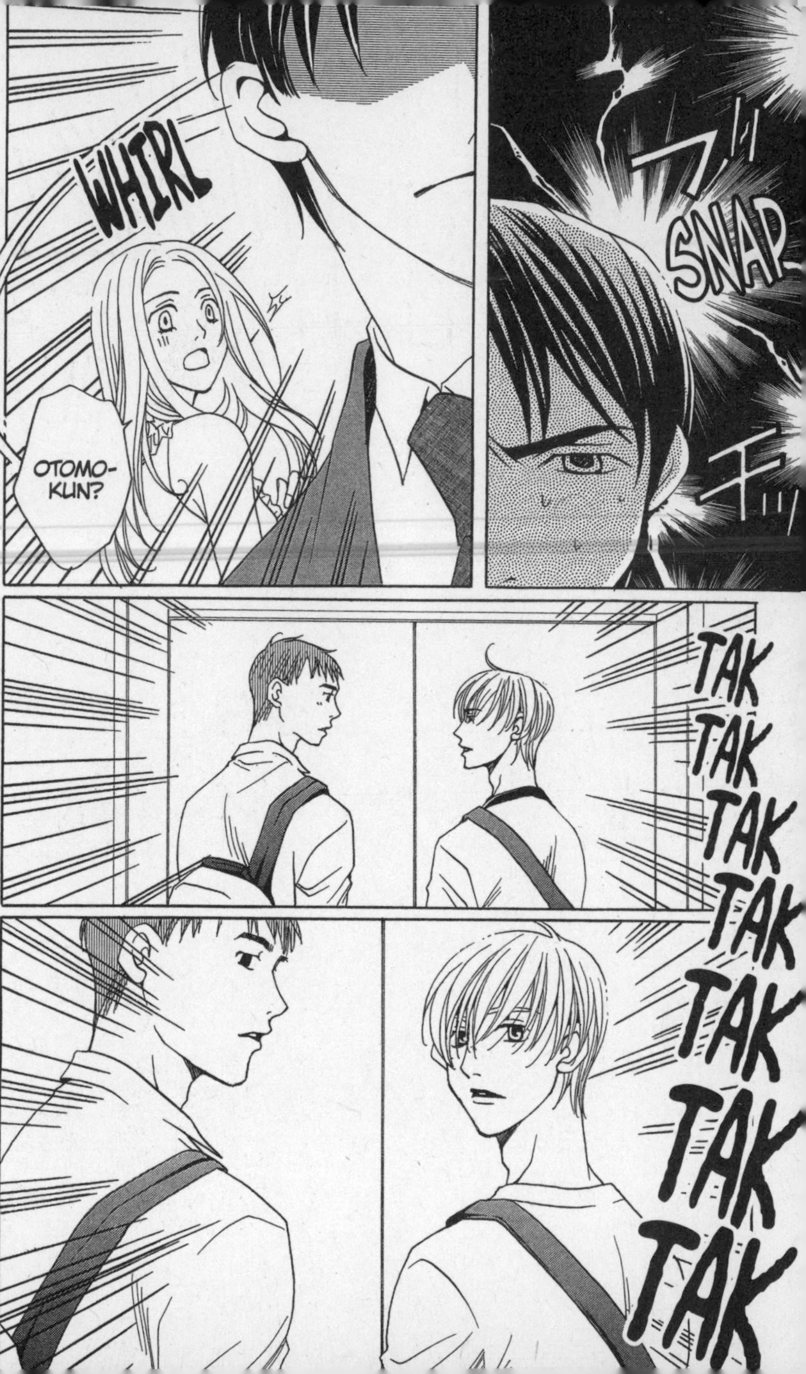
SNAP
WHIRL
OTOMO-KUN?
TAK TAK TAK TAK TAK TAK TAK TAK

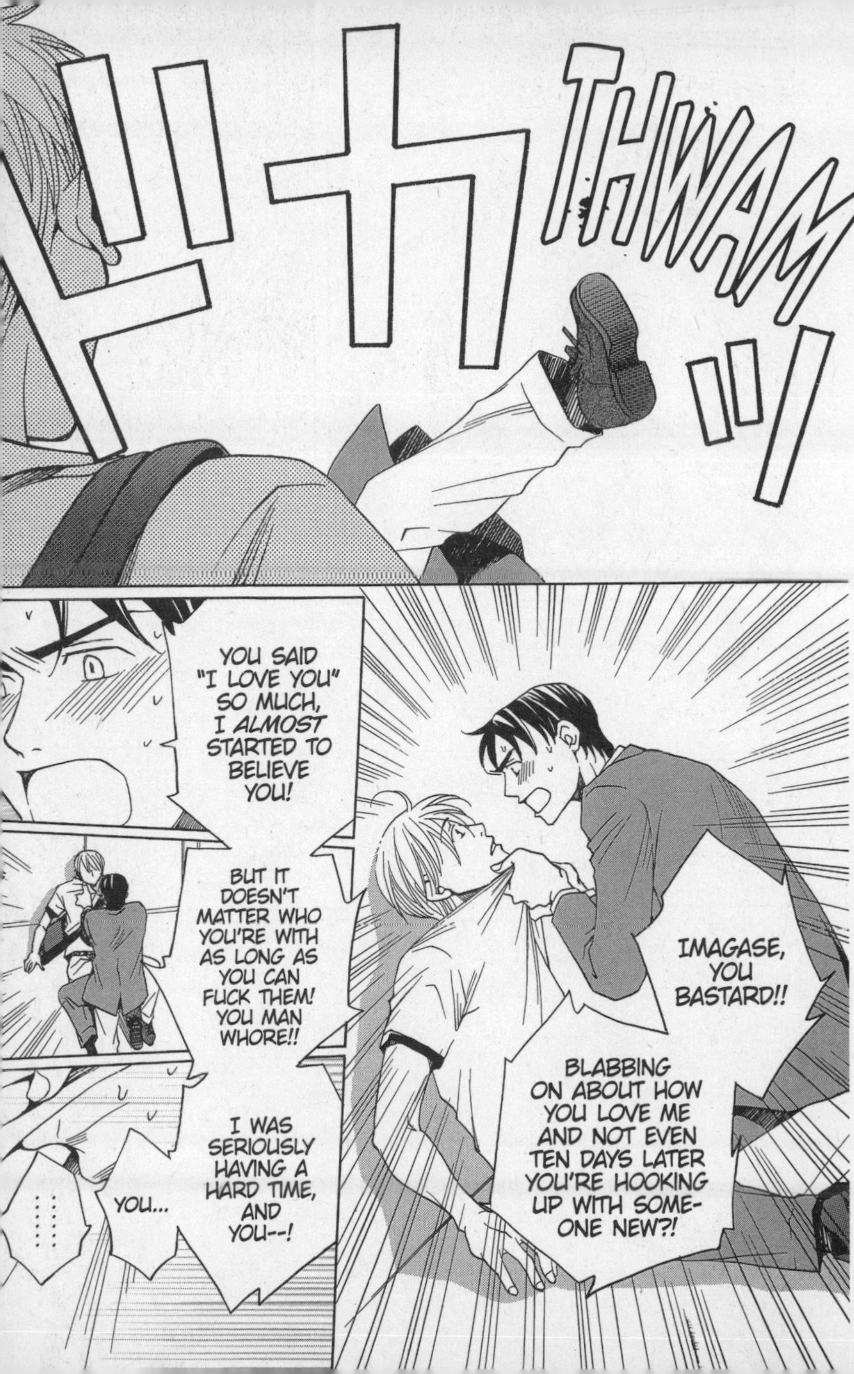
ドカッ
THWAM
IMAGASE, YOU BASTARD!!
BLABBING ON ABOUT HOW YOU LOVE ME AND NOT EVEN TEN DAYS LATER YOU'RE HOOKING UP WITH SOME-ONE NEW?!
YOU SAID "I LOVE YOU" SO MUCH, I *ALMOST* STARTED TO BELIEVE YOU!
BUT IT DOESN'T MATTER WHO YOU'RE WITH AS LONG AS YOU CAN FUCK THEM! YOU MAN WHORE!!
I WAS SERIOUSLY HAVING A HARD TIME, AND YOU--!
YOU...
......

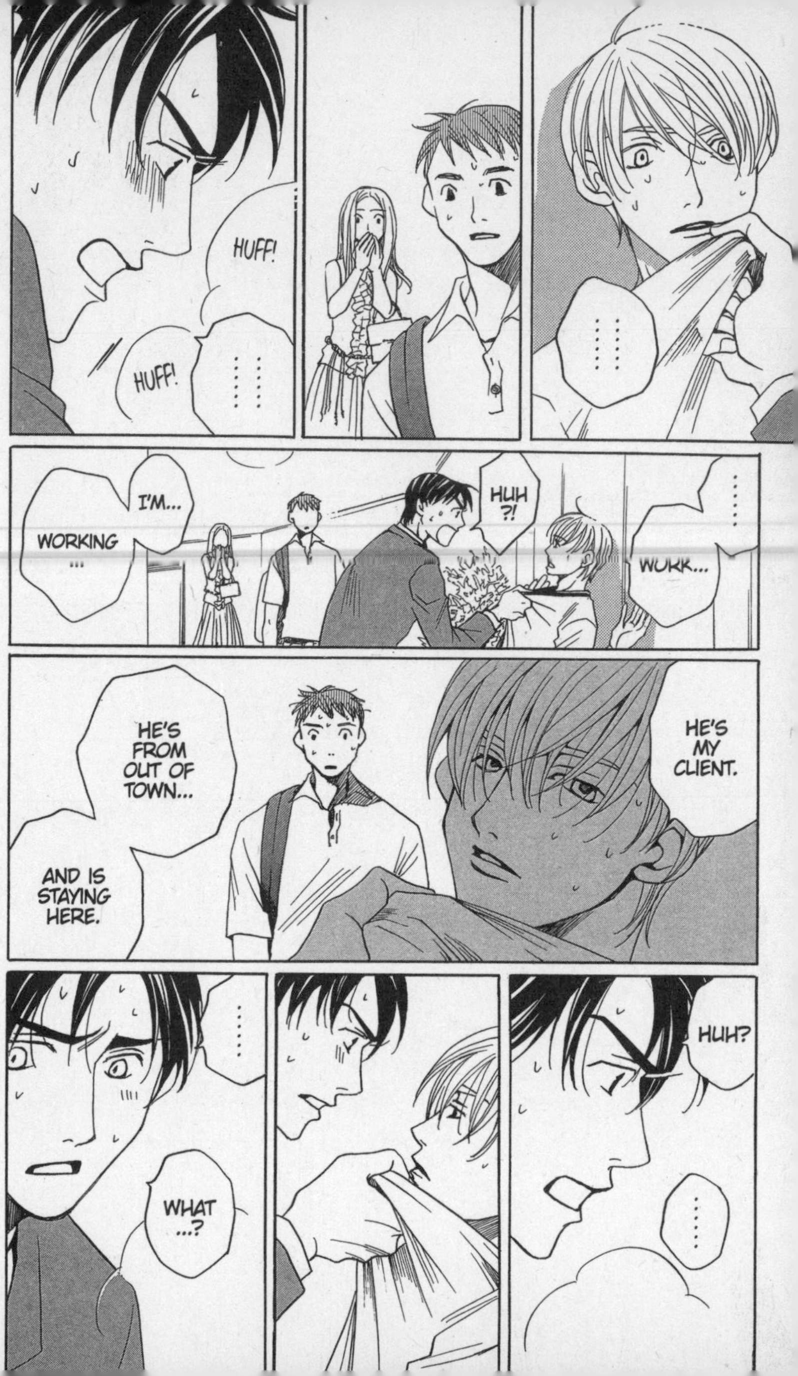
......
HUFF!
......
HUFF!
......
WURK...
HUH ?!
I'M... WORKING ...
HE'S MY CLIENT.
HE'S FROM OUT OF TOWN...
AND IS STAYING HERE.
HUH?
......
......
WHAT ...?

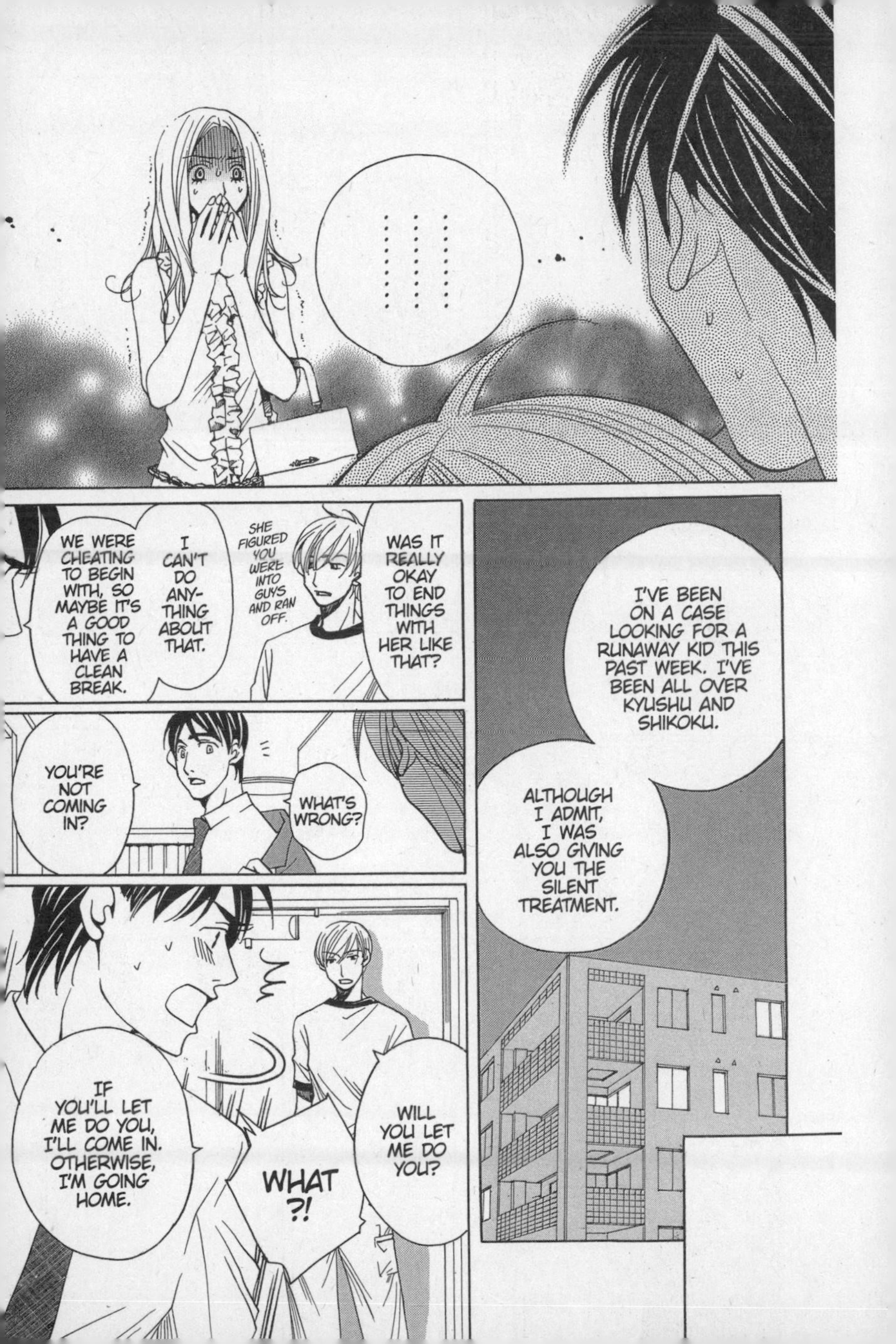
......
I'VE BEEN ON A CASE LOOKING FOR A RUNAWAY KID THIS PAST WEEK. I'VE BEEN ALL OVER KYUSHU AND SHIKOKU.
ALTHOUGH I ADMIT, I WAS ALSO GIVING YOU THE SILENT TREATMENT.
WAS IT REALLY OKAY TO END THINGS WITH HER LIKE THAT?
SHE FIGURED YOU WERE INTO GUYS AND RAN OFF.
I CAN'T DO ANYTHING ABOUT THAT.
WE WERE CHEATING TO BEGIN WITH, SO MAYBE IT'S A GOOD THING TO HAVE A CLEAN BREAK.
WHAT'S WRONG?
YOU'RE NOT COMING IN?
WILL YOU LET ME DO YOU?
WHAT ?!
IF YOU'LL LET ME DO YOU, I'LL COME IN. OTHERWISE, I'M GOING HOME.

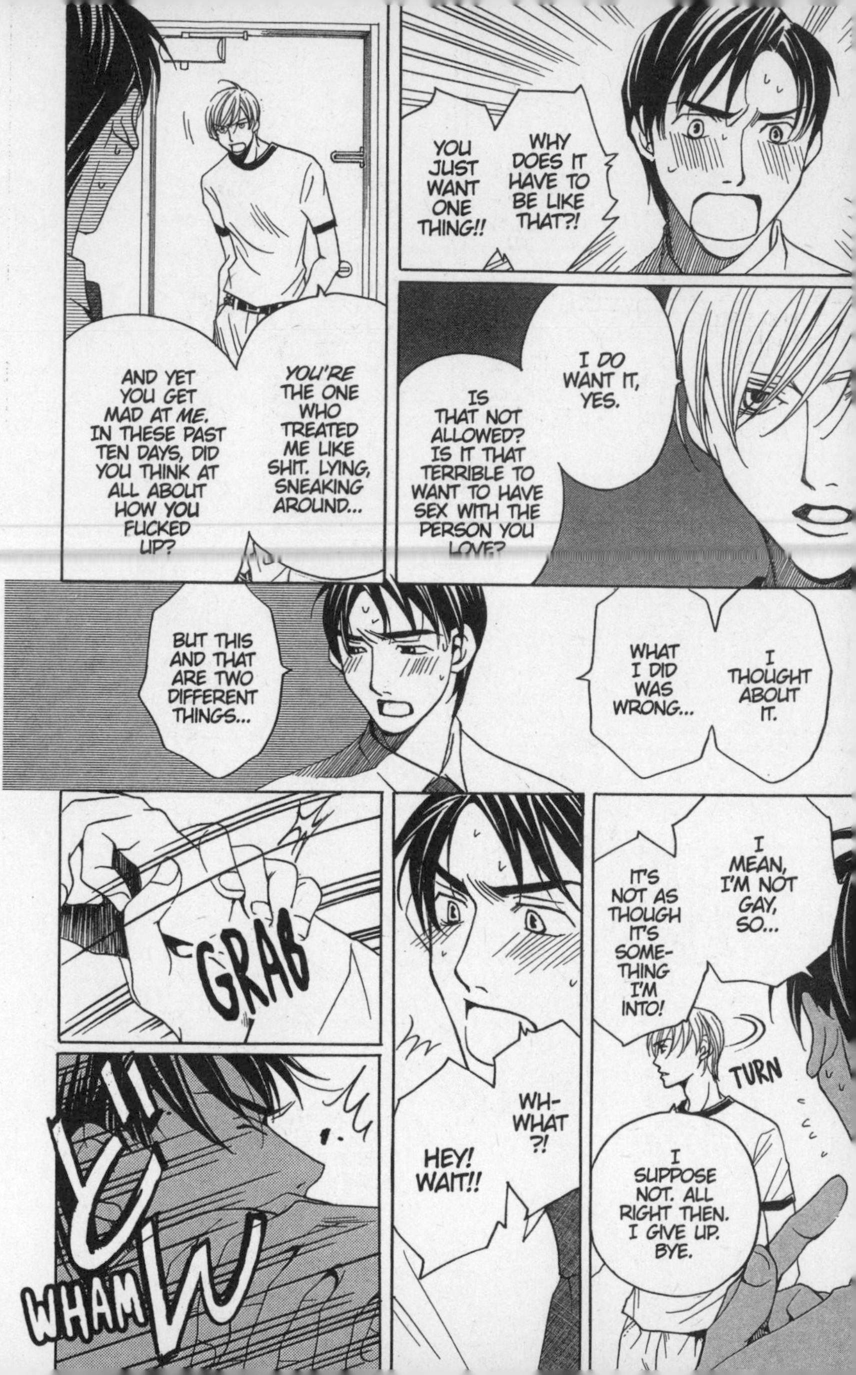
WHY DOES IT HAVE TO BE LIKE THAT?!
YOU JUST WANT ONE THING!!
I *DO* WANT IT, YES.
IS THAT NOT ALLOWED? IS IT THAT TERRIBLE TO WANT TO HAVE SEX WITH THE PERSON YOU LOVE?
YOU'RE THE ONE WHO TREATED ME LIKE SHIT. LYING, SNEAKING AROUND...
AND YET YOU GET MAD AT *ME*. IN THESE PAST TEN DAYS, DID YOU THINK AT ALL ABOUT HOW YOU FUCKED UP?
I THOUGHT ABOUT IT.
WHAT I DID WAS WRONG...
BUT THIS AND THAT ARE TWO DIFFERENT THINGS...
I MEAN, I'M NOT GAY, SO...
IT'S NOT AS THOUGH IT'S SOME-THING I'M INTO!
TURN
I SUPPOSE NOT. ALL RIGHT THEN. I GIVE UP. BYE.
WH-WHAT?!
HEY! WAIT!!
GRAB
WHAM

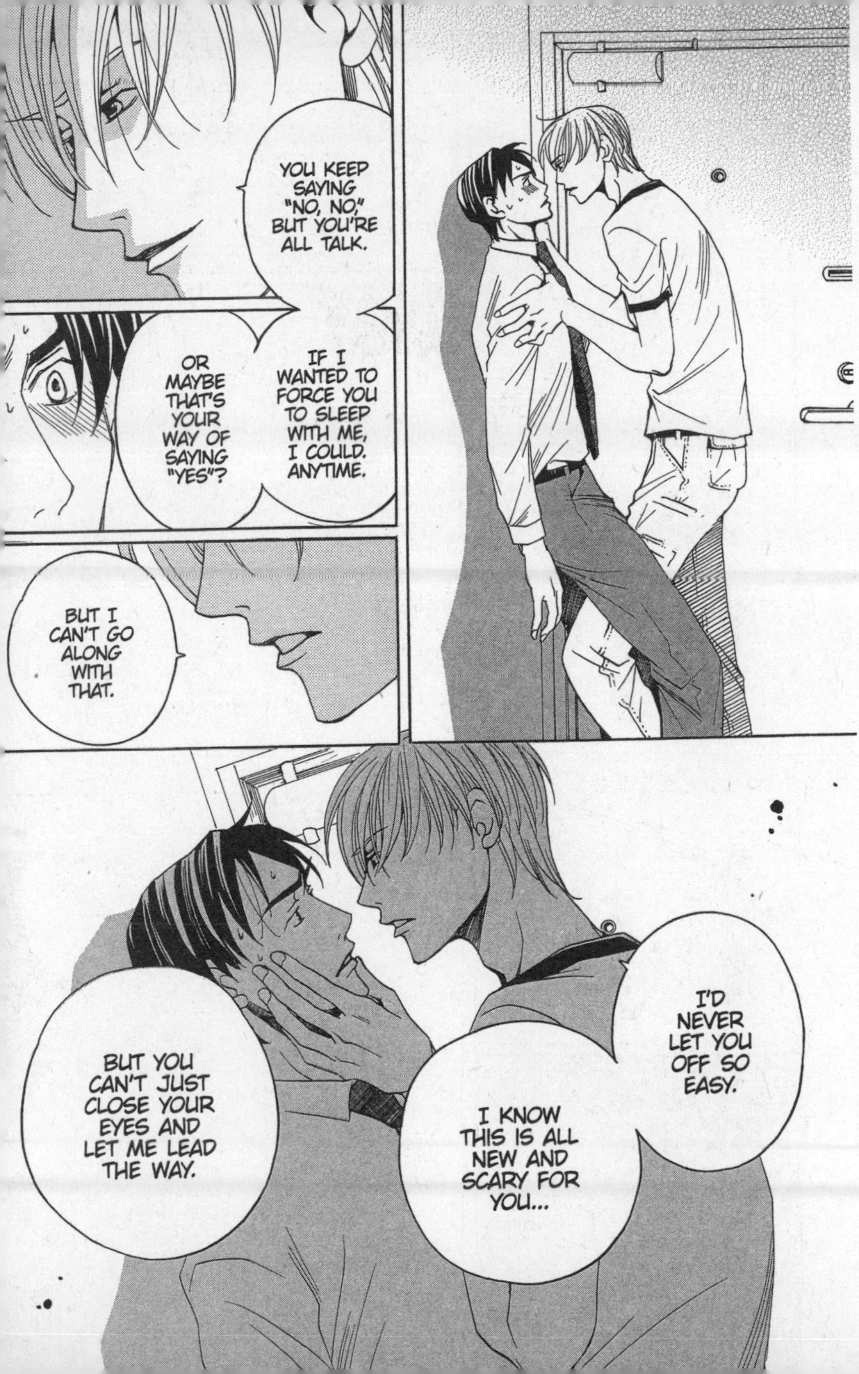
YOU KEEP SAYING "NO, NO," BUT YOU'RE ALL TALK.
IF I WANTED TO FORCE YOU TO SLEEP WITH ME, I COULD. ANYTIME.
OR MAYBE THAT'S YOUR WAY OF SAYING "YES"?
BUT I CAN'T GO ALONG WITH THAT.
I'D NEVER LET YOU OFF SO EASY.
I KNOW THIS IS ALL NEW AND SCARY FOR YOU...
BUT YOU CAN'T JUST CLOSE YOUR EYES AND LET ME LEAD THE WAY.

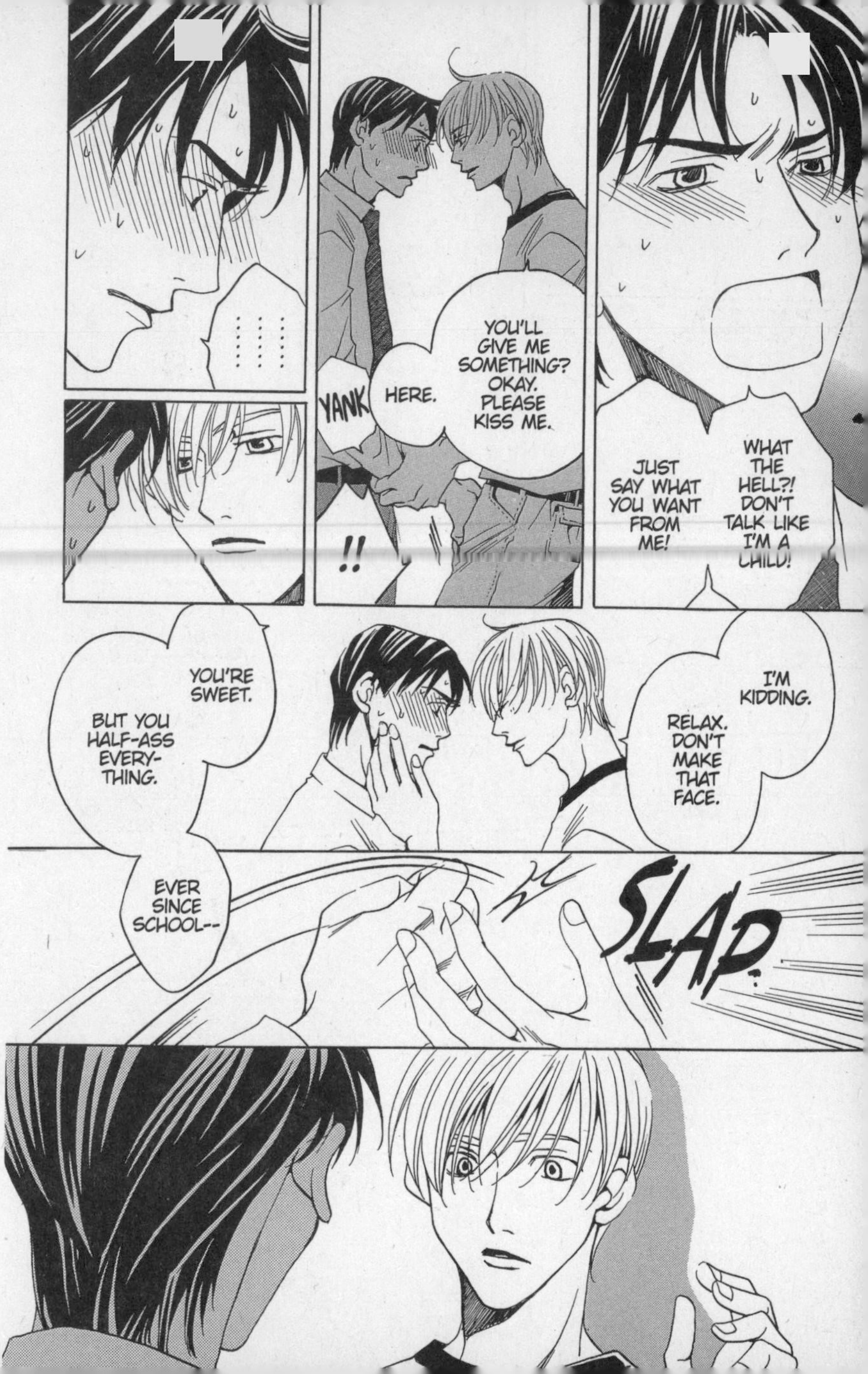
WHAT THE HELL?! DON'T TALK LIKE I'M A CHILD!
JUST SAY WHAT YOU WANT FROM ME!
YOU'LL GIVE ME SOMETHING? OKAY. PLEASE KISS ME.
HERE.
YANK
!!
......
I'M KIDDING.
RELAX. DON'T MAKE THAT FACE.
YOU'RE SWEET.
BUT YOU HALF-ASS EVERY-THING.
EVER SINCE SCHOOL--
SLAP

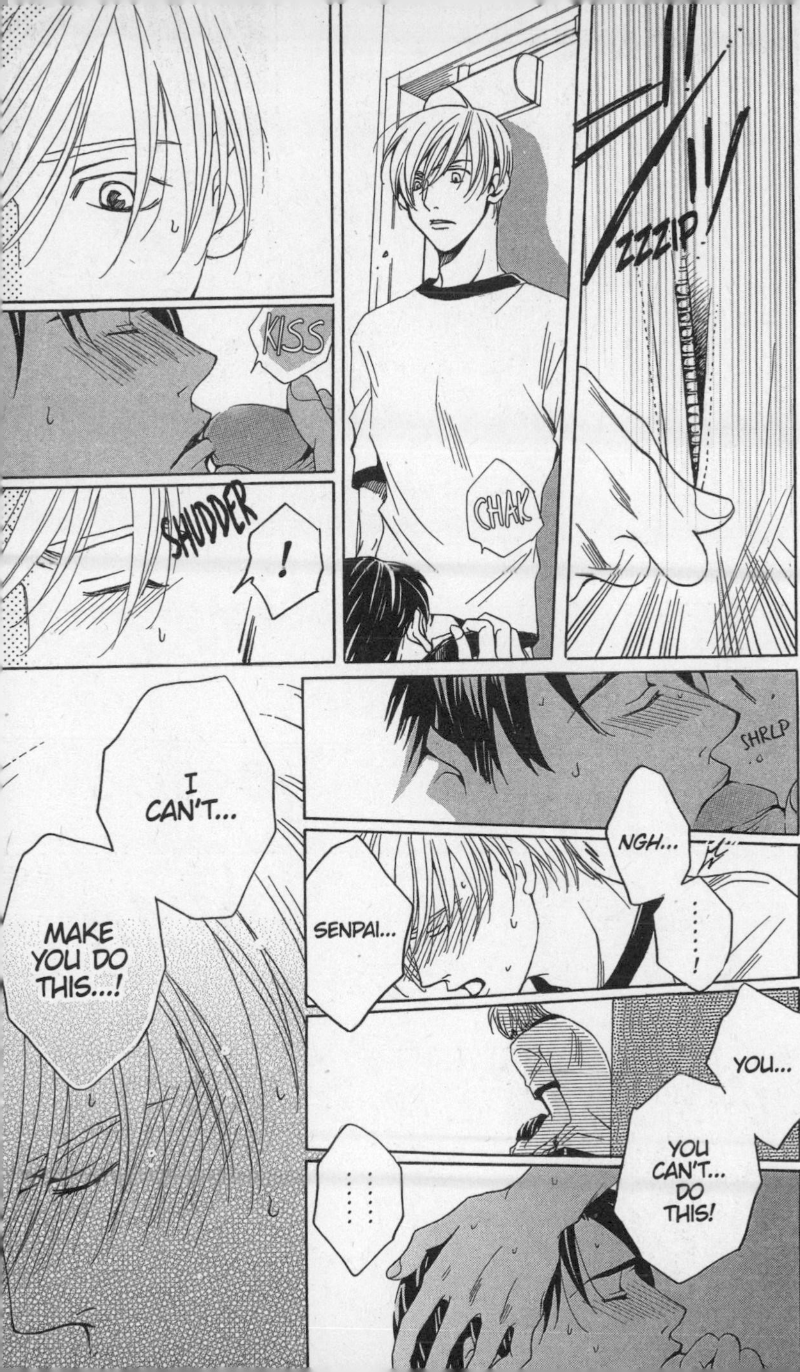
ZZZIP!!
CHAK
KISS
SHUDDER
!
SHRLP
NGH...
......!
SENPAI...
YOU...
YOU CAN'T... DO THIS!
......
I CAN'T...
MAKE YOU DO THIS...!

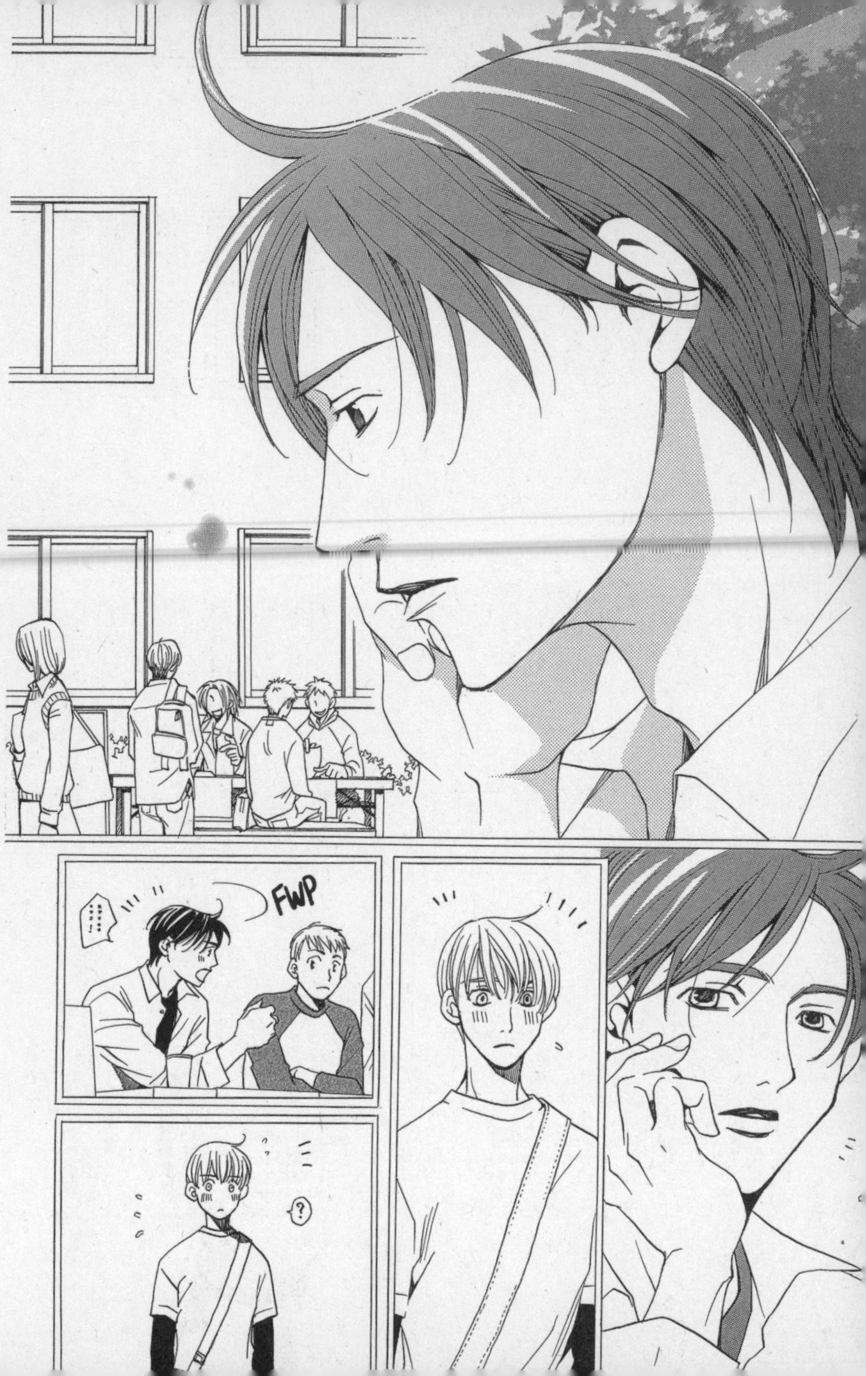
FWP
?

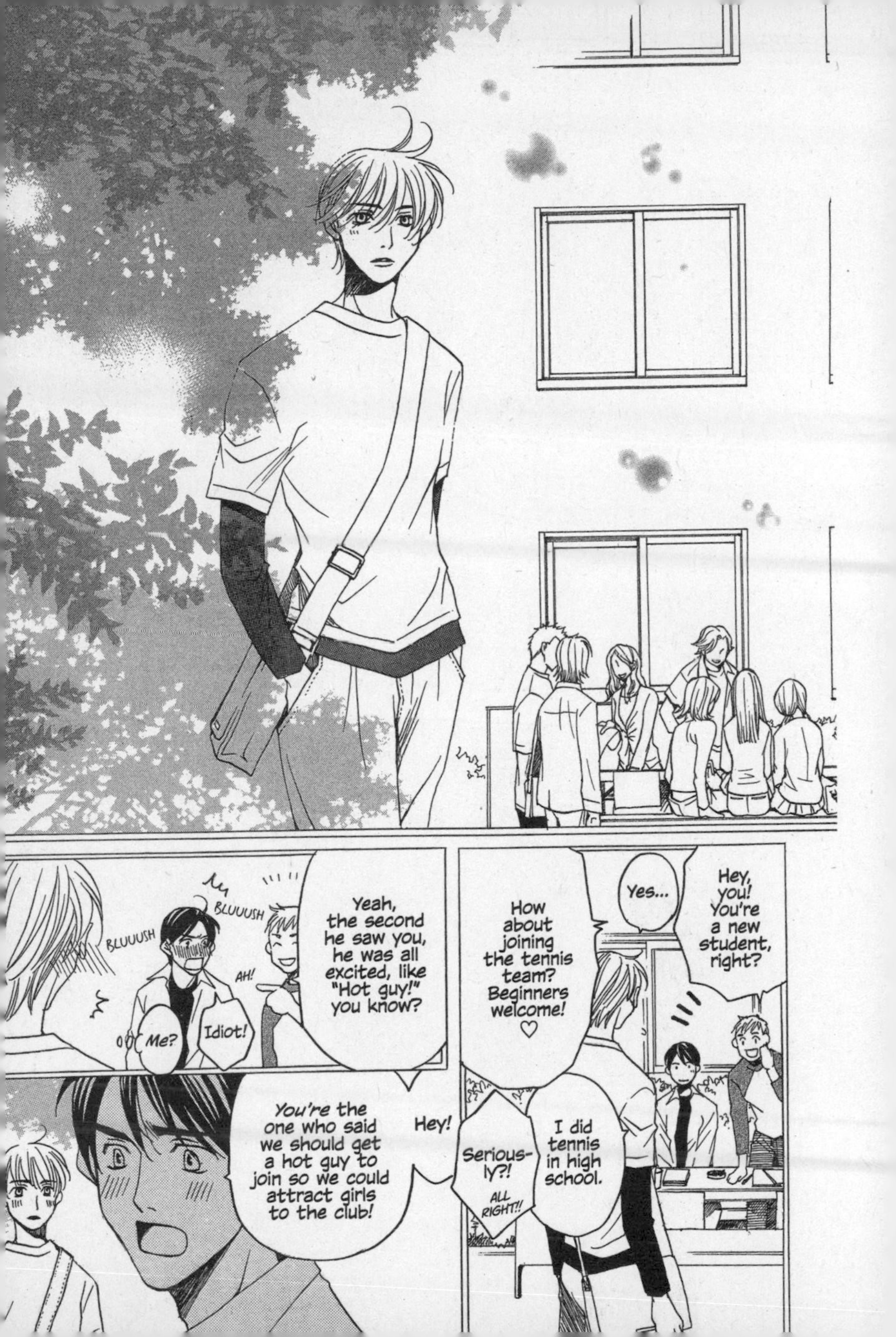
Hey, you! You're a new student, right?
Yes...
How about joining the tennis team? Beginners welcome! ♡
I did tennis in high school.
Serious-ly?!
ALL RIGHT!!
Yeah, the second he saw you, he was all excited, like "Hot guy!" you know?
BLUUUSH
AH!
Idiot!
BLUUUSH
Me?
Hey!
You're the one who said we should get a hot guy to join so we could attract girls to the club!

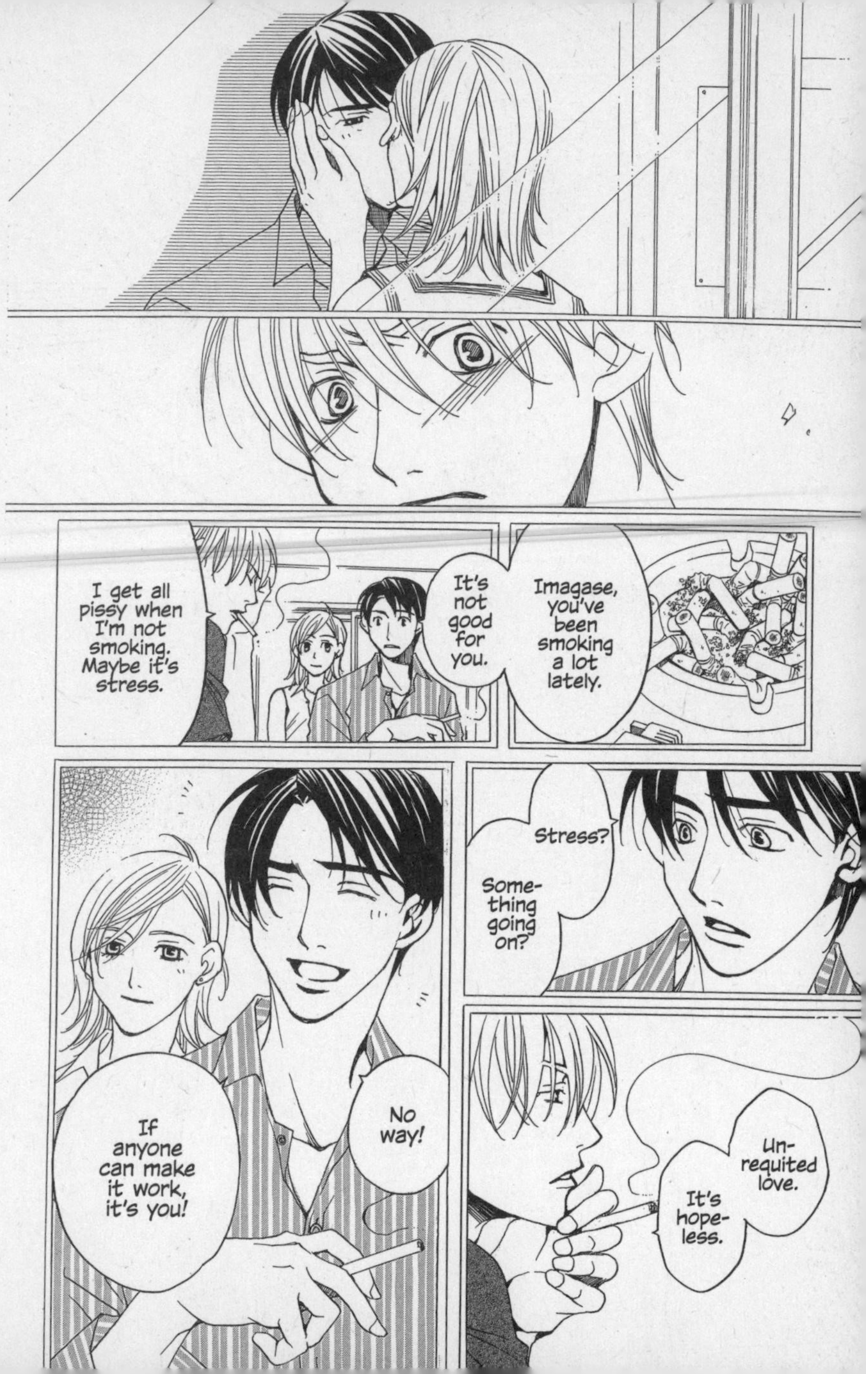
Imagase, you've been smoking a lot lately.
It's not good for you.
I get all pissy when I'm not smoking. Maybe it's stress.
Stress?
Some-thing going on?
Un-requited love.
It's hope-less.
No way!
If anyone can make it work, it's you!

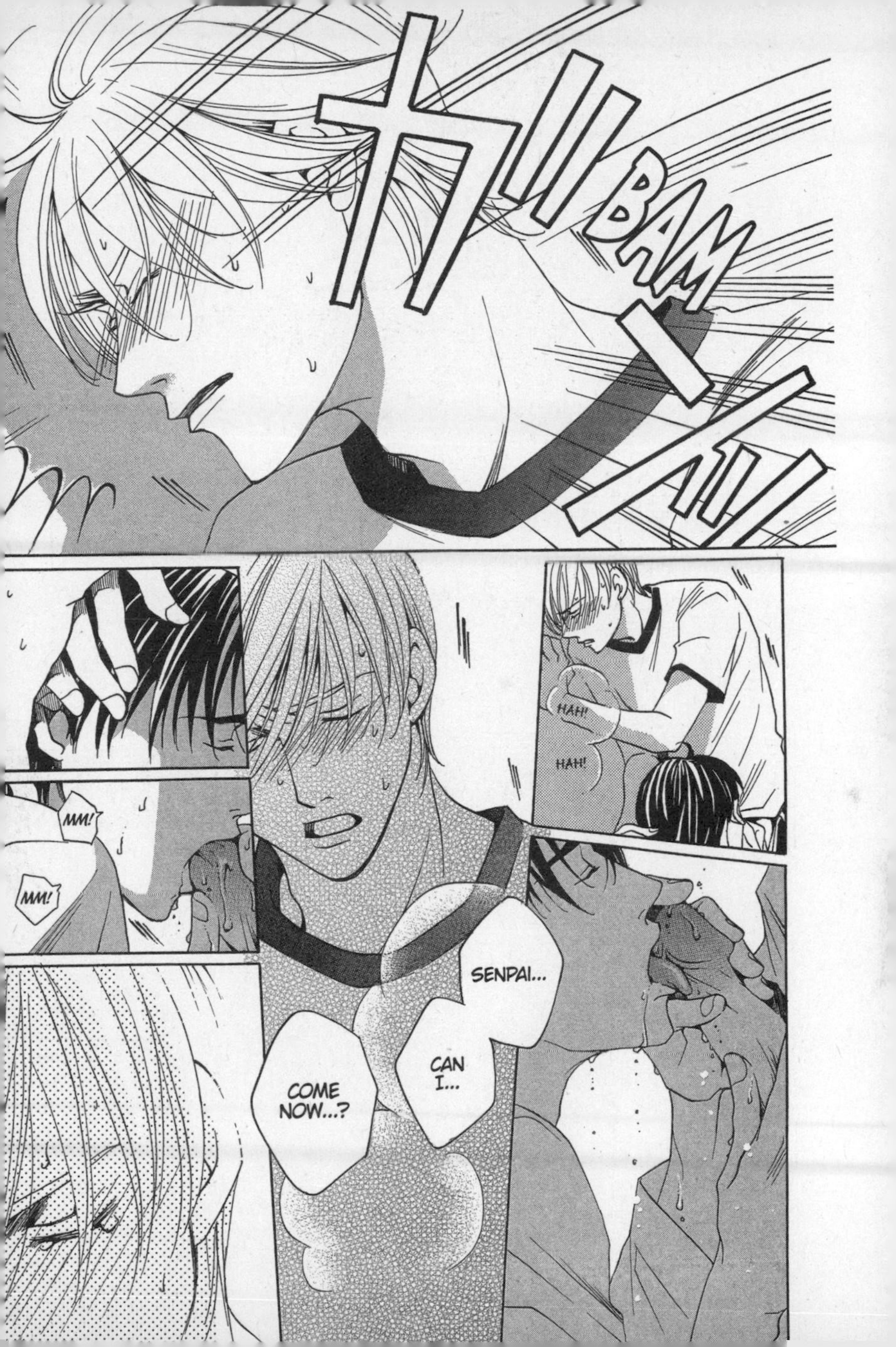
BAM
HAH!
HAH!
SENPAI...
CAN I...
COME NOW...?
MM!
MM!

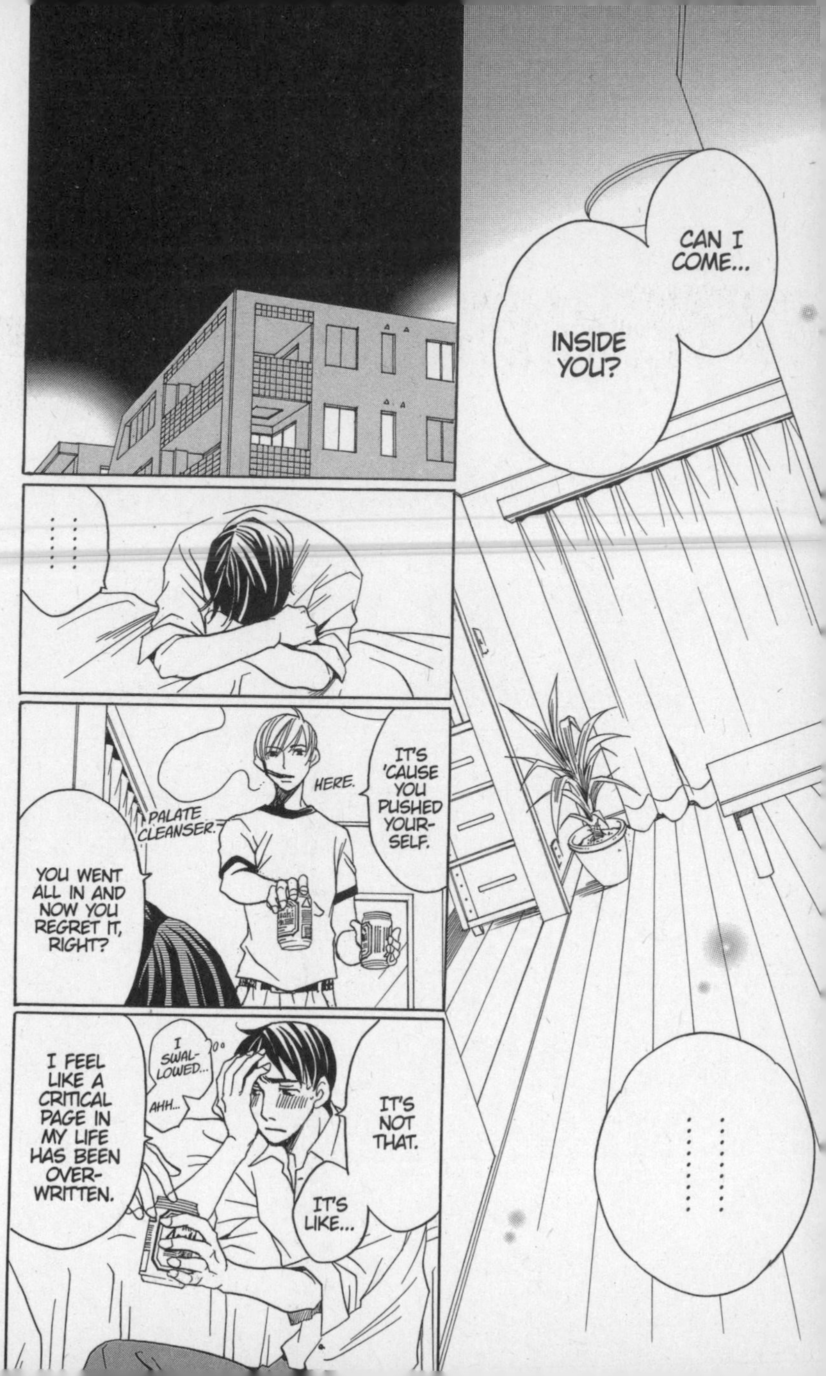
CAN I COME...
INSIDE YOU?
......
......
IT'S 'CAUSE YOU PUSHED YOURSELF.
HERE.
PALATE CLEANSER.
YOU WENT ALL IN AND NOW YOU REGRET IT, RIGHT?
IT'S NOT THAT.
IT'S LIKE...
I SWALLOWED...
AHH...
I FEEL LIKE A CRITICAL PAGE IN MY LIFE HAS BEEN OVERWRITTEN.

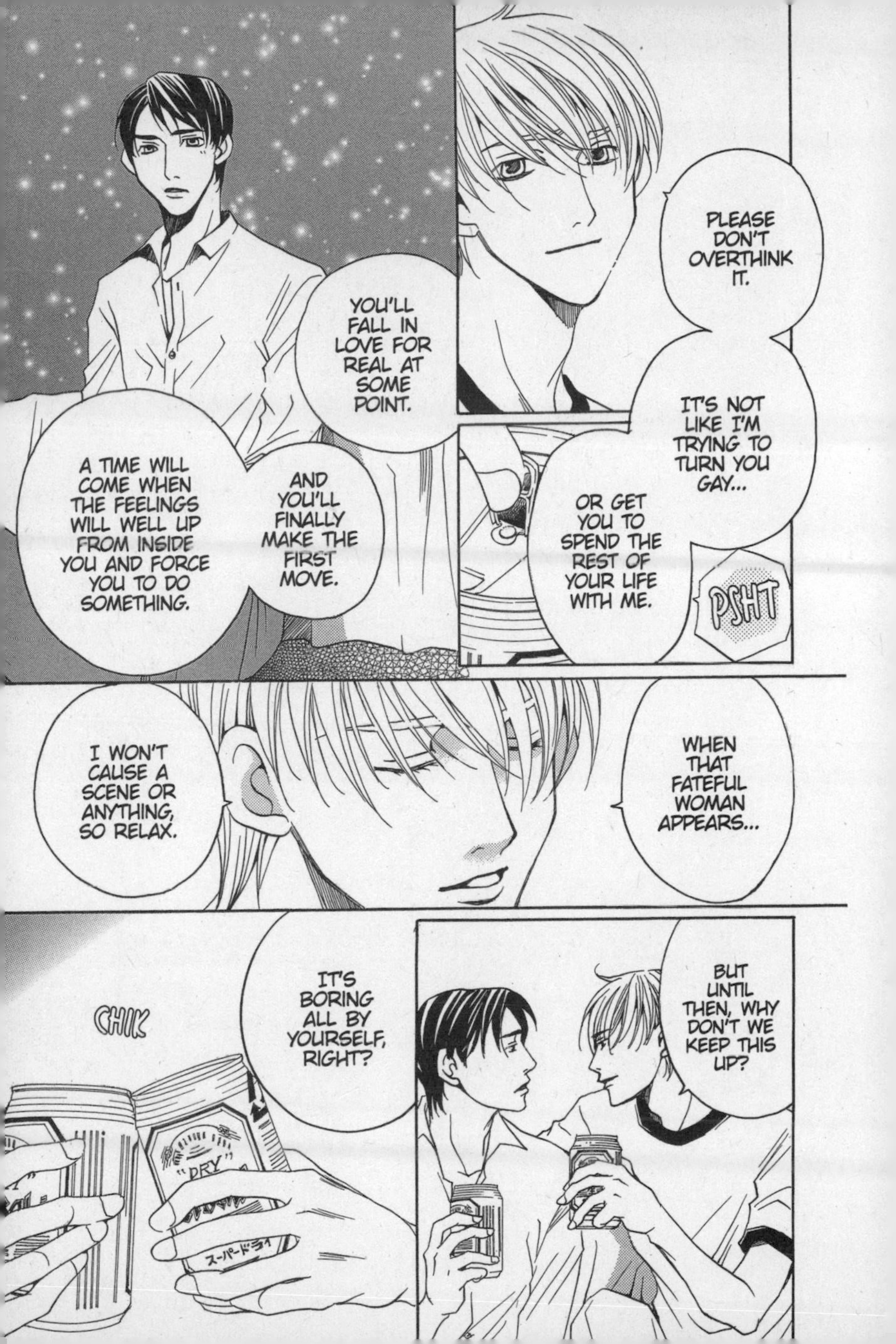
PLEASE DON'T OVERTHINK IT.
IT'S NOT LIKE I'M TRYING TO TURN YOU GAY...
OR GET YOU TO SPEND THE REST OF YOUR LIFE WITH ME.
PSHT
YOU'LL FALL IN LOVE FOR REAL AT SOME POINT.
AND YOU'LL FINALLY MAKE THE FIRST MOVE.
A TIME WILL COME WHEN THE FEELINGS WILL WELL UP FROM INSIDE YOU AND FORCE YOU TO DO SOMETHING.
WHEN THAT FATEFUL WOMAN APPEARS...
I WON'T CAUSE A SCENE OR ANYTHING, SO RELAX.
BUT UNTIL THEN, WHY DON'T WE KEEP THIS UP?
IT'S BORING ALL BY YOURSELF, RIGHT?
CHIK
"DRY"
スーパードライ

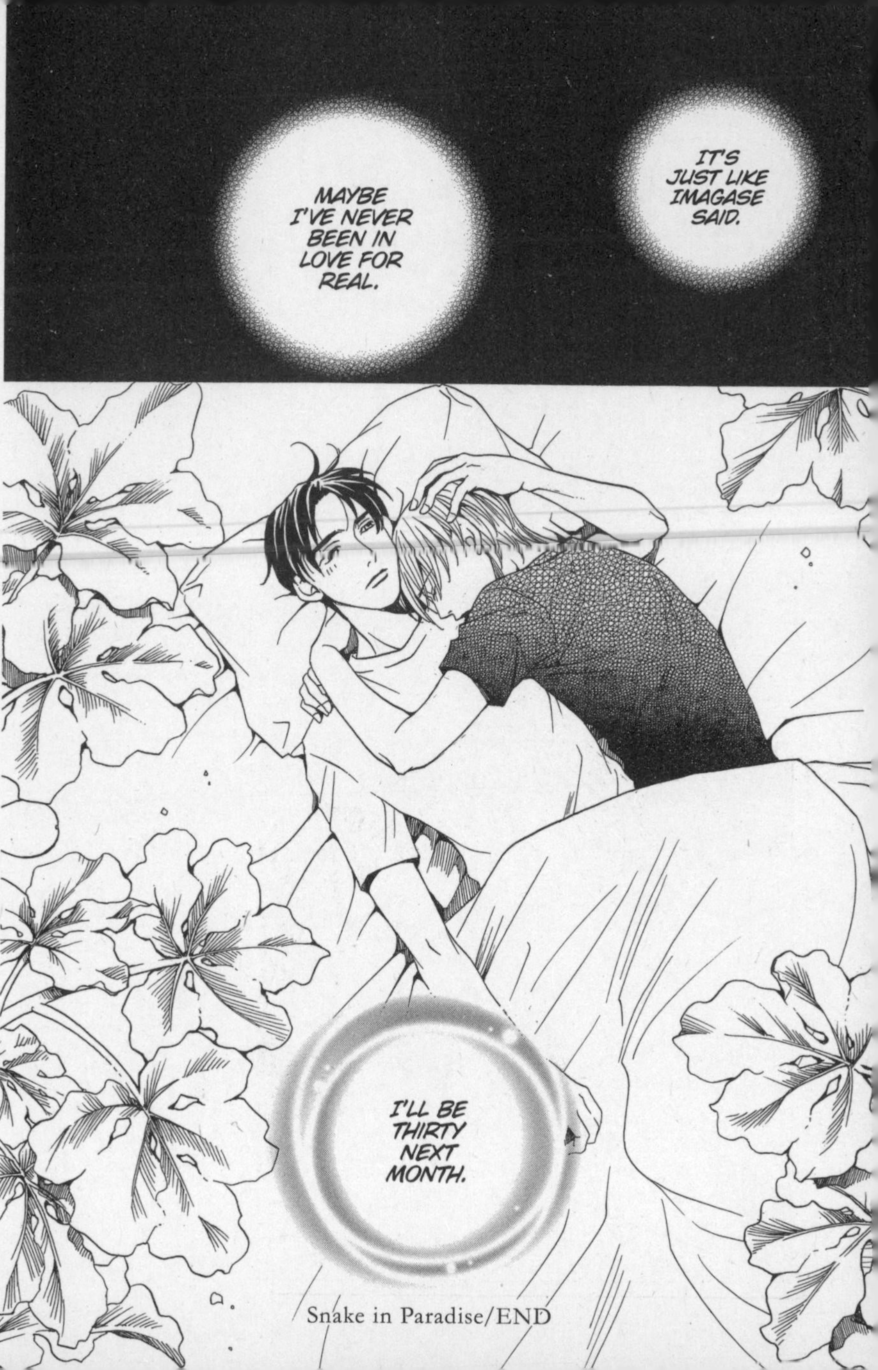
IT'S JUST LIKE IMAGASE SAID.
MAYBE I'VE NEVER BEEN IN LOVE FOR REAL.
I'LL BE THIRTY NEXT MONTH.

Snake in Paradise/END

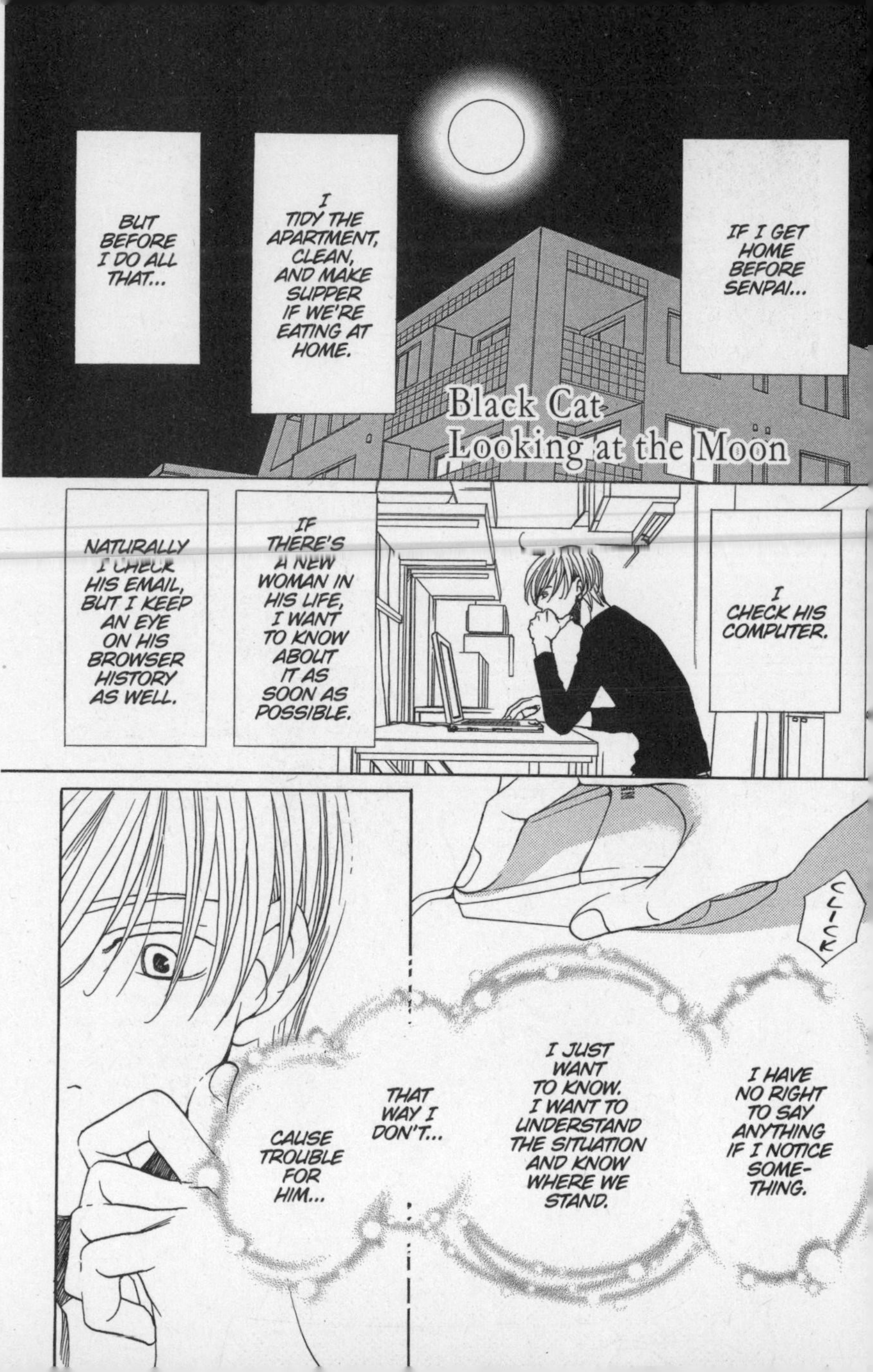
IF I GET HOME BEFORE SENPAI...
I TIDY THE APARTMENT, CLEAN, AND MAKE SUPPER IF WE'RE EATING AT HOME.
BUT BEFORE I DO ALL THAT...
Black Cat Looking at the Moon
I CHECK HIS COMPUTER.
IF THERE'S A NEW WOMAN IN HIS LIFE, I WANT TO KNOW ABOUT IT AS SOON AS POSSIBLE.
NATURALLY I CHECK HIS EMAIL, BUT I KEEP AN EYE ON HIS BROWSER HISTORY AS WELL.
CLICK
I HAVE NO RIGHT TO SAY ANYTHING IF I NOTICE SOME-THING.
I JUST WANT TO KNOW. I WANT TO UNDERSTAND THE SITUATION AND KNOW WHERE WE STAND.
THAT WAY I DON'T...
CAUSE TROUBLE FOR HIM...

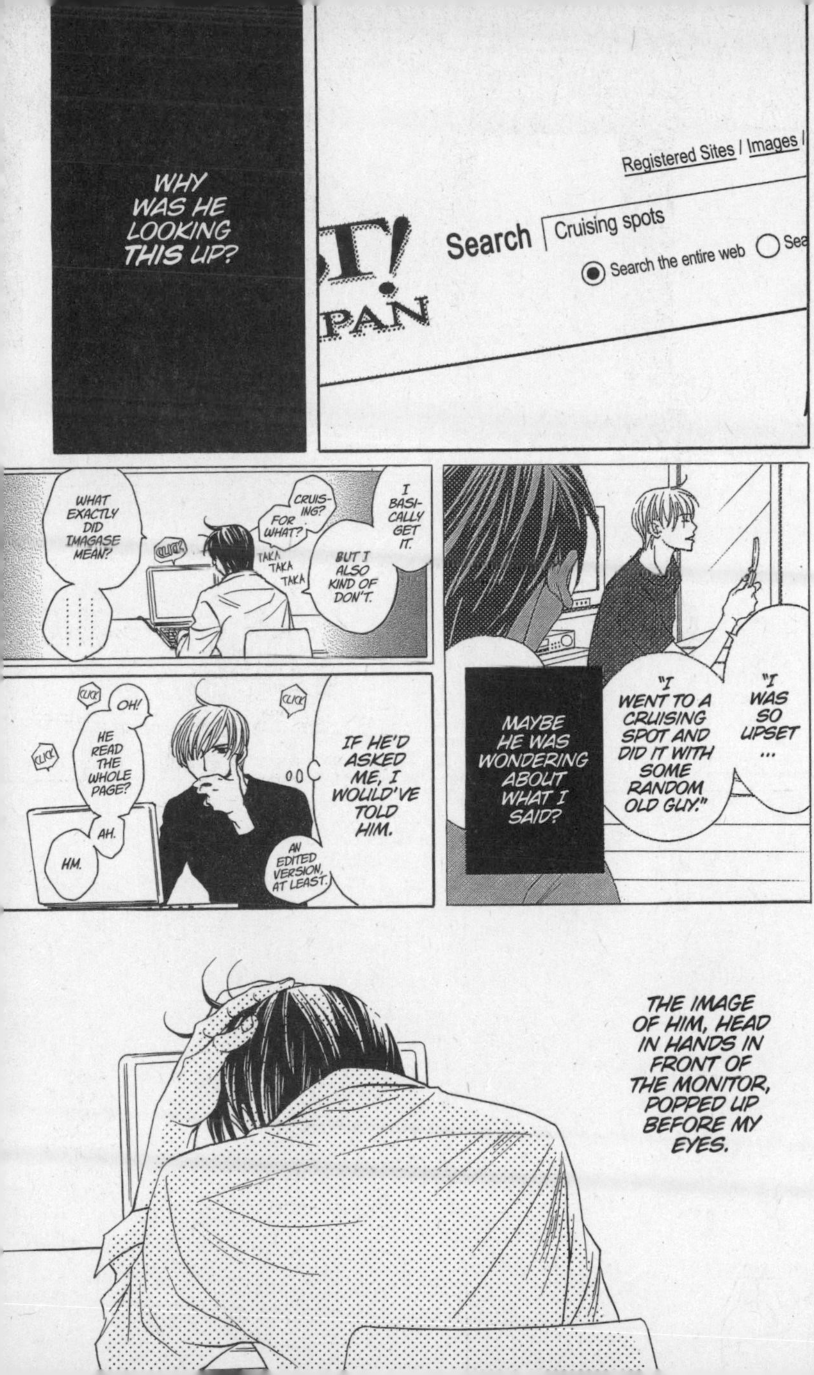
Registered Sites / Images /
Search
Cruising spots
Search the entire web
WHY WAS HE LOOKING THIS UP?
"I WAS SO UPSET...
"I WENT TO A CRUISING SPOT AND DID IT WITH SOME RANDOM OLD GUY."
MAYBE HE WAS WONDERING ABOUT WHAT I SAID?
I BASICALLY GET IT.
BUT I ALSO KIND OF DON'T.
CRUISING? FOR WHAT?
TAKA TAKA TAKA
CLICK
WHAT EXACTLY DID IMAGASE MEAN?
......
IF HE'D ASKED ME, I WOULD'VE TOLD HIM.
AN EDITED VERSION, AT LEAST.
CLICK
OH!
HE READ THE WHOLE PAGE?
CLICK
AH.
HM.
THE IMAGE OF HIM, HEAD IN HANDS IN FRONT OF THE MONITOR, POPPED UP BEFORE MY EYES.

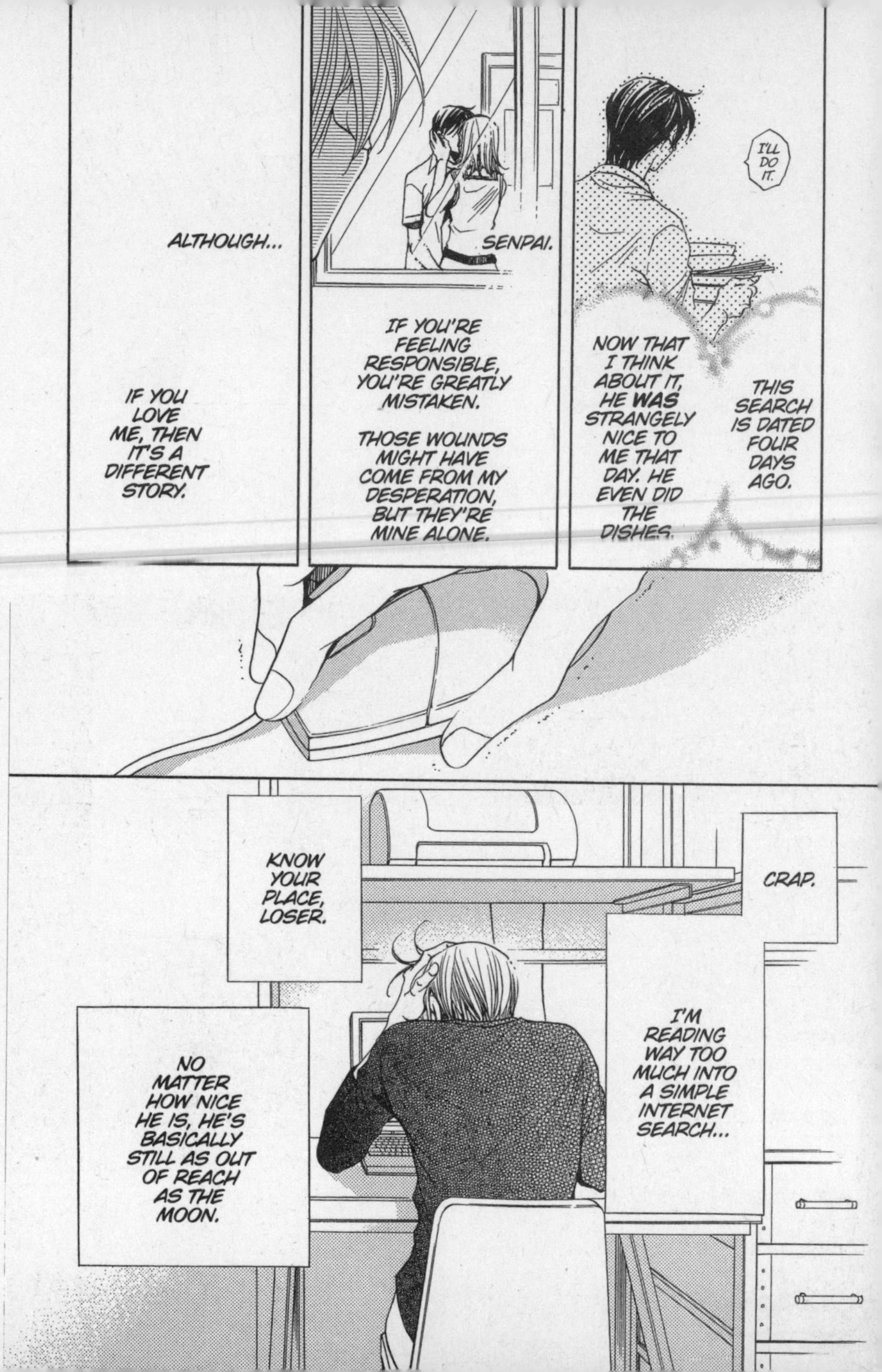
I'LL DO IT.
THIS SEARCH IS DATED FOUR DAYS AGO.
NOW THAT I THINK ABOUT IT, HE **WAS** STRANGELY NICE TO ME THAT DAY. HE EVEN DID THE DISHES.
SENPAI.
IF YOU'RE FEELING RESPONSIBLE, YOU'RE GREATLY MISTAKEN.
THOSE WOUNDS MIGHT HAVE COME FROM MY DESPERATION, BUT THEY'RE MINE ALONE.
ALTHOUGH...
IF YOU LOVE ME, THEN IT'S A DIFFERENT STORY.
CRAP.
I'M READING WAY TOO MUCH INTO A SIMPLE INTERNET SEARCH...
KNOW YOUR PLACE, LOSER.
NO MATTER HOW NICE HE IS, HE'S BASICALLY STILL AS OUT OF REACH AS THE MOON.

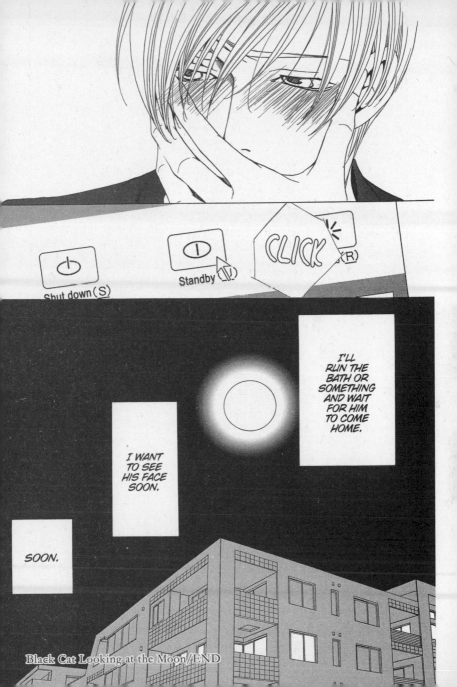

CLICK

Shut down (S)

Standby (U)

(R)

I'LL RUN THE BATH OR SOMETHING AND WAIT FOR HIM TO COME HOME.

I WANT TO SEE HIS FACE SOON.

SOON.

Black Cat Looking at the Moon/END

The Black Cat's Cold Fingertips

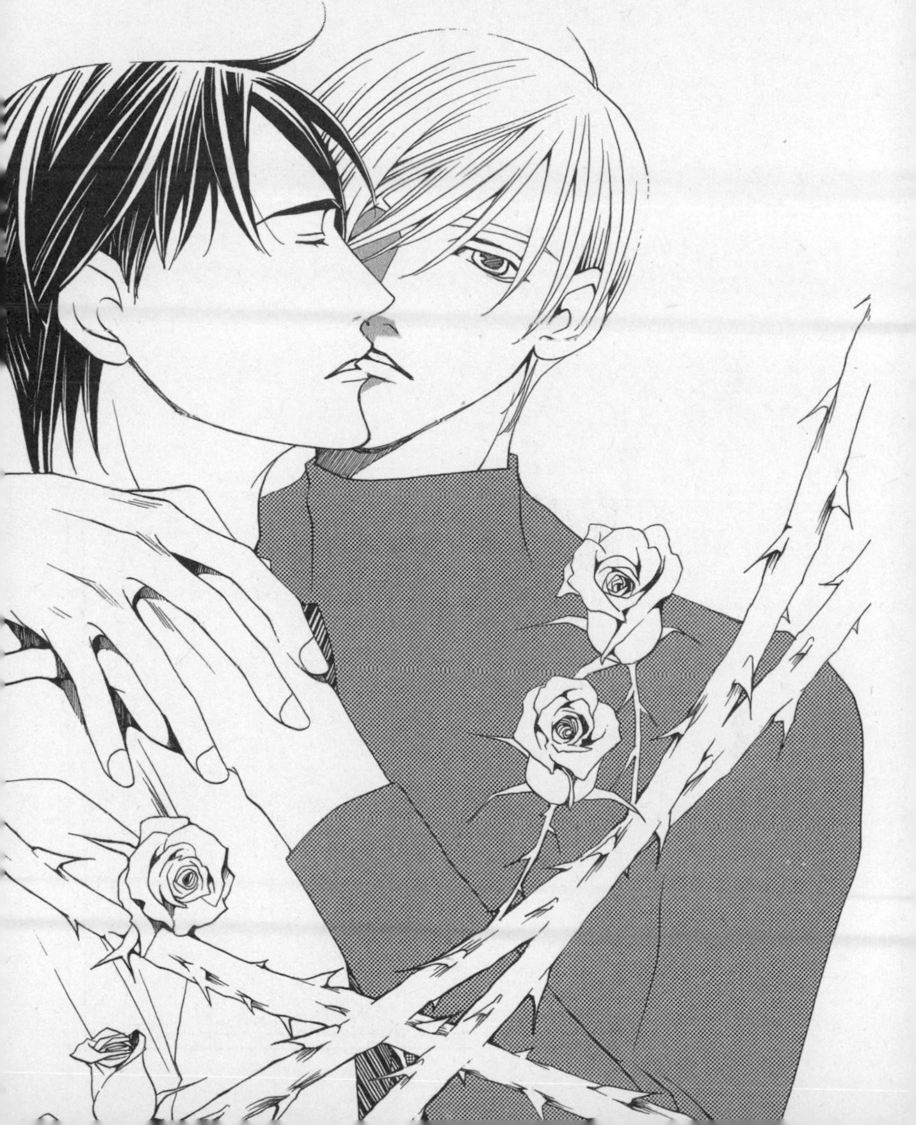

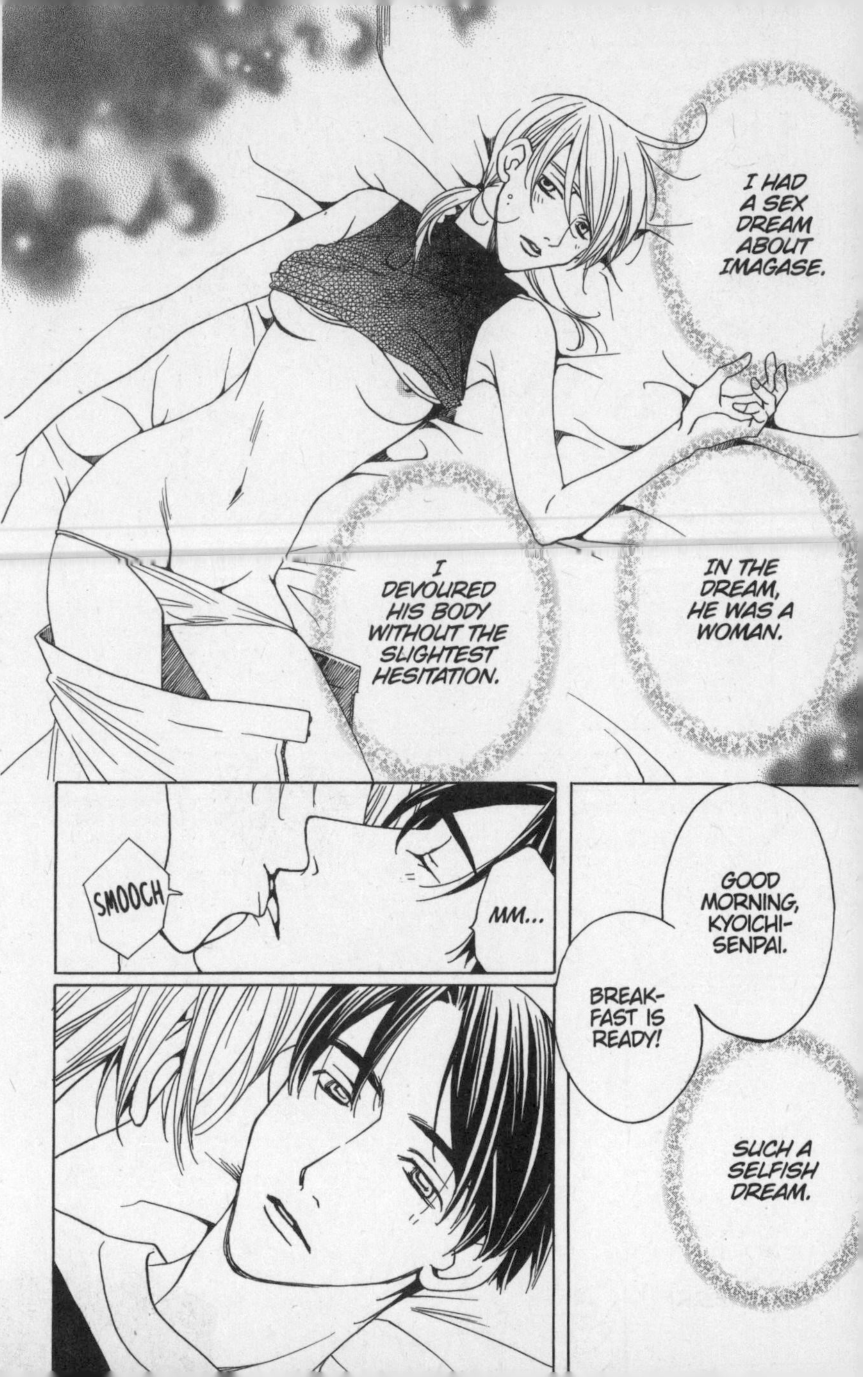
I HAD A SEX DREAM ABOUT IMAGASE.
IN THE DREAM, HE WAS A WOMAN.
I DEVOURED HIS BODY WITHOUT THE SLIGHTEST HESITATION.
GOOD MORNING, KYOICHI-SENPAI.
BREAK-FAST IS READY!
SUCH A SELFISH DREAM.
MM...
SMOOCH

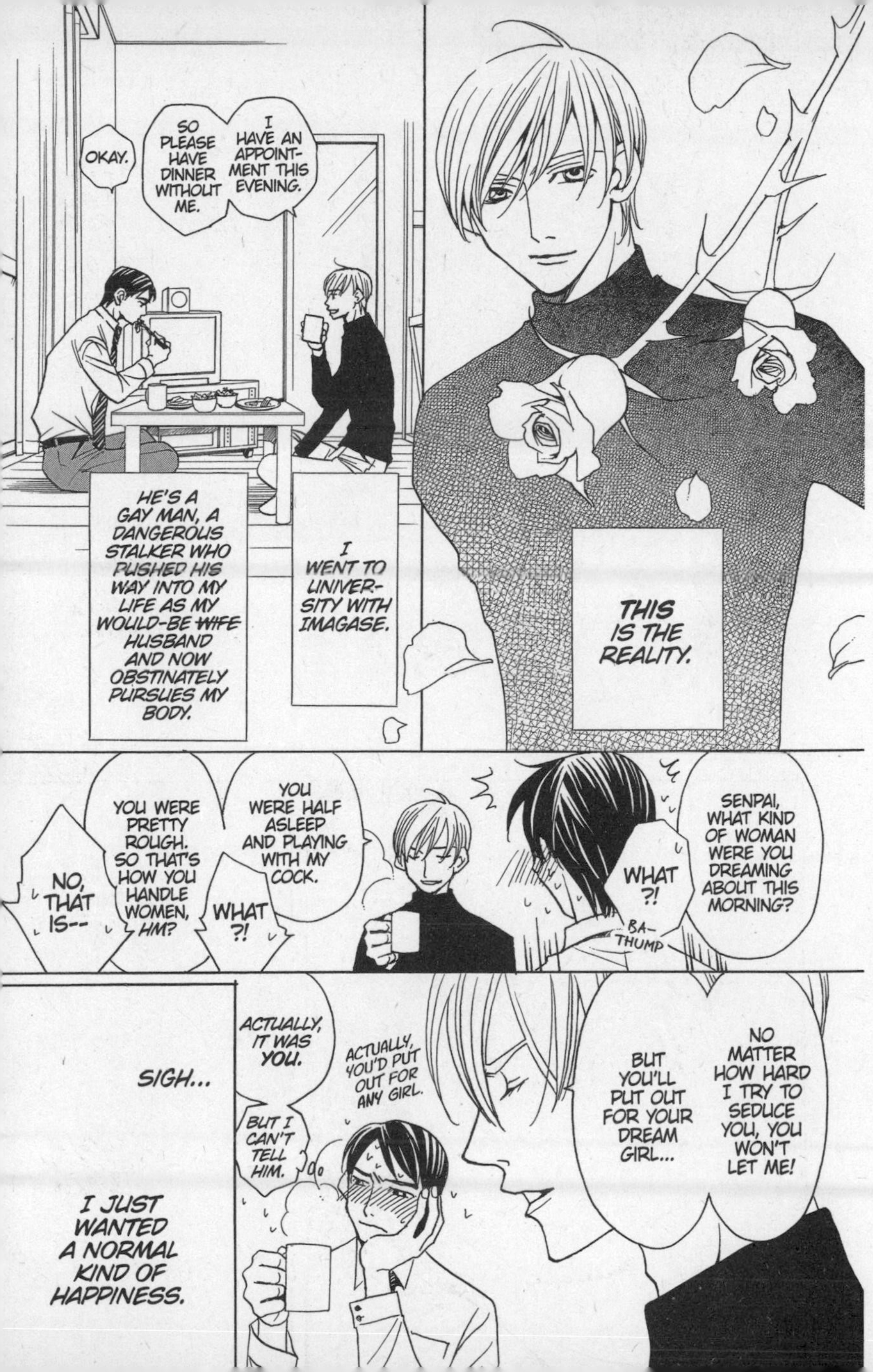
THIS IS THE REALITY.
I HAVE AN APPOINTMENT THIS EVENING.
SO PLEASE HAVE DINNER WITHOUT ME.
OKAY.
I WENT TO UNIVERSITY WITH IMAGASE.
HE'S A GAY MAN, A DANGEROUS STALKER WHO PUSHED HIS WAY INTO MY LIFE AS MY WOULD-BE ~~WIFE~~ HUSBAND AND NOW OBSTINATELY PURSUES MY BODY.
SENPAI, WHAT KIND OF WOMAN WERE YOU DREAMING ABOUT THIS MORNING?
WHAT ?!
BA-THUMP
YOU WERE HALF ASLEEP AND PLAYING WITH MY COCK.
YOU WERE PRETTY ROUGH. SO THAT'S HOW YOU HANDLE WOMEN, HM?
WHAT ?!
NO, THAT IS--
NO MATTER HOW HARD I TRY TO SEDUCE YOU, YOU WON'T LET ME!
BUT YOU'LL PUT OUT FOR YOUR DREAM GIRL...
ACTUALLY, IT WAS YOU.
ACTUALLY, YOU'D PUT OUT FOR ANY GIRL.
BUT I CAN'T TELL HIM.
SIGH...
I JUST WANTED A NORMAL KIND OF HAPPINESS.

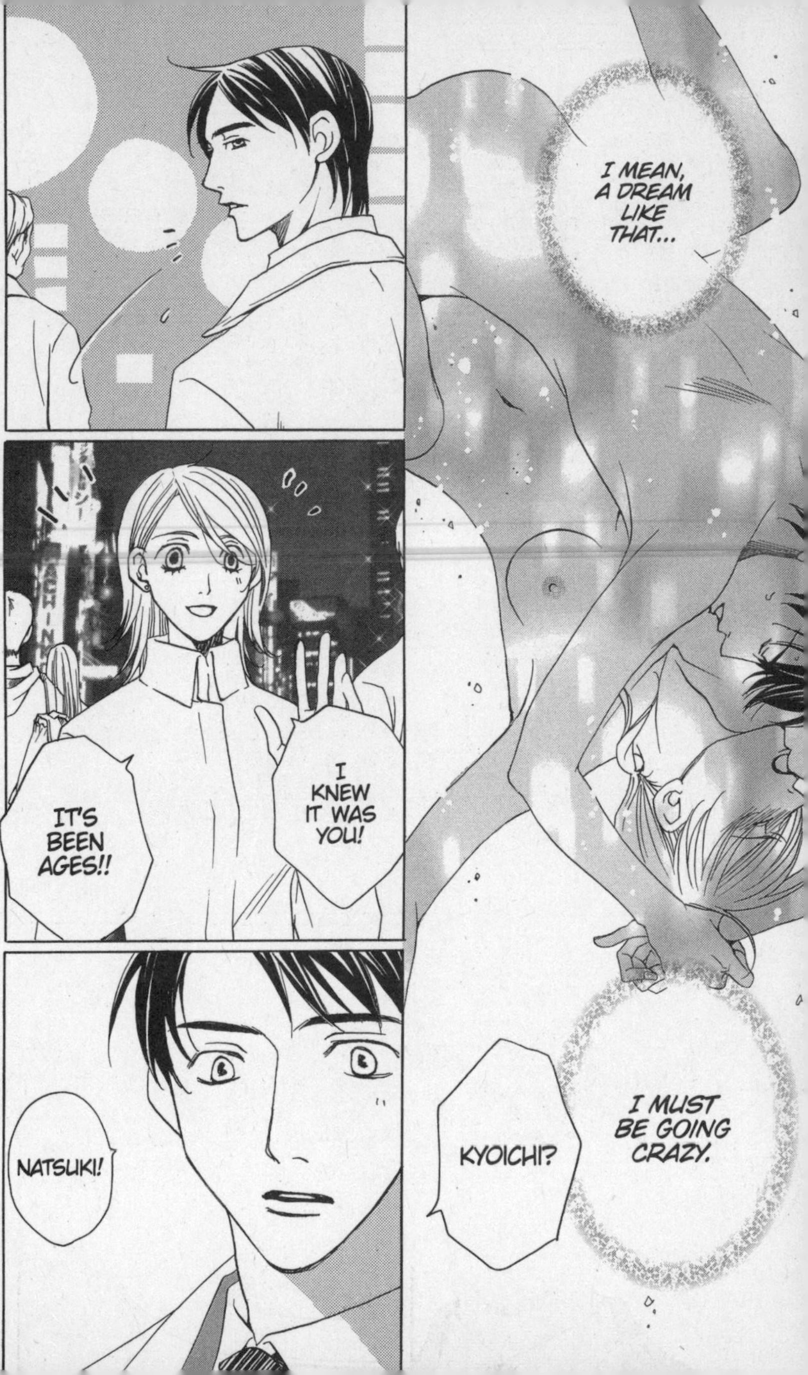
I MEAN, A DREAM LIKE THAT...
I MUST BE GOING CRAZY.
KYOICHI?
I KNEW IT WAS YOU!
IT'S BEEN AGES!!
NATSUKI!

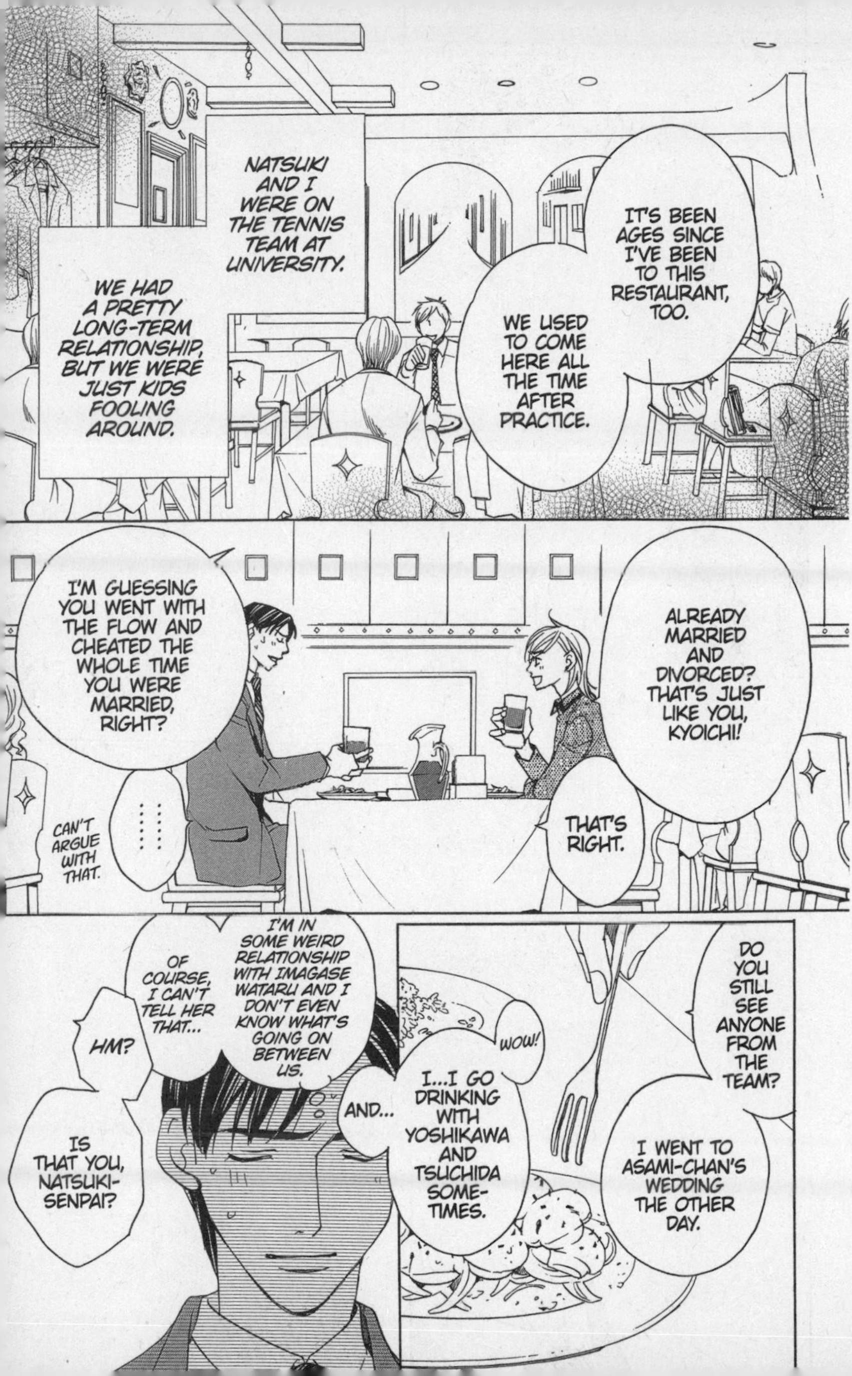
IT'S BEEN AGES SINCE I'VE BEEN TO THIS RESTAURANT, TOO.
WE USED TO COME HERE ALL THE TIME AFTER PRACTICE.
NATSUKI AND I WERE ON THE TENNIS TEAM AT UNIVERSITY.
WE HAD A PRETTY LONG-TERM RELATIONSHIP, BUT WE WERE JUST KIDS FOOLING AROUND.
ALREADY MARRIED AND DIVORCED? THAT'S JUST LIKE YOU, KYOICHI!
THAT'S RIGHT.
I'M GUESSING YOU WENT WITH THE FLOW AND CHEATED THE WHOLE TIME YOU WERE MARRIED, RIGHT?
......
CAN'T ARGUE WITH THAT.
DO YOU STILL SEE ANYONE FROM THE TEAM?
I WENT TO ASAMI-CHAN'S WEDDING THE OTHER DAY.
WOW!
I'M IN SOME WEIRD RELATIONSHIP WITH IMAGASE WATARU AND I DON'T EVEN KNOW WHAT'S GOING ON BETWEEN US.
OF COURSE, I CAN'T TELL HER THAT...
AND...
I...I GO DRINKING WITH YOSHIKAWA AND TSUCHIDA SOMETIMES.
HM?
IS THAT YOU, NATSUKI-SENPAI?

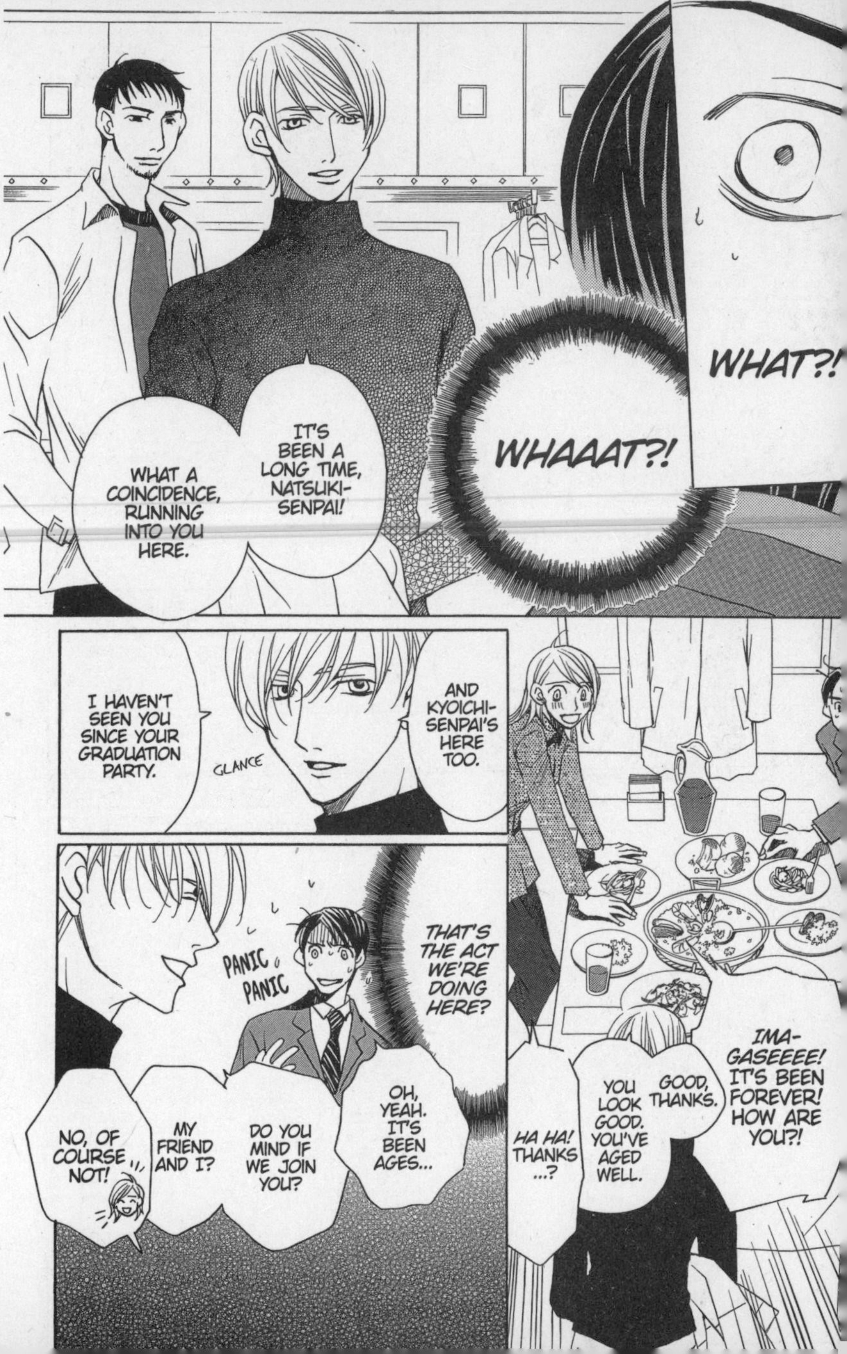
WHAT?!
WHAAAT?!
IT'S BEEN A LONG TIME, NATSUKI-SENPAI!
WHAT A COINCIDENCE, RUNNING INTO YOU HERE.
IMA-GASEEEE! IT'S BEEN FOREVER! HOW ARE YOU?!
GOOD, THANKS.
YOU LOOK GOOD. YOU'VE AGED WELL.
HA HA! THANKS ...?
AND KYOICHI-SENPAI'S HERE TOO.
GLANCE
I HAVEN'T SEEN YOU SINCE YOUR GRADUATION PARTY.
THAT'S THE ACT WE'RE DOING HERE?
PANIC PANIC
OH, YEAH. IT'S BEEN AGES...
DO YOU MIND IF WE JOIN YOU?
MY FRIEND AND I?
NO, OF COURSE NOT!

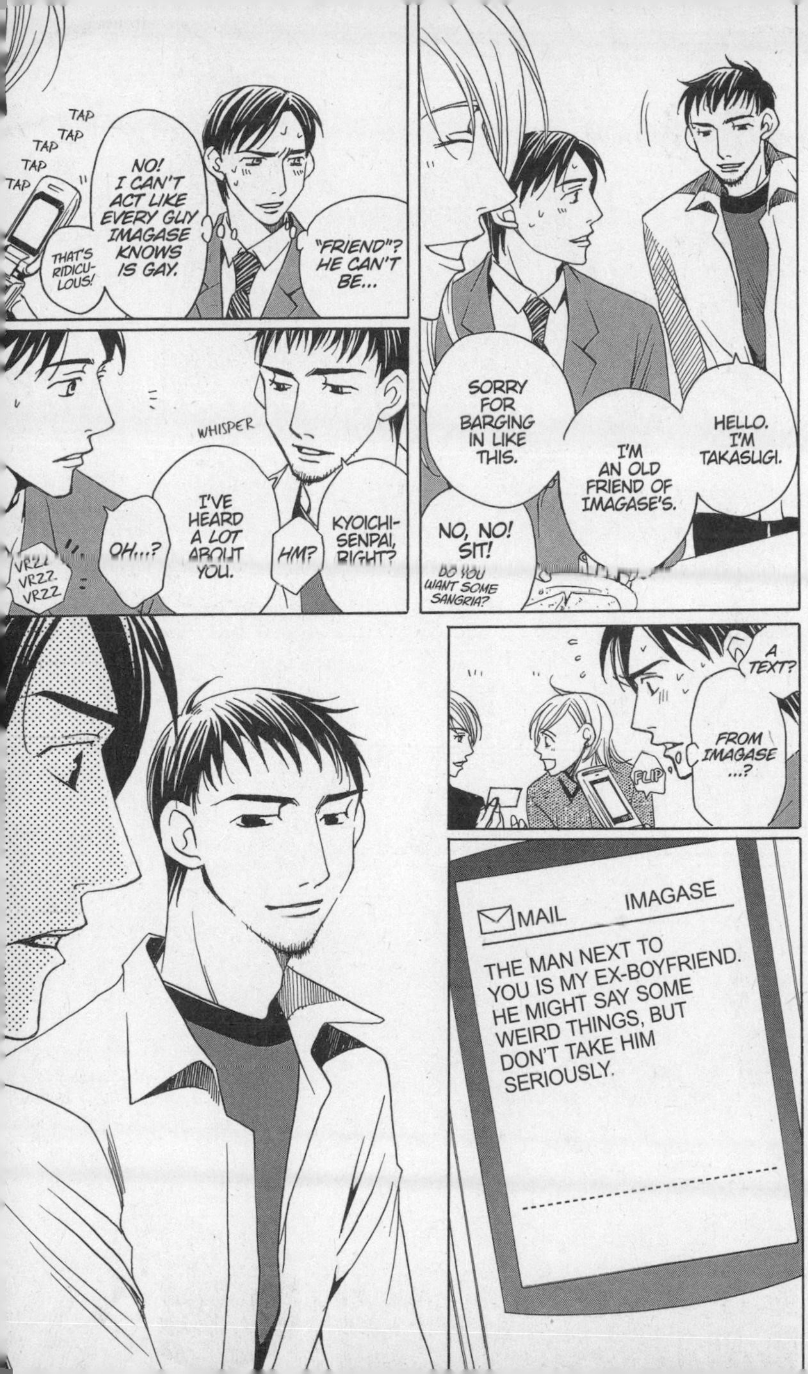
HELLO. I'M TAKASUGI.
I'M AN OLD FRIEND OF IMAGASE'S.
SORRY FOR BARGING IN LIKE THIS.
NO, NO! SIT!
DO YOU WANT SOME SANGRIA?
"FRIEND"? HE CAN'T BE...
NO! I CAN'T ACT LIKE EVERY GUY IMAGASE KNOWS IS GAY.
THAT'S RIDICULOUS!
TAP TAP TAP TAP TAP
KYOICHI-SENPAI, RIGHT?
HM?
I'VE HEARD A LOT ABOUT YOU.
WHISPER
OH...?
VRZZ VRZZ VRZZ
A TEXT?
FROM IMAGASE ...?
FLIP
MAIL IMAGASE
THE MAN NEXT TO YOU IS MY EX-BOYFRIEND. HE MIGHT SAY SOME WEIRD THINGS, BUT DON'T TAKE HIM SERIOUSLY.

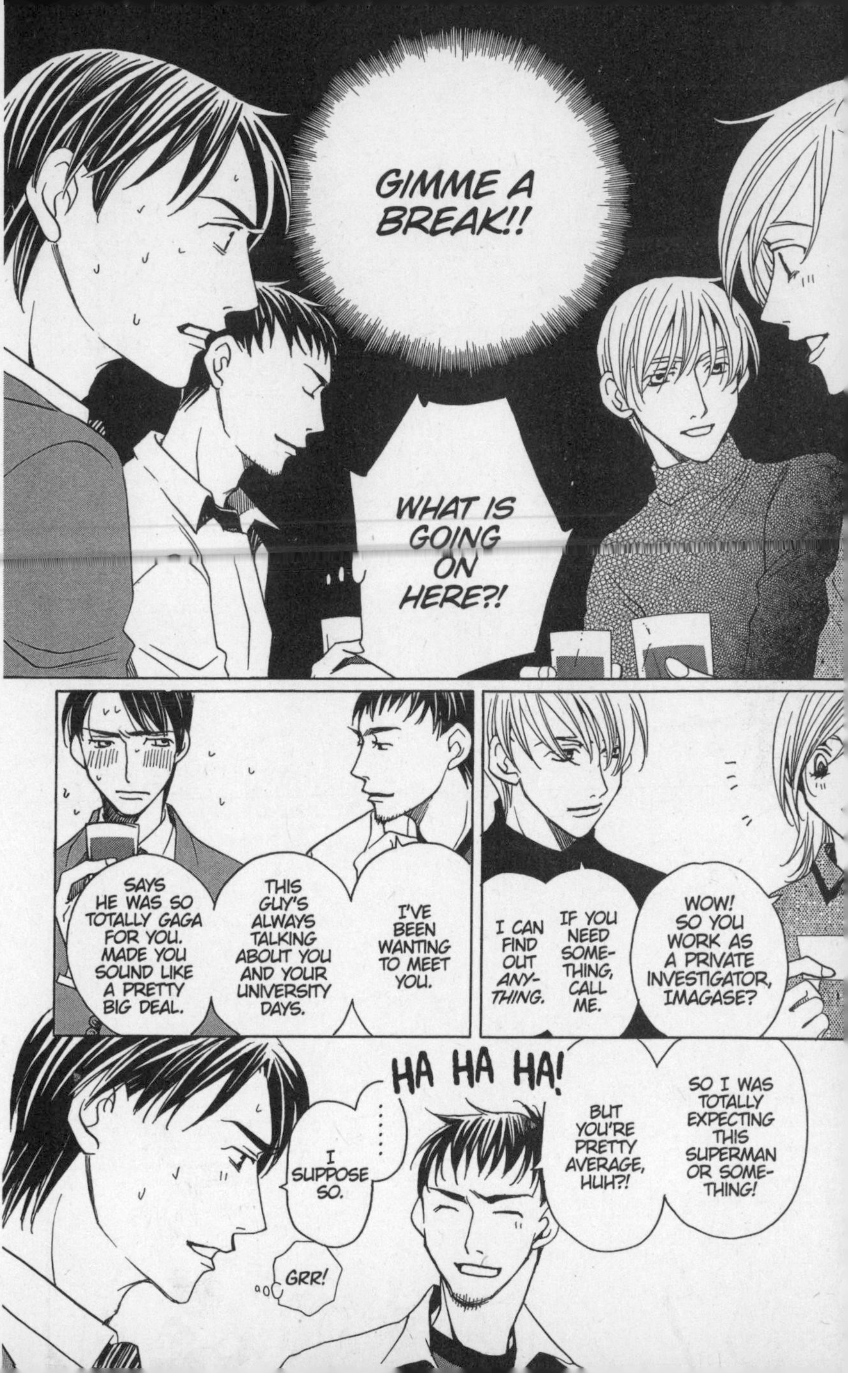
GIMME A BREAK!!
WHAT IS GOING ON HERE?!
WOW! SO YOU WORK AS A PRIVATE INVESTIGATOR, IMAGASE?
IF YOU NEED SOME-THING, CALL ME.
I CAN FIND OUT ANY-THING.
I'VE BEEN WANTING TO MEET YOU.
THIS GUY'S ALWAYS TALKING ABOUT YOU AND YOUR UNIVERSITY DAYS.
SAYS HE WAS SO TOTALLY GAGA FOR YOU. MADE YOU SOUND LIKE A PRETTY BIG DEAL.
SO I WAS TOTALLY EXPECTING THIS SUPERMAN OR SOME-THING!
BUT YOU'RE PRETTY AVERAGE, HUH?!
HA HA HA!
......
I SUPPOSE SO.
GRR!

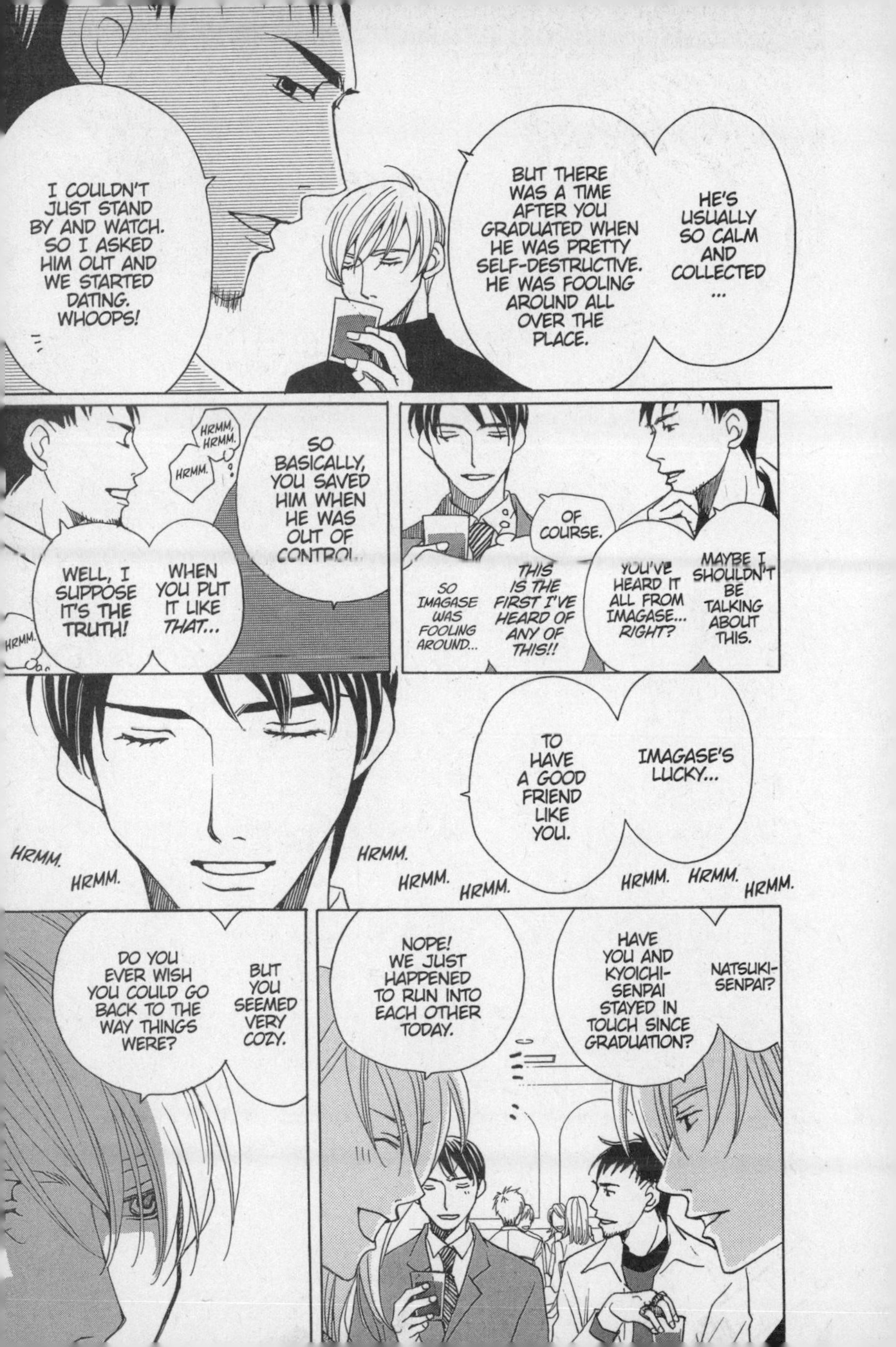
HE'S USUALLY SO CALM AND COLLECTED ...
BUT THERE WAS A TIME AFTER YOU GRADUATED WHEN HE WAS PRETTY SELF-DESTRUCTIVE. HE WAS FOOLING AROUND ALL OVER THE PLACE.
I COULDN'T JUST STAND BY AND WATCH. SO I ASKED HIM OUT AND WE STARTED DATING. WHOOPS!
MAYBE I SHOULDN'T BE TALKING ABOUT THIS.
YOU'VE HEARD IT ALL FROM IMAGASE... RIGHT?
OF COURSE.
THIS IS THE FIRST I'VE HEARD OF ANY OF THIS!!
SO IMAGASE WAS FOOLING AROUND...
SO BASICALLY, YOU SAVED HIM WHEN HE WAS OUT OF CONTROL.
HRMM, HRMM.
HRMM.
WHEN YOU PUT IT LIKE THAT...
WELL, I SUPPOSE IT'S THE TRUTH!
HRMM.
IMAGASE'S LUCKY...
TO HAVE A GOOD FRIEND LIKE YOU.
HRMM. HRMM. HRMM.
HRMM. HRMM. HRMM.
HRMM. HRMM.
NATSUKI-SENPAI?
HAVE YOU AND KYOICHI-SENPAI STAYED IN TOUCH SINCE GRADUATION?
NOPE! WE JUST HAPPENED TO RUN INTO EACH OTHER TODAY.
BUT YOU SEEMED VERY COZY.
DO YOU EVER WISH YOU COULD GO BACK TO THE WAY THINGS WERE?

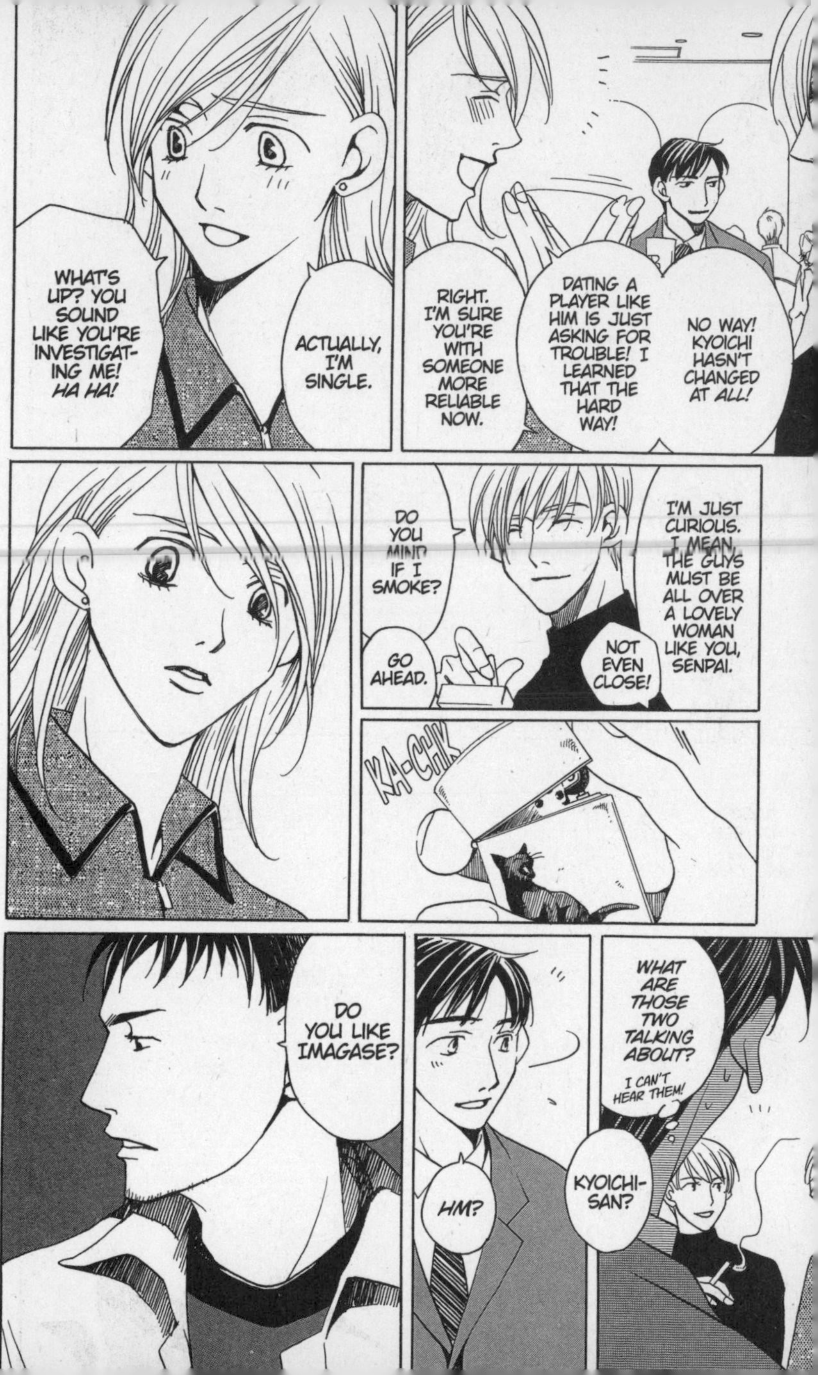
NO WAY! KYOICHI HASN'T CHANGED AT ALL!
DATING A PLAYER LIKE HIM IS JUST ASKING FOR TROUBLE! I LEARNED THAT THE HARD WAY!
RIGHT. I'M SURE YOU'RE WITH SOMEONE MORE RELIABLE NOW.
ACTUALLY, I'M SINGLE.
WHAT'S UP? YOU SOUND LIKE YOU'RE INVESTIGATING ME! HA HA!
I'M JUST CURIOUS. I MEAN, THE GUYS MUST BE ALL OVER A LOVELY WOMAN LIKE YOU, SENPAI.
NOT EVEN CLOSE!
DO YOU MIND IF I SMOKE?
GO AHEAD.
KA-CHK
WHAT ARE THOSE TWO TALKING ABOUT?
I CAN'T HEAR THEM!
KYOICHI-SAN?
HM?
DO YOU LIKE IMAGASE?

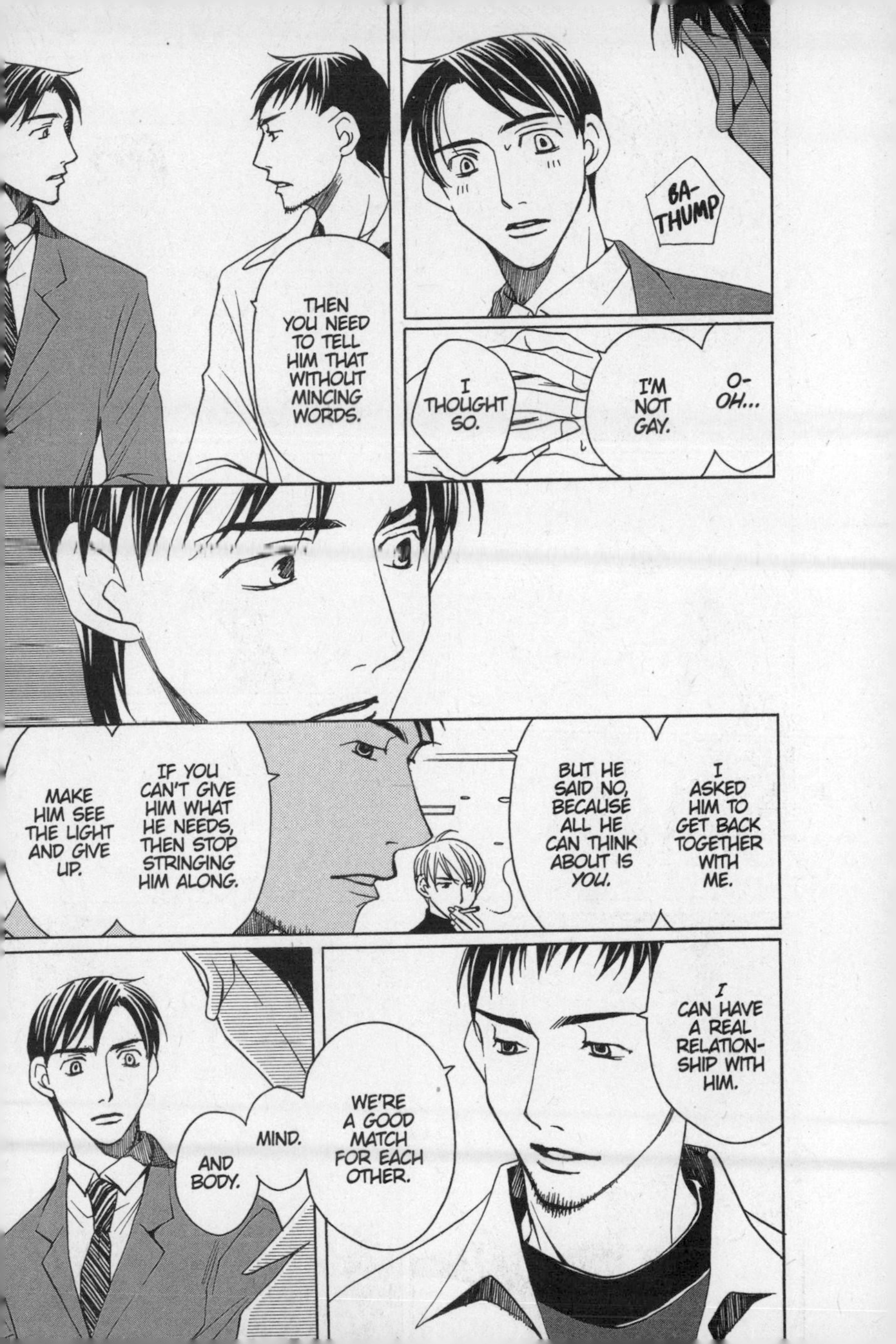
BA-THUMP
O-OH...
I'M NOT GAY.
I THOUGHT SO.
THEN YOU NEED TO TELL HIM THAT WITHOUT MINCING WORDS.
I ASKED HIM TO GET BACK TOGETHER WITH ME.
BUT HE SAID NO, BECAUSE ALL HE CAN THINK ABOUT IS *YOU.*
IF YOU CAN'T GIVE HIM WHAT HE NEEDS, THEN STOP STRINGING HIM ALONG.
MAKE HIM SEE THE LIGHT AND GIVE UP.
I CAN HAVE A REAL RELATIONSHIP WITH HIM.
WE'RE A GOOD MATCH FOR EACH OTHER.
MIND.
AND BODY.

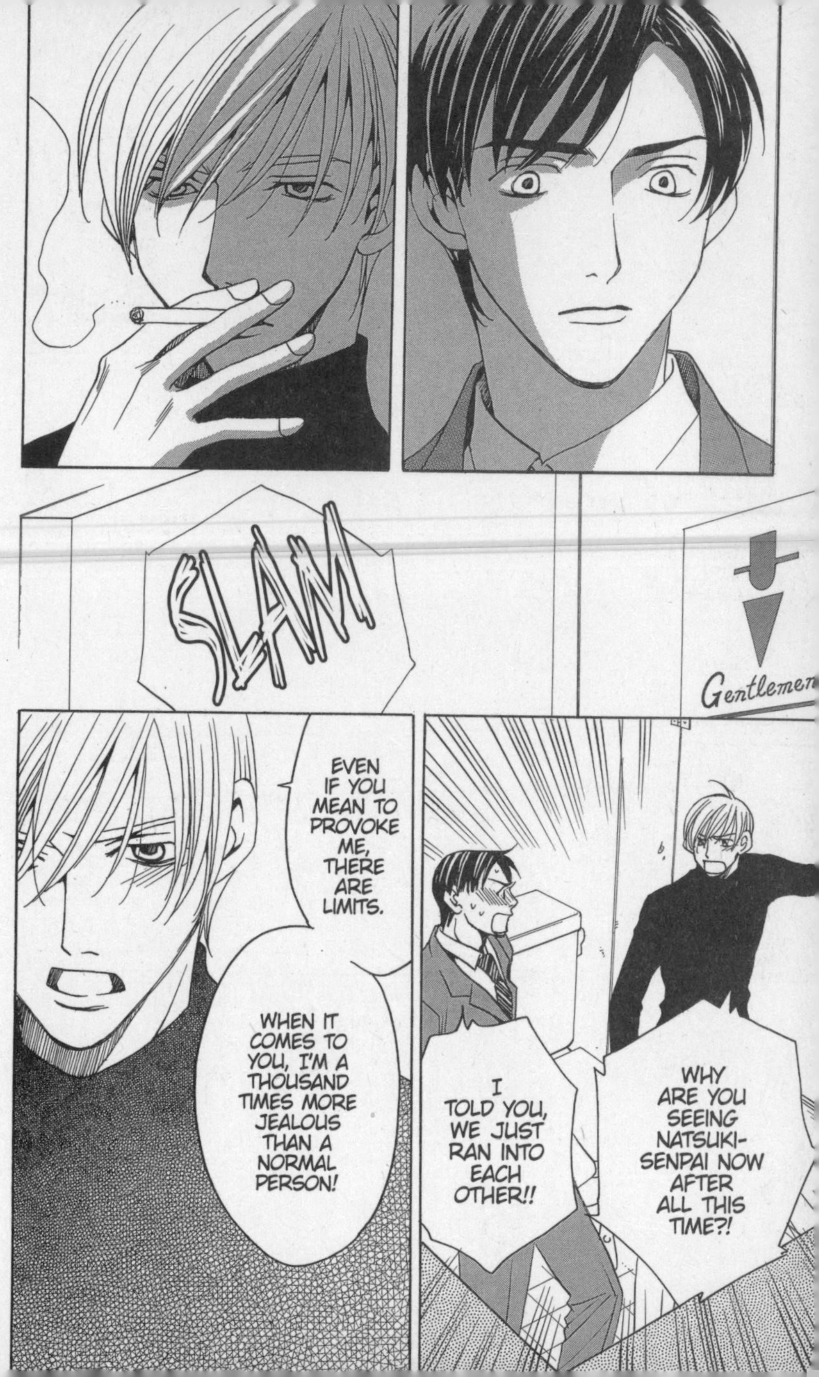
Gentlemen
SLAM
WHY ARE YOU SEEING NATSUKI-SENPAI NOW AFTER ALL THIS TIME?!
I TOLD YOU, WE JUST RAN INTO EACH OTHER!!
EVEN IF YOU MEAN TO PROVOKE ME, THERE ARE LIMITS.
WHEN IT COMES TO YOU, I'M A THOUSAND TIMES MORE JEALOUS THAN A NORMAL PERSON!

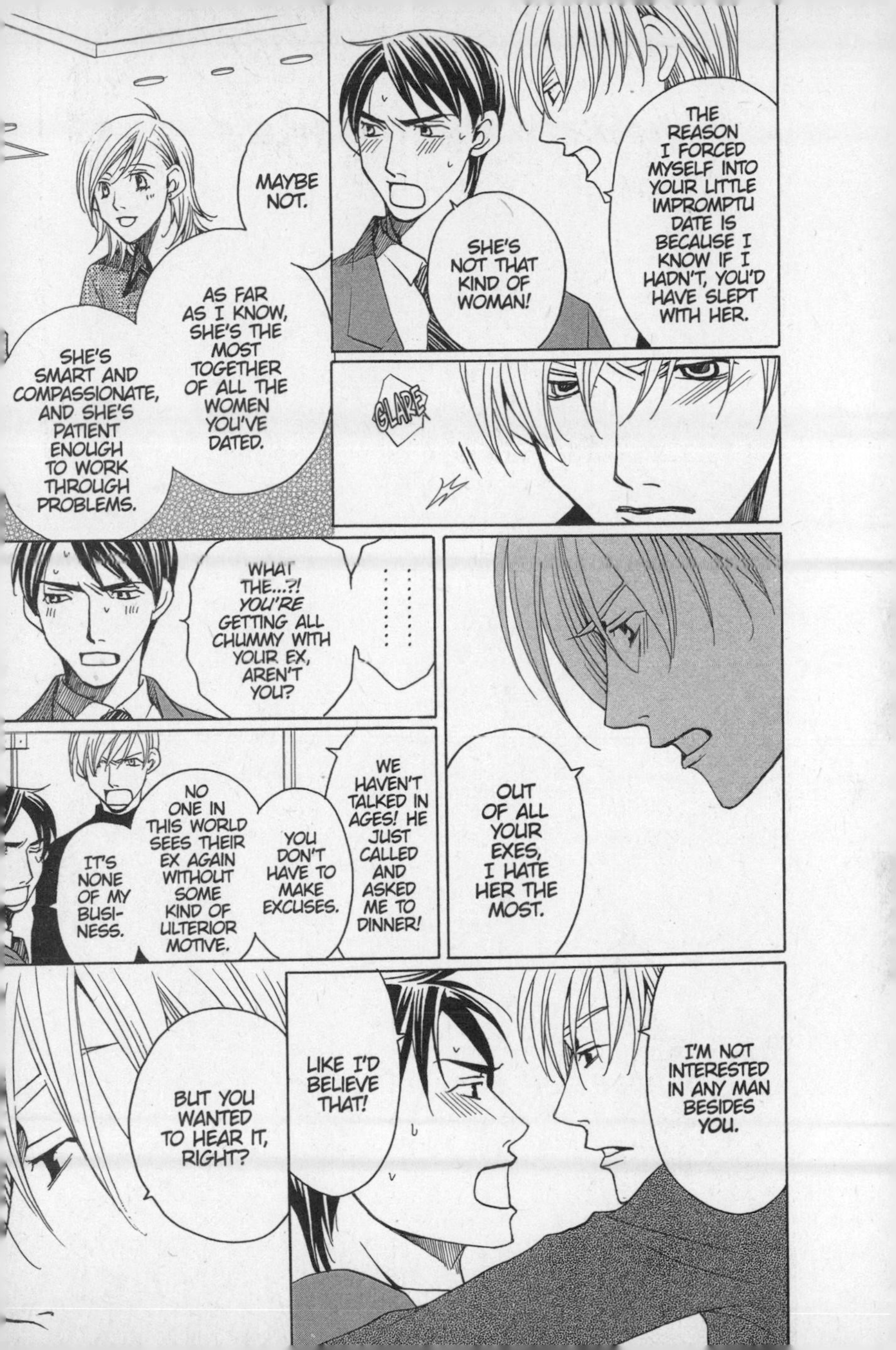
THE REASON I FORCED MYSELF INTO YOUR LITTLE IMPROMPTU DATE IS BECAUSE I KNOW IF I HADN'T, YOU'D HAVE SLEPT WITH HER.
SHE'S NOT THAT KIND OF WOMAN!
GLARE
MAYBE NOT.
AS FAR AS I KNOW, SHE'S THE MOST TOGETHER OF ALL THE WOMEN YOU'VE DATED.
SHE'S SMART AND COMPASSIONATE, AND SHE'S PATIENT ENOUGH TO WORK THROUGH PROBLEMS.
OUT OF ALL YOUR EXES, I HATE HER THE MOST.
WHAT THE...?! *YOU'RE* GETTING ALL CHUMMY WITH YOUR EX, AREN'T YOU?
......
WE HAVEN'T TALKED IN AGES! HE JUST CALLED AND ASKED ME TO DINNER!
YOU DON'T HAVE TO MAKE EXCUSES.
NO ONE IN THIS WORLD SEES THEIR EX AGAIN WITHOUT SOME KIND OF ULTERIOR MOTIVE.
IT'S NONE OF MY BUSINESS.
I'M NOT INTERESTED IN ANY MAN BESIDES YOU.
LIKE I'D BELIEVE THAT!
BUT YOU WANTED TO HEAR IT, RIGHT?

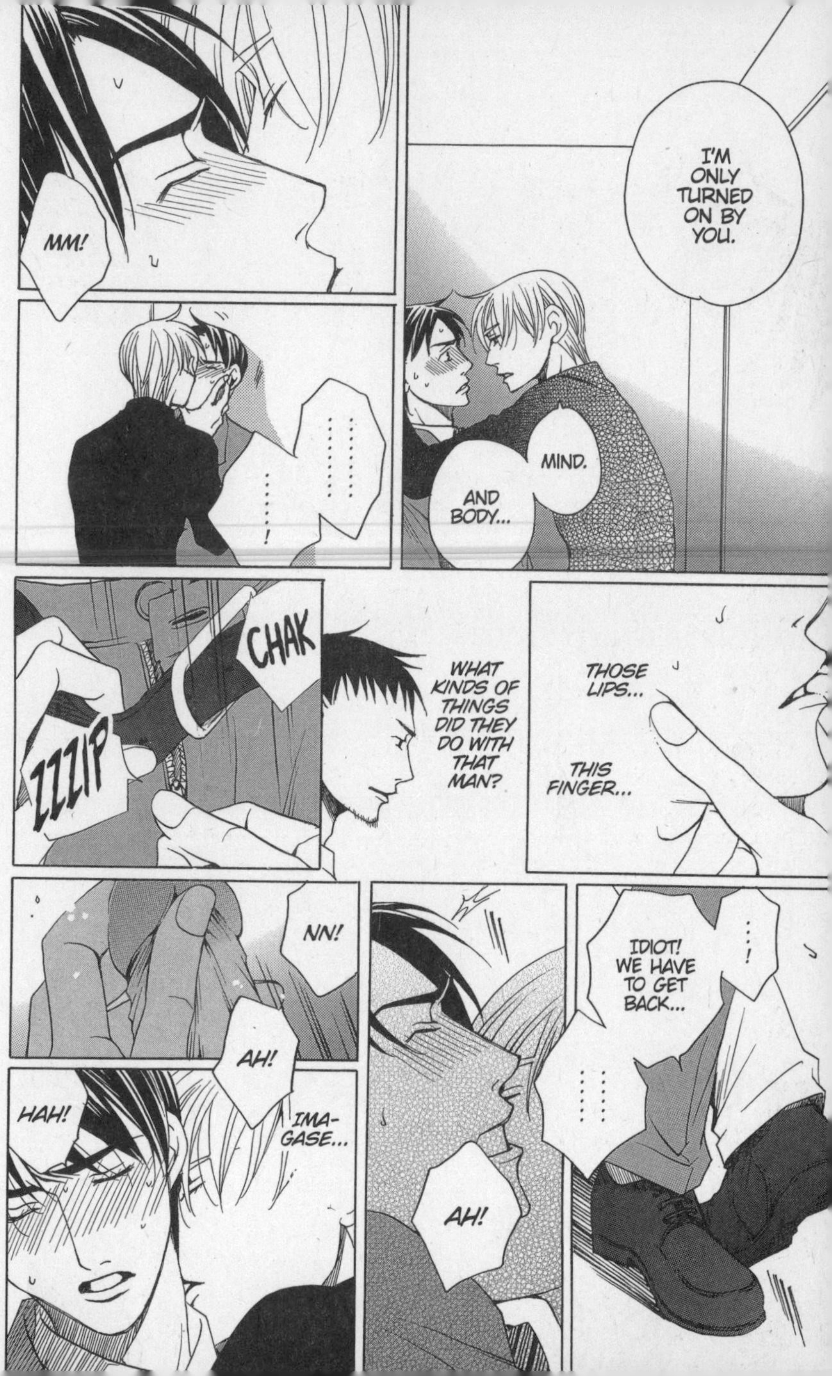
I'M ONLY TURNED ON BY YOU.
MIND.
AND BODY...
MM!
......!
THOSE LIPS...
THIS FINGER...
WHAT KINDS OF THINGS DID THEY DO WITH THAT MAN?
CHAK
ZZZIP
...!
IDIOT! WE HAVE TO GET BACK...
......
AH!
NN!
AH!
HAH!
IMA-GASE...

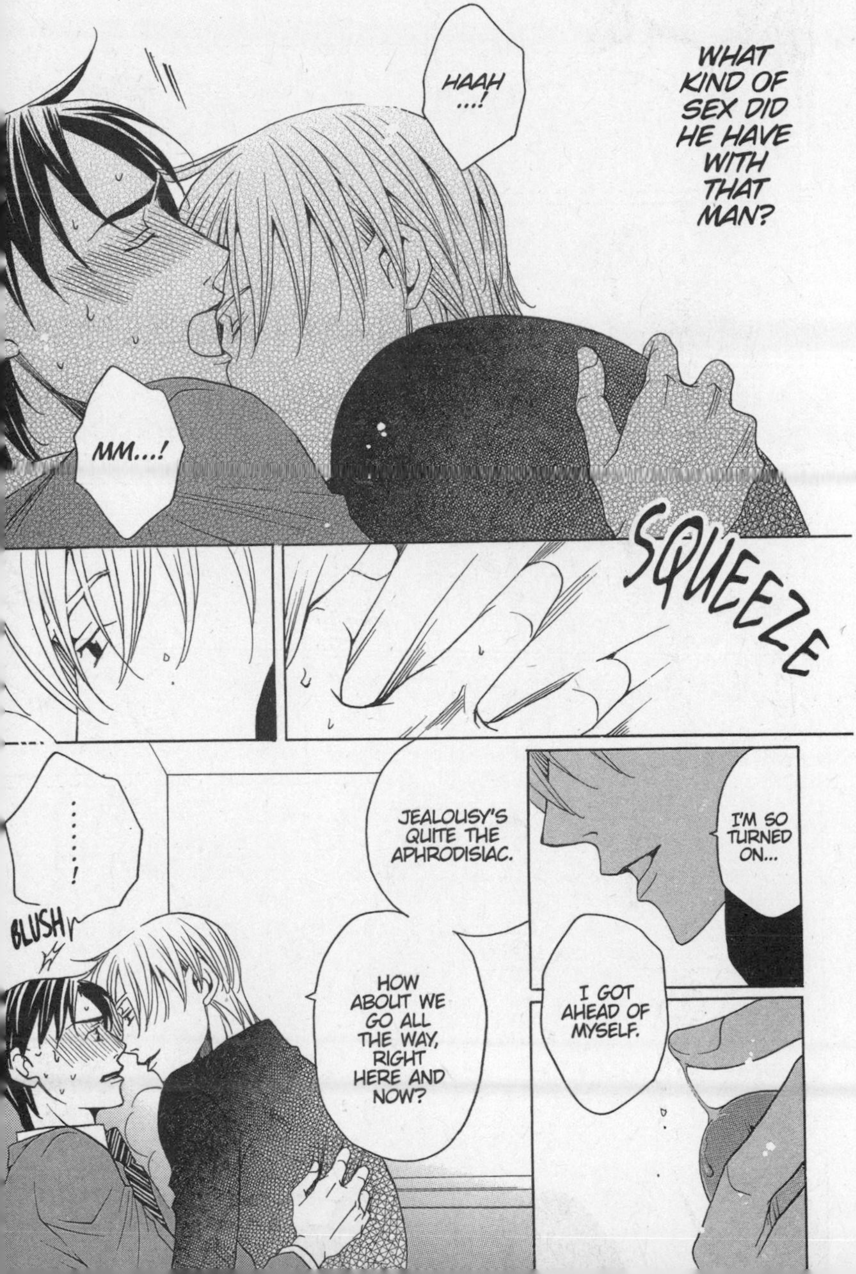
WHAT KIND OF SEX DID HE HAVE WITH THAT MAN?
HAAH ...!
SQUEEZE
MM...!
I'M SO TURNED ON...
I GOT AHEAD OF MYSELF.
JEALOUSY'S QUITE THE APHRODISIAC.
HOW ABOUT WE GO ALL THE WAY, RIGHT HERE AND NOW?
......!
BLUSH

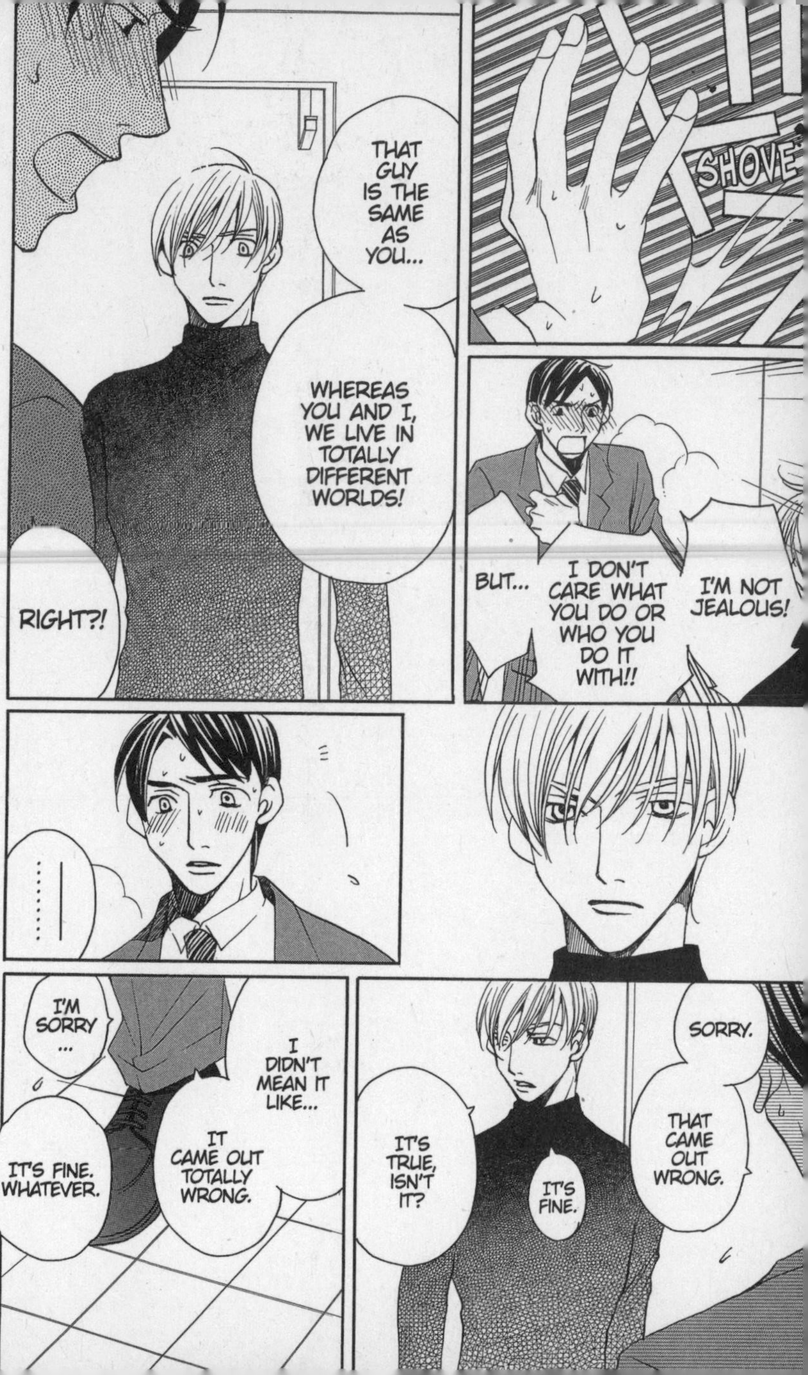
SHOVE
I'M NOT JEALOUS!
I DON'T CARE WHAT YOU DO OR WHO YOU DO IT WITH!!
BUT...
THAT GUY IS THE SAME AS YOU...
WHEREAS YOU AND I, WE LIVE IN TOTALLY DIFFERENT WORLDS!
RIGHT?!
......
SORRY.
THAT CAME OUT WRONG.
IT'S FINE.
IT'S TRUE, ISN'T IT?
I DIDN'T MEAN IT LIKE...
IT CAME OUT TOTALLY WRONG.
I'M SORRY...
IT'S FINE. WHATEVER.

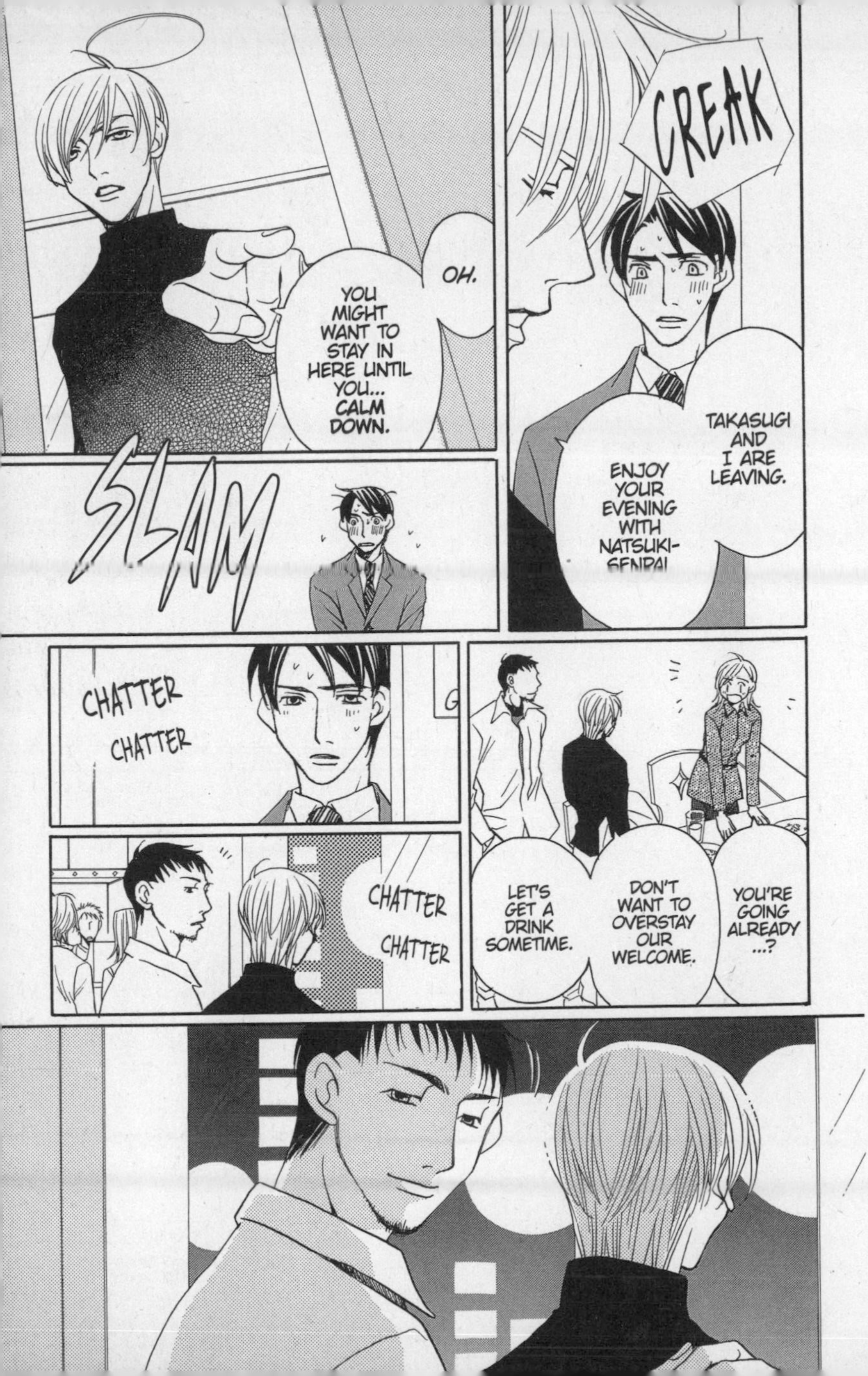
CREAK
TAKASUGI AND I ARE LEAVING.
ENJOY YOUR EVENING WITH NATSUKI-SENPAI
OH.
YOU MIGHT WANT TO STAY IN HERE UNTIL YOU... CALM DOWN.
SLAM
YOU'RE GOING ALREADY ...?
DON'T WANT TO OVERSTAY OUR WELCOME.
LET'S GET A DRINK SOMETIME.
CHATTER
CHATTER
CHATTER
CHATTER

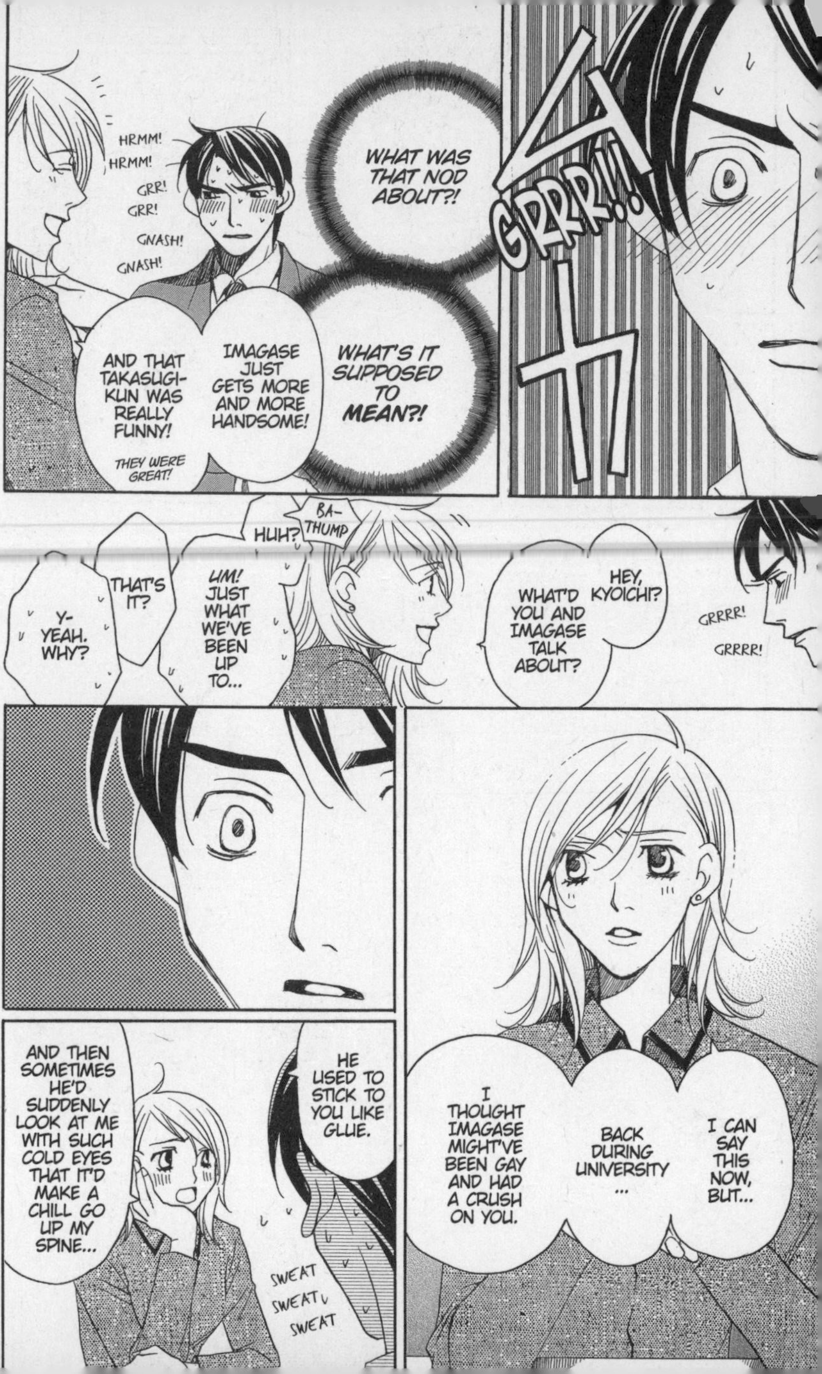
GRRR!!
WHAT WAS THAT NOD ABOUT?!
WHAT'S IT SUPPOSED TO MEAN?!
HRMM!
HRMM!
GRR!
GRR!
GNASH!
GNASH!
IMAGASE JUST GETS MORE AND MORE HANDSOME!
AND THAT TAKASUGI-KUN WAS REALLY FUNNY!
THEY WERE GREAT!
GRRRR!
GRRRR!
HEY, KYOICHI? WHAT'D YOU AND IMAGASE TALK ABOUT?
BA-THUMP
HUH?
UM! JUST WHAT WE'VE BEEN UP TO...
THAT'S IT?
Y-YEAH. WHY?
I CAN SAY THIS NOW, BUT...
BACK DURING UNIVERSITY...
I THOUGHT IMAGASE MIGHT'VE BEEN GAY AND HAD A CRUSH ON YOU.
HE USED TO STICK TO YOU LIKE GLUE.
AND THEN SOMETIMES HE'D SUDDENLY LOOK AT ME WITH SUCH COLD EYES THAT IT'D MAKE A CHILL GO UP MY SPINE...
SWEAT
SWEAT
SWEAT

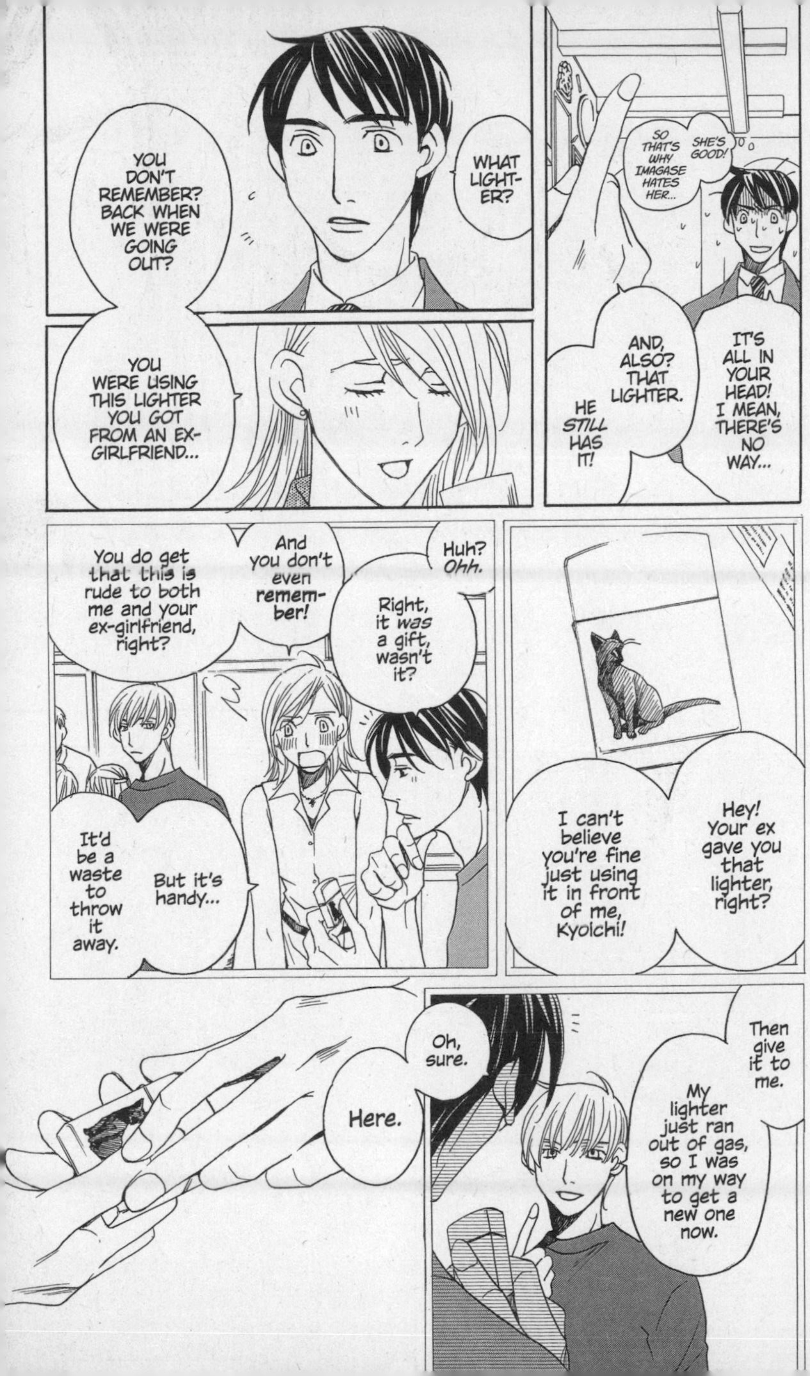
SHE'S GOOD!
SO THAT'S WHY IMAGASE HATES HER...
IT'S ALL IN YOUR HEAD! I MEAN, THERE'S NO WAY...
AND, ALSO? THAT LIGHTER.
HE *STILL* HAS IT!
WHAT LIGHTER?
YOU DON'T REMEMBER? BACK WHEN WE WERE GOING OUT?
YOU WERE USING THIS LIGHTER YOU GOT FROM AN EX-GIRLFRIEND...
Hey! Your ex gave you that lighter, right?
I can't believe you're fine just using it in front of me, Kyoichi!
Huh? *Ohh.*
Right, it *was* a gift, wasn't it?
And you don't even remember!
You do get that this is rude to both me and your ex-girlfriend, right?
But it's handy...
It'd be a waste to throw it away.
Then give it to me.
My lighter just ran out of gas, so I was on my way to get a new one now.
Oh, sure.
Here.

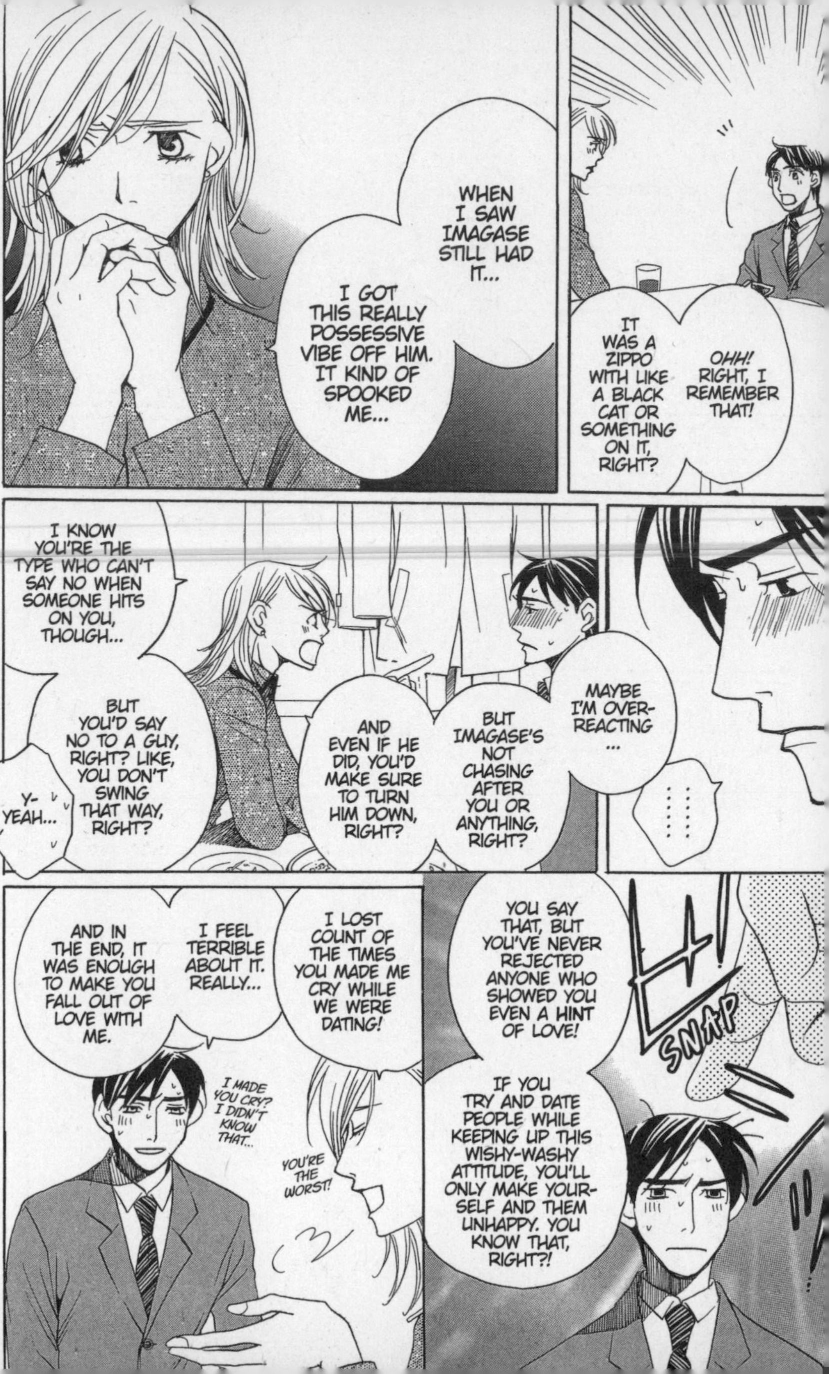
IT WAS A ZIPPO WITH LIKE A BLACK CAT OR SOMETHING ON IT, RIGHT?
OHH! RIGHT, I REMEMBER THAT!
WHEN I SAW IMAGASE STILL HAD IT...
I GOT THIS REALLY POSSESSIVE VIBE OFF HIM. IT KIND OF SPOOKED ME...
I KNOW YOU'RE THE TYPE WHO CAN'T SAY NO WHEN SOMEONE HITS ON YOU, THOUGH...
BUT YOU'D SAY NO TO A GUY, RIGHT? LIKE, YOU DON'T SWING THAT WAY, RIGHT?
Y-YEAH...
BUT IMAGASE'S NOT CHASING AFTER YOU OR ANYTHING, RIGHT?
AND EVEN IF HE DID, YOU'D MAKE SURE TO TURN HIM DOWN, RIGHT?
MAYBE I'M OVER-REACTING ...
......
SNAP
YOU SAY THAT, BUT YOU'VE NEVER REJECTED ANYONE WHO SHOWED YOU EVEN A HINT OF LOVE!
IF YOU TRY AND DATE PEOPLE WHILE KEEPING UP THIS WISHY-WASHY ATTITUDE, YOU'LL ONLY MAKE YOURSELF AND THEM UNHAPPY. YOU KNOW THAT, RIGHT?!
I LOST COUNT OF THE TIMES YOU MADE ME CRY WHILE WE WERE DATING!
I FEEL TERRIBLE ABOUT IT. REALLY...
AND IN THE END, IT WAS ENOUGH TO MAKE YOU FALL OUT OF LOVE WITH ME.
I MADE YOU CRY? I DIDN'T KNOW THAT...
YOU'RE THE WORST!

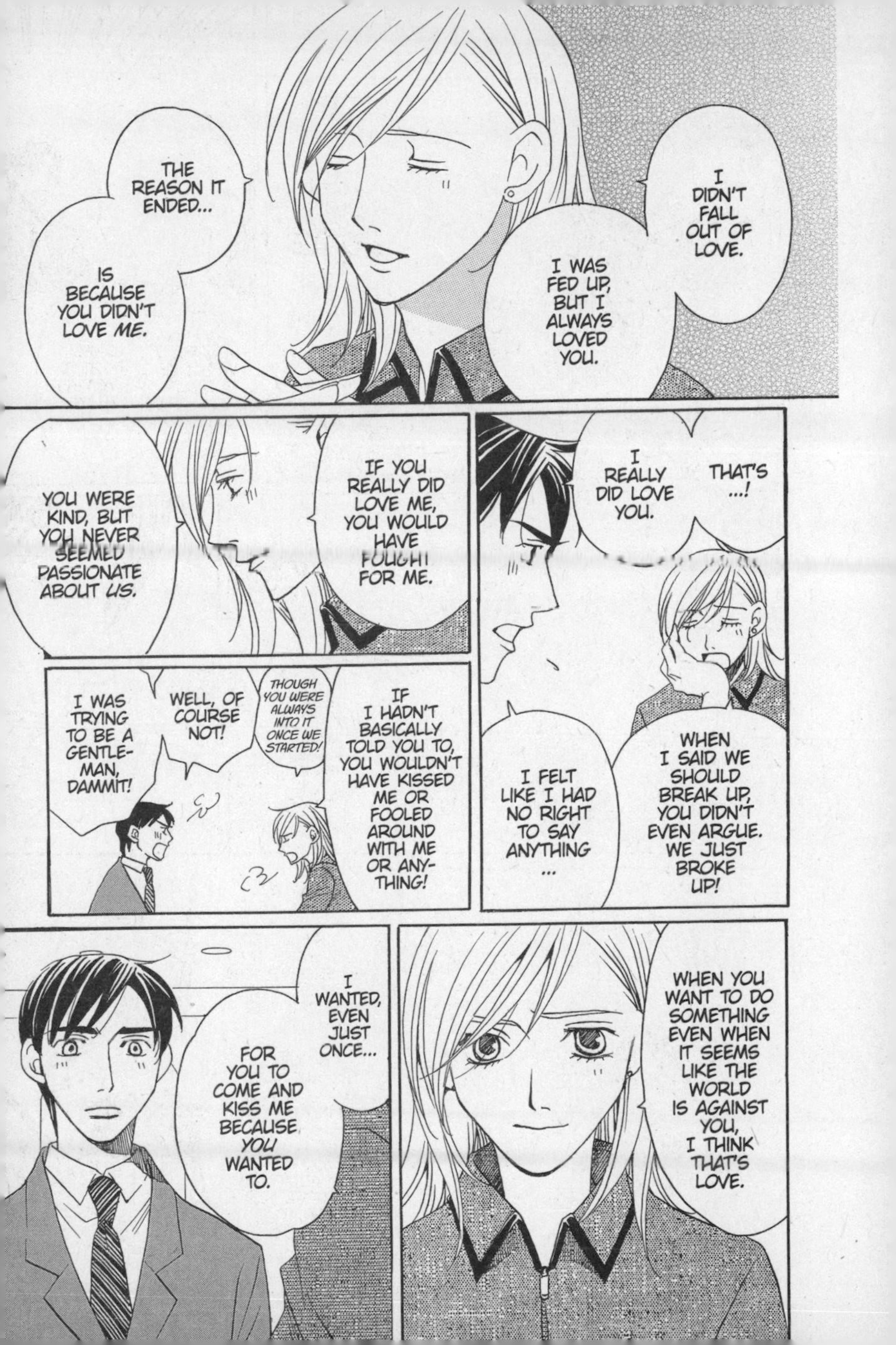
I DIDN'T FALL OUT OF LOVE.
I WAS FED UP, BUT I ALWAYS LOVED YOU.
THE REASON IT ENDED...
IS BECAUSE YOU DIDN'T LOVE ME.
THAT'S ...!
I REALLY DID LOVE YOU.
WHEN I SAID WE SHOULD BREAK UP, YOU DIDN'T EVEN ARGUE. WE JUST BROKE UP!
I FELT LIKE I HAD NO RIGHT TO SAY ANYTHING ...
IF YOU REALLY DID LOVE ME, YOU WOULD HAVE FOUGHT FOR ME.
YOU WERE KIND, BUT YOU NEVER SEEMED PASSIONATE ABOUT US.
IF I HADN'T BASICALLY TOLD YOU TO, YOU WOULDN'T HAVE KISSED ME OR FOOLED AROUND WITH ME OR ANY-THING!
THOUGH YOU WERE ALWAYS INTO IT ONCE WE STARTED!
WELL, OF COURSE NOT!
I WAS TRYING TO BE A GENTLE-MAN, DAMMIT!
WHEN YOU WANT TO DO SOMETHING EVEN WHEN IT SEEMS LIKE THE WORLD IS AGAINST YOU, I THINK THAT'S LOVE.
I WANTED, EVEN JUST ONCE...
FOR YOU TO COME AND KISS ME BECAUSE YOU WANTED TO.

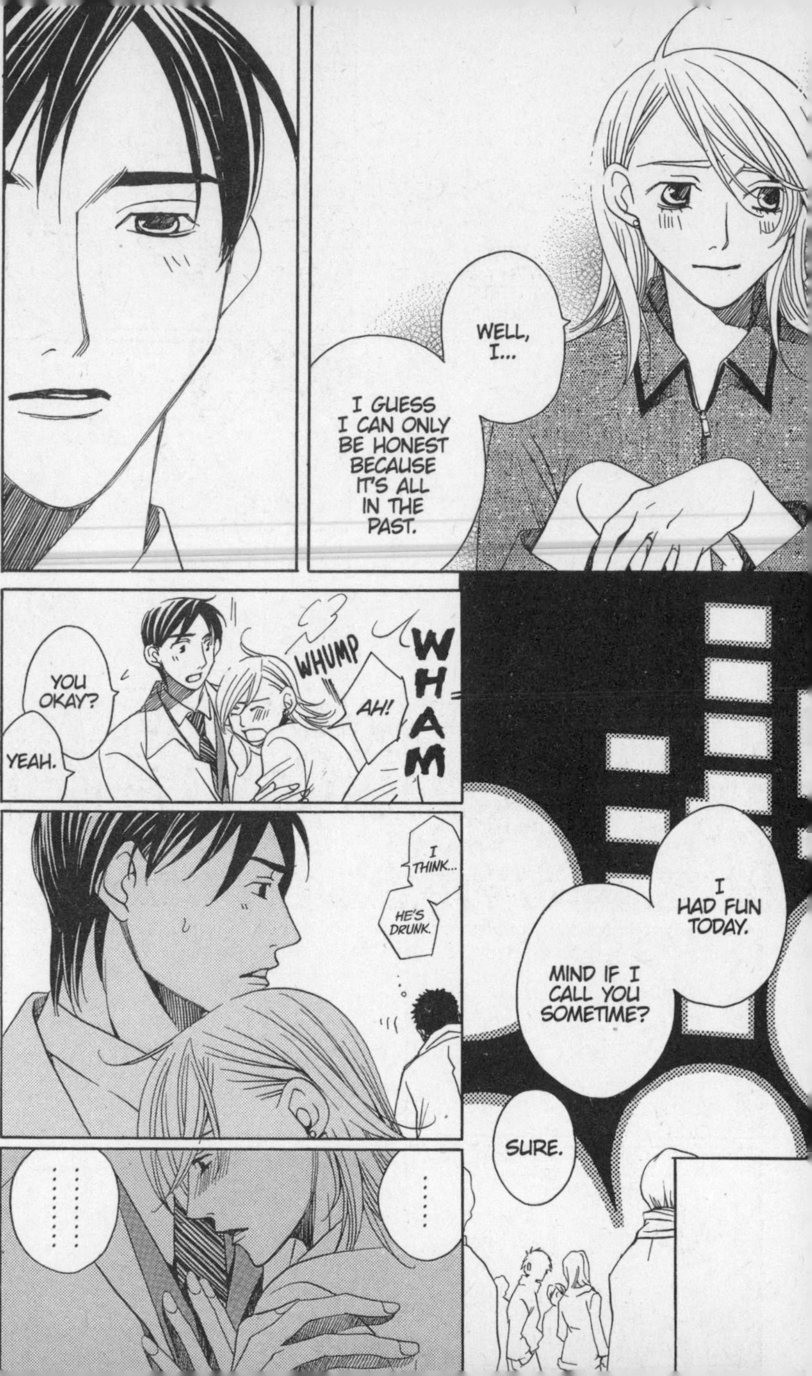
WELL, I...
I GUESS I CAN ONLY BE HONEST BECAUSE IT'S ALL IN THE PAST.
I HAD FUN TODAY.
MIND IF I CALL YOU SOMETIME?
SURE.
WHAM
WHUMP
AH!
YOU OKAY?
YEAH.
I THINK...
HE'S DRUNK.
......
......

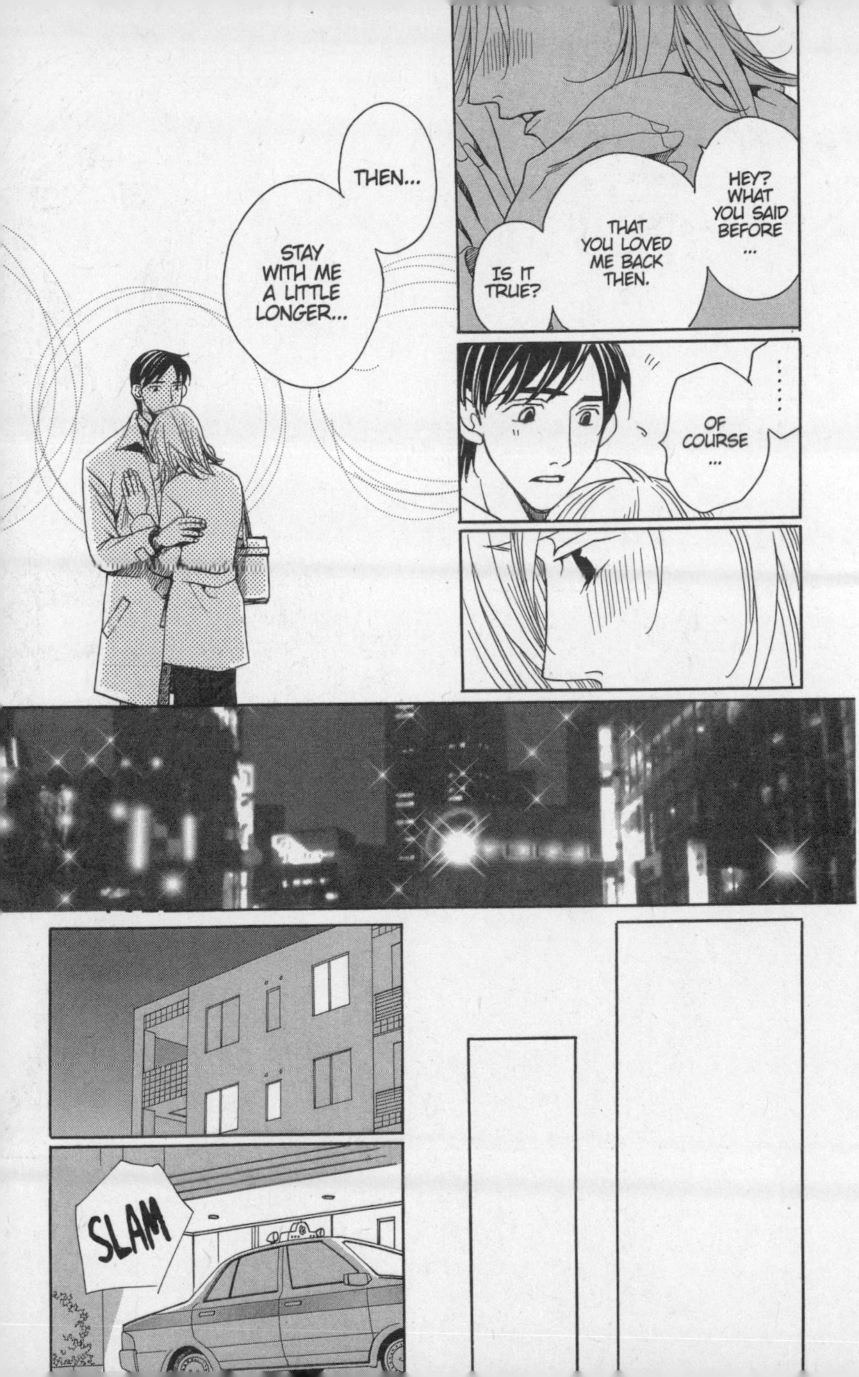
HEY? WHAT YOU SAID BEFORE ...
THAT YOU LOVED ME BACK THEN.
IS IT TRUE?
......
OF COURSE ...
THEN...
STAY WITH ME A LITTLE LONGER...
SLAM

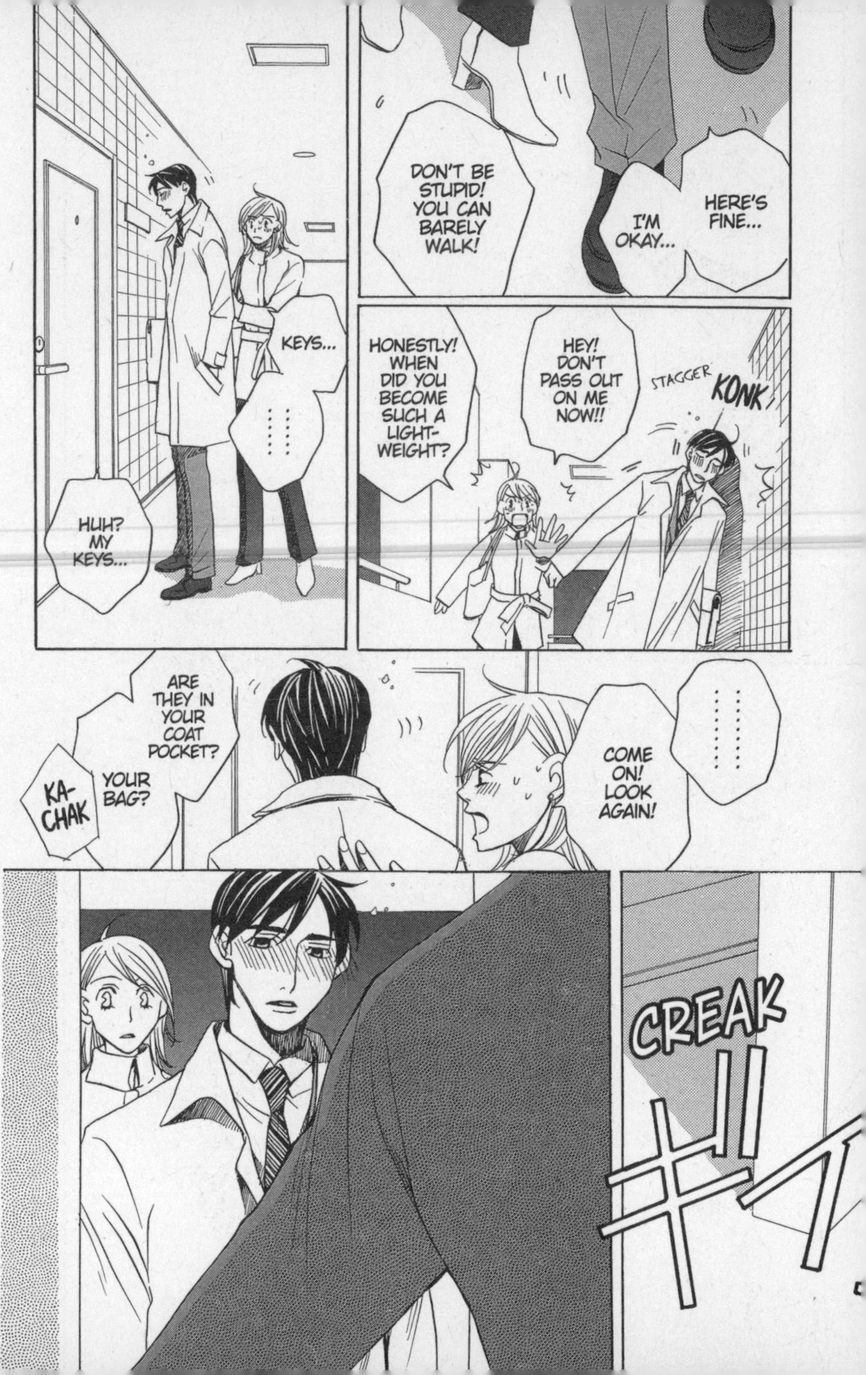
HERE'S FINE...
I'M OKAY...
DON'T BE STUPID! YOU CAN BARELY WALK!
KONK
STAGGER
HEY! DON'T PASS OUT ON ME NOW!!
HONESTLY! WHEN DID YOU BECOME SUCH A LIGHT-WEIGHT?
KEYS...
......
HUH? MY KEYS...
......
COME ON! LOOK AGAIN!
ARE THEY IN YOUR COAT POCKET?
YOUR BAG?
KA-CHAK
CREAK
ギイ

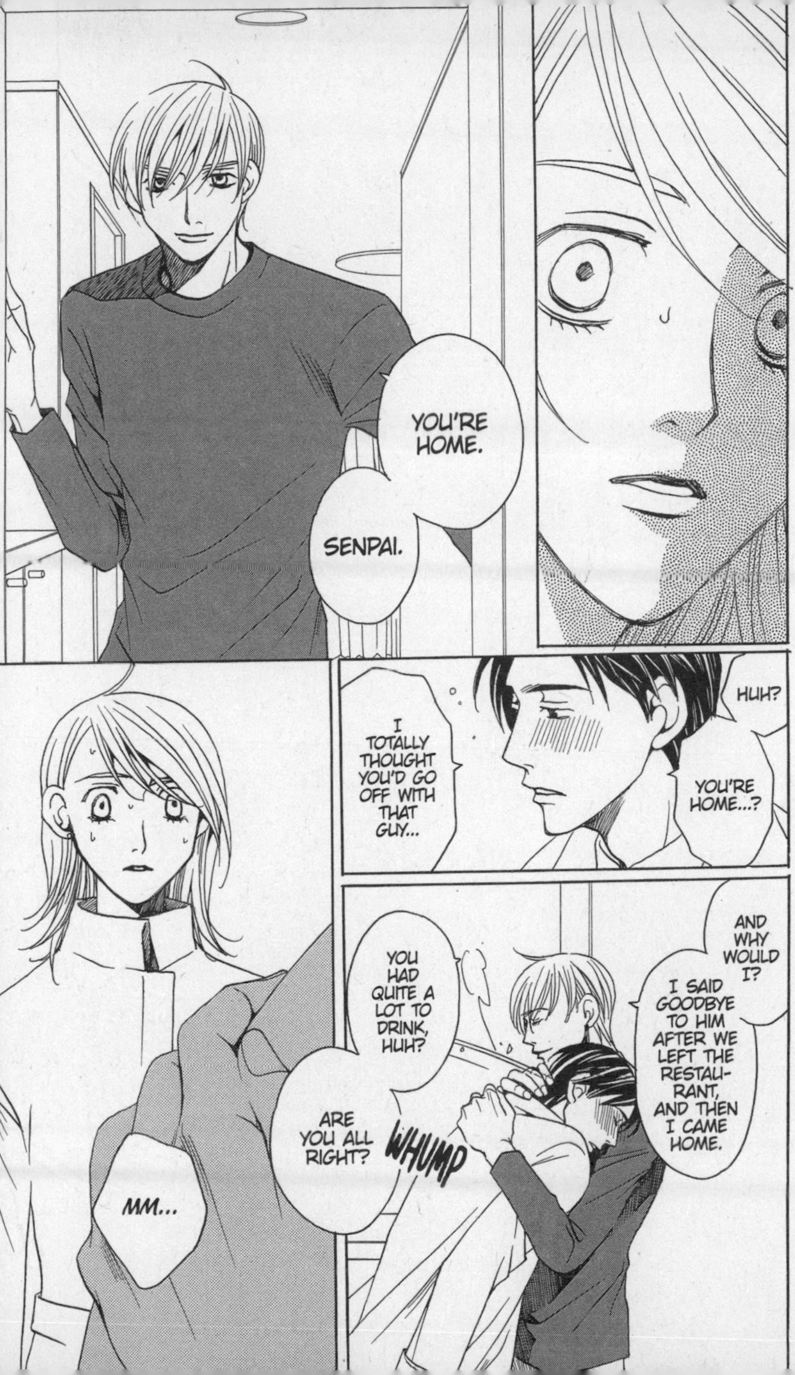
YOU'RE HOME.
SENPAI.
HUH?
YOU'RE HOME...?
I TOTALLY THOUGHT YOU'D GO OFF WITH THAT GUY...
AND WHY WOULD I?
I SAID GOODBYE TO HIM AFTER WE LEFT THE RESTAU-RANT, AND THEN I CAME HOME.
YOU HAD QUITE A LOT TO DRINK, HUH?
WHUMP
ARE YOU ALL RIGHT?
MM...

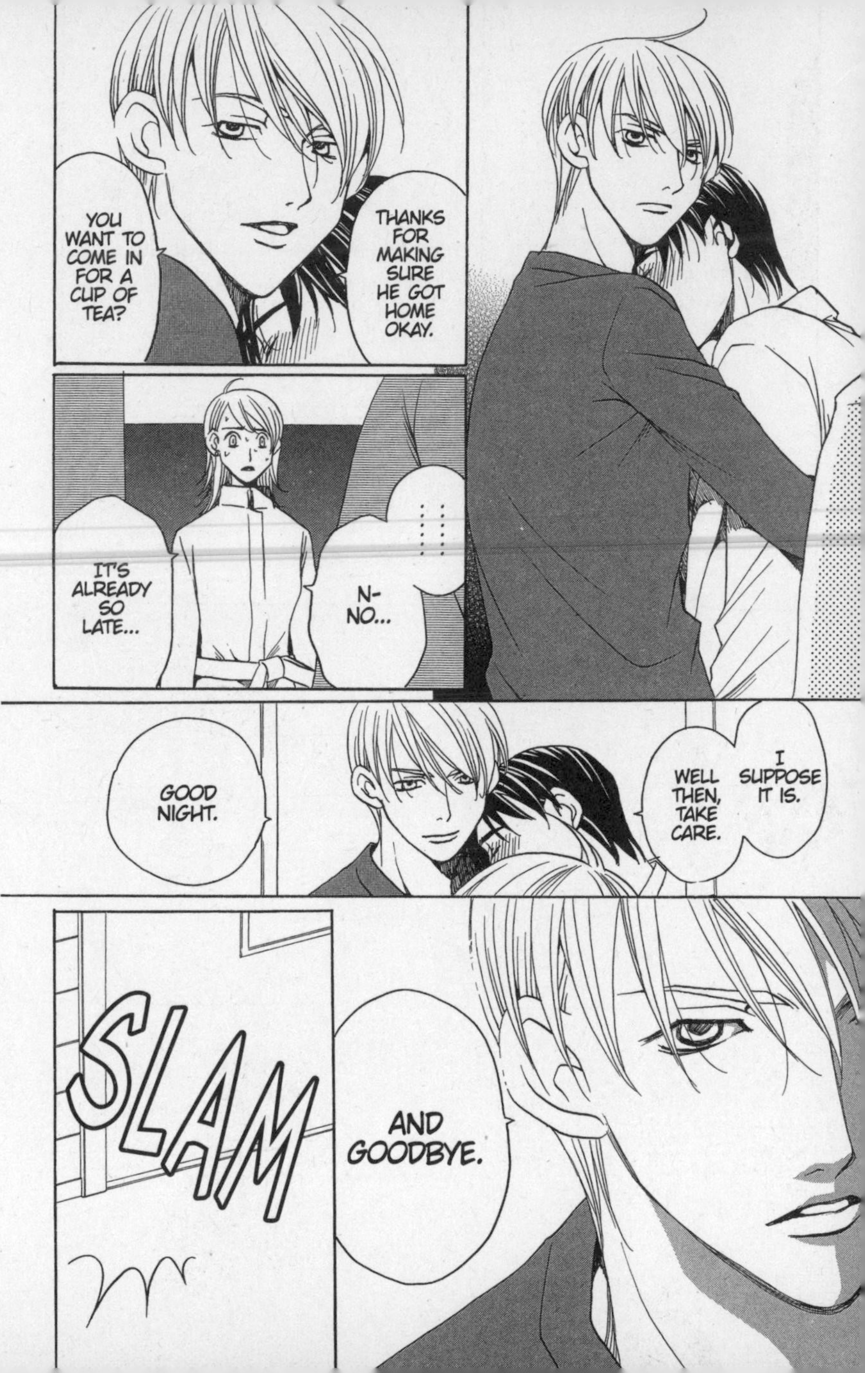
THANKS FOR MAKING SURE HE GOT HOME OKAY.
YOU WANT TO COME IN FOR A CUP OF TEA?
......
N-NO...
IT'S ALREADY SO LATE...
I SUPPOSE IT IS.
WELL THEN, TAKE CARE.
GOOD NIGHT.
AND GOODBYE.
SLAM

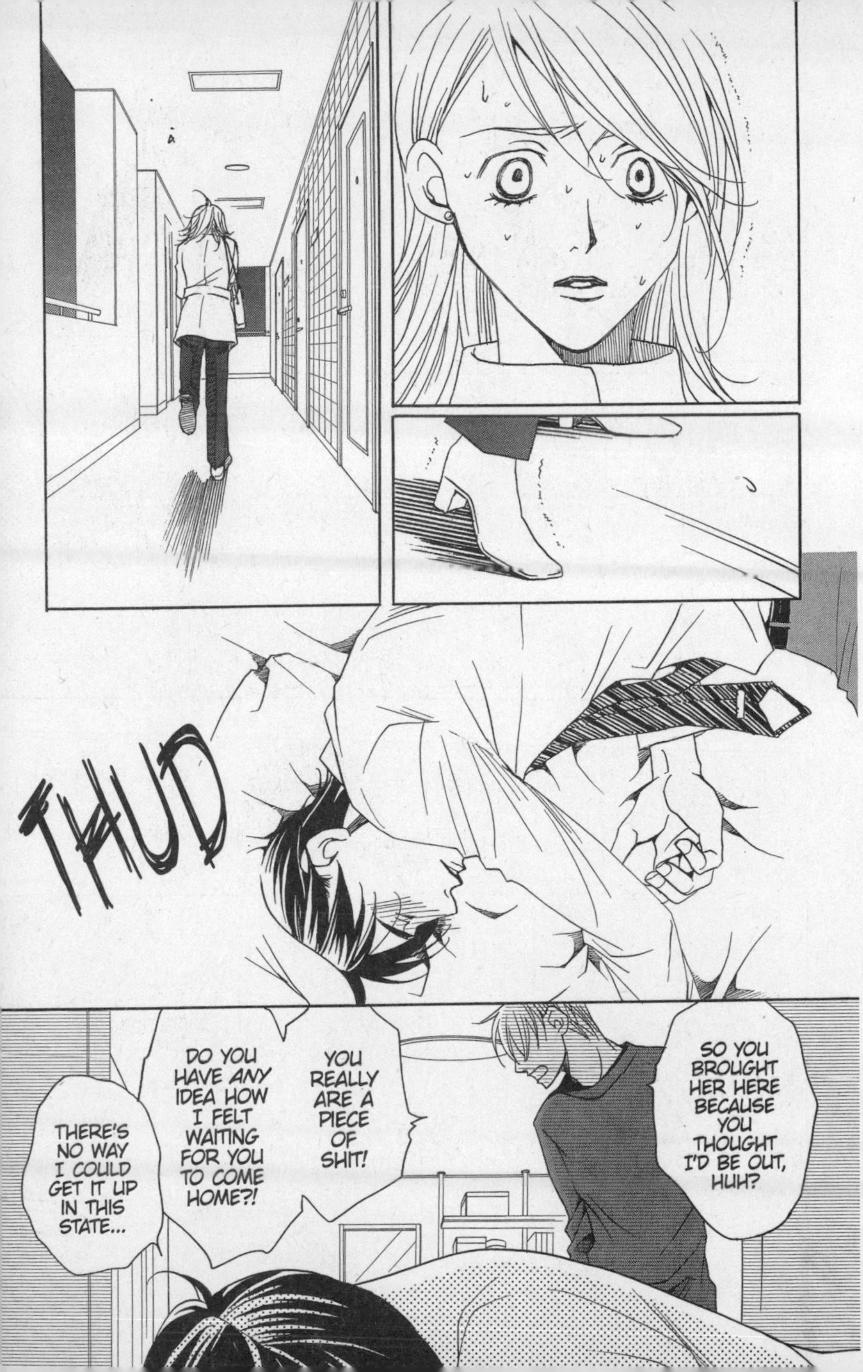
THUD
SO YOU BROUGHT HER HERE BECAUSE YOU THOUGHT I'D BE OUT, HUH?
YOU REALLY ARE A PIECE OF SHIT!
DO YOU HAVE ANY IDEA HOW I FELT WAITING FOR YOU TO COME HOME?!
THERE'S NO WAY I COULD GET IT UP IN THIS STATE...

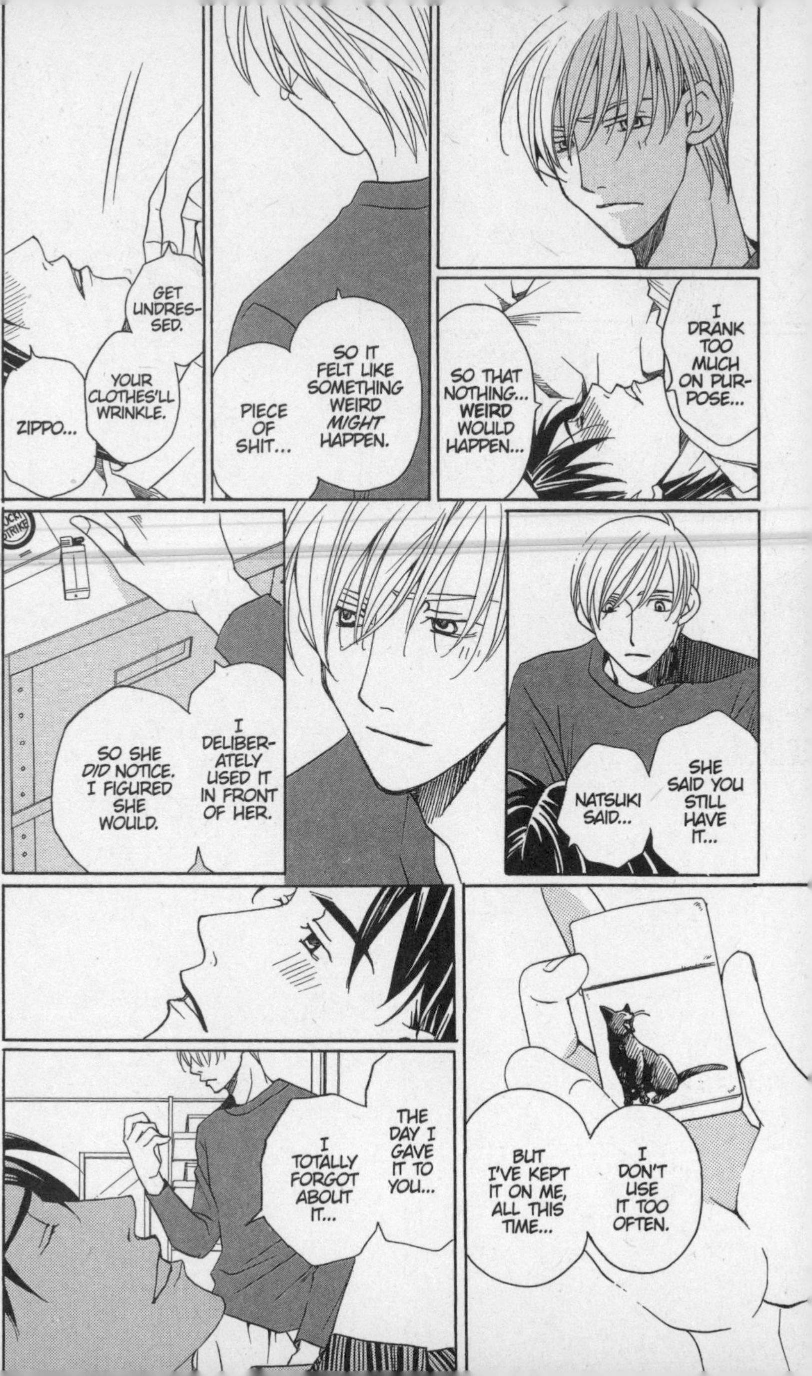
I DRANK TOO MUCH ON PURPOSE...
SO THAT NOTHING... WEIRD WOULD HAPPEN...
SO IT FELT LIKE SOMETHING WEIRD *MIGHT* HAPPEN.
PIECE OF SHIT...
GET UNDRESSED.
YOUR CLOTHES'LL WRINKLE.
ZIPPO...
SHE SAID YOU STILL HAVE IT...
NATSUKI SAID...
I DELIBERATELY USED IT IN FRONT OF HER.
SO SHE *DID* NOTICE. I FIGURED SHE WOULD.
I DON'T USE IT TOO OFTEN.
BUT I'VE KEPT IT ON ME, ALL THIS TIME...
THE DAY I GAVE IT TO YOU...
I TOTALLY FORGOT ABOUT IT...

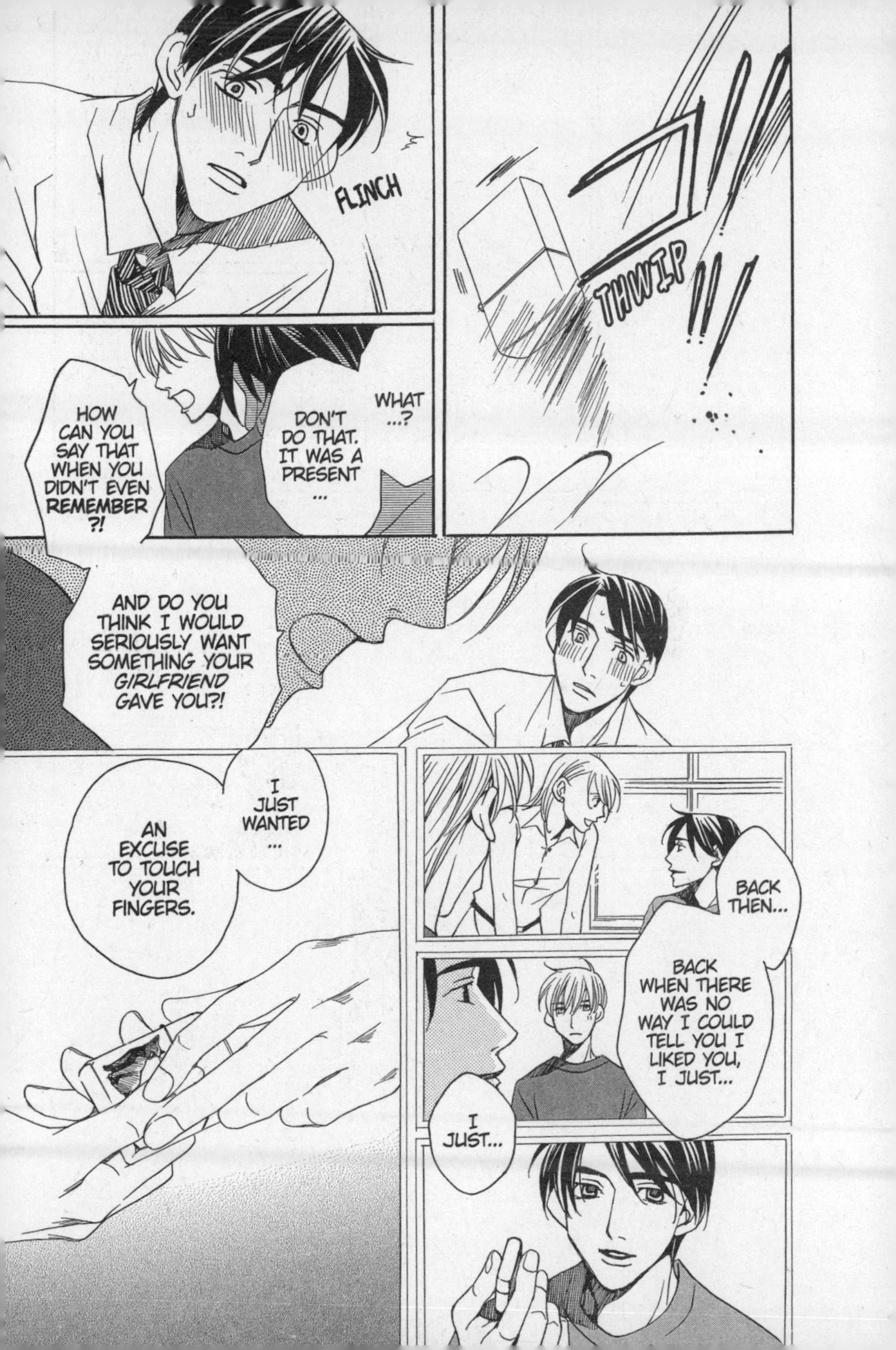
THWIP!!
FLINCH
WHAT ...?
DON'T DO THAT. IT WAS A PRESENT ...
HOW CAN YOU SAY THAT WHEN YOU DIDN'T EVEN REMEMBER ?!
AND DO YOU THINK I WOULD SERIOUSLY WANT SOMETHING YOUR *GIRLFRIEND* GAVE YOU?!
BACK THEN...
BACK WHEN THERE WAS NO WAY I COULD TELL YOU I LIKED YOU, I JUST...
I JUST...
I JUST WANTED ...
AN EXCUSE TO TOUCH YOUR FINGERS.

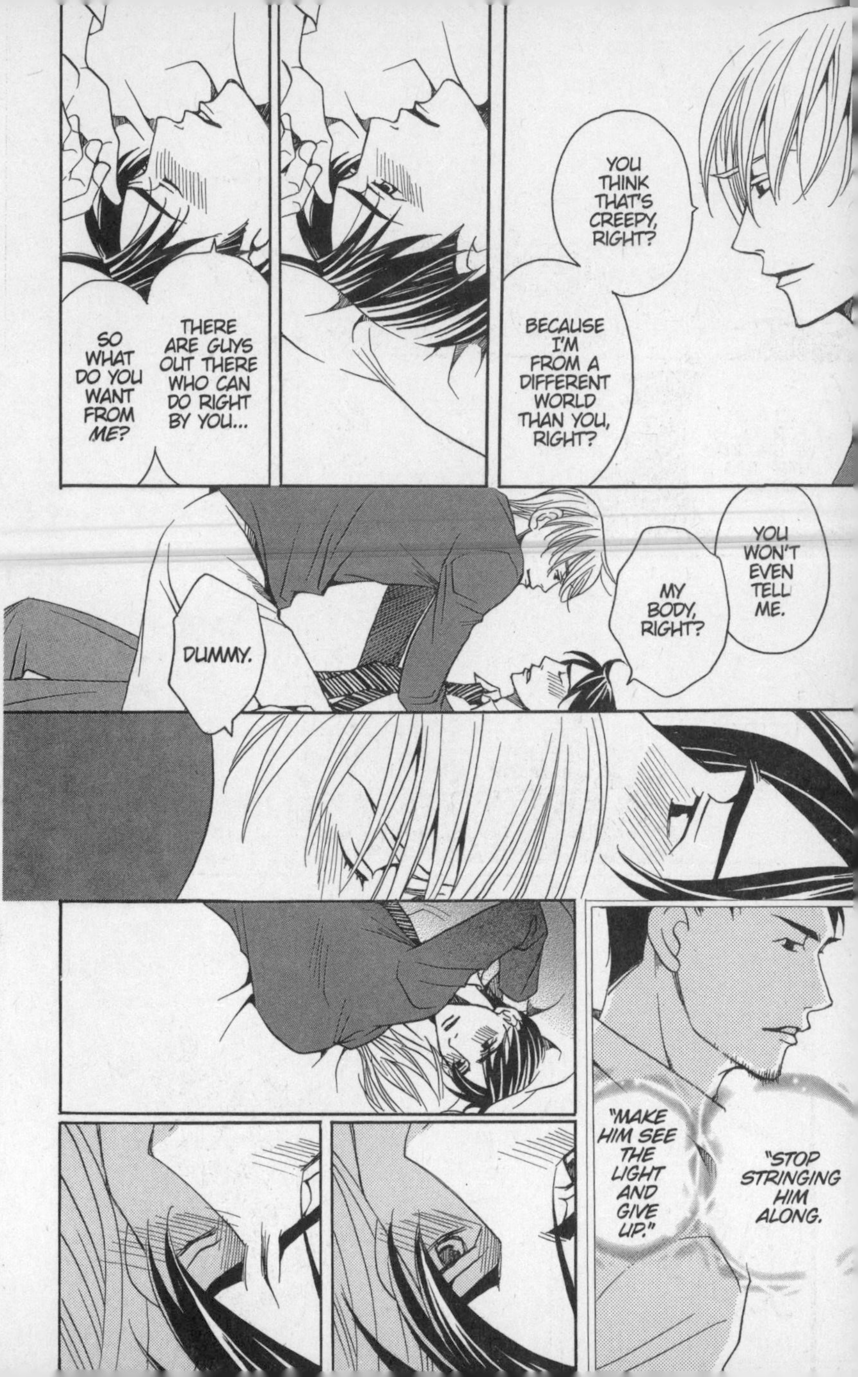
YOU THINK THAT'S CREEPY, RIGHT?
BECAUSE I'M FROM A DIFFERENT WORLD THAN YOU, RIGHT?
THERE ARE GUYS OUT THERE WHO CAN DO RIGHT BY YOU...
SO WHAT DO YOU WANT FROM ME?
YOU WON'T EVEN TELL ME.
MY BODY, RIGHT?
DUMMY.
"STOP STRINGING HIM ALONG.
"MAKE HIM SEE THE LIGHT AND GIVE UP."

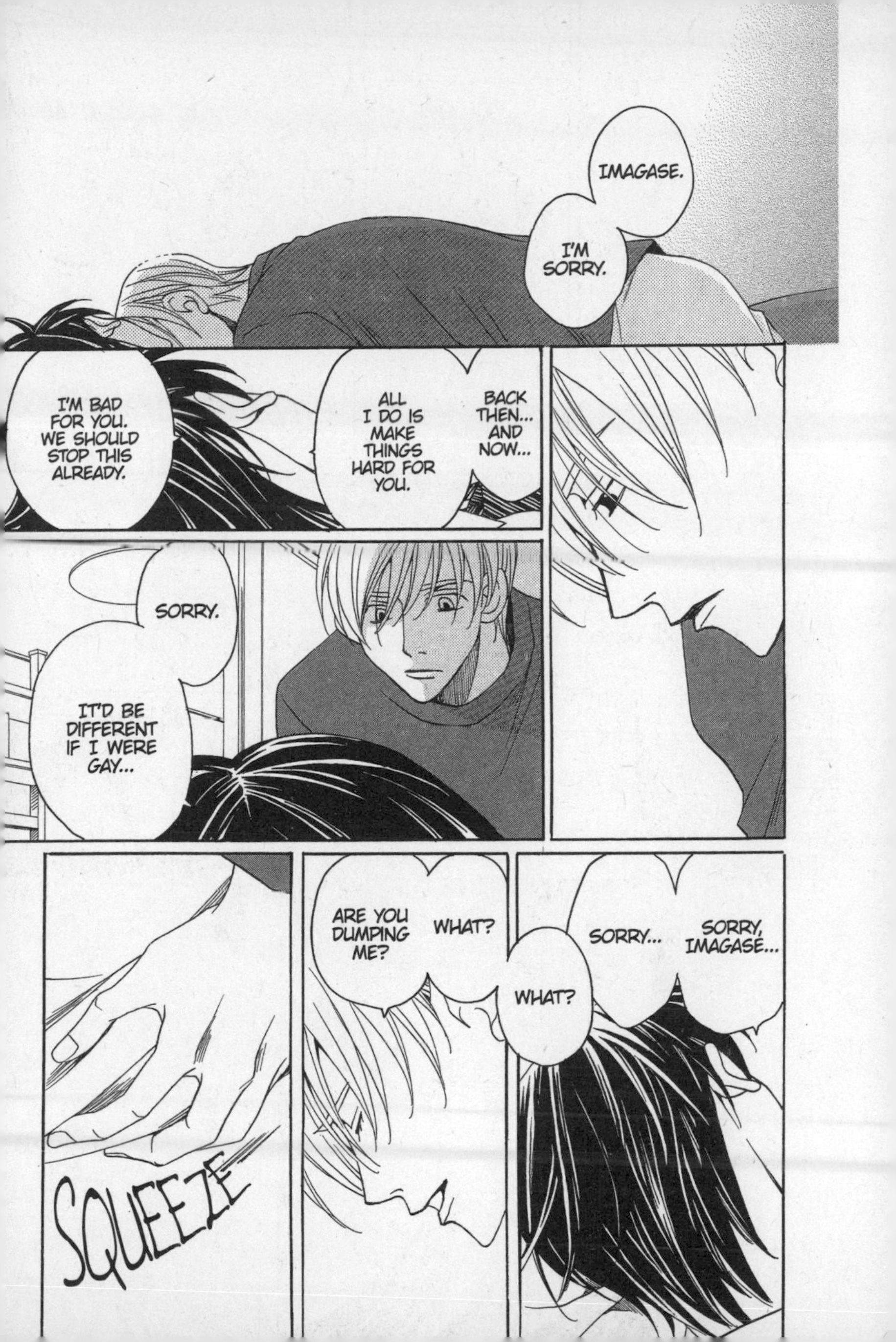
IMAGASE.
I'M SORRY.
BACK THEN... AND NOW...
ALL I DO IS MAKE THINGS HARD FOR YOU.
I'M BAD FOR YOU. WE SHOULD STOP THIS ALREADY.
SORRY.
IT'D BE DIFFERENT IF I WERE GAY...
SORRY, IMAGASE...
SORRY...
WHAT?
WHAT?
ARE YOU DUMPING ME?
SQUEEZE

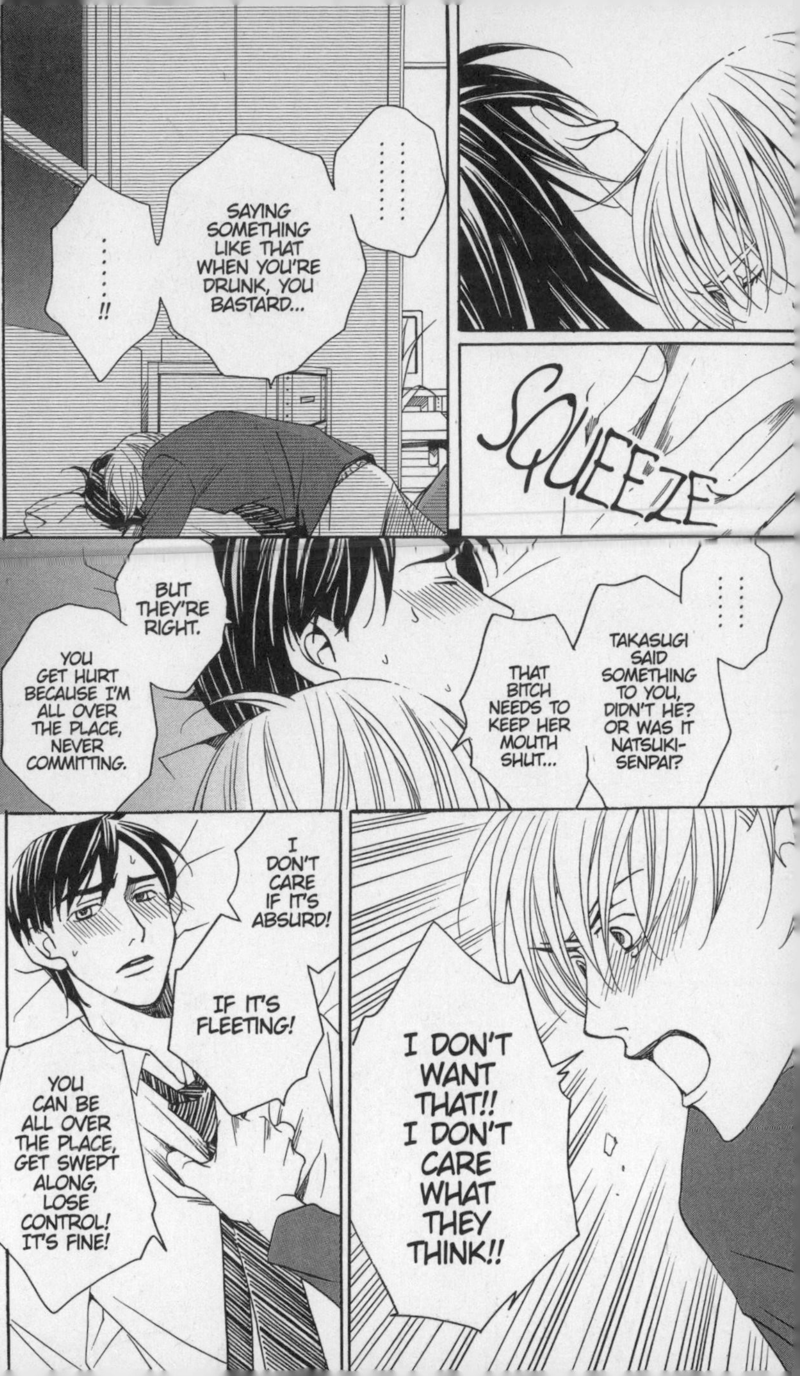
SQUEEZE
......
SAYING SOMETHING LIKE THAT WHEN YOU'RE DRUNK, YOU BASTARD...
......!!
......
TAKASUGI SAID SOMETHING TO YOU, DIDN'T HE? OR WAS IT NATSUKI-SENPAI?
THAT BITCH NEEDS TO KEEP HER MOUTH SHUT...
BUT THEY'RE RIGHT.
YOU GET HURT BECAUSE I'M ALL OVER THE PLACE, NEVER COMMITTING.
I DON'T WANT THAT!! I DON'T CARE WHAT THEY THINK!!
I DON'T CARE IF IT'S ABSURD!
IF IT'S FLEETING!
YOU CAN BE ALL OVER THE PLACE, GET SWEPT ALONG, LOSE CONTROL! IT'S FINE!

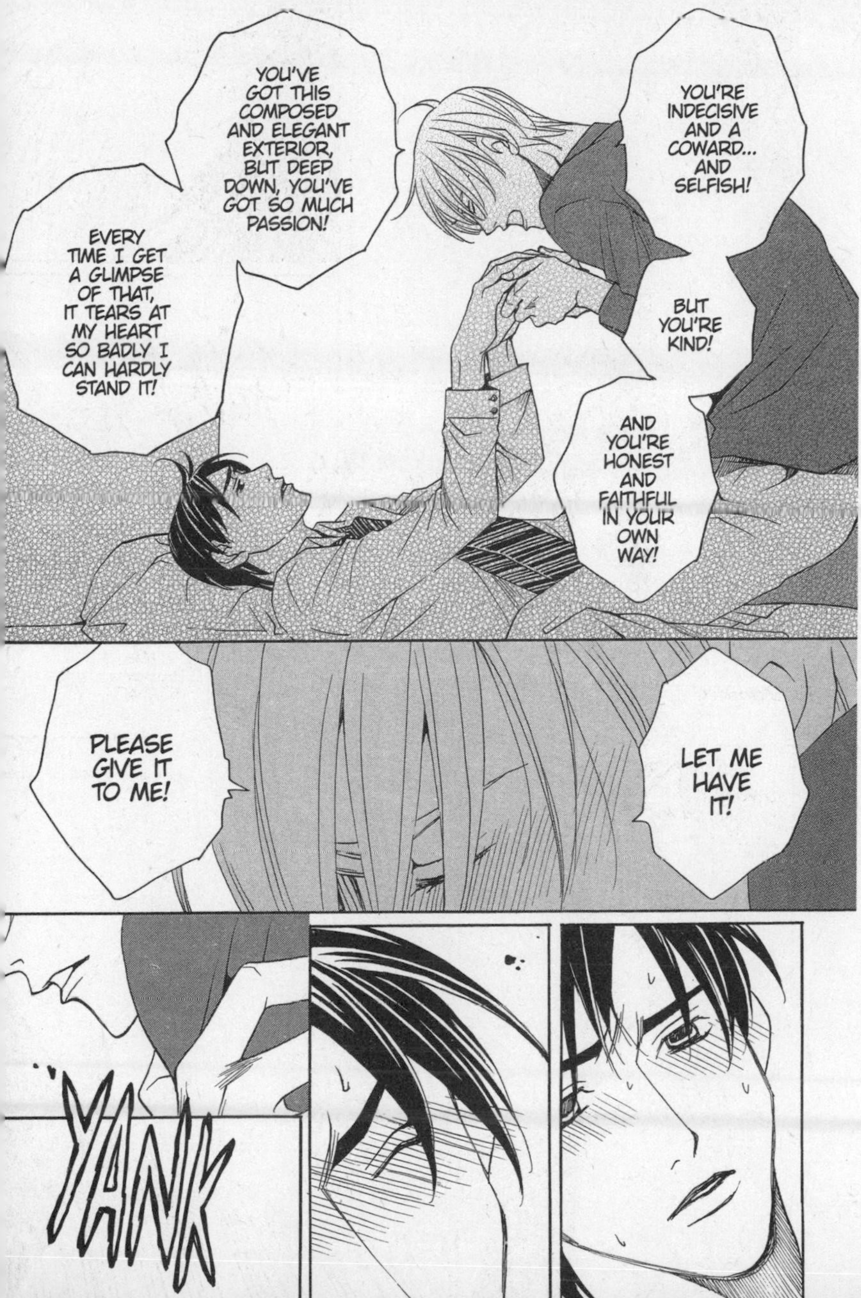
YOU'RE INDECISIVE AND A COWARD... AND SELFISH!
BUT YOU'RE KIND!
AND YOU'RE HONEST AND FAITHFUL IN YOUR OWN WAY!
YOU'VE GOT THIS COMPOSED AND ELEGANT EXTERIOR, BUT DEEP DOWN, YOU'VE GOT SO MUCH PASSION!
EVERY TIME I GET A GLIMPSE OF THAT, IT TEARS AT MY HEART SO BADLY I CAN HARDLY STAND IT!
LET ME HAVE IT!
PLEASE GIVE IT TO ME!
YANK

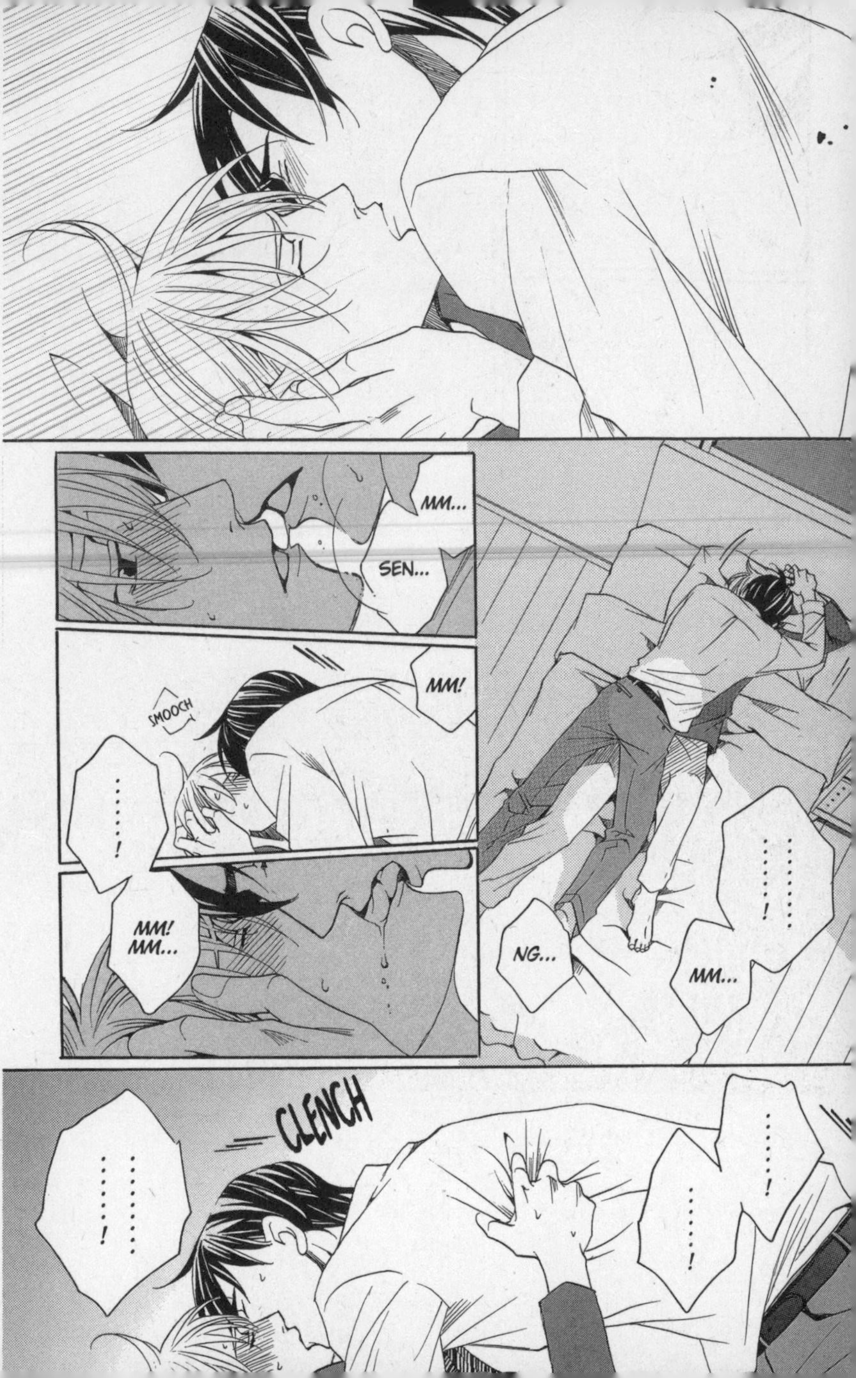
......!
MM...
NG...
MM...
SEN...
MM!
SMOOCH
......!
MM! MM...
......!
......!
CLENCH
....!

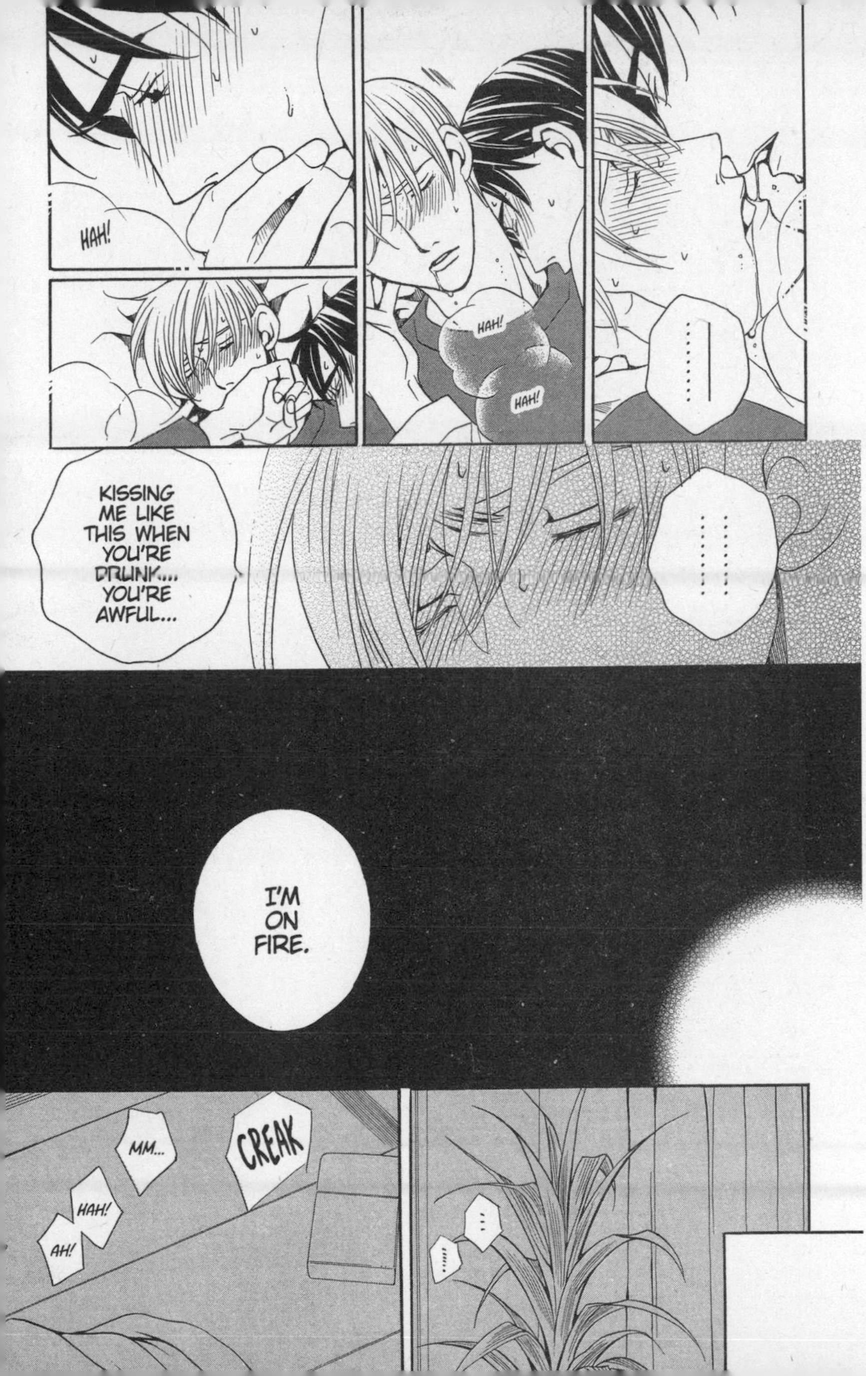
......
HAH!
HAH!
HAH!
......
KISSING ME LIKE THIS WHEN YOU'RE DRUNK... YOU'RE AWFUL...
I'M ON FIRE.
...
......
CREAK
MM...
HAH!
AH!

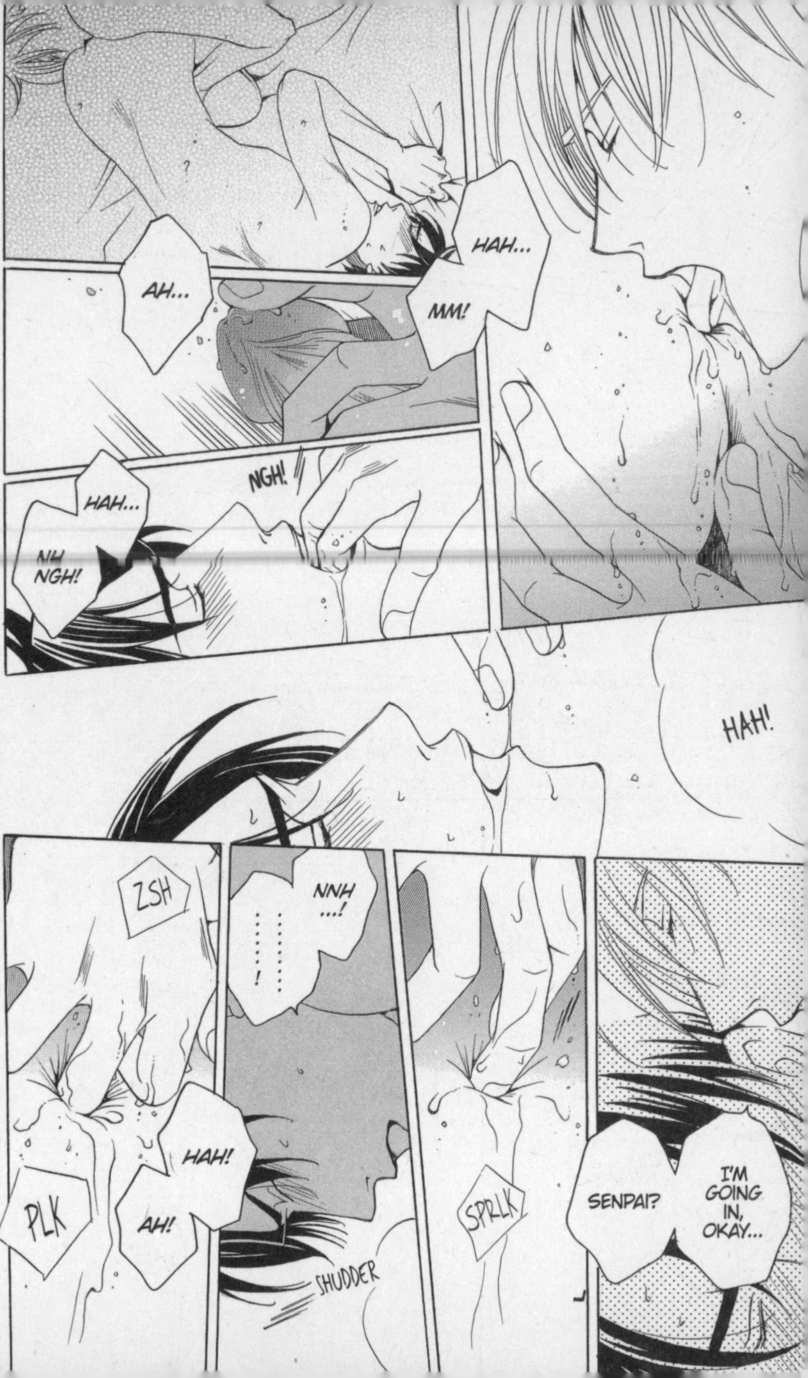
HAH...
MM!
AH...
NGH!
HAH...
NH NGH!
HAH!
I'M GOING IN, OKAY...
SENPAI?
SPRLK
NNH ...!
......!
SHUDDER
ZSH
HAH!
AH!
PLK

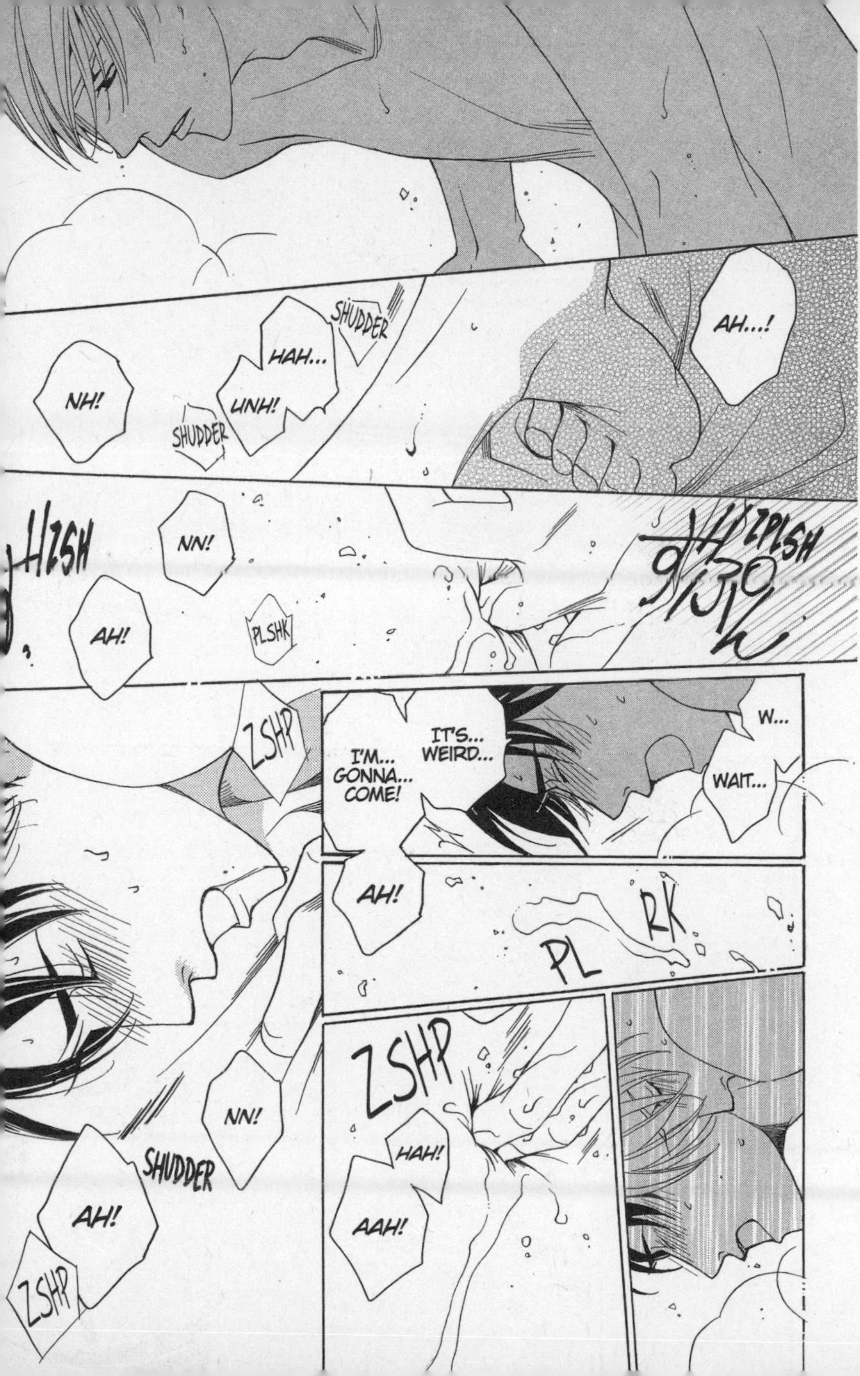
AH...!
SHUDDER
HAH...
UNH!
SHUDDER
NH!
ZPLSH
NN!
PLSHK
AH!
HZSH
W...
WAIT...
IT'S... WEIRD...
I'M... GONNA... COME!
AH!
RK
PL
ZSHP
HAH!
AAH!
ZSHP
NN!
SHUDDER
AH!
ZSHP

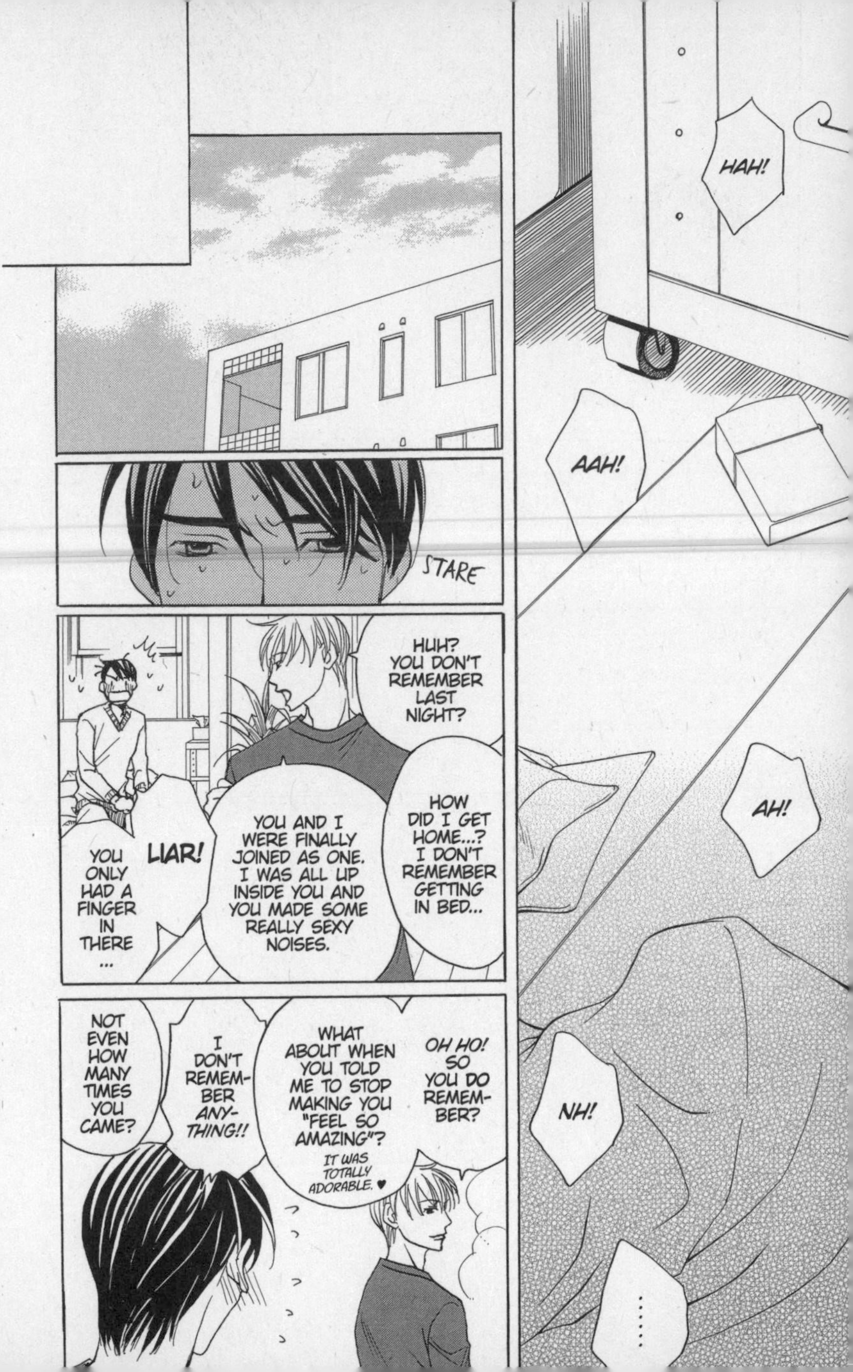
HAH!
AAH!
AH!
NH!
......
STARE
HUH? YOU DON'T REMEMBER LAST NIGHT?
HOW DID I GET HOME...? I DON'T REMEMBER GETTING IN BED...
YOU AND I WERE FINALLY JOINED AS ONE. I WAS ALL UP INSIDE YOU AND YOU MADE SOME REALLY SEXY NOISES.
LIAR!
YOU ONLY HAD A FINGER IN THERE ...
OH HO! SO YOU DO REMEMBER?
WHAT ABOUT WHEN YOU TOLD ME TO STOP MAKING YOU "FEEL SO AMAZING"?
IT WAS TOTALLY ADORABLE. ♥
I DON'T REMEMBER ANYTHING!!
NOT EVEN HOW MANY TIMES YOU CAME?

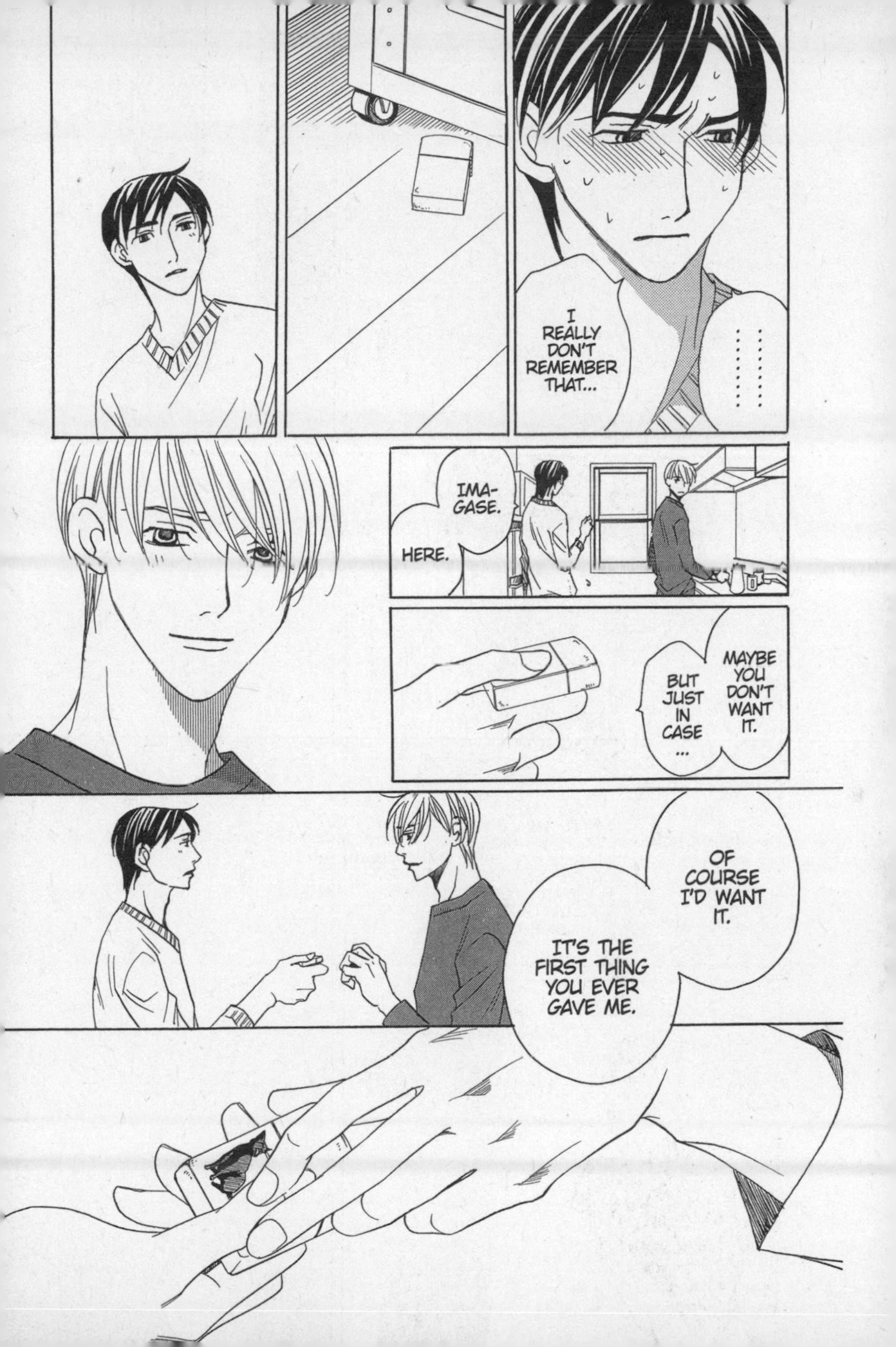
......
I REALLY DON'T REMEMBER THAT...
IMA-GASE.
HERE.
MAYBE YOU DON'T WANT IT.
BUT JUST IN CASE...
OF COURSE I'D WANT IT.
IT'S THE FIRST THING YOU EVER GAVE ME.

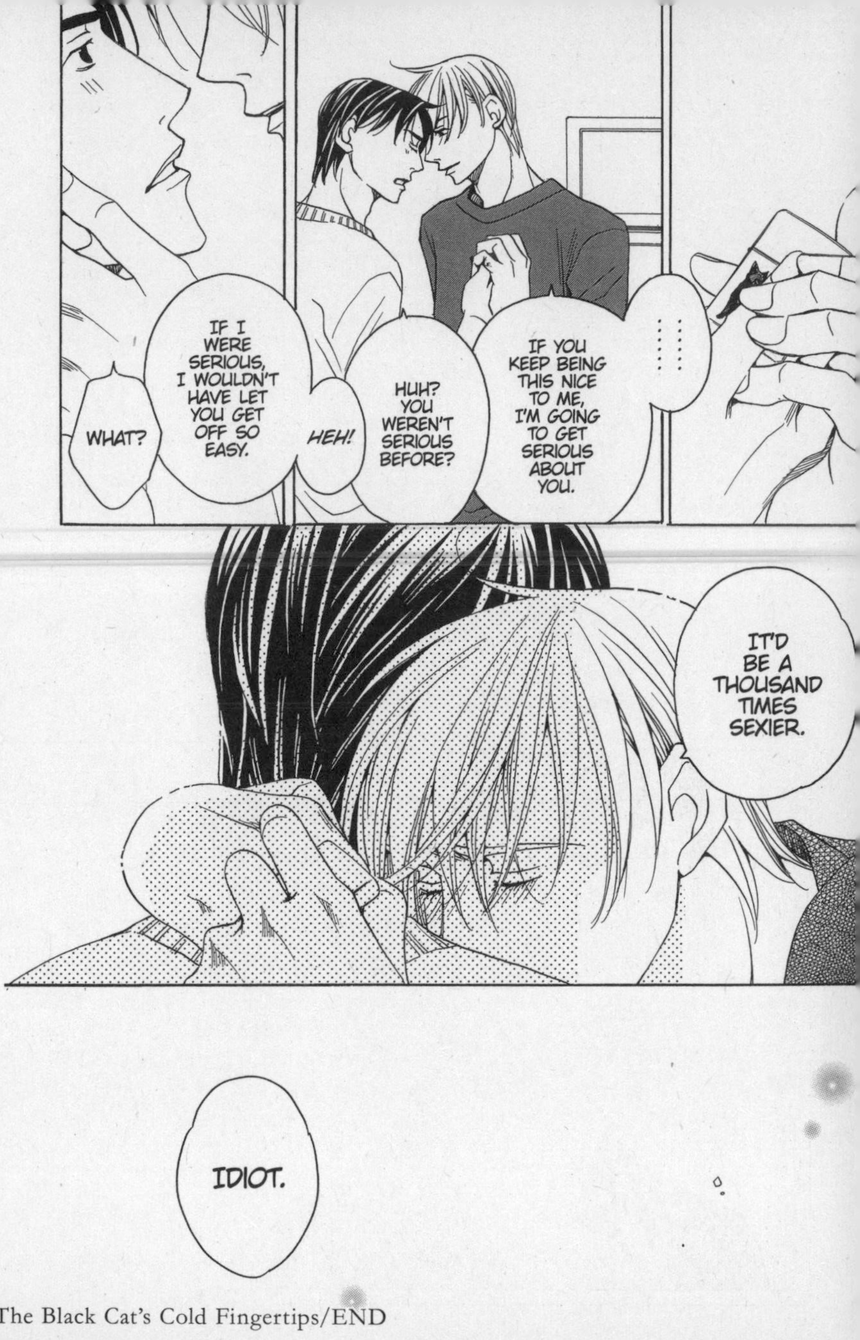
......
IF YOU KEEP BEING THIS NICE TO ME, I'M GOING TO GET SERIOUS ABOUT YOU.
HUH? YOU WEREN'T SERIOUS BEFORE?
HEH!
IF I WERE SERIOUS, I WOULDN'T HAVE LET YOU GET OFF SO EASY.
WHAT?
IT'D BE A THOUSAND TIMES SEXIER.
IDIOT.

The Black Cat's Cold Fingertips/END

Mouse, Thoughtful at a Dead End

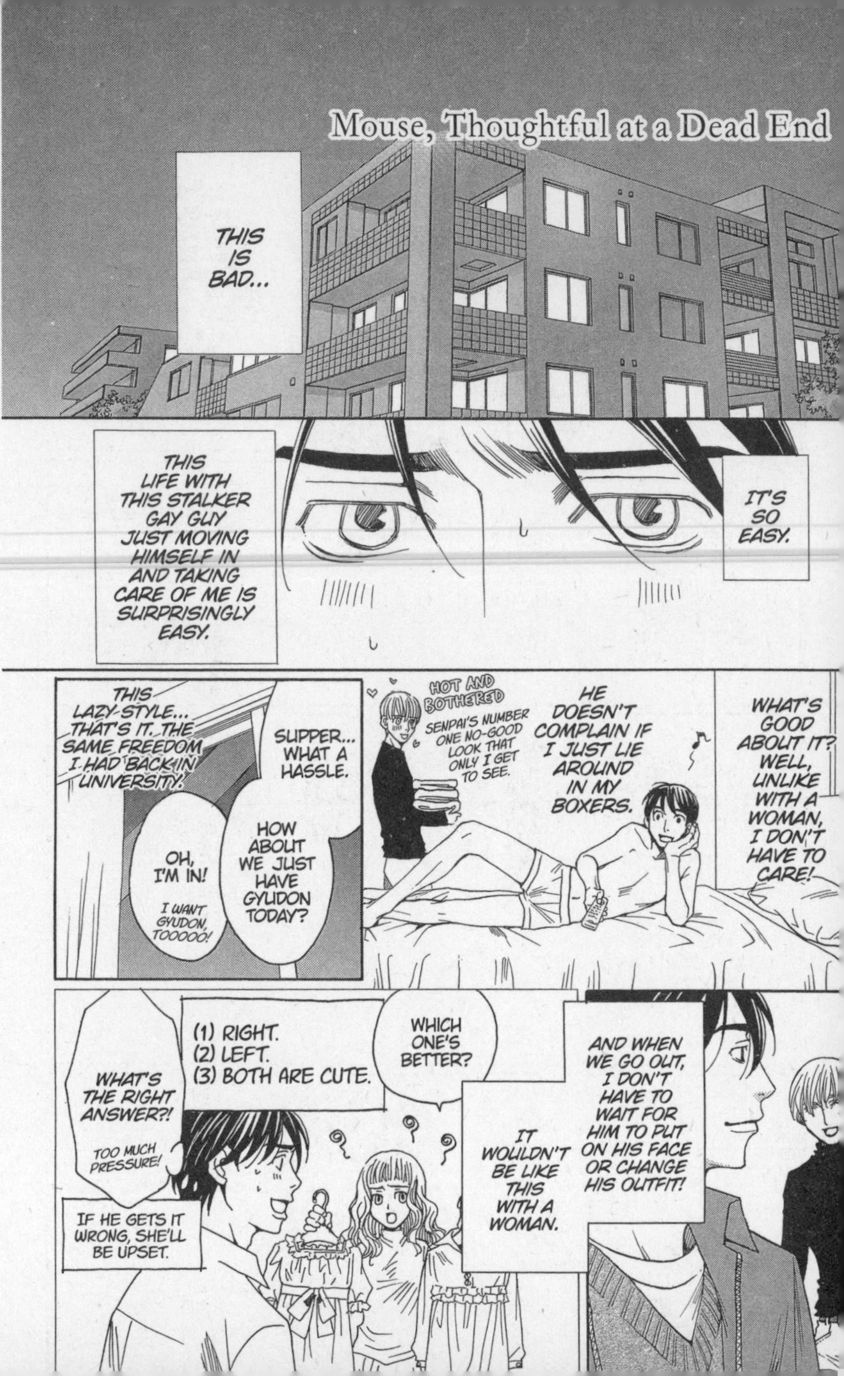

THIS IS BAD...
IT'S SO EASY.
THIS LIFE WITH THIS STALKER GAY GUY JUST MOVING HIMSELF IN AND TAKING CARE OF ME IS SURPRISINGLY EASY.
WHAT'S GOOD ABOUT IT? WELL, UNLIKE WITH A WOMAN, I DON'T HAVE TO CARE!
HE DOESN'T COMPLAIN IF I JUST LIE AROUND IN MY BOXERS.
HOT AND BOTHERED
SENPAI'S NUMBER ONE NO-GOOD LOOK THAT ONLY I GET TO SEE.
SUPPER... WHAT A HASSLE.
THIS LAZY-STYLE... THAT'S IT. THE SAME FREEDOM I HAD BACK IN UNIVERSITY!
HOW ABOUT WE JUST HAVE GYUDON TODAY?
OH, I'M IN!
I WANT GYUDON, TOOOOO!
AND WHEN WE GO OUT, I DON'T HAVE TO WAIT FOR HIM TO PUT ON HIS FACE OR CHANGE HIS OUTFIT!
IT WOULDN'T BE LIKE THIS WITH A WOMAN.
WHICH ONE'S BETTER?
(1) RIGHT.
(2) LEFT.
(3) BOTH ARE CUTE.
WHAT'S THE RIGHT ANSWER?!
TOO MUCH PRESSURE!
IF HE GETS IT WRONG, SHE'LL BE UPSET.

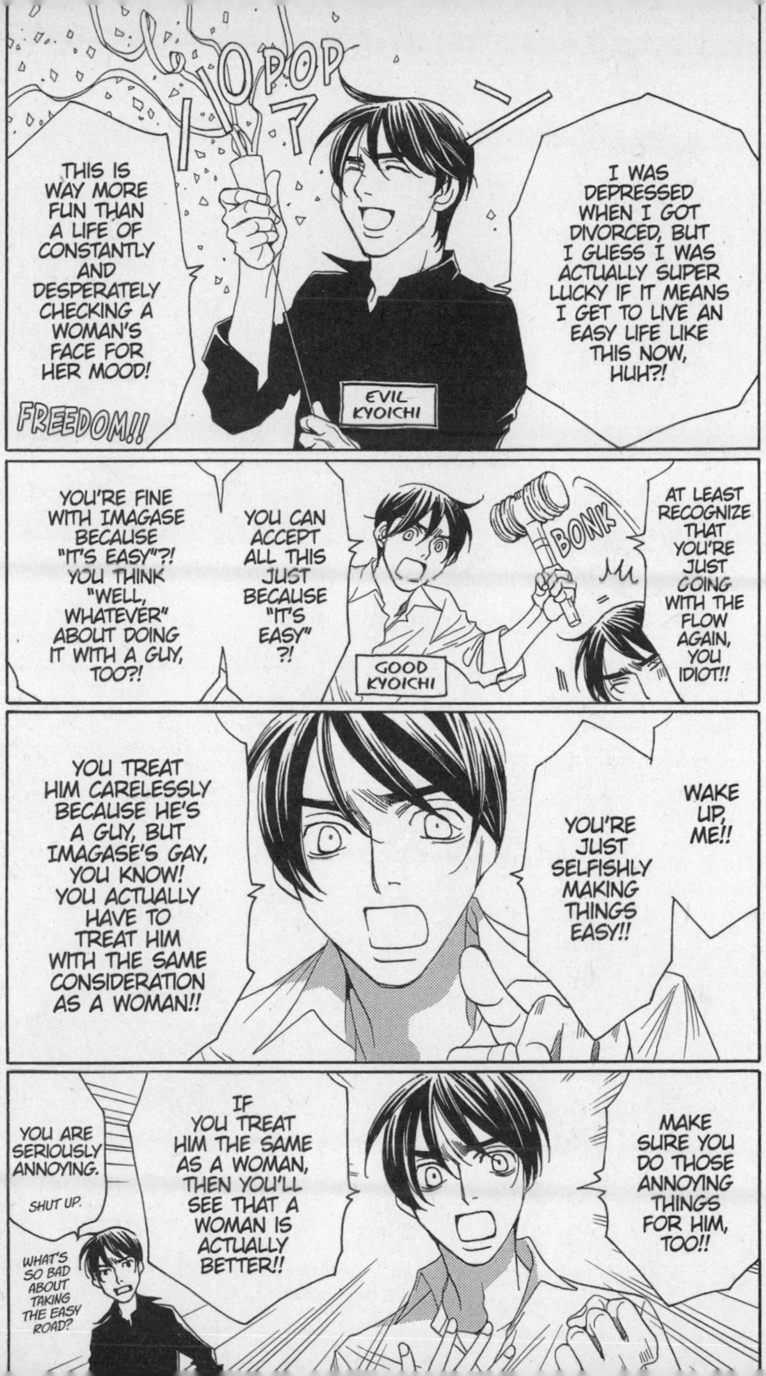

POP
I WAS DEPRESSED WHEN I GOT DIVORCED, BUT I GUESS I WAS ACTUALLY SUPER LUCKY IF IT MEANS I GET TO LIVE AN EASY LIFE LIKE THIS NOW, HUH?!
THIS IS WAY MORE FUN THAN A LIFE OF CONSTANTLY AND DESPERATELY CHECKING A WOMAN'S FACE FOR HER MOOD!
EVIL KYOICHI
FREEDOM!!
AT LEAST RECOGNIZE THAT YOU'RE JUST GOING WITH THE FLOW AGAIN, YOU IDIOT!!
BONK
GOOD KYOICHI
YOU CAN ACCEPT ALL THIS JUST BECAUSE "IT'S EASY"?!
YOU'RE FINE WITH IMAGASE BECAUSE "IT'S EASY"?! YOU THINK "WELL, WHATEVER" ABOUT DOING IT WITH A GUY, TOO?!
WAKE UP, ME!!
YOU'RE JUST SELFISHLY MAKING THINGS EASY!!
YOU TREAT HIM CARELESSLY BECAUSE HE'S A GUY, BUT IMAGASE'S GAY, YOU KNOW! YOU ACTUALLY HAVE TO TREAT HIM WITH THE SAME CONSIDERATION AS A WOMAN!!
MAKE SURE YOU DO THOSE ANNOYING THINGS FOR HIM, TOO!!
IF YOU TREAT HIM THE SAME AS A WOMAN, THEN YOU'LL SEE THAT A WOMAN IS ACTUALLY BETTER!!
YOU ARE SERIOUSLY ANNOYING.
SHUT UP.
WHAT'S SO BAD ABOUT TAKING THE EASY ROAD?

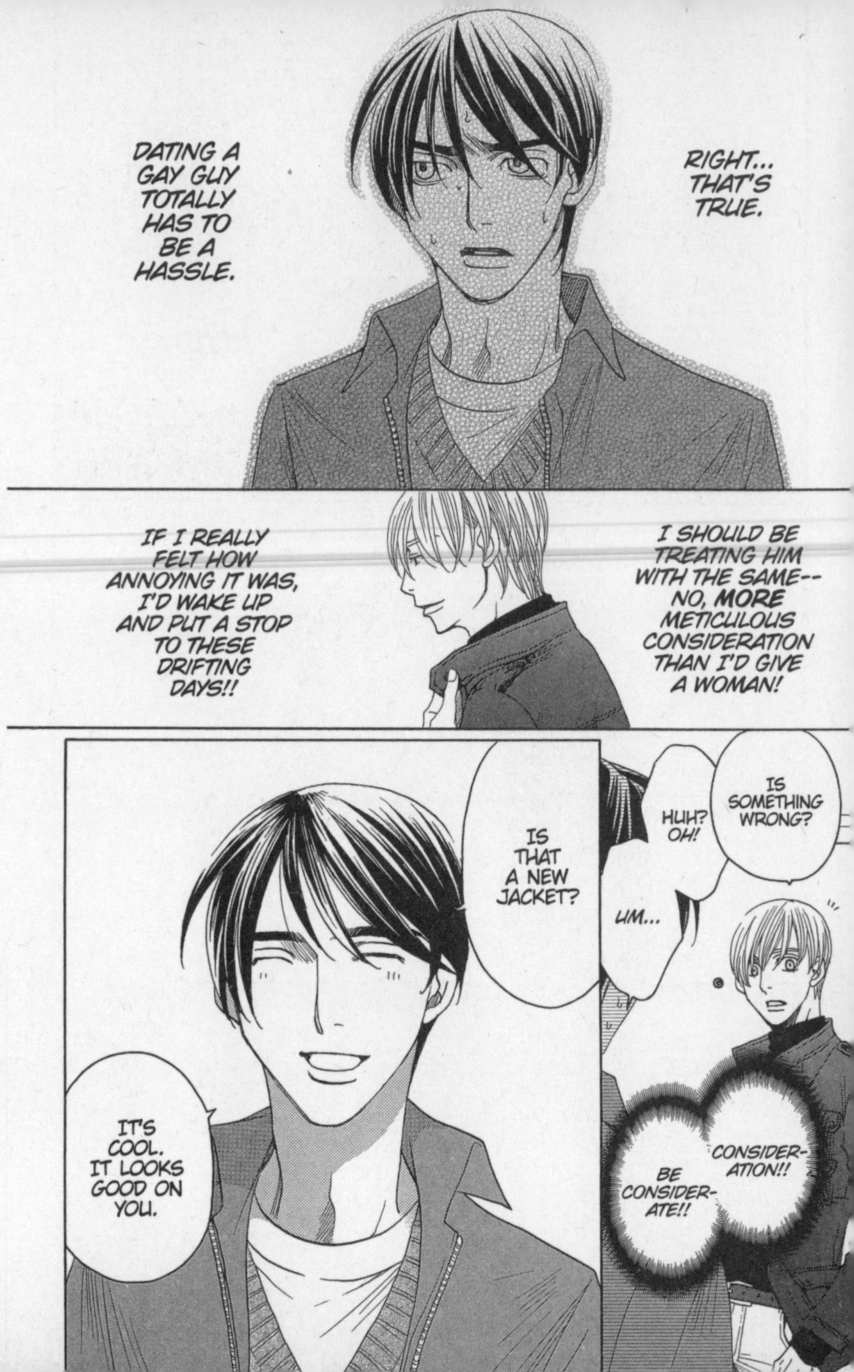
RIGHT... THAT'S TRUE.
DATING A GAY GUY TOTALLY HAS TO BE A HASSLE.
I SHOULD BE TREATING HIM WITH THE SAME-- NO, **MORE** METICULOUS CONSIDERATION THAN I'D GIVE A WOMAN!
IF I REALLY FELT HOW ANNOYING IT WAS, I'D WAKE UP AND PUT A STOP TO THESE DRIFTING DAYS!!
IS SOMETHING WRONG?
HUH? OH!
UM...
CONSIDER-ATION!!
BE CONSIDER-ATE!!
IS THAT A NEW JACKET?
IT'S COOL. IT LOOKS GOOD ON YOU.

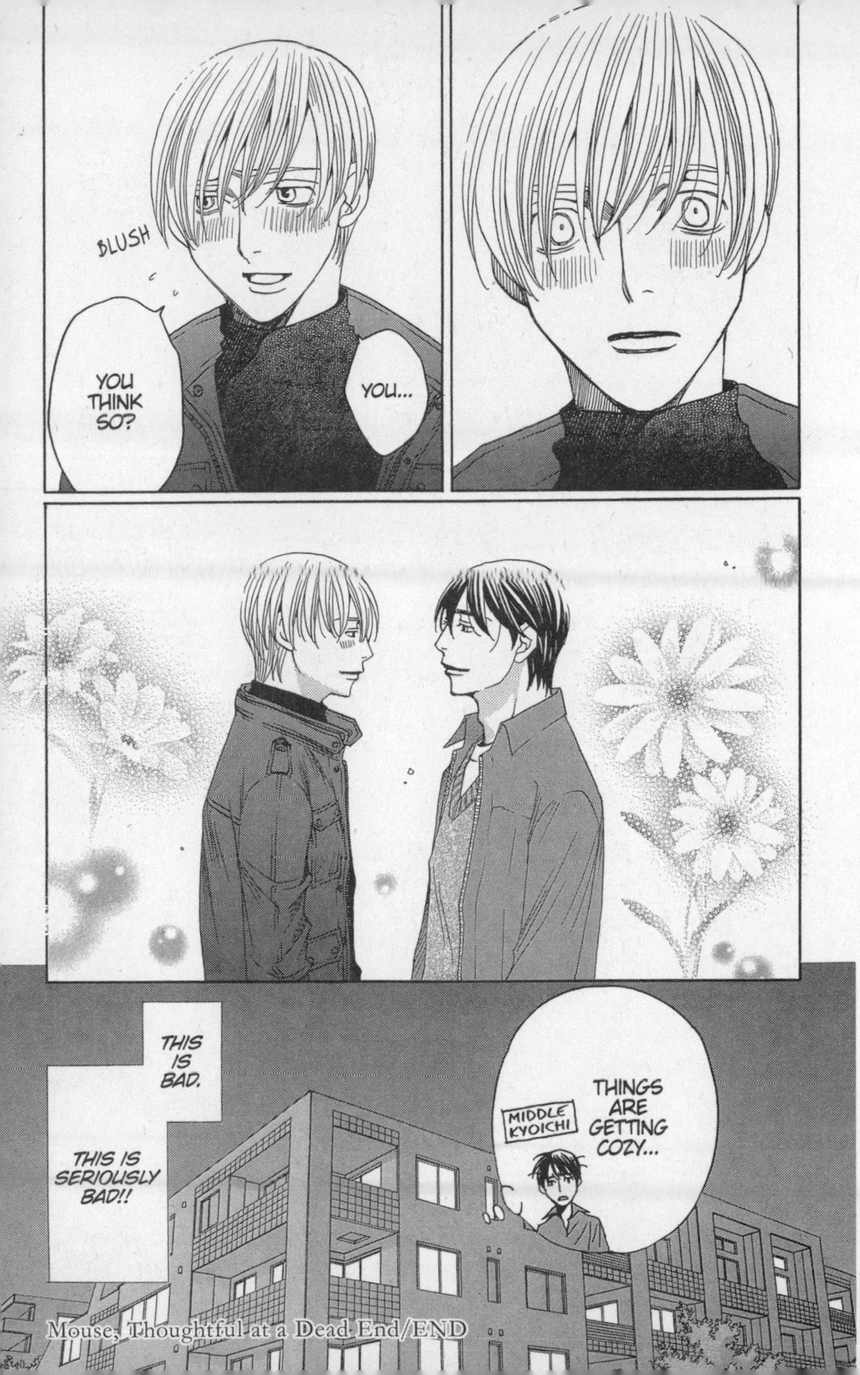
BLUSH
YOU...
YOU THINK SO?
MIDDLE KYOICHI
THINGS ARE GETTING COZY...
THIS IS BAD.
THIS IS SERIOUSLY BAD!!
Mouse, Thoughtful at a Dead End/END

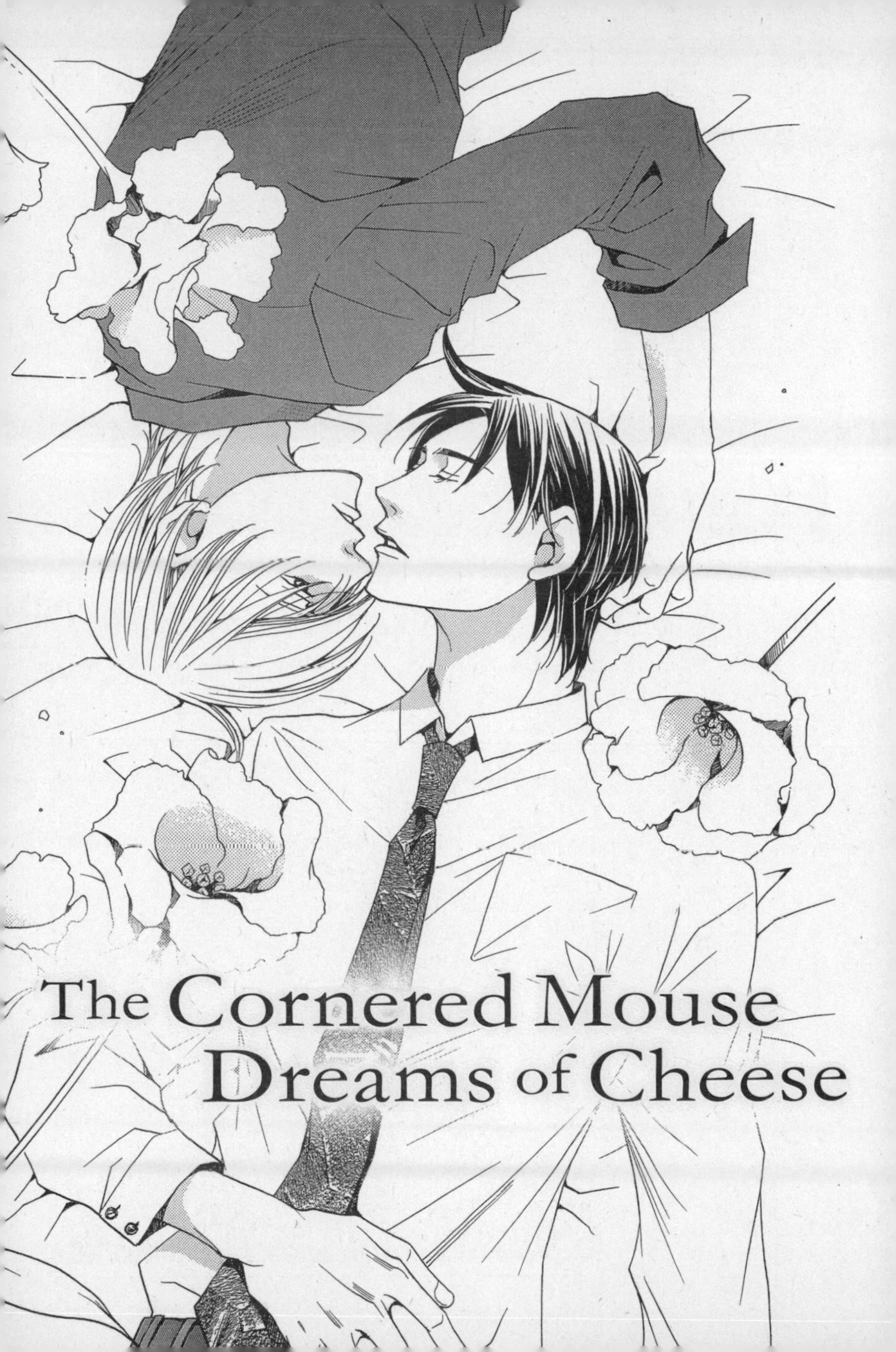
The Cornered Mouse
Dreams of Cheese

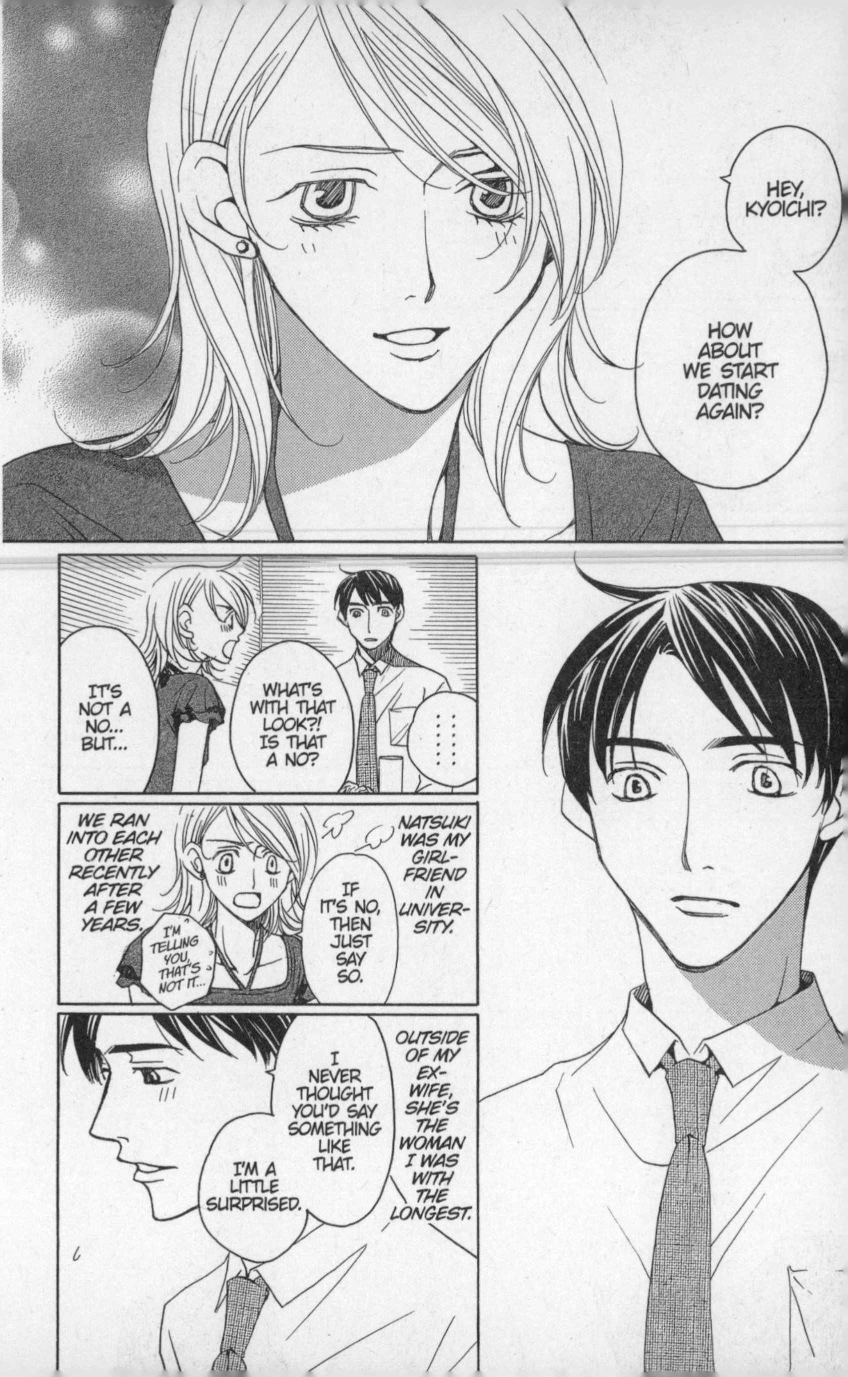
HEY, KYOICHI?
HOW ABOUT WE START DATING AGAIN?
......
WHAT'S WITH THAT LOOK?! IS THAT A NO?
IT'S NOT A NO... BUT...
NATSUKI WAS MY GIRL-FRIEND IN UNIVER-SITY.
IF IT'S NO, THEN JUST SAY SO.
WE RAN INTO EACH OTHER RECENTLY AFTER A FEW YEARS.
I'M TELLING YOU, THAT'S NOT IT...
OUTSIDE OF MY EX-WIFE, SHE'S THE WOMAN I WAS WITH THE LONGEST.
I NEVER THOUGHT YOU'D SAY SOMETHING LIKE THAT.
I'M A LITTLE SURPRISED.

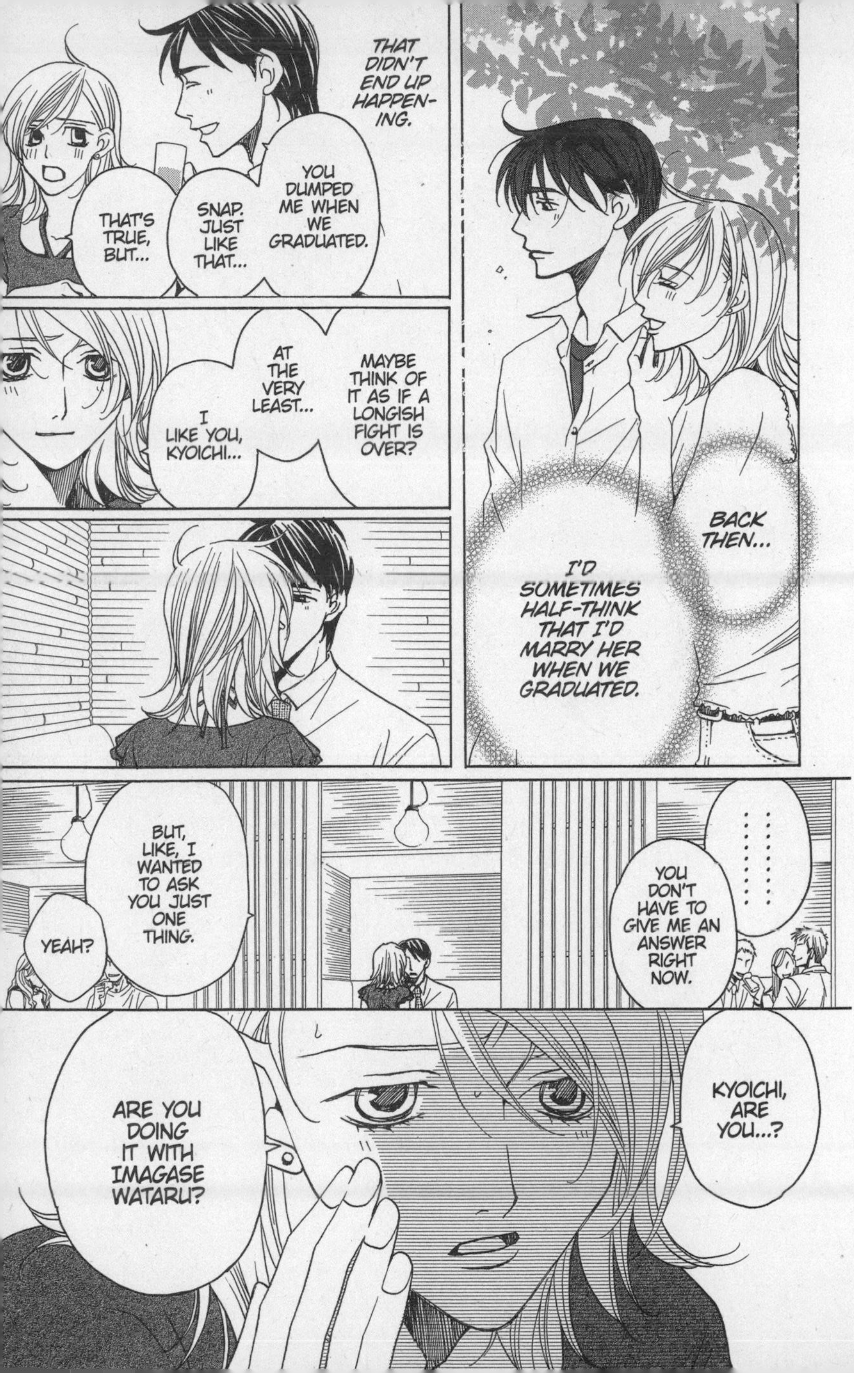
BACK THEN...
I'D SOMETIMES HALF-THINK THAT I'D MARRY HER WHEN WE GRADUATED.
THAT DIDN'T END UP HAPPENING.
YOU DUMPED ME WHEN WE GRADUATED.
SNAP. JUST LIKE THAT...
THAT'S TRUE, BUT...
MAYBE THINK OF IT AS IF A LONGISH FIGHT IS OVER?
AT THE VERY LEAST...
I LIKE YOU, KYOICHI...
......
YOU DON'T HAVE TO GIVE ME AN ANSWER RIGHT NOW.
BUT, LIKE, I WANTED TO ASK YOU JUST ONE THING.
YEAH?
KYOICHI, ARE YOU...?
ARE YOU DOING IT WITH IMAGASE WATARU?

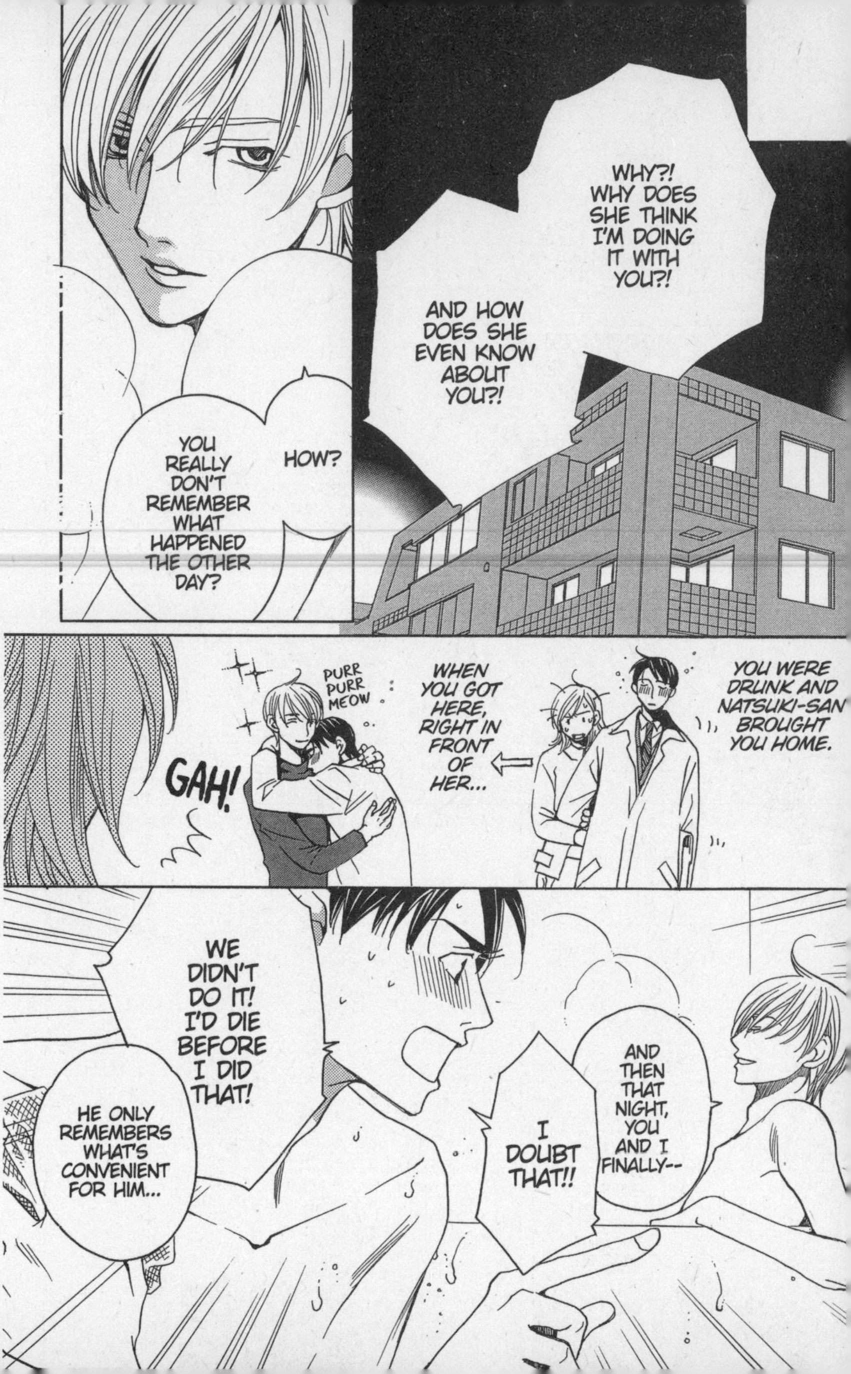

WHY?! WHY DOES SHE THINK I'M DOING IT WITH YOU?!
AND HOW DOES SHE EVEN KNOW ABOUT YOU?!
HOW?
YOU REALLY DON'T REMEMBER WHAT HAPPENED THE OTHER DAY?
YOU WERE DRUNK AND NATSUKI-SAN BROUGHT YOU HOME.
WHEN YOU GOT HERE, RIGHT IN FRONT OF HER...
PURR PURR MEOW
GAH!
AND THEN THAT NIGHT, YOU AND I FINALLY--
I DOUBT THAT!!
WE DIDN'T DO IT! I'D DIE BEFORE I DID THAT!
HE ONLY REMEMBERS WHAT'S CONVENIENT FOR HIM...

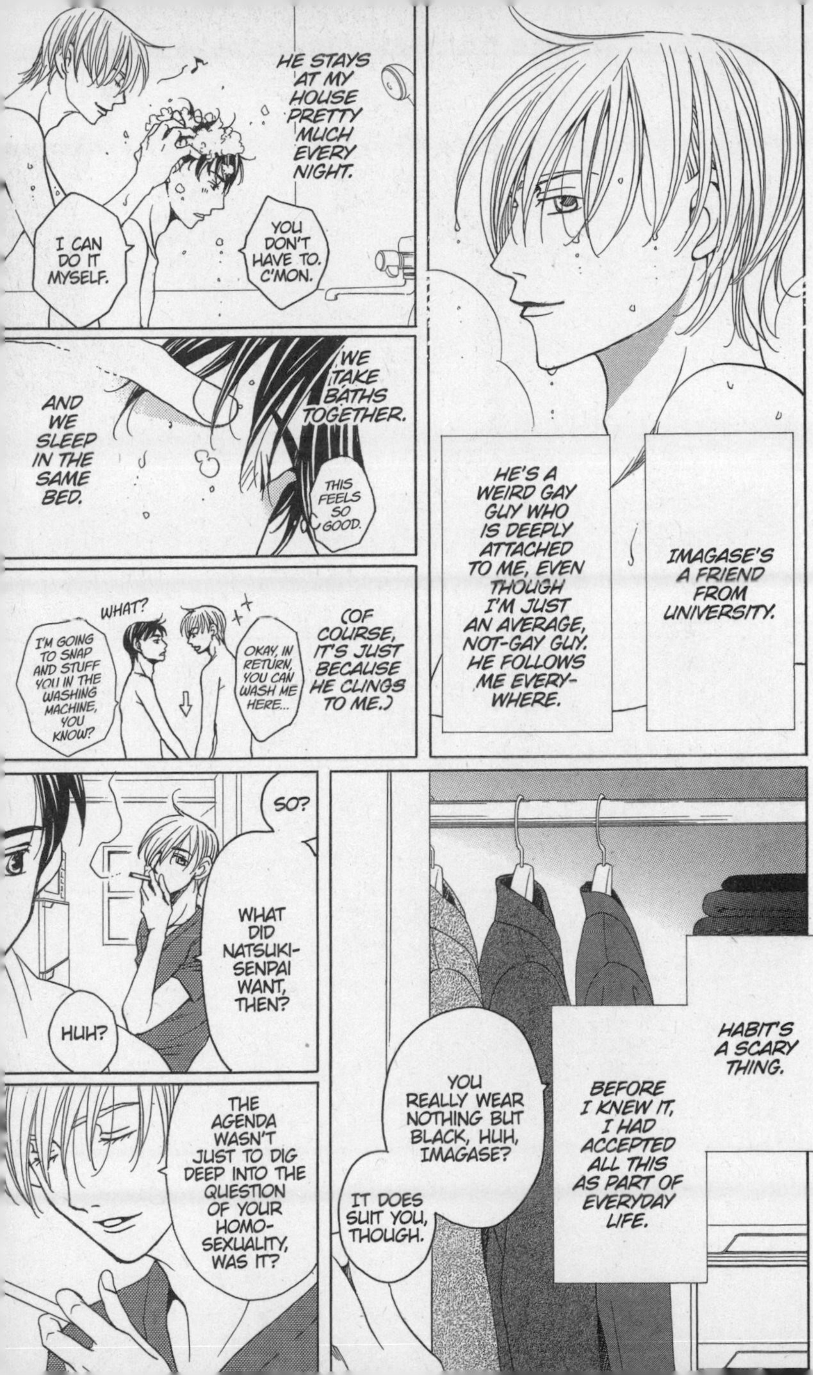
IMAGASE'S A FRIEND FROM UNIVERSITY.
HE'S A WEIRD GAY GUY WHO IS DEEPLY ATTACHED TO ME, EVEN THOUGH I'M JUST AN AVERAGE, NOT-GAY GUY. HE FOLLOWS ME EVERYWHERE.
HE STAYS AT MY HOUSE PRETTY MUCH EVERY NIGHT.
YOU DON'T HAVE TO. C'MON.
I CAN DO IT MYSELF.
WE TAKE BATHS TOGETHER.
THIS FEELS SO GOOD.
AND WE SLEEP IN THE SAME BED.
(OF COURSE, IT'S JUST BECAUSE HE CLINGS TO ME.)
OKAY, IN RETURN, YOU CAN WASH ME HERE...
WHAT?
I'M GOING TO SNAP AND STUFF YOU IN THE WASHING MACHINE, YOU KNOW?
HABIT'S A SCARY THING.
BEFORE I KNEW IT, I HAD ACCEPTED ALL THIS AS PART OF EVERYDAY LIFE.
YOU REALLY WEAR NOTHING BUT BLACK, HUH, IMAGASE?
IT DOES SUIT YOU, THOUGH.
SO?
WHAT DID NATSUKI-SENPAI WANT, THEN?
HUH?
THE AGENDA WASN'T JUST TO DIG DEEP INTO THE QUESTION OF YOUR HOMOSEXUALITY, WAS IT?

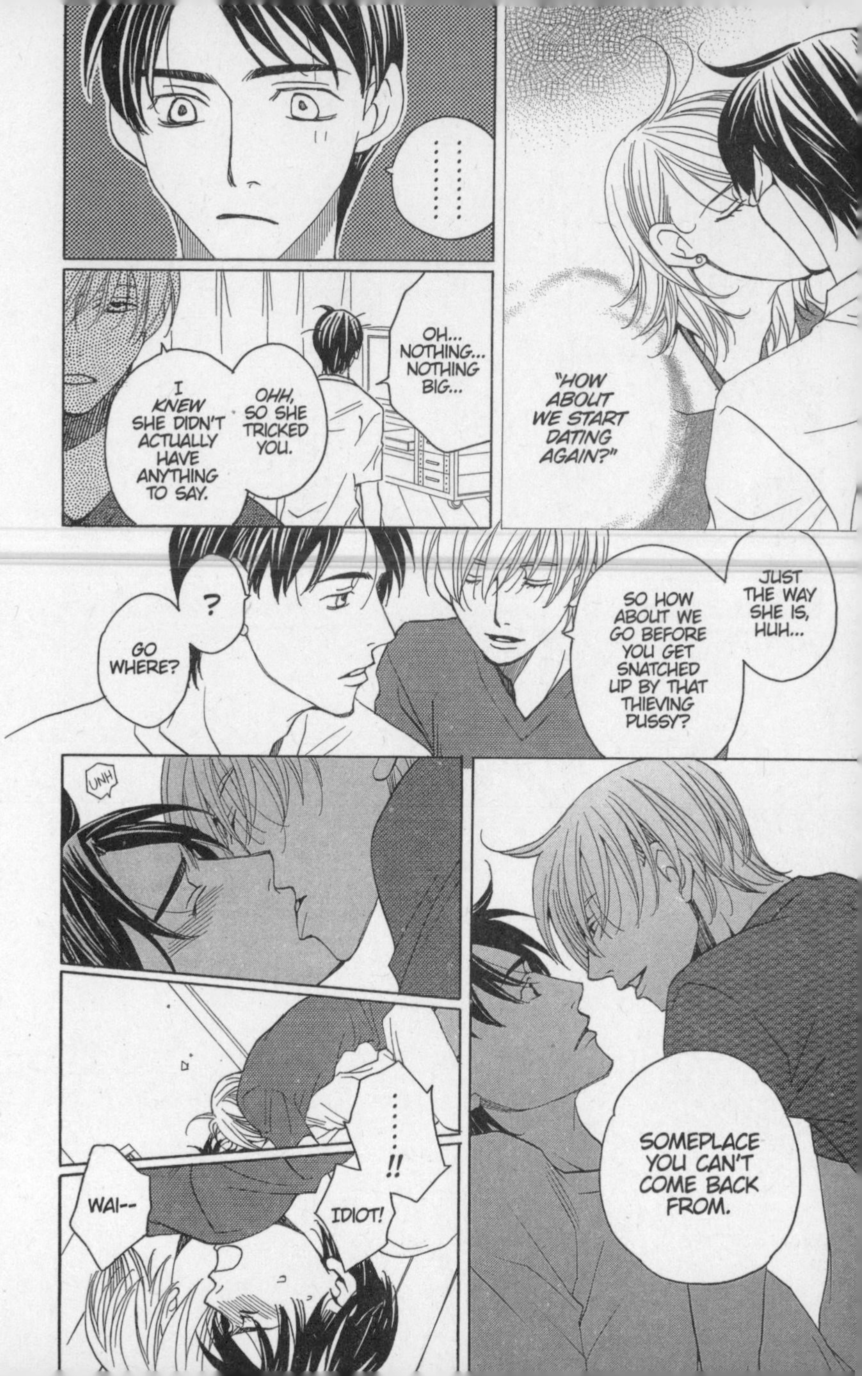
"HOW ABOUT WE START DATING AGAIN?"
......
OH... NOTHING... NOTHING BIG...
OHH, SO SHE TRICKED YOU.
I KNEW SHE DIDN'T ACTUALLY HAVE ANYTHING TO SAY.
JUST THE WAY SHE IS, HUH...
SO HOW ABOUT WE GO BEFORE YOU GET SNATCHED UP BY THAT THIEVING PUSSY?
?
GO WHERE?
SOMEPLACE YOU CAN'T COME BACK FROM.
UNH
......
!!
IDIOT!
WAI--

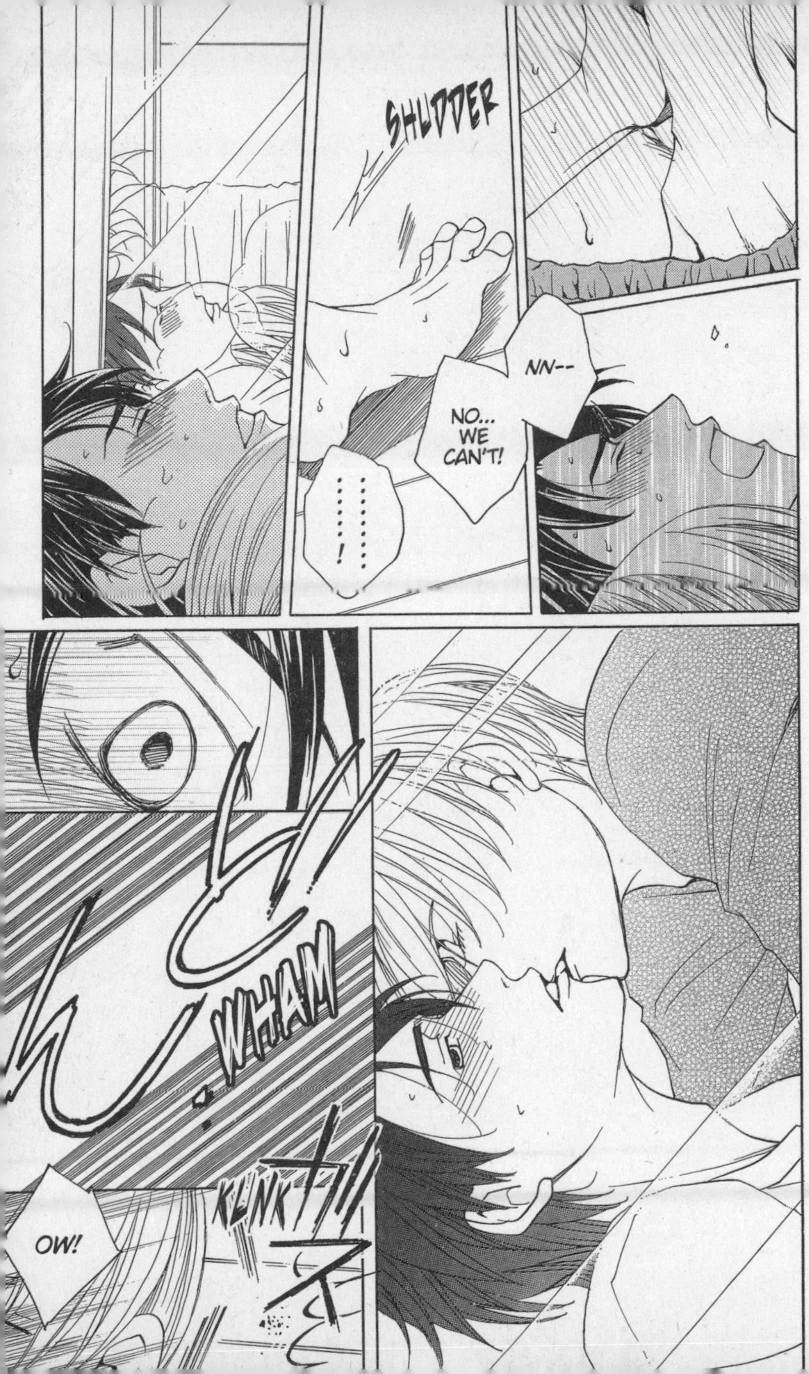
NN--
NO... WE CAN'T!
SHUDDER
......!
WHAM
KLNK
OW!

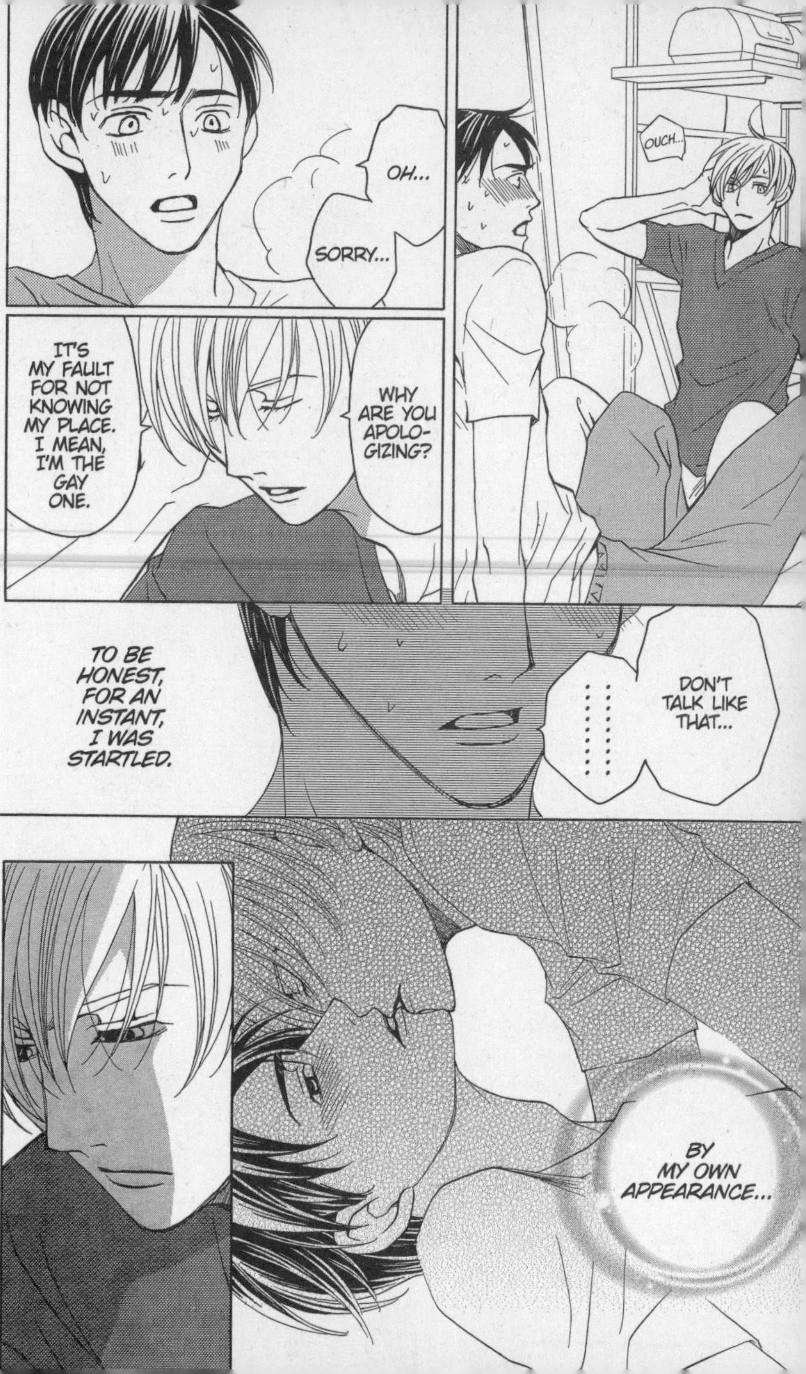
OUCH...
OH...
SORRY...
WHY ARE YOU APOLOGIZING?
IT'S MY FAULT FOR NOT KNOWING MY PLACE. I MEAN, I'M THE GAY ONE.
DON'T TALK LIKE THAT...
......
TO BE HONEST, FOR AN INSTANT, I WAS STARTLED.
BY MY OWN APPEARANCE...

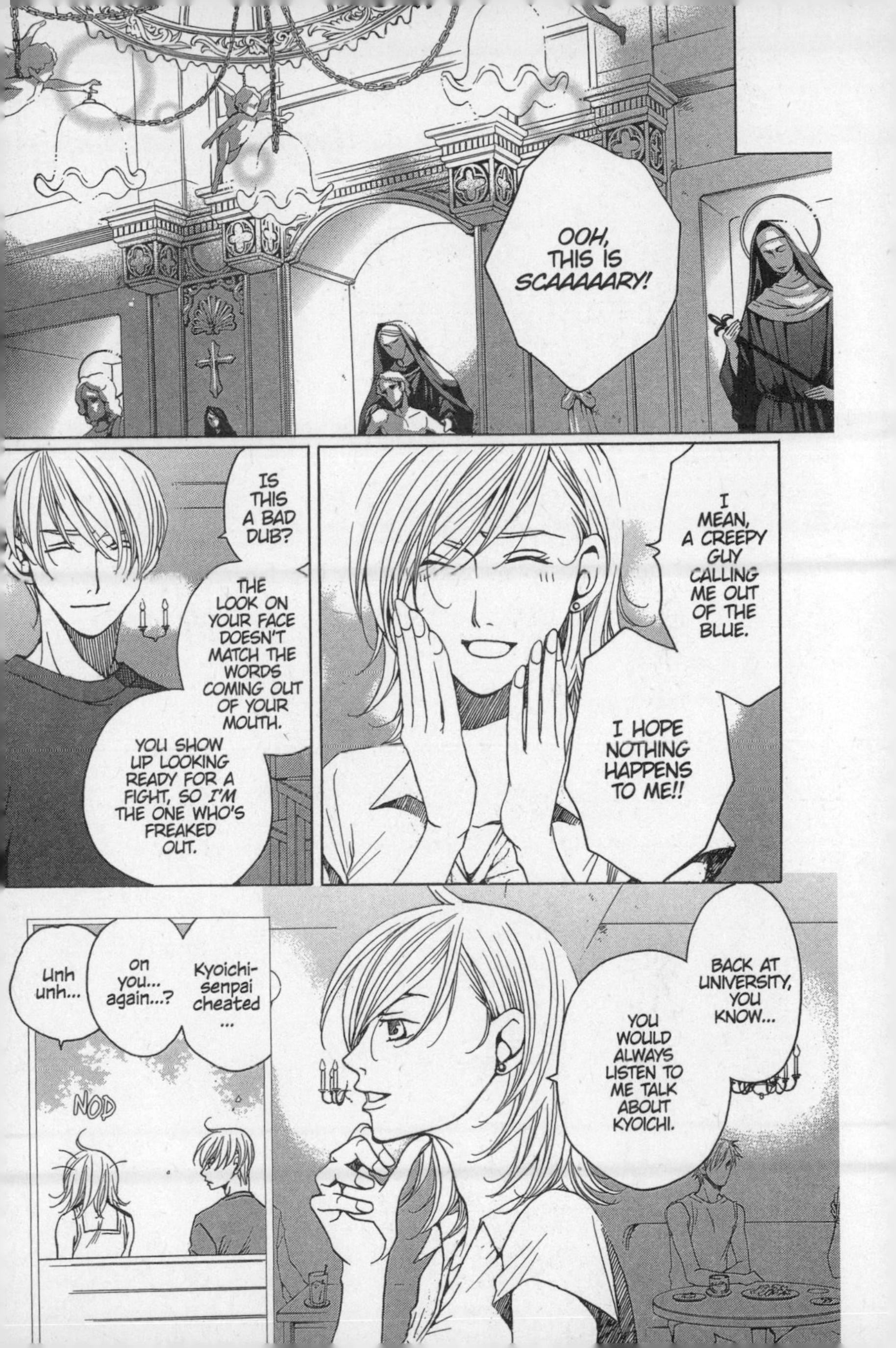
OOH, THIS IS SCAAAAARY!
I MEAN, A CREEPY GUY CALLING ME OUT OF THE BLUE.
I HOPE NOTHING HAPPENS TO ME!!
IS THIS A BAD DUB?
THE LOOK ON YOUR FACE DOESN'T MATCH THE WORDS COMING OUT OF YOUR MOUTH.
YOU SHOW UP LOOKING READY FOR A FIGHT, SO I'M THE ONE WHO'S FREAKED OUT.
BACK AT UNIVERSITY, YOU KNOW...
YOU WOULD ALWAYS LISTEN TO ME TALK ABOUT KYOICHI.
Kyoichi-senpai cheated ...
on you... again...?
Unh unh...
NOD

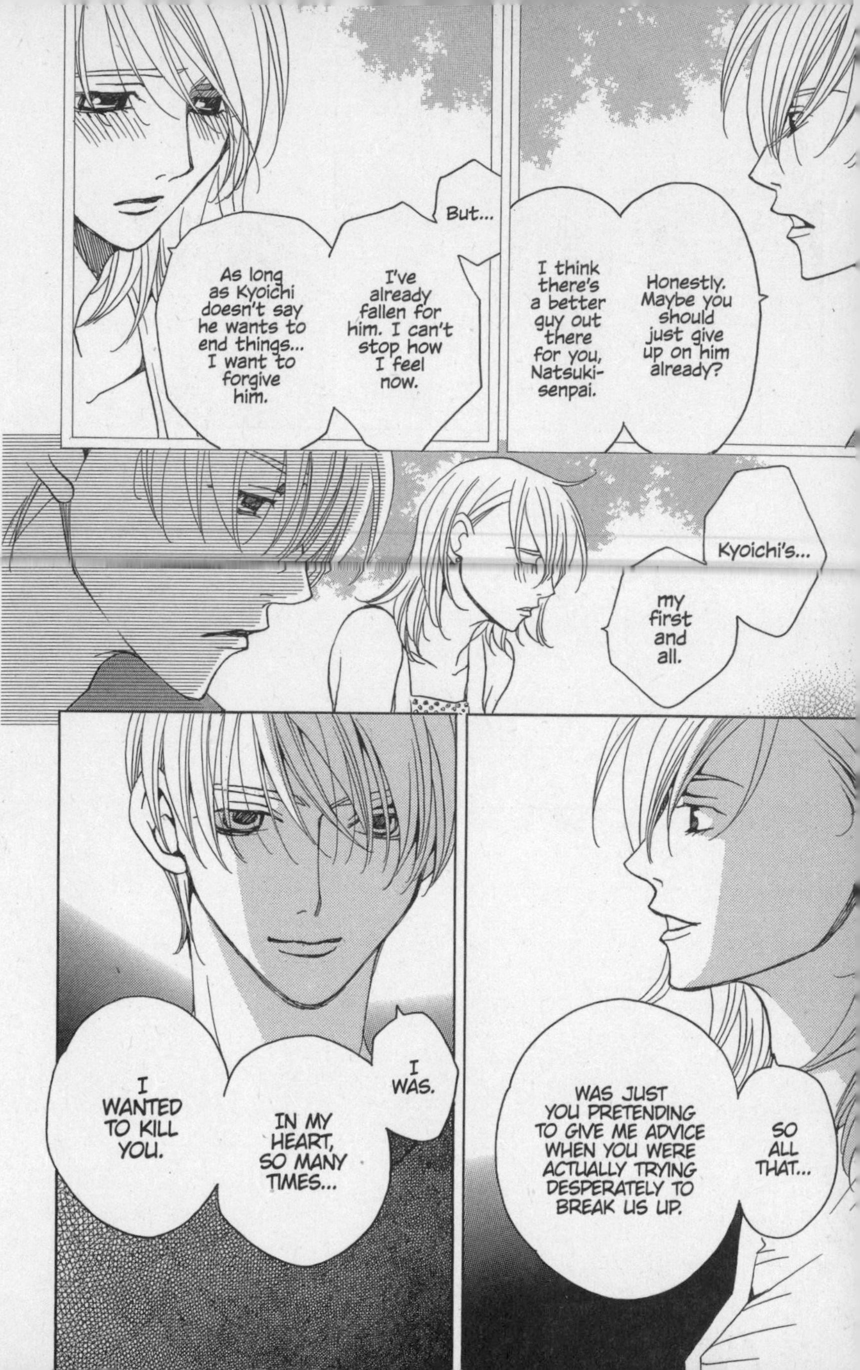
Honestly. Maybe you should just give up on him already?
I think there's a better guy out there for you, Natsuki-senpai.
But...
I've already fallen for him. I can't stop how I feel now.
As long as Kyoichi doesn't say he wants to end things... I want to forgive him.
Kyoichi's...
my first and all.
SO ALL THAT...
WAS JUST YOU PRETENDING TO GIVE ME ADVICE WHEN YOU WERE ACTUALLY TRYING DESPERATELY TO BREAK US UP.
I WAS.
IN MY HEART, SO MANY TIMES...
I WANTED TO KILL YOU.

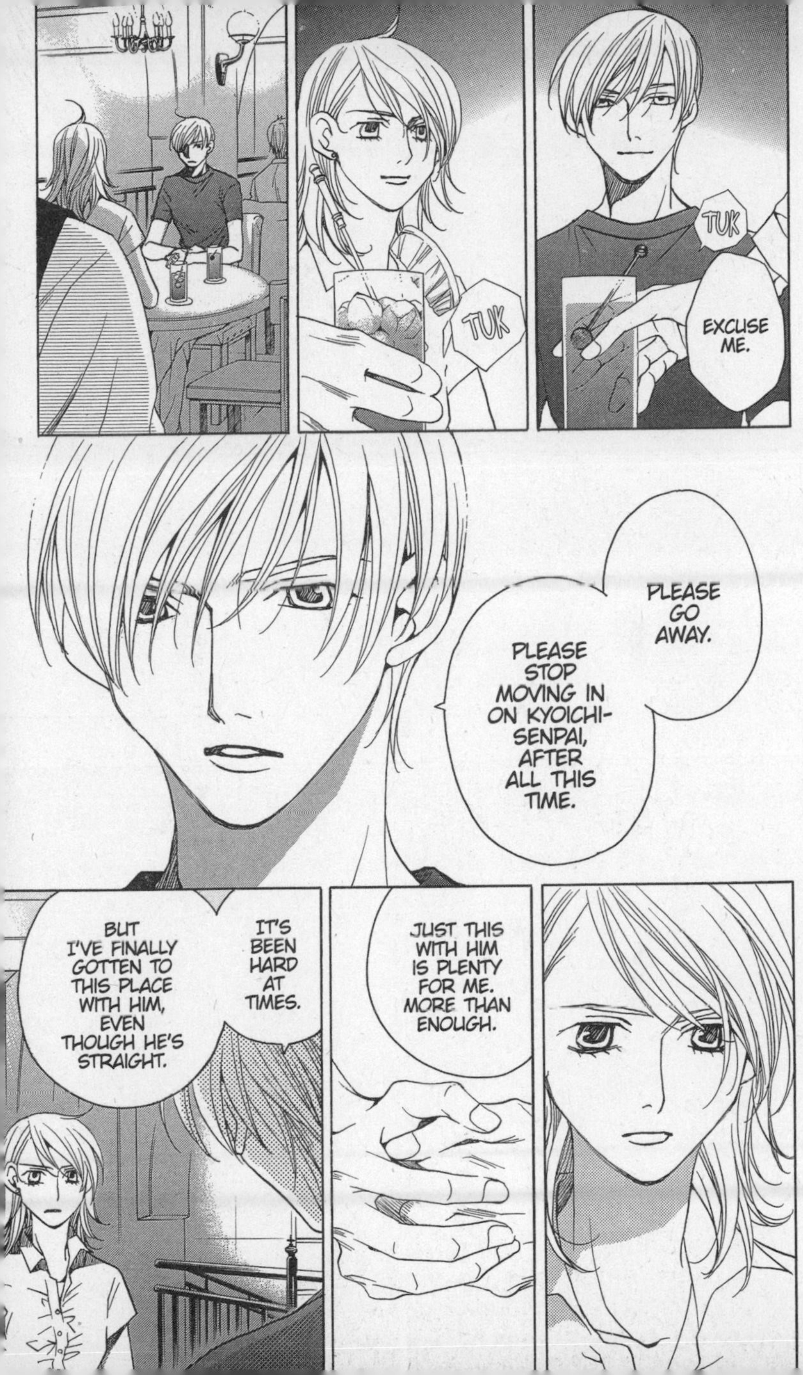
TUK
EXCUSE ME.
TUK
PLEASE GO AWAY.
PLEASE STOP MOVING IN ON KYOICHI-SENPAI, AFTER ALL THIS TIME.
JUST THIS WITH HIM IS PLENTY FOR ME. MORE THAN ENOUGH.
IT'S BEEN HARD AT TIMES.
BUT I'VE FINALLY GOTTEN TO THIS PLACE WITH HIM, EVEN THOUGH HE'S STRAIGHT.

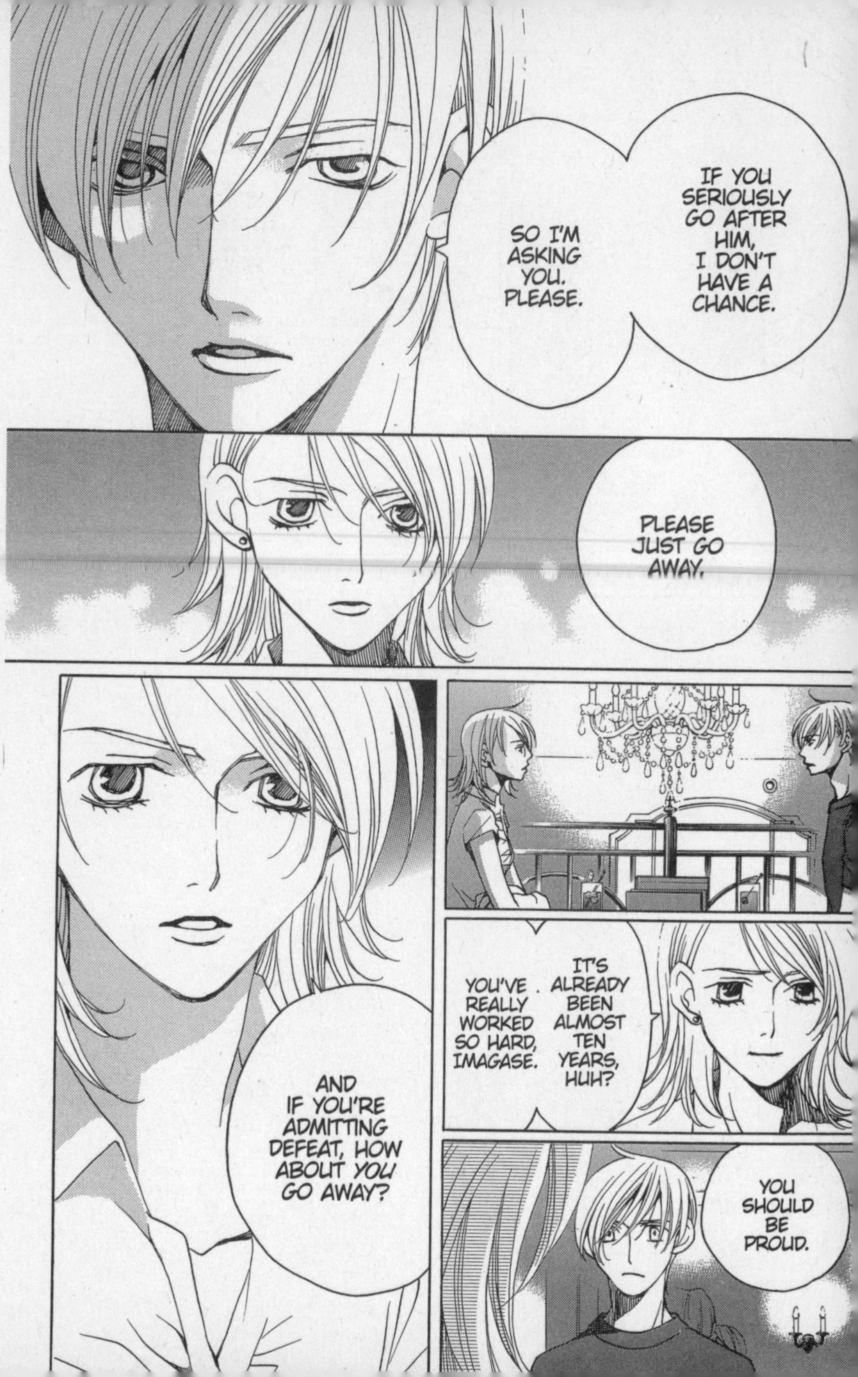
IF YOU SERIOUSLY GO AFTER HIM, I DON'T HAVE A CHANCE.
SO I'M ASKING YOU. PLEASE.
PLEASE JUST GO AWAY.
IT'S ALREADY BEEN ALMOST TEN YEARS, HUH?
YOU'VE REALLY WORKED SO HARD, IMAGASE.
YOU SHOULD BE PROUD.
AND IF YOU'RE ADMITTING DEFEAT, HOW ABOUT *YOU* GO AWAY?

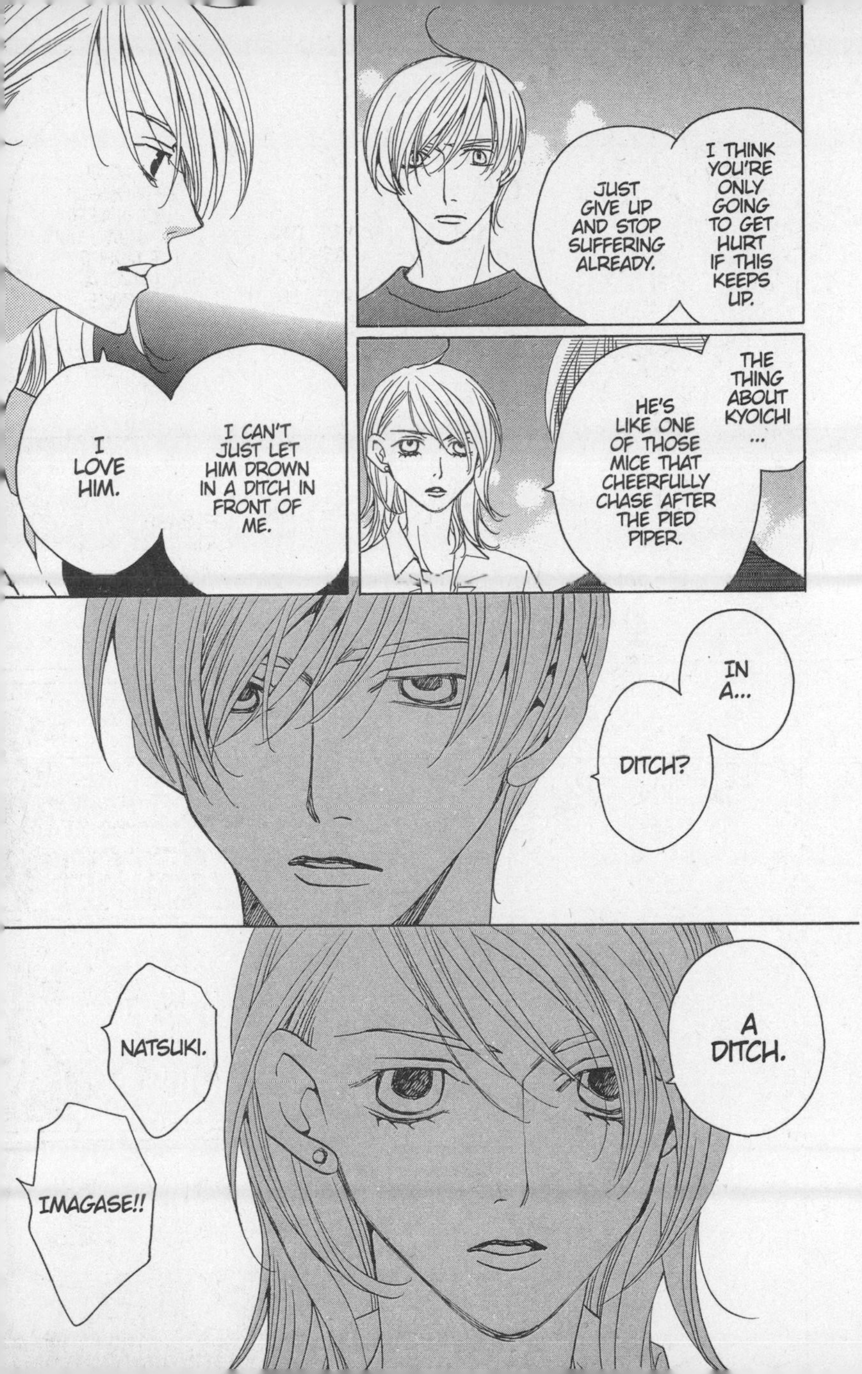
I THINK YOU'RE ONLY GOING TO GET HURT IF THIS KEEPS UP.
JUST GIVE UP AND STOP SUFFERING ALREADY.
THE THING ABOUT KYOICHI ...
HE'S LIKE ONE OF THOSE MICE THAT CHEERFULLY CHASE AFTER THE PIED PIPER.
I CAN'T JUST LET HIM DROWN IN A DITCH IN FRONT OF ME.
I LOVE HIM.
IN A...
DITCH?
A DITCH.
NATSUKI.
IMAGASE!!

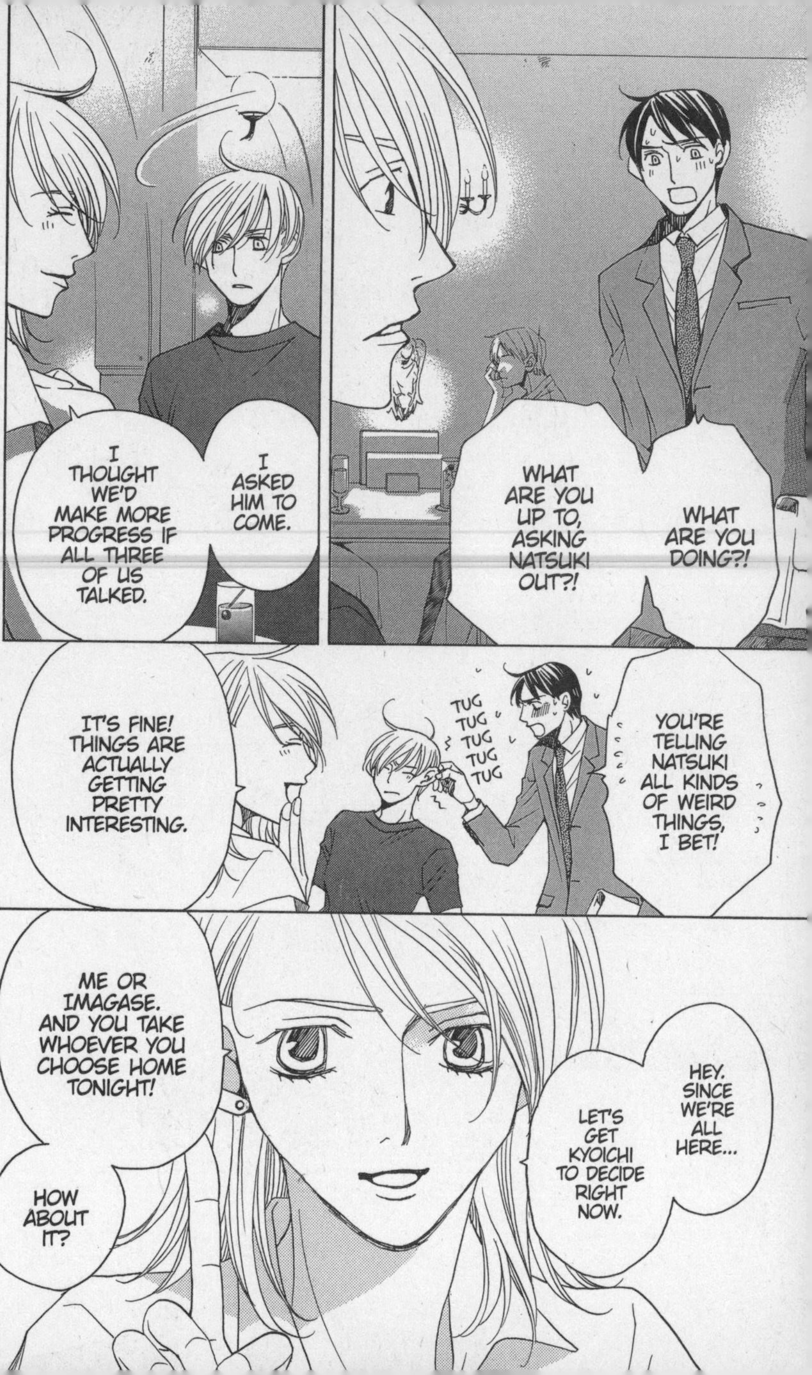
WHAT ARE YOU DOING?!
WHAT ARE YOU UP TO, ASKING NATSUKI OUT?!
I ASKED HIM TO COME.
I THOUGHT WE'D MAKE MORE PROGRESS IF ALL THREE OF US TALKED.
YOU'RE TELLING NATSUKI ALL KINDS OF WEIRD THINGS, I BET!
TUG TUG TUG TUG TUG
IT'S FINE! THINGS ARE ACTUALLY GETTING PRETTY INTERESTING.
HEY. SINCE WE'RE ALL HERE...
LET'S GET KYOICHI TO DECIDE RIGHT NOW.
ME OR IMAGASE. AND YOU TAKE WHOEVER YOU CHOOSE HOME TONIGHT!
HOW ABOUT IT?

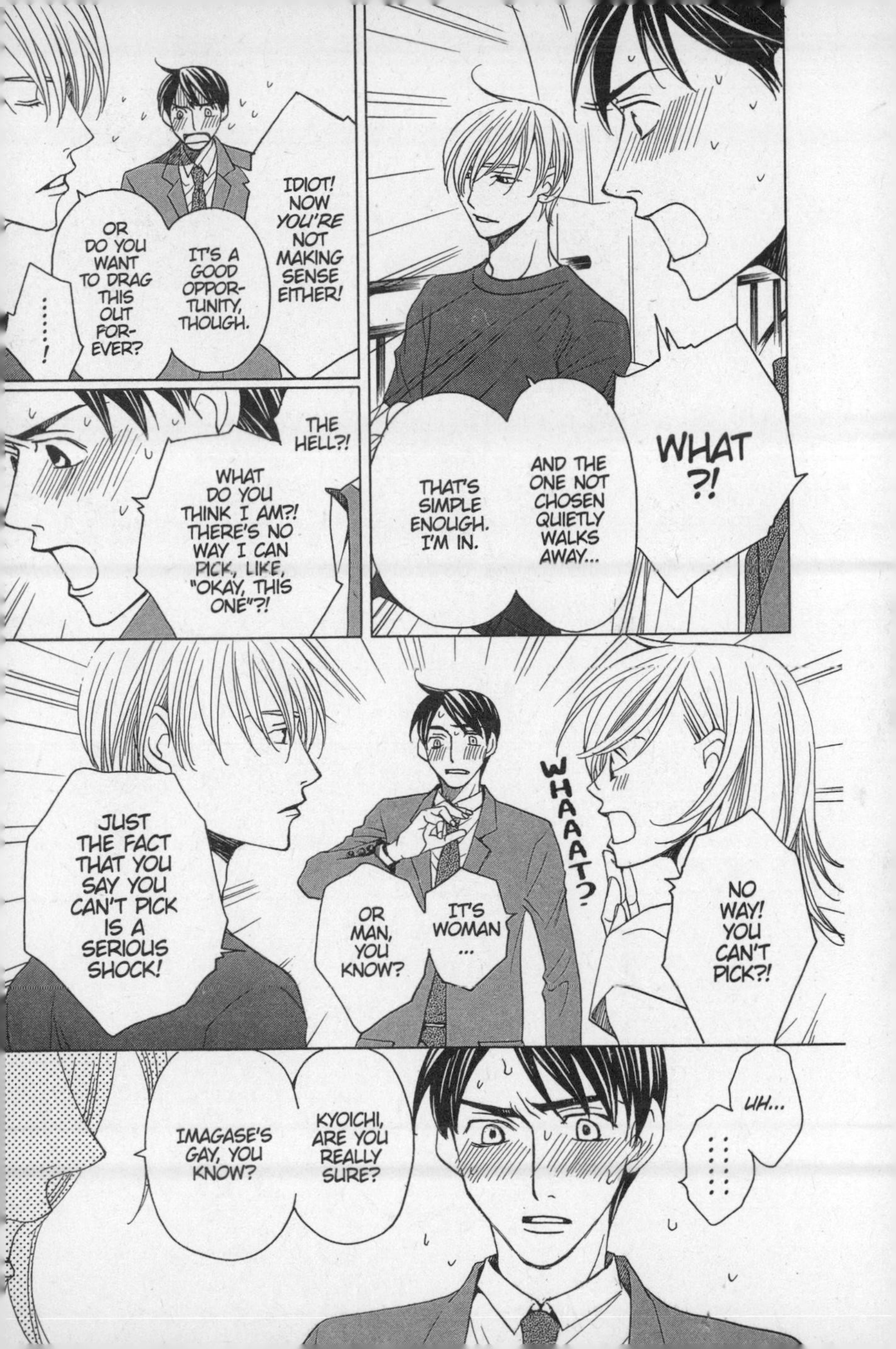
WHAT?!
AND THE ONE NOT CHOSEN QUIETLY WALKS AWAY...
THAT'S SIMPLE ENOUGH. I'M IN.
IDIOT! NOW YOU'RE NOT MAKING SENSE EITHER!
IT'S A GOOD OPPORTUNITY, THOUGH.
OR DO YOU WANT TO DRAG THIS OUT FOREVER?
......!
THE HELL?!
WHAT DO YOU THINK I AM?! THERE'S NO WAY I CAN PICK, LIKE, "OKAY, THIS ONE"?!
NO WAY! YOU CAN'T PICK?!
WHAAAT?
IT'S WOMAN...
OR MAN, YOU KNOW?
JUST THE FACT THAT YOU SAY YOU CAN'T PICK IS A SERIOUS SHOCK!
UH...
......
KYOICHI, ARE YOU REALLY SURE?
IMAGASE'S GAY, YOU KNOW?

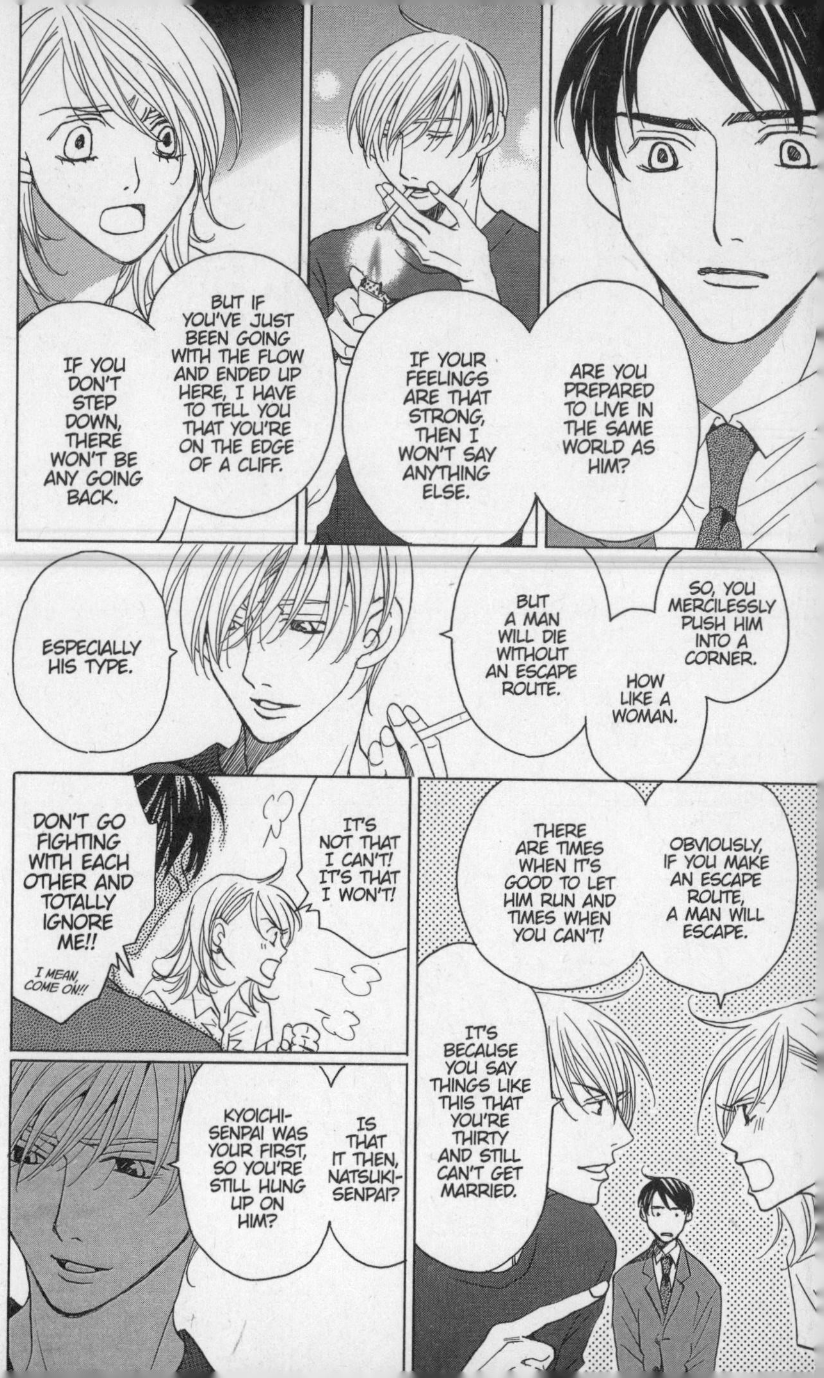
ARE YOU PREPARED TO LIVE IN THE SAME WORLD AS HIM?
IF YOUR FEELINGS ARE THAT STRONG, THEN I WON'T SAY ANYTHING ELSE.
BUT IF YOU'VE JUST BEEN GOING WITH THE FLOW AND ENDED UP HERE, I HAVE TO TELL YOU THAT YOU'RE ON THE EDGE OF A CLIFF.
IF YOU DON'T STEP DOWN, THERE WON'T BE ANY GOING BACK.
SO, YOU MERCILESSLY PUSH HIM INTO A CORNER.
HOW LIKE A WOMAN.
BUT A MAN WILL DIE WITHOUT AN ESCAPE ROUTE.
ESPECIALLY HIS TYPE.
OBVIOUSLY, IF YOU MAKE AN ESCAPE ROUTE, A MAN WILL ESCAPE.
THERE ARE TIMES WHEN IT'S GOOD TO LET HIM RUN AND TIMES WHEN YOU CAN'T!
IT'S BECAUSE YOU SAY THINGS LIKE THIS THAT YOU'RE THIRTY AND STILL CAN'T GET MARRIED.
IT'S NOT THAT I CAN'T! IT'S THAT I WON'T!
DON'T GO FIGHTING WITH EACH OTHER AND TOTALLY IGNORE ME!!
I MEAN, COME ON!!
IS THAT IT THEN, NATSUKI-SENPAI?
KYOICHI-SENPAI WAS YOUR FIRST, SO YOU'RE STILL HUNG UP ON HIM?

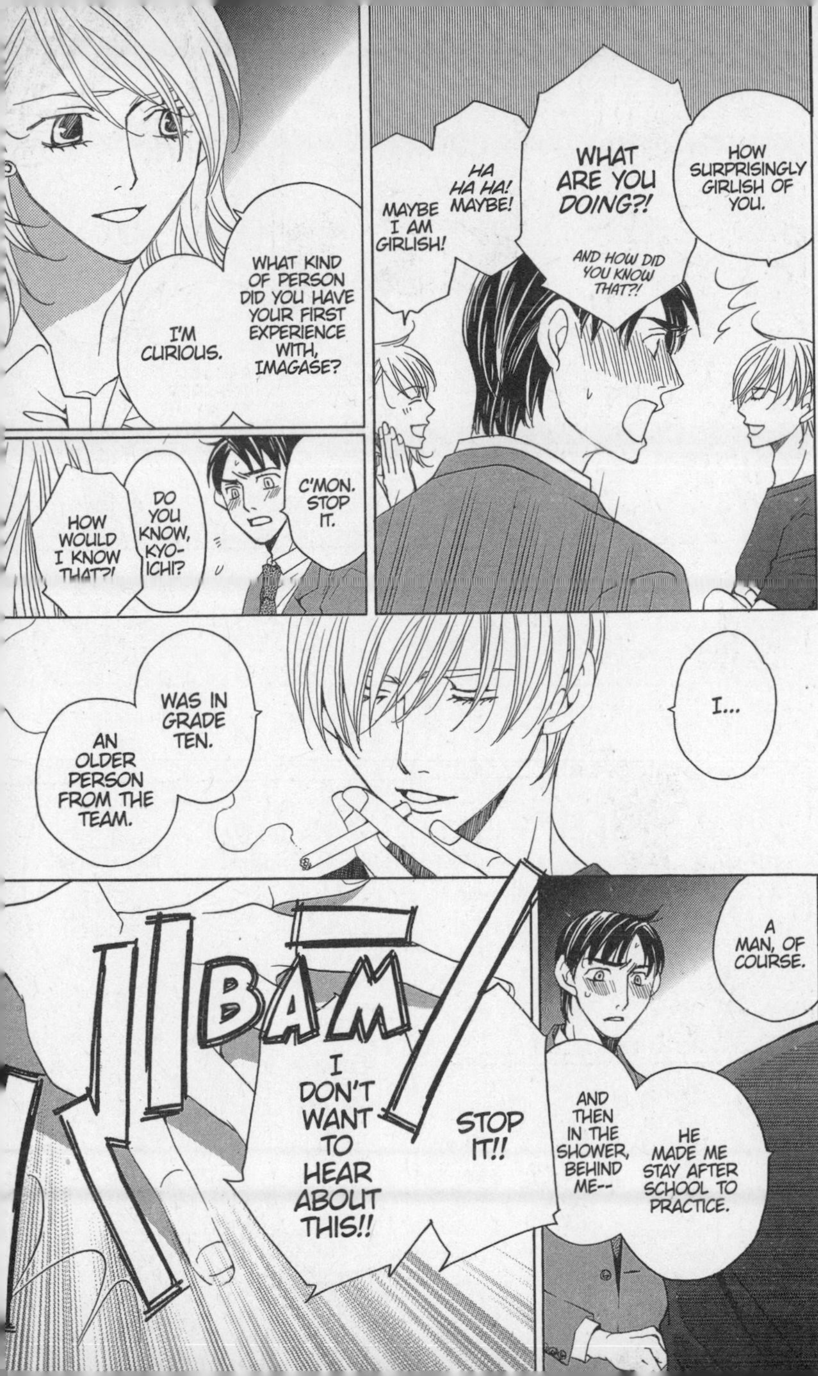

HOW SURPRISINGLY GIRLISH OF YOU.
WHAT ARE YOU DOING?!
AND HOW DID YOU KNOW THAT?!
HA HA HA! MAYBE!
MAYBE I AM GIRLISH!
WHAT KIND OF PERSON DID YOU HAVE YOUR FIRST EXPERIENCE WITH, IMAGASE?
I'M CURIOUS.
C'MON. STOP IT.
DO YOU KNOW, KYO-ICHI?
HOW WOULD I KNOW THAT?!
I...
WAS IN GRADE TEN.
AN OLDER PERSON FROM THE TEAM.
A MAN, OF COURSE.
HE MADE ME STAY AFTER SCHOOL TO PRACTICE.
AND THEN IN THE SHOWER, BEHIND ME--
STOP IT!!
BAM
I DON'T WANT TO HEAR ABOUT THIS!!

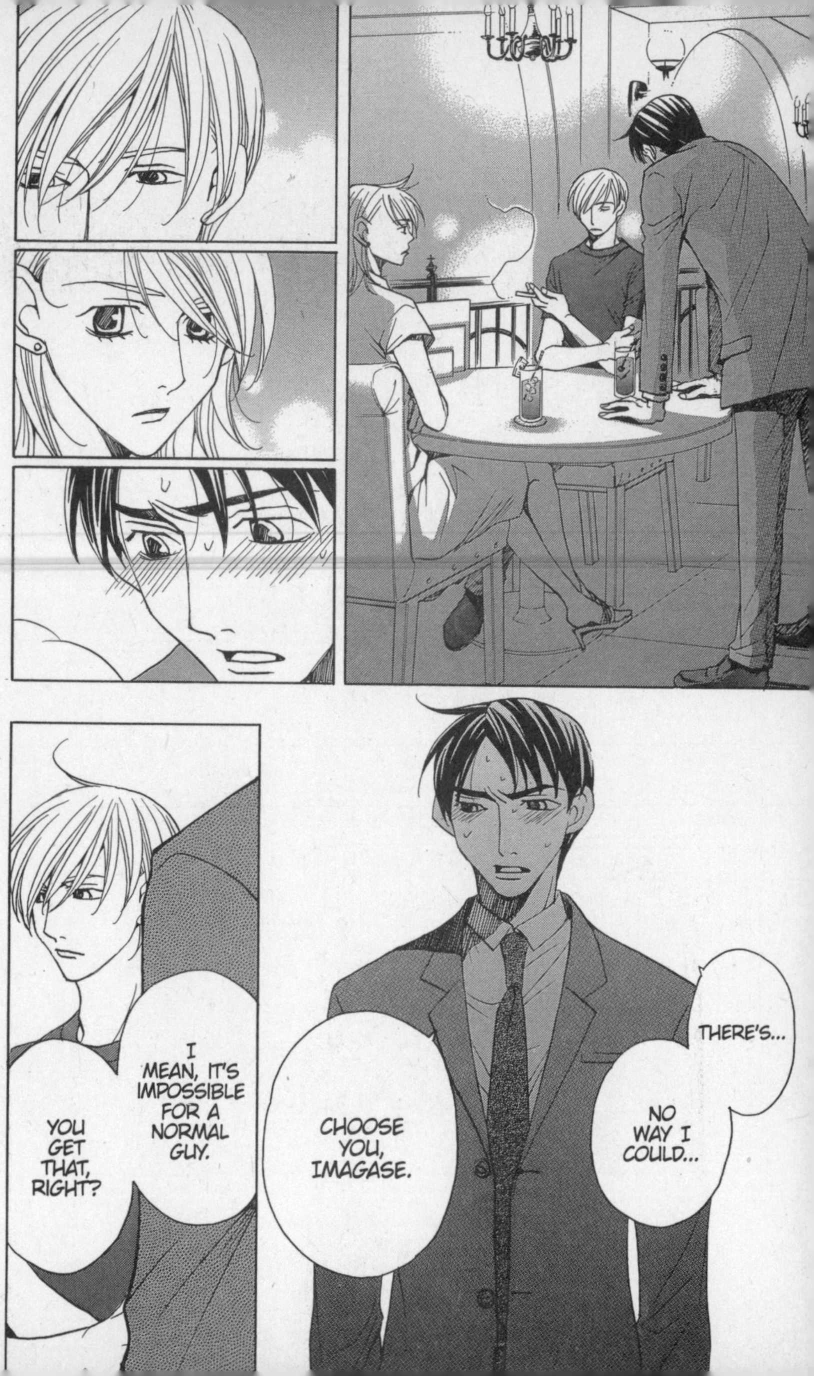
THERE'S...
NO WAY I COULD...
CHOOSE YOU, IMAGASE.
I MEAN, IT'S IMPOSSIBLE FOR A NORMAL GUY.
YOU GET THAT, RIGHT?

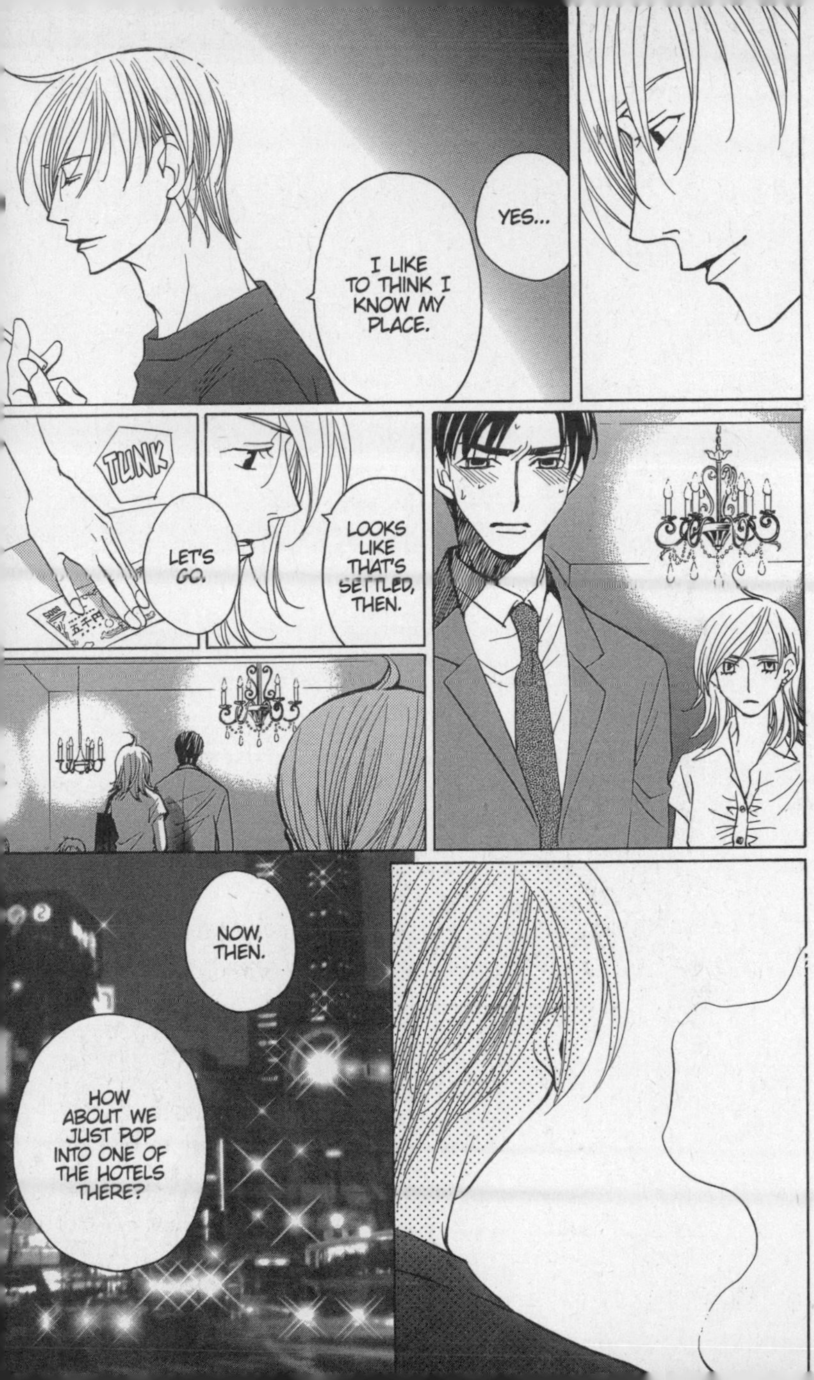
YES...
I LIKE TO THINK I KNOW MY PLACE.
LOOKS LIKE THAT'S SETTLED, THEN.
TUNK
LET'S GO.
NOW, THEN.
HOW ABOUT WE JUST POP INTO ONE OF THE HOTELS THERE?

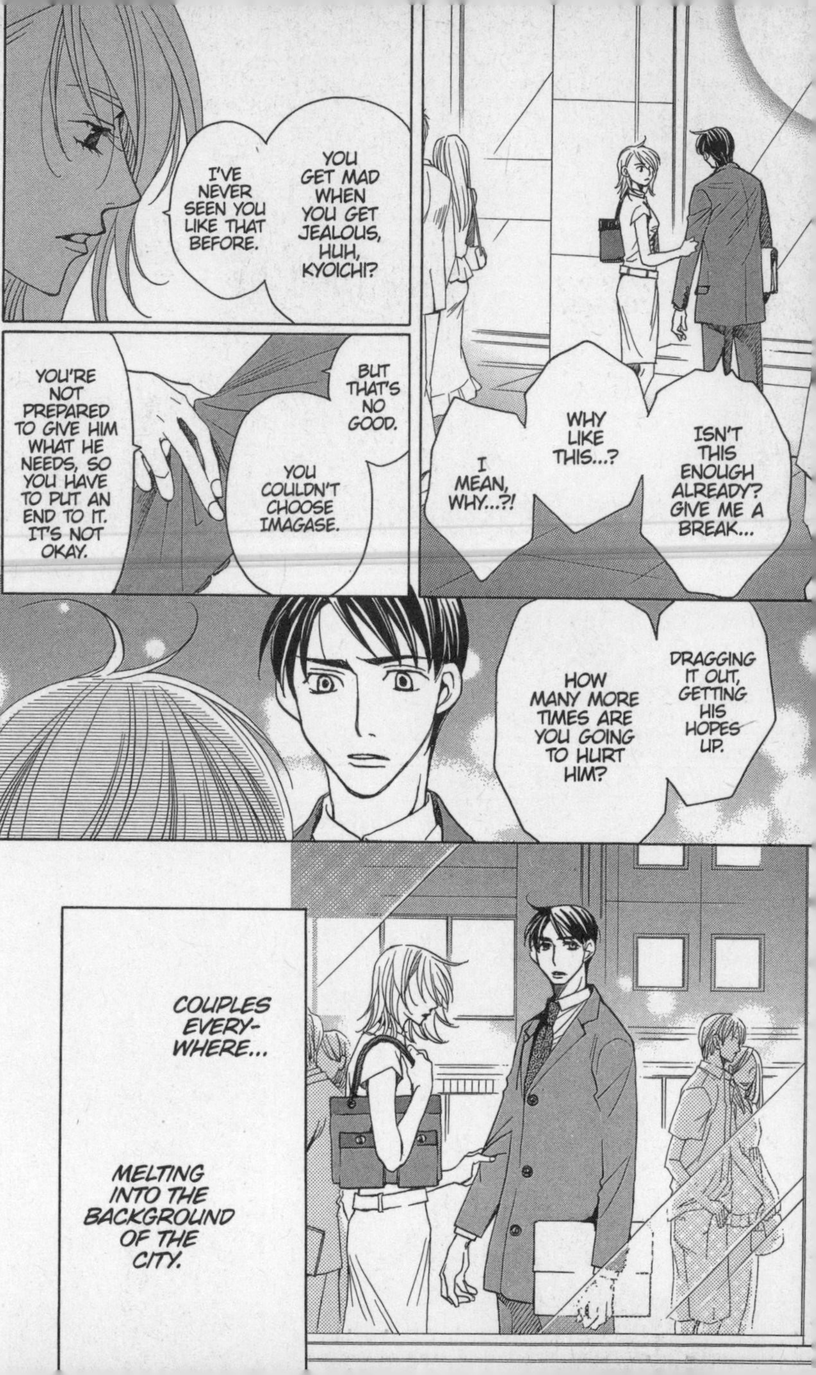
ISN'T THIS ENOUGH ALREADY? GIVE ME A BREAK...
WHY LIKE THIS...?
I MEAN, WHY...?!
YOU GET MAD WHEN YOU GET JEALOUS, HUH, KYOICHI?
I'VE NEVER SEEN YOU LIKE THAT BEFORE.
BUT THAT'S NO GOOD.
YOU COULDN'T CHOOSE IMAGASE.
YOU'RE NOT PREPARED TO GIVE HIM WHAT HE NEEDS, SO YOU HAVE TO PUT AN END TO IT. IT'S NOT OKAY.
DRAGGING IT OUT, GETTING HIS HOPES UP.
HOW MANY MORE TIMES ARE YOU GOING TO HURT HIM?
COUPLES EVERY-WHERE...
MELTING INTO THE BACKGROUND OF THE CITY.

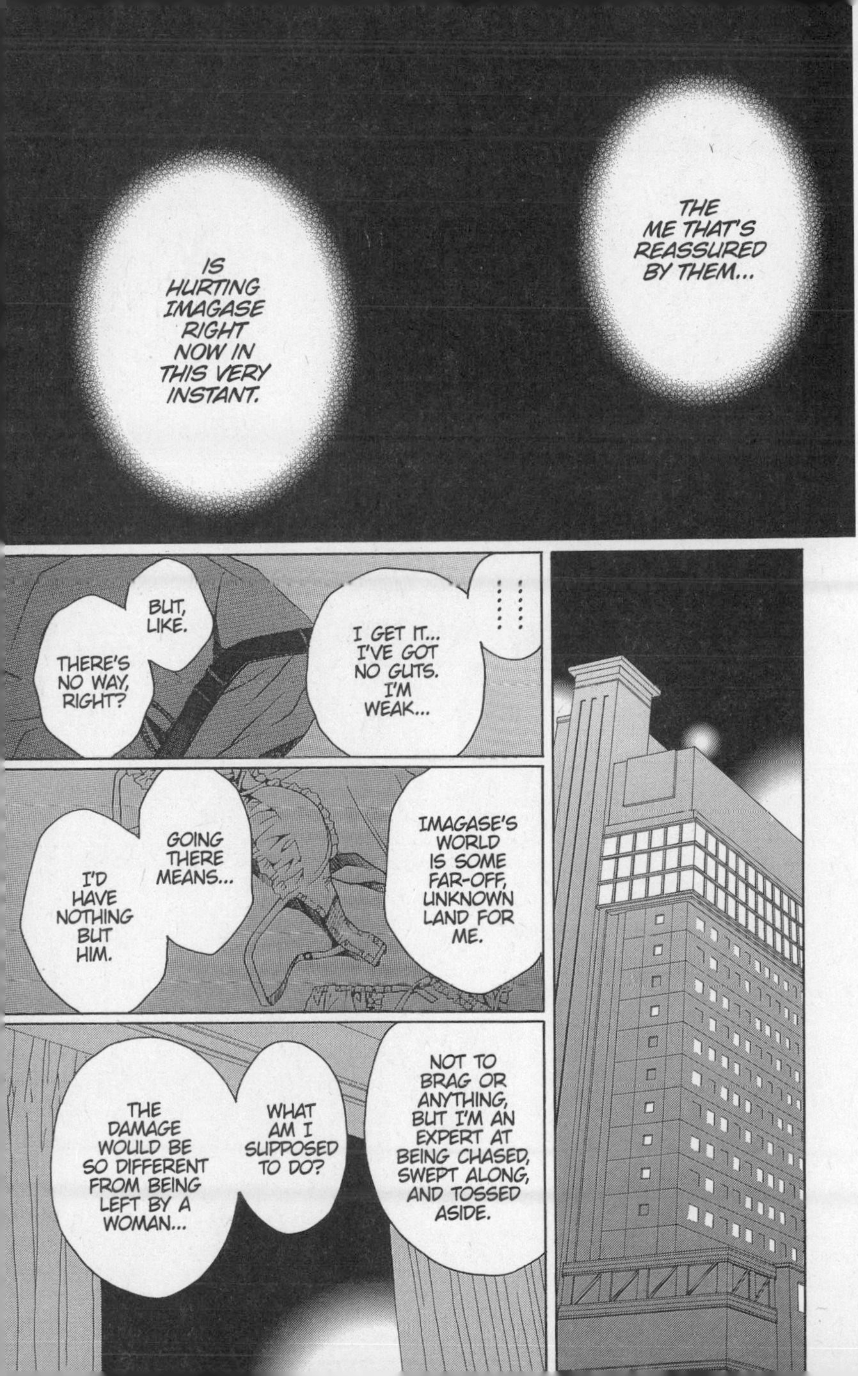
THE ME THAT'S REASSURED BY THEM...
IS HURTING IMAGASE RIGHT NOW IN THIS VERY INSTANT.
......
I GET IT... I'VE GOT NO GUTS. I'M WEAK...
BUT, LIKE.
THERE'S NO WAY, RIGHT?
IMAGASE'S WORLD IS SOME FAR-OFF, UNKNOWN LAND FOR ME.
GOING THERE MEANS...
I'D HAVE NOTHING BUT HIM.
NOT TO BRAG OR ANYTHING, BUT I'M AN EXPERT AT BEING CHASED, SWEPT ALONG, AND TOSSED ASIDE.
WHAT AM I SUPPOSED TO DO?
THE DAMAGE WOULD BE SO DIFFERENT FROM BEING LEFT BY A WOMAN...

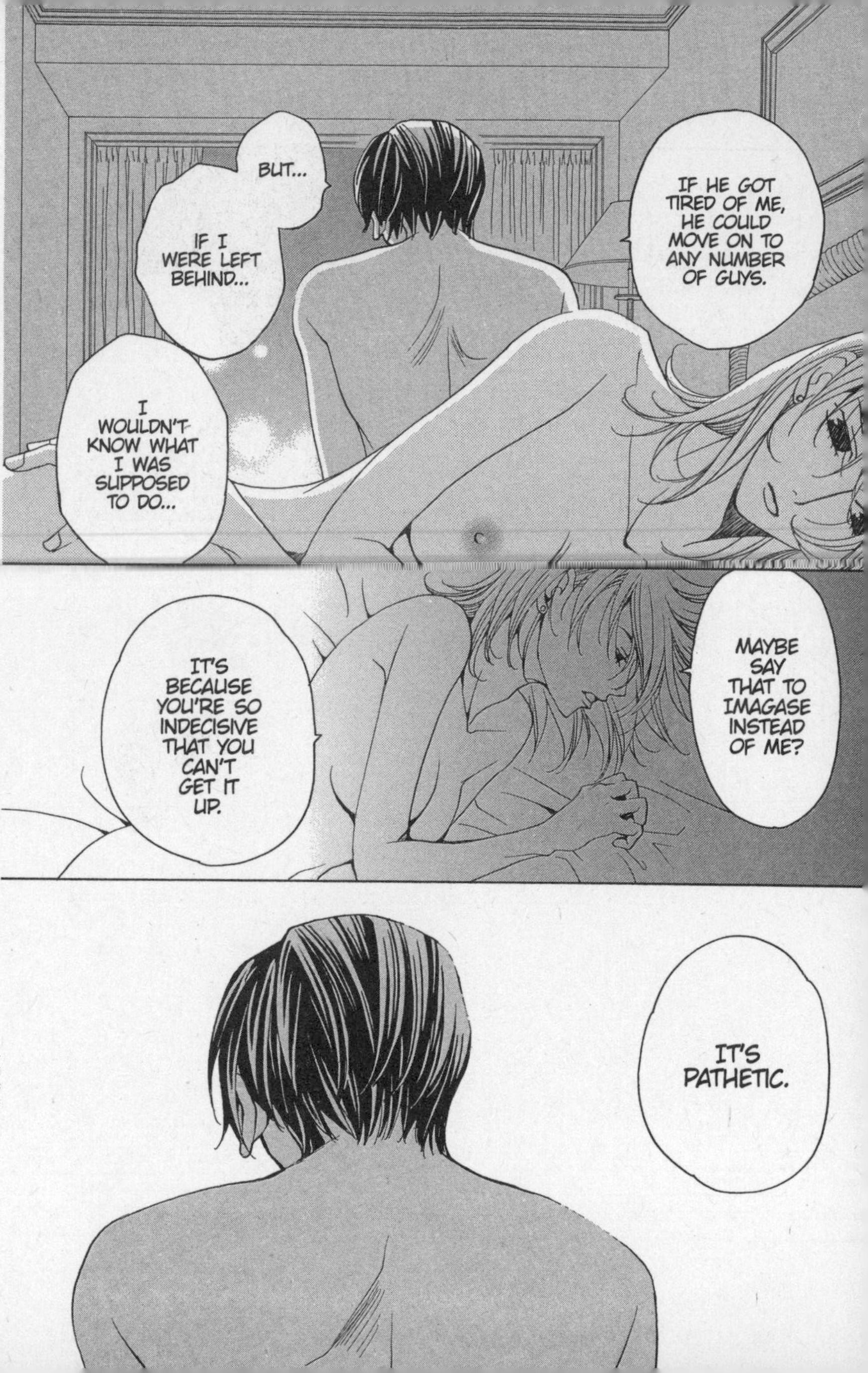
IF HE GOT TIRED OF ME, HE COULD MOVE ON TO ANY NUMBER OF GUYS.
BUT...
IF I WERE LEFT BEHIND...
I WOULDN'T KNOW WHAT I WAS SUPPOSED TO DO...
MAYBE SAY THAT TO IMAGASE INSTEAD OF ME?
IT'S BECAUSE YOU'RE SO INDECISIVE THAT YOU CAN'T GET IT UP.
IT'S PATHETIC.

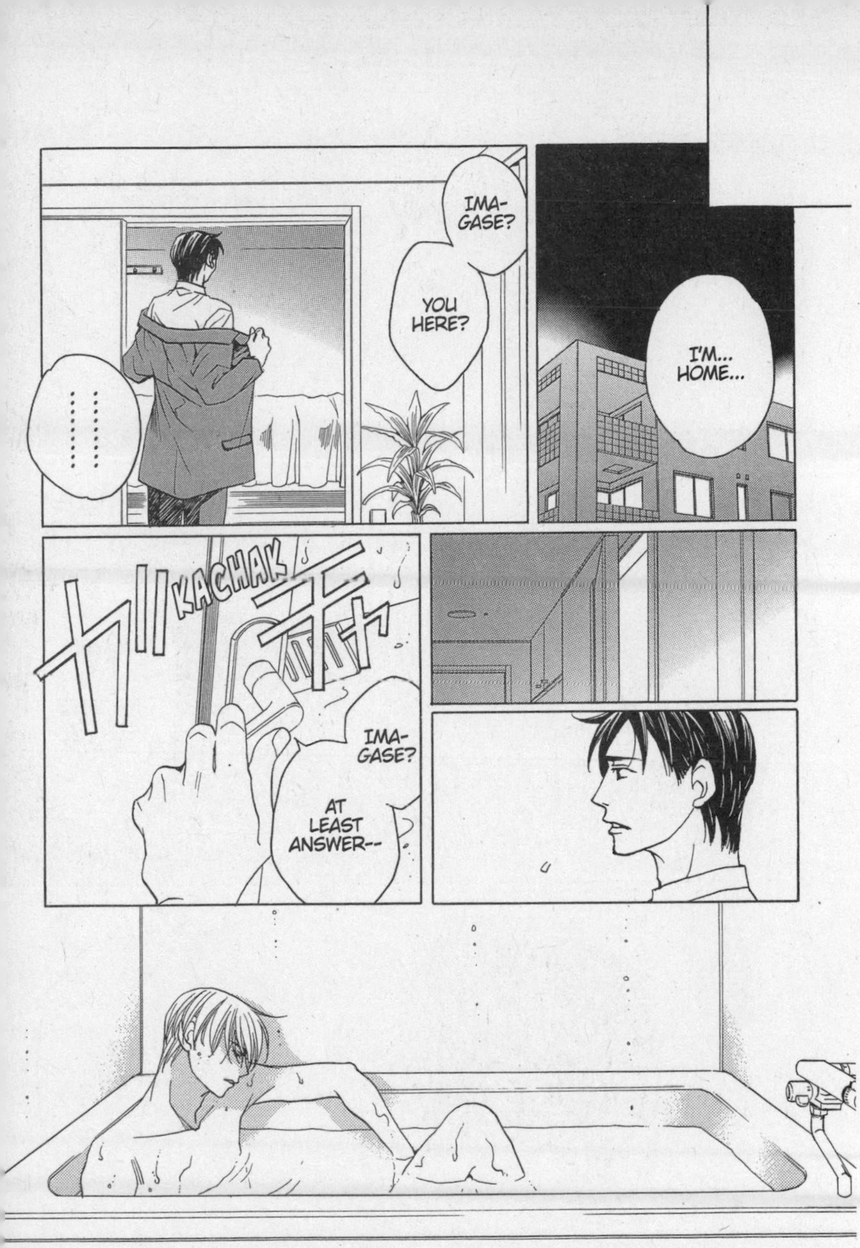
I'M... HOME...
IMA-GASE?
YOU HERE?
......
KACHAK
IMA-GASE?
AT LEAST ANSWER--

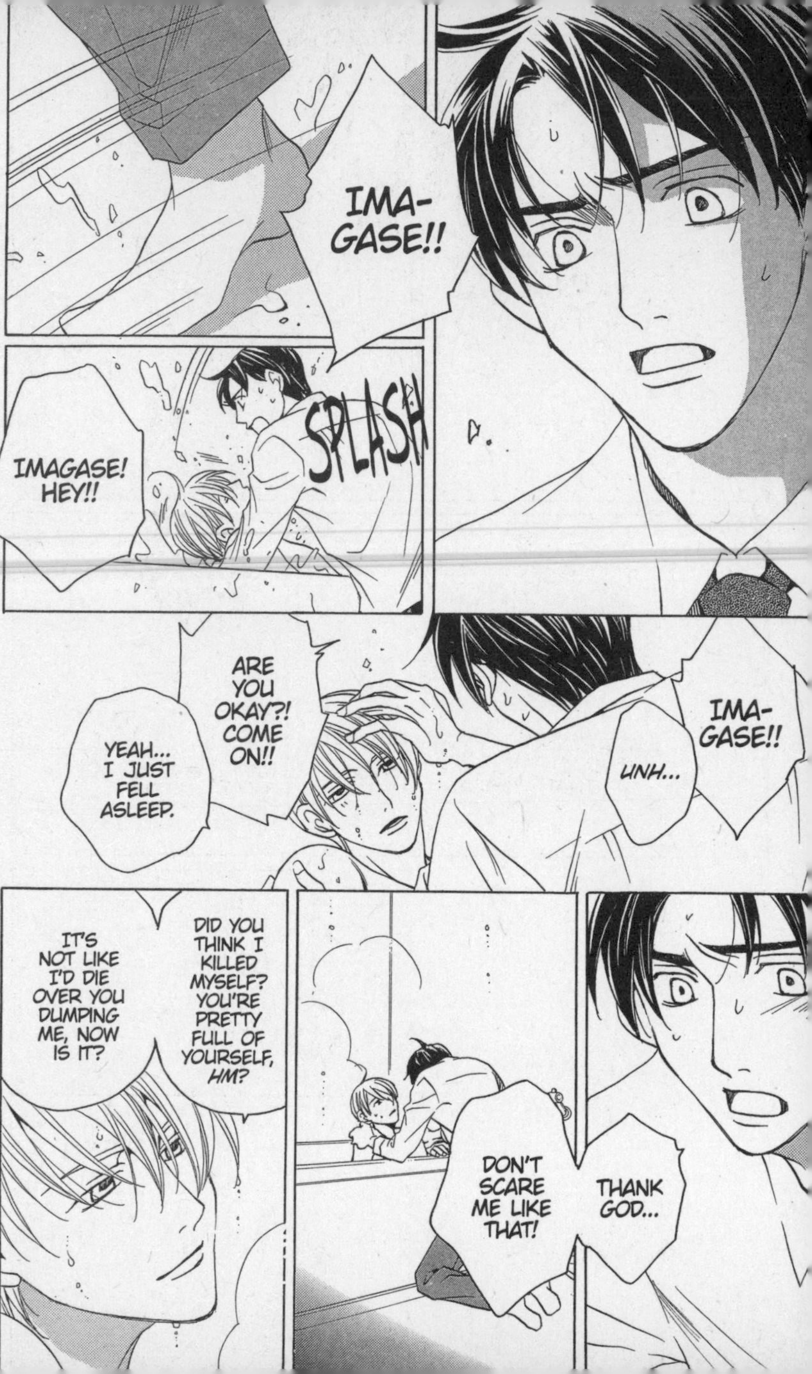
IMA-GASE!!
IMAGASE! HEY!!
SPLASH
IMA-GASE!!
UNH...
ARE YOU OKAY?! COME ON!!
YEAH... I JUST FELL ASLEEP.
THANK GOD...
DON'T SCARE ME LIKE THAT!
DID YOU THINK I KILLED MYSELF? YOU'RE PRETTY FULL OF YOURSELF, HM?
IT'S NOT LIKE I'D DIE OVER YOU DUMPING ME, NOW IS IT?

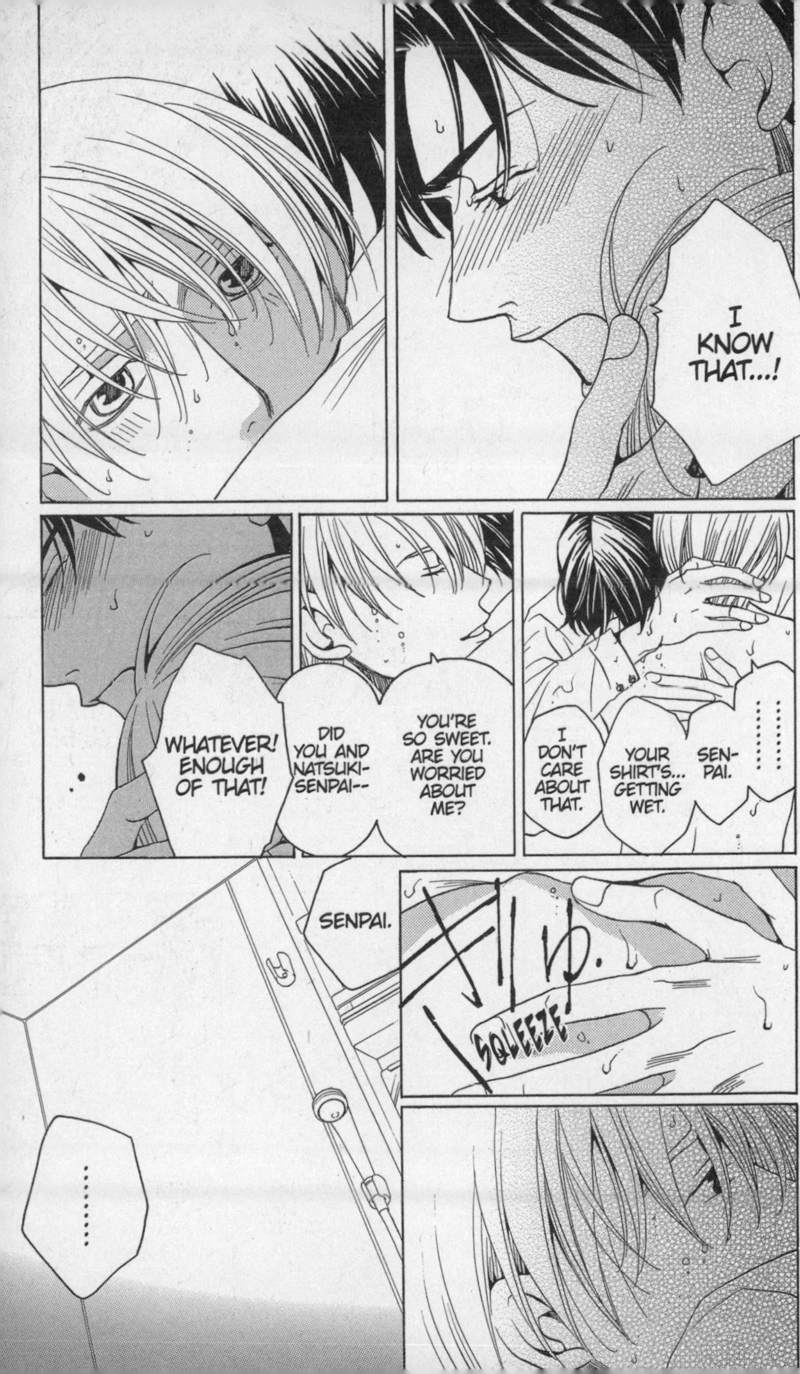
I KNOW THAT...!
......
SEN-PAI.
YOUR SHIRT'S... GETTING WET.
I DON'T CARE ABOUT THAT.
YOU'RE SO SWEET. ARE YOU WORRIED ABOUT ME?
DID YOU AND NATSUKI-SENPAI--
WHATEVER! ENOUGH OF THAT!
SQUEEZE
SENPAI.
......

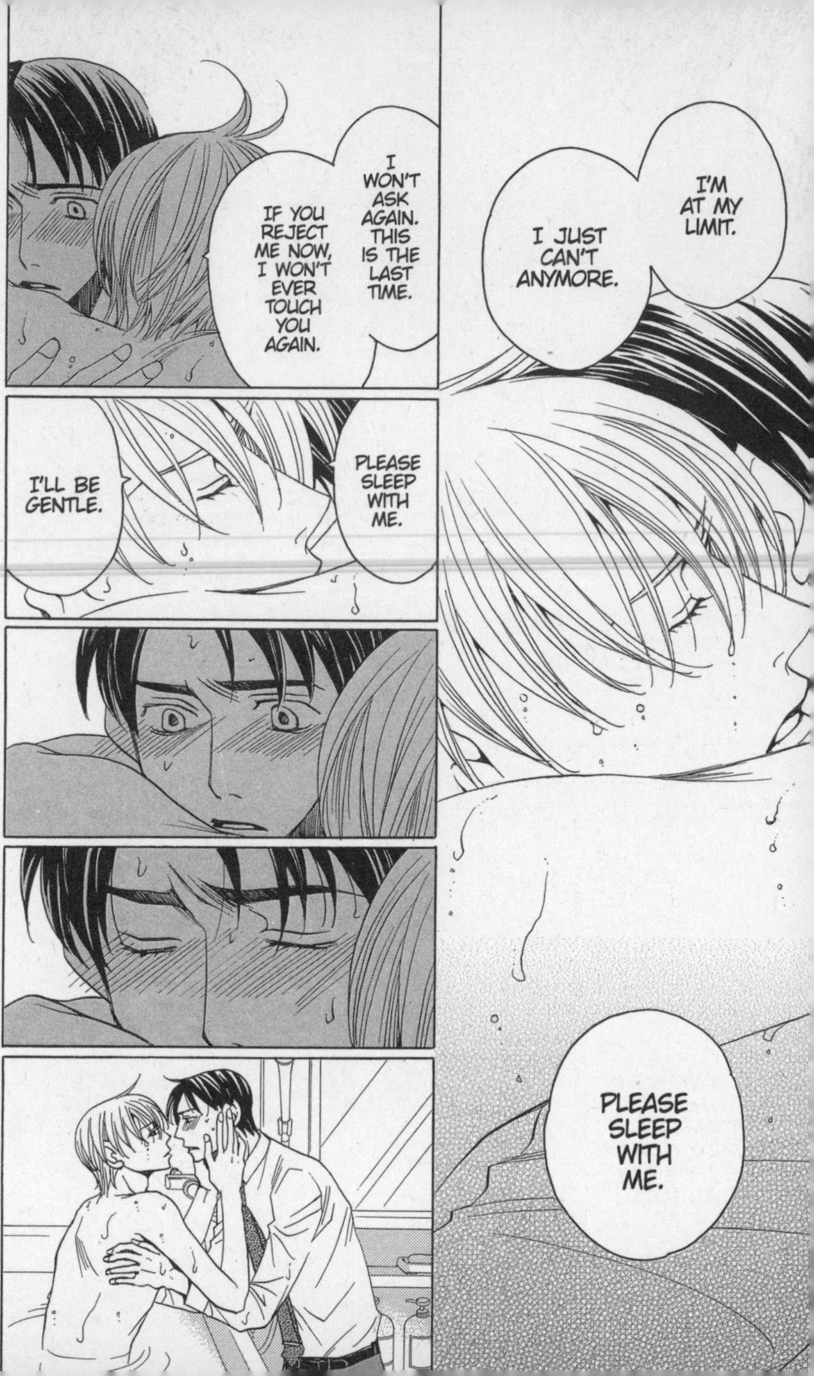
I'M AT MY LIMIT.
I JUST CAN'T ANYMORE.
PLEASE SLEEP WITH ME.
I WON'T ASK AGAIN. THIS IS THE LAST TIME.
IF YOU REJECT ME NOW, I WON'T EVER TOUCH YOU AGAIN.
PLEASE SLEEP WITH ME.
I'LL BE GENTLE.

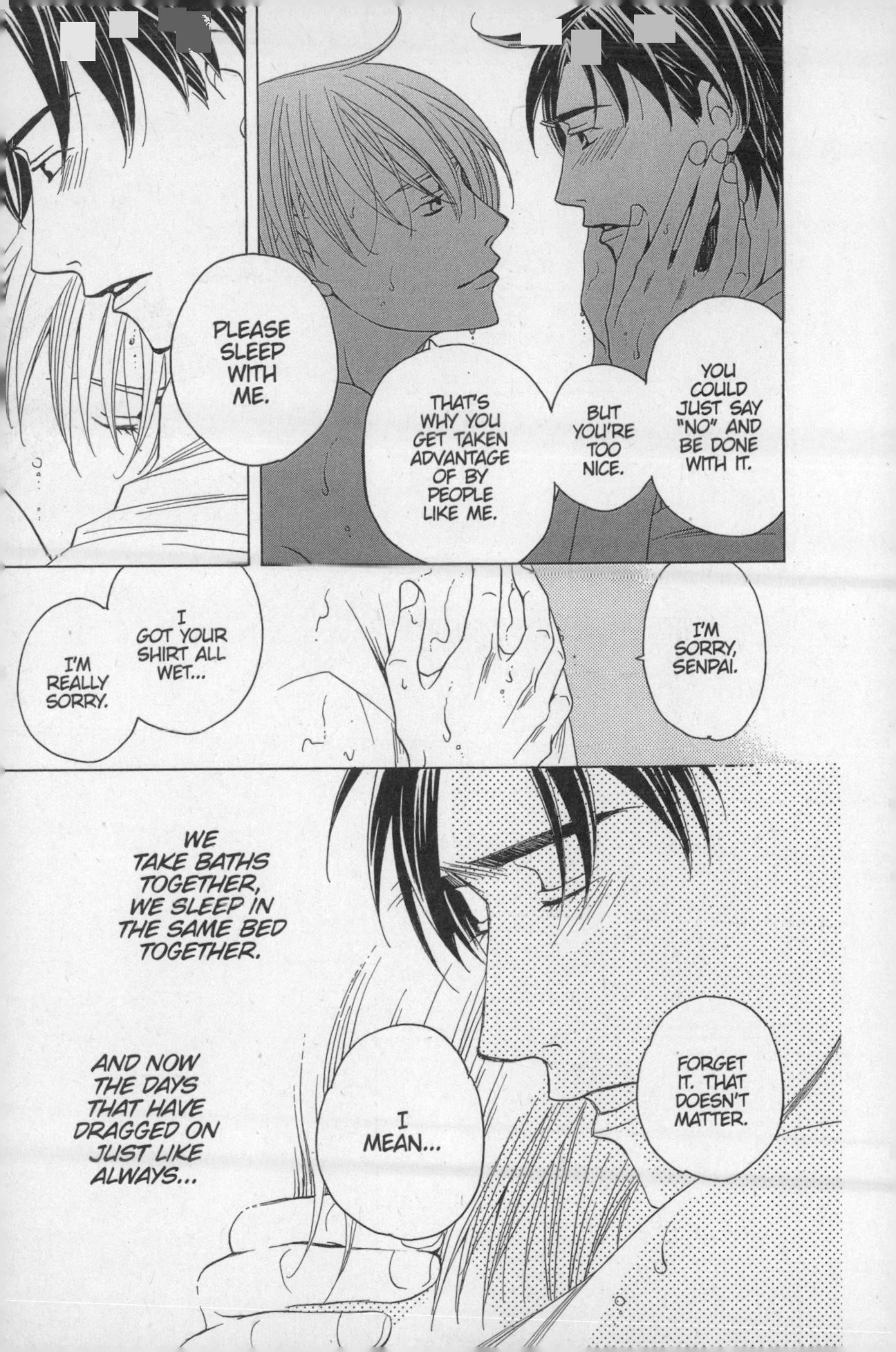
YOU COULD JUST SAY "NO" AND BE DONE WITH IT.
BUT YOU'RE TOO NICE.
THAT'S WHY YOU GET TAKEN ADVANTAGE OF BY PEOPLE LIKE ME.
PLEASE SLEEP WITH ME.
I'M SORRY, SENPAI.
I GOT YOUR SHIRT ALL WET...
I'M REALLY SORRY.
FORGET IT. THAT DOESN'T MATTER.
I MEAN...
WE TAKE BATHS TOGETHER, WE SLEEP IN THE SAME BED TOGETHER.
AND NOW THE DAYS THAT HAVE DRAGGED ON JUST LIKE ALWAYS...

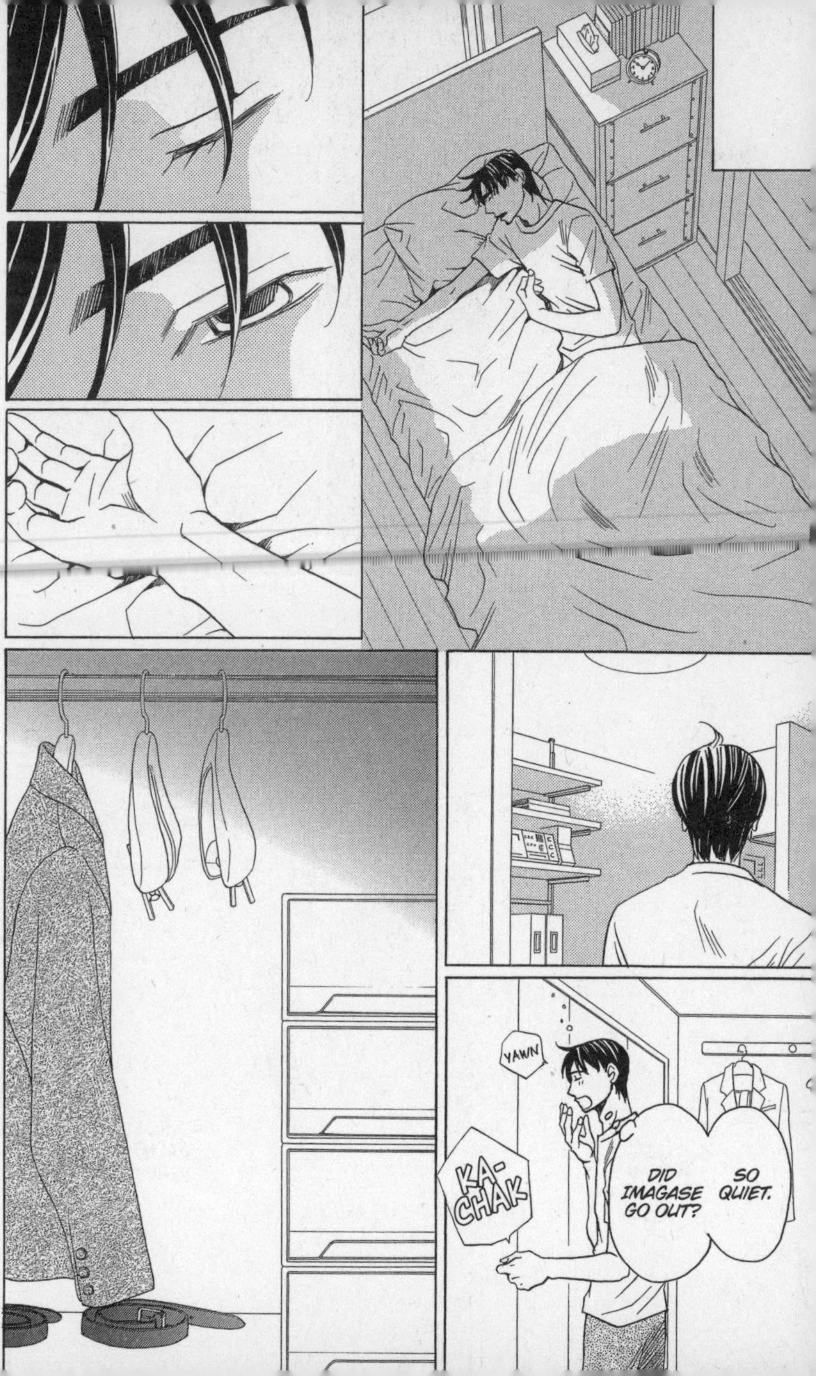
YAWN
KA-CHAK
SO QUIET.
DID IMAGASE GO OUT?

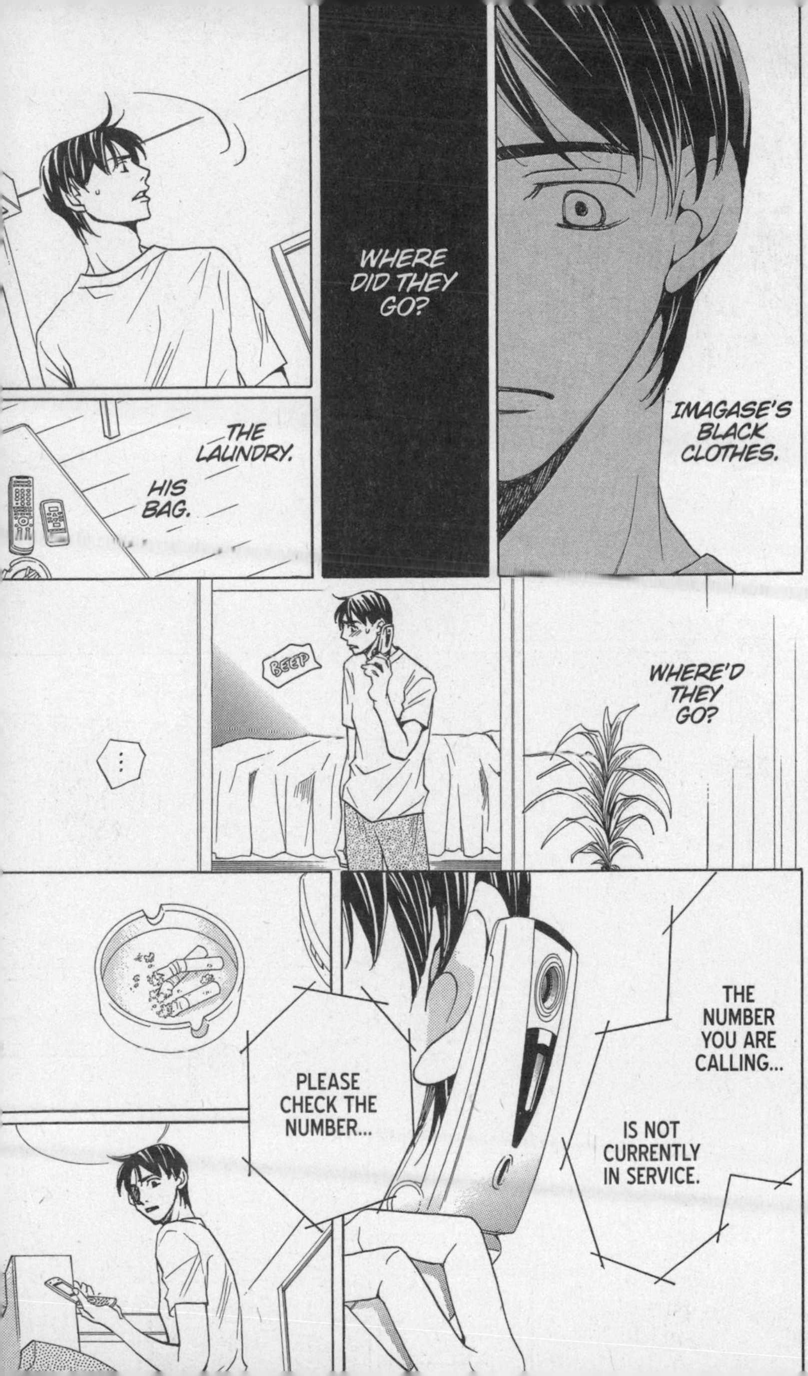
IMAGASE'S BLACK CLOTHES.
WHERE DID THEY GO?
THE LAUNDRY.
HIS BAG.
WHERE'D THEY GO?
BEEP
...
THE NUMBER YOU ARE CALLING...
IS NOT CURRENTLY IN SERVICE.
PLEASE CHECK THE NUMBER...

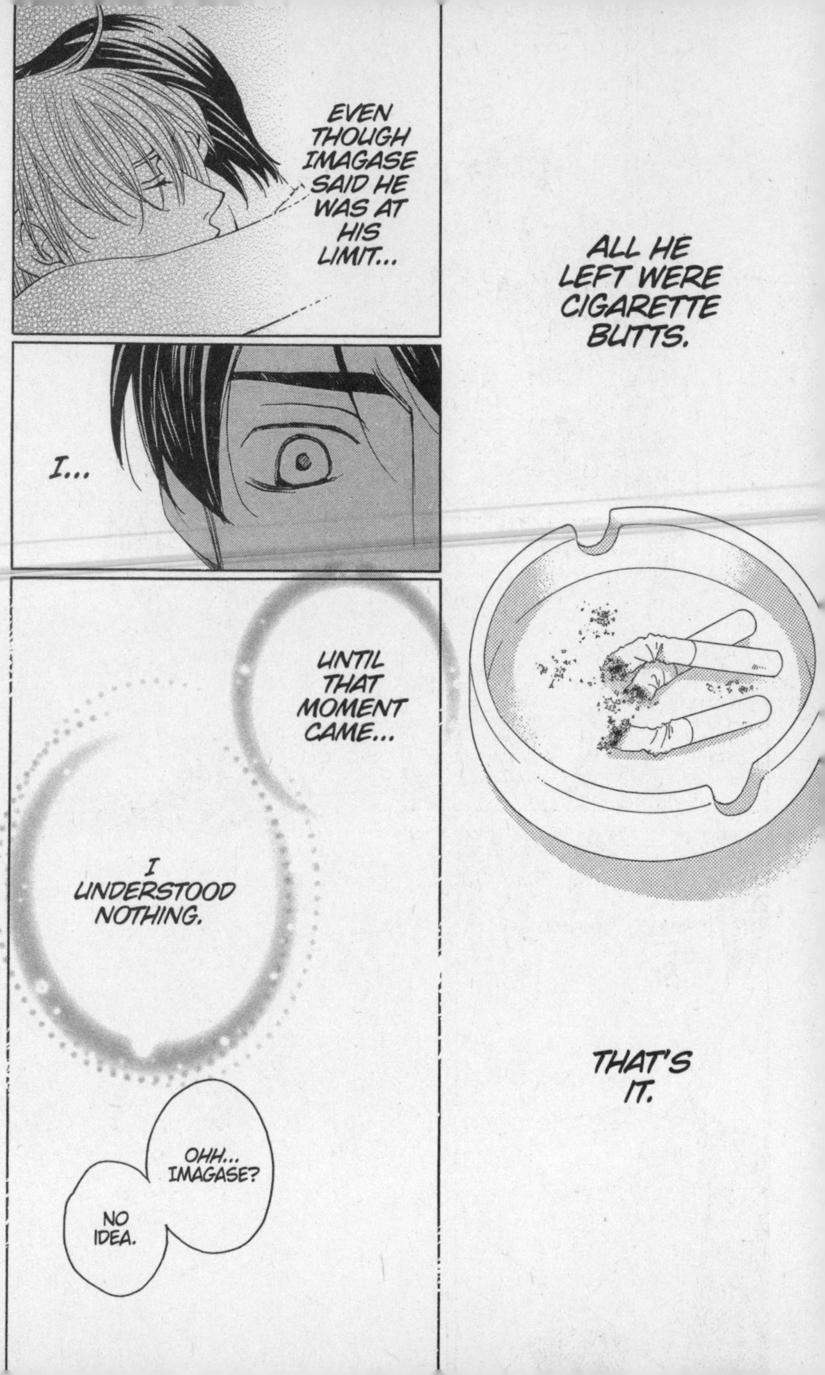
ALL HE LEFT WERE CIGARETTE BUTTS.
THAT'S IT.
EVEN THOUGH IMAGASE SAID HE WAS AT HIS LIMIT...
I...
UNTIL THAT MOMENT CAME...
I UNDERSTOOD NOTHING.
OHH... IMAGASE?
NO IDEA.

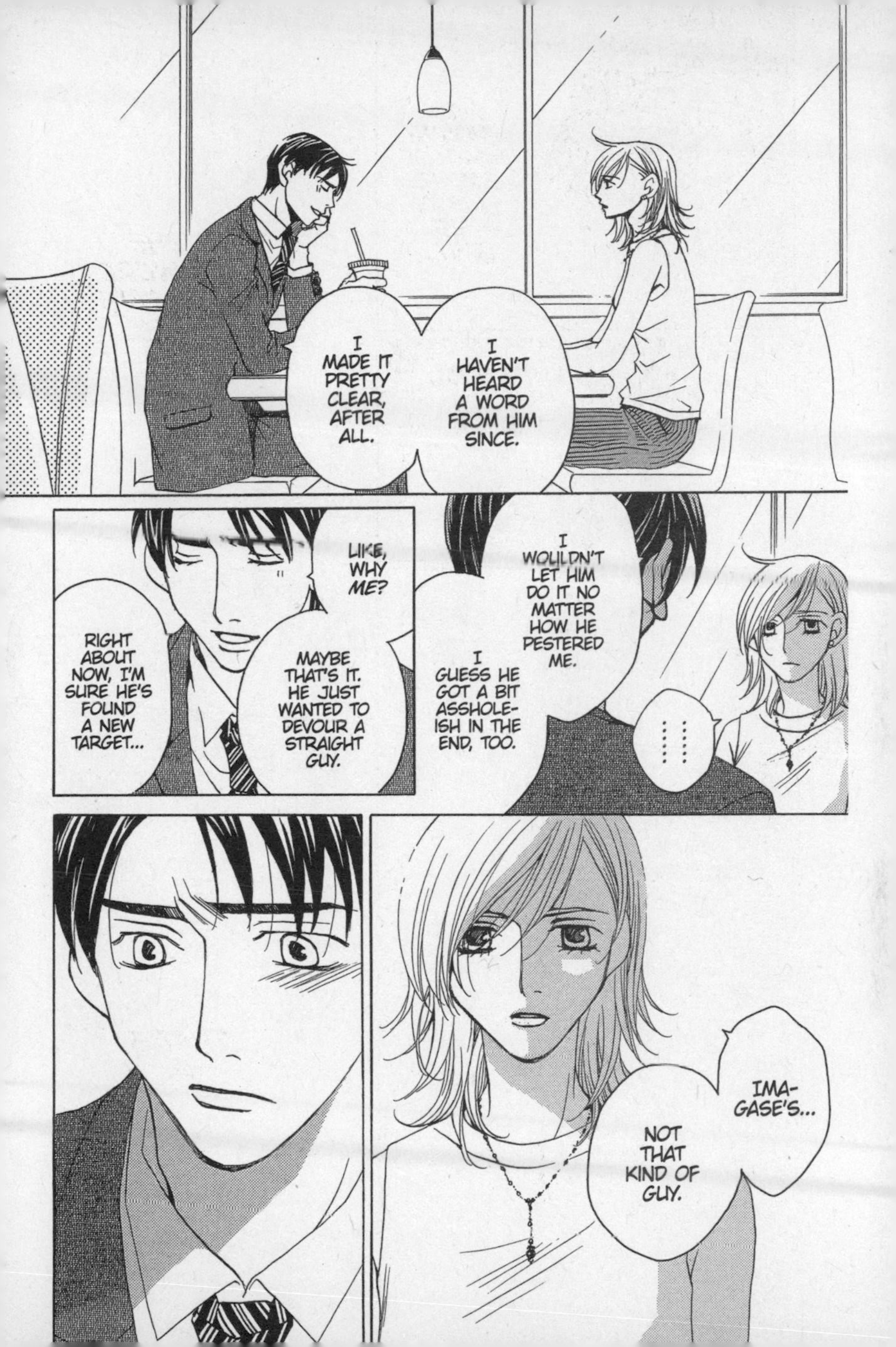
I HAVEN'T HEARD A WORD FROM HIM SINCE.
I MADE IT PRETTY CLEAR, AFTER ALL.
I WOULDN'T LET HIM DO IT NO MATTER HOW HE PESTERED ME.
I GUESS HE GOT A BIT ASSHOLE-ISH IN THE END, TOO.
......
LIKE, WHY ME?
MAYBE THAT'S IT. HE JUST WANTED TO DEVOUR A STRAIGHT GUY.
RIGHT ABOUT NOW, I'M SURE HE'S FOUND A NEW TARGET...
IMA-GASE'S...
NOT THAT KIND OF GUY.

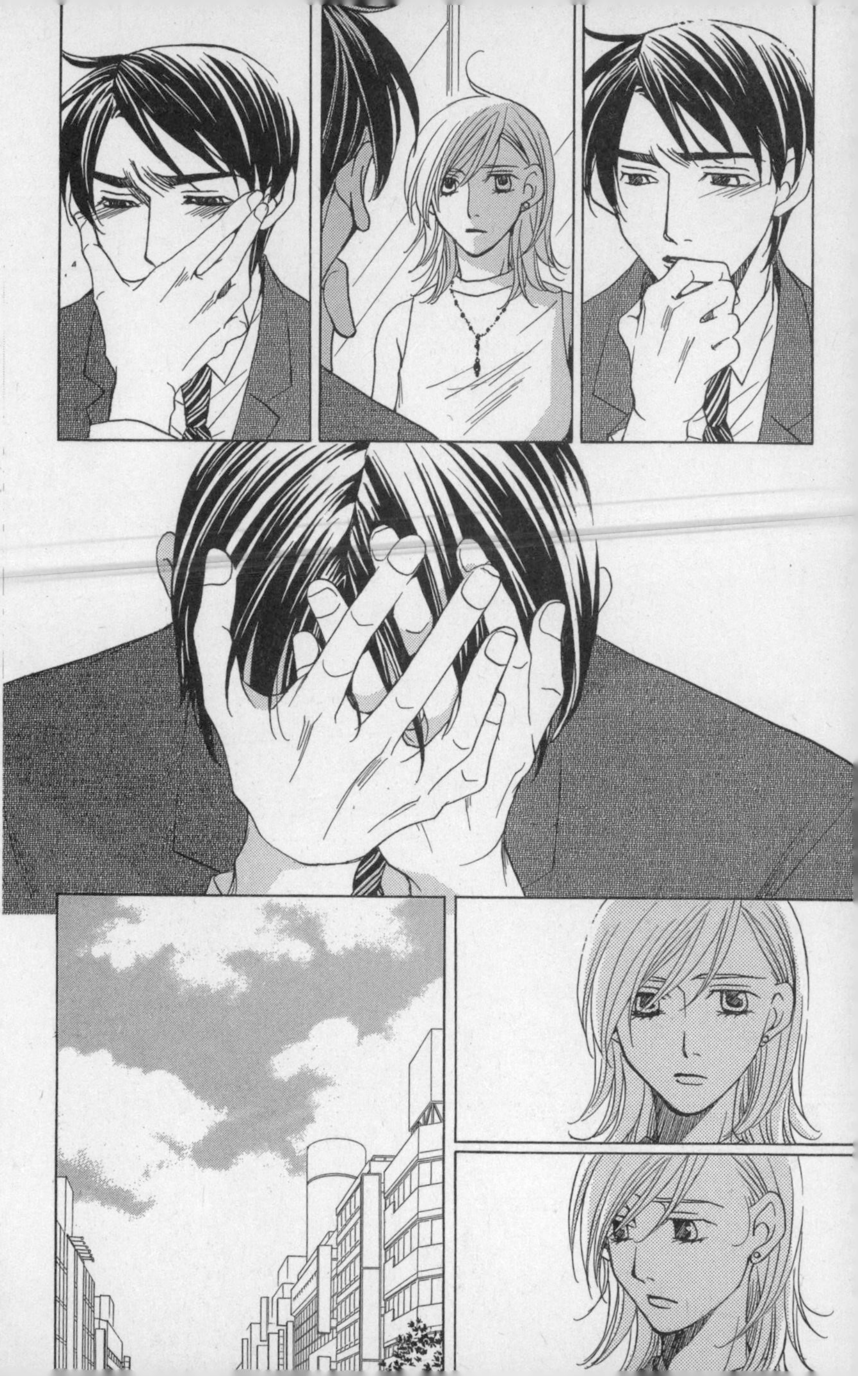

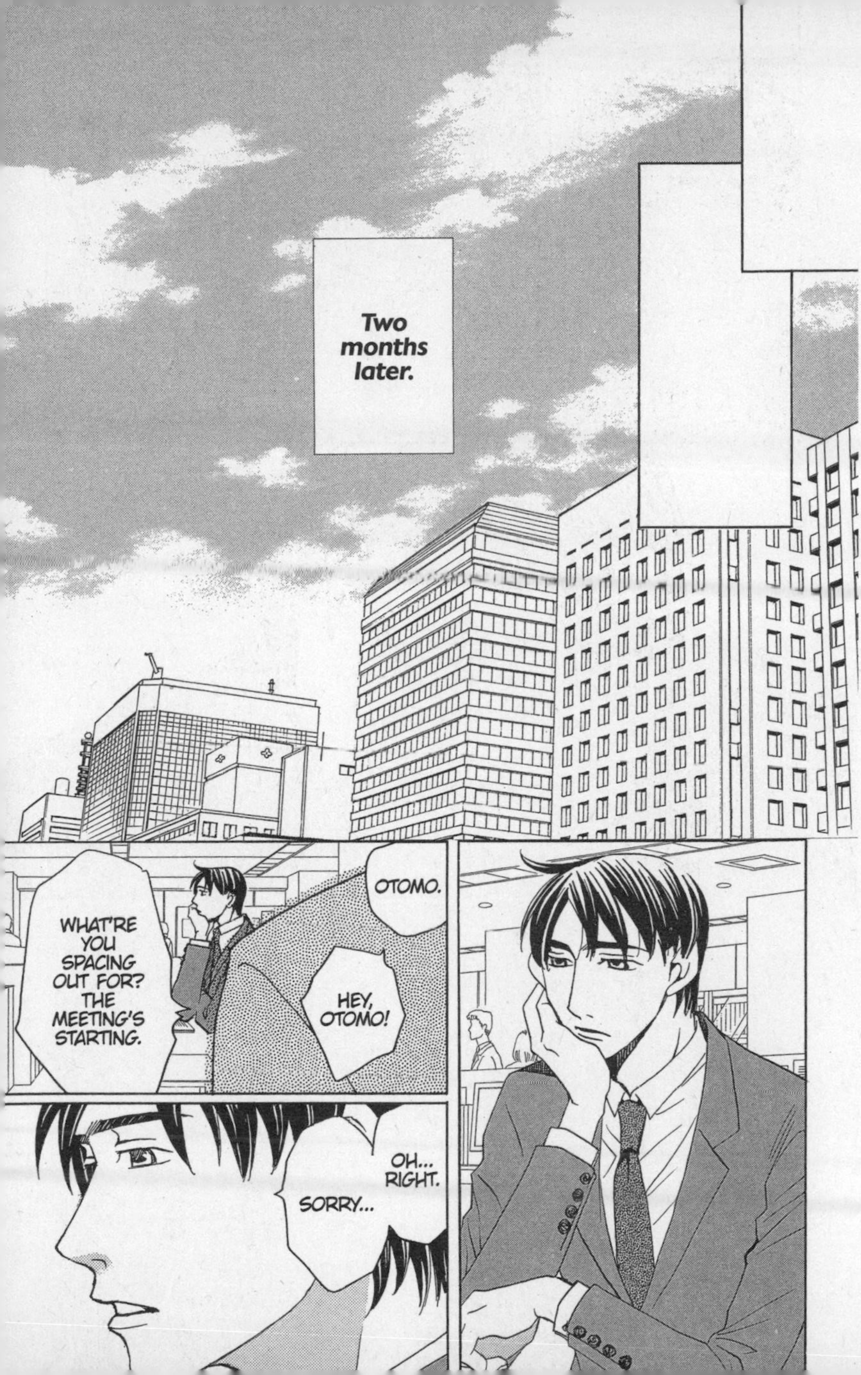
Two months later.
OTOMO.
HEY, OTOMO!
WHAT'RE YOU SPACING OUT FOR? THE MEETING'S STARTING.
OH... RIGHT.
SORRY...

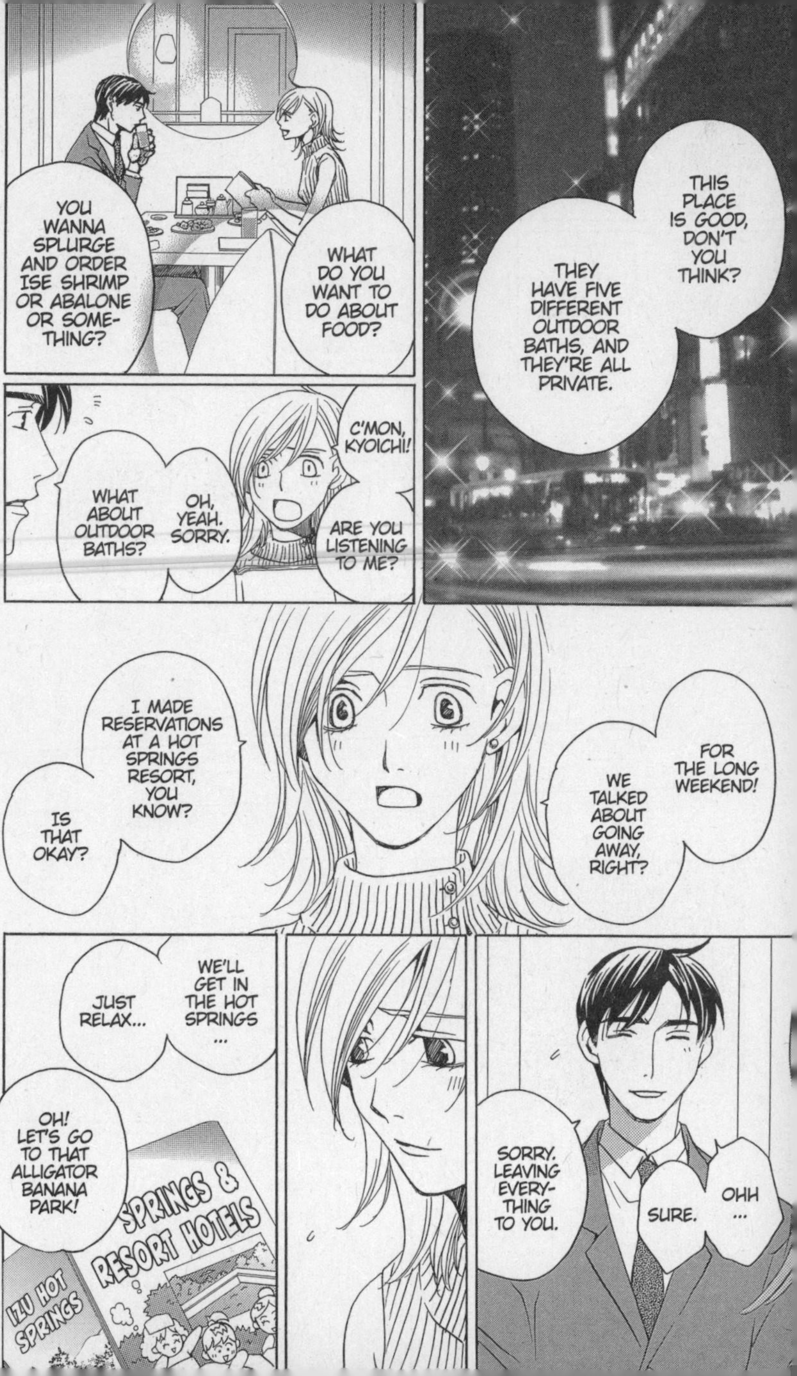
THIS PLACE IS GOOD, DON'T YOU THINK?
THEY HAVE FIVE DIFFERENT OUTDOOR BATHS, AND THEY'RE ALL PRIVATE.
WHAT DO YOU WANT TO DO ABOUT FOOD?
YOU WANNA SPLURGE AND ORDER ISE SHRIMP OR ABALONE OR SOME-THING?
C'MON, KYOICHI!
ARE YOU LISTENING TO ME?
OH, YEAH. SORRY.
WHAT ABOUT OUTDOOR BATHS?
FOR THE LONG WEEKEND!
WE TALKED ABOUT GOING AWAY, RIGHT?
I MADE RESERVATIONS AT A HOT SPRINGS RESORT, YOU KNOW?
IS THAT OKAY?
OHH ...
SURE.
SORRY. LEAVING EVERY-THING TO YOU.
WE'LL GET IN THE HOT SPRINGS ...
JUST RELAX...
OH! LET'S GO TO THAT ALLIGATOR BANANA PARK!
SPRINGS & RESORT HOTELS
IZU HOT SPRINGS

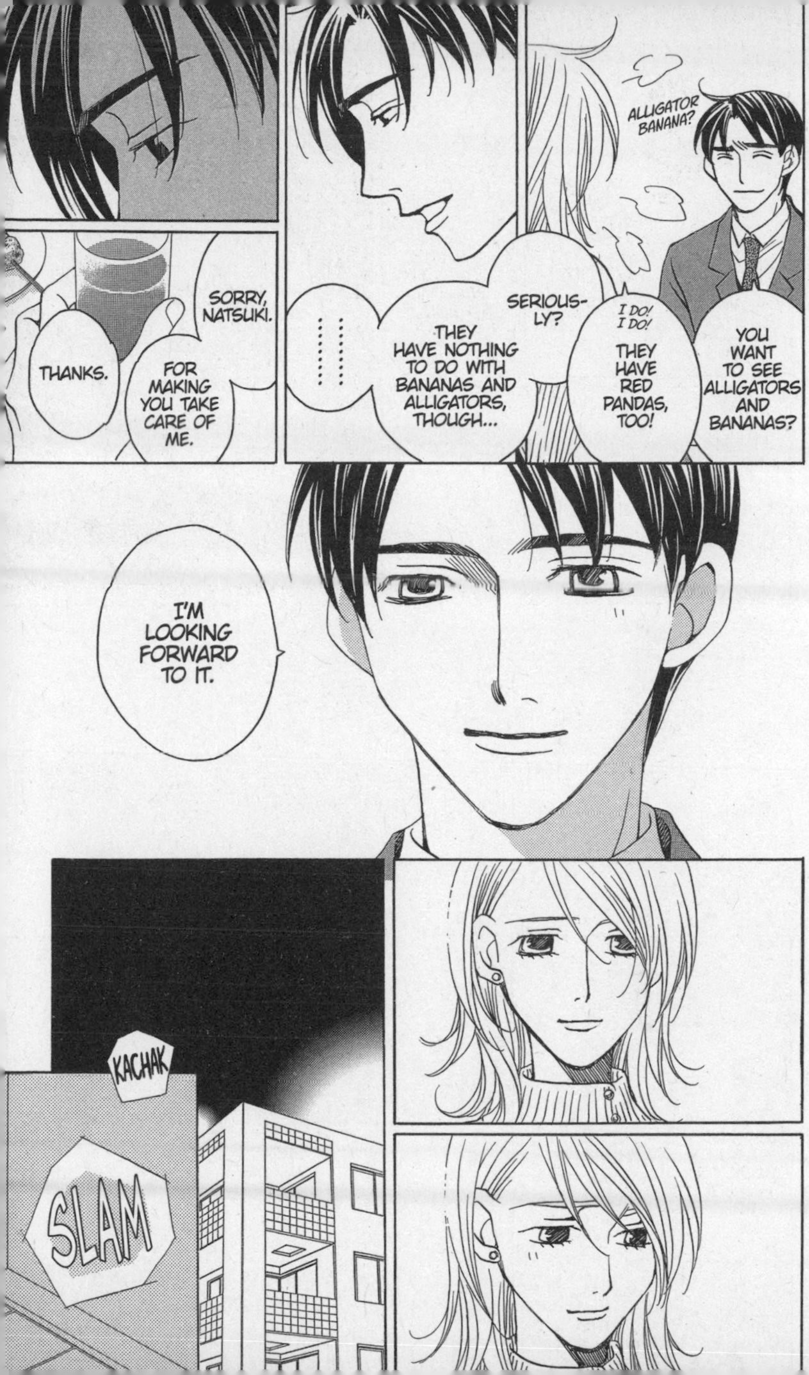

ALLIGATOR BANANA?
YOU WANT TO SEE ALLIGATORS AND BANANAS?
I DO! I DO!
THEY HAVE RED PANDAS, TOO!
SERIOUS-LY?
THEY HAVE NOTHING TO DO WITH BANANAS AND ALLIGATORS, THOUGH...
......
SORRY, NATSUKI.
FOR MAKING YOU TAKE CARE OF ME.
THANKS.
I'M LOOKING FORWARD TO IT.
KACHAK
SLAM

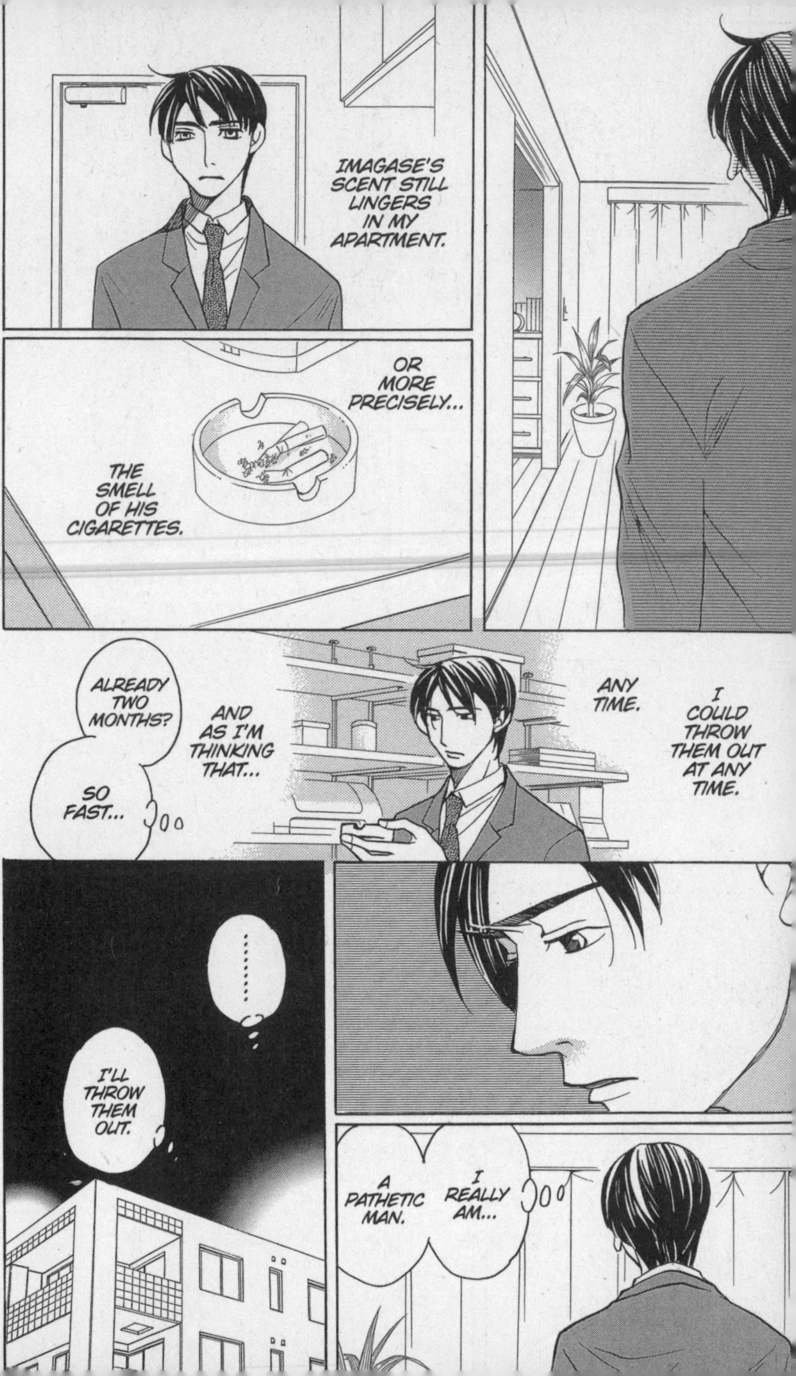
IMAGASE'S SCENT STILL LINGERS IN MY APARTMENT.
OR MORE PRECISELY...
THE SMELL OF HIS CIGARETTES.
I COULD THROW THEM OUT AT ANY TIME.
ANY TIME.
AND AS I'M THINKING THAT...
ALREADY TWO MONTHS?
SO FAST...
I REALLY AM...
A PATHETIC MAN.
......
I'LL THROW THEM OUT.

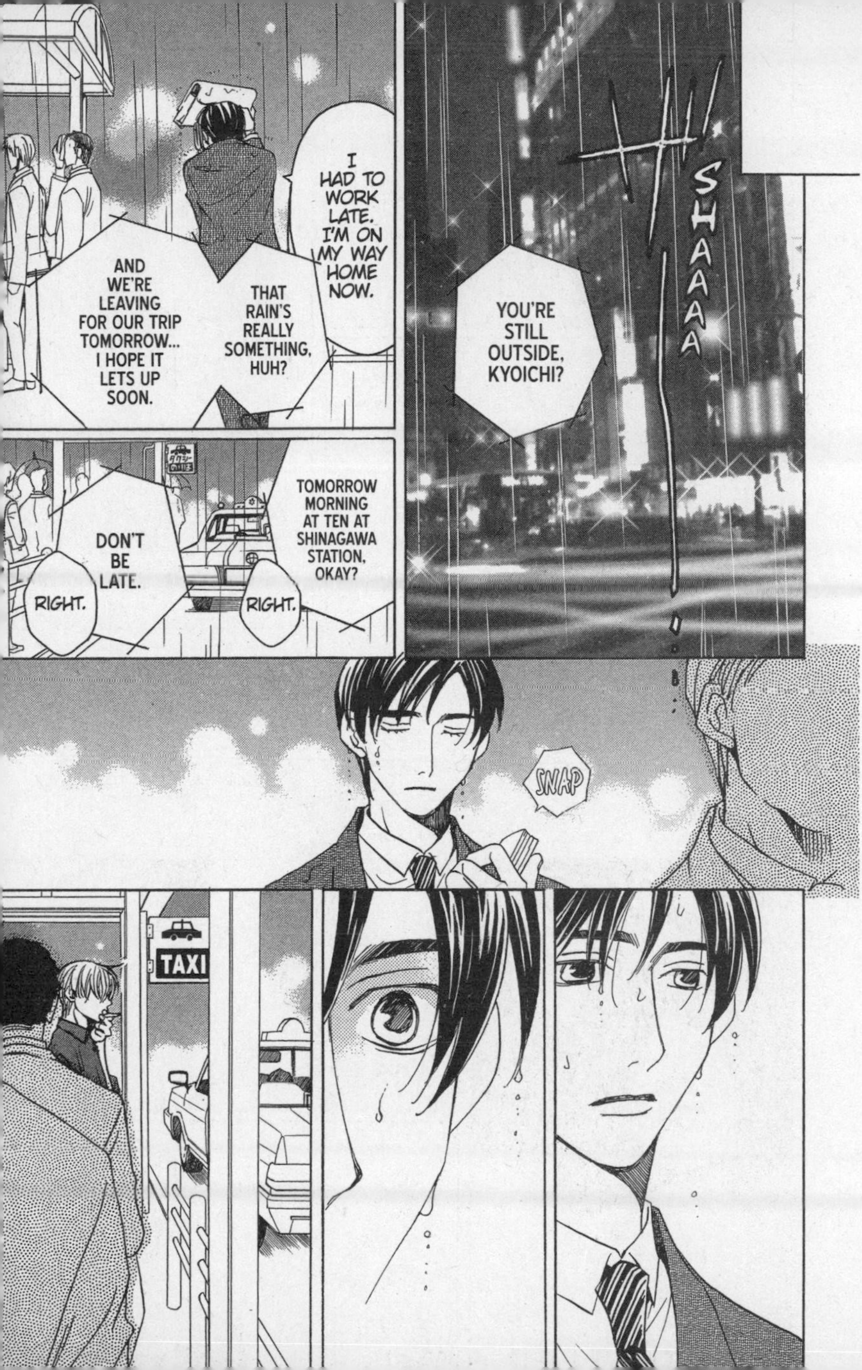
SHAAAA
YOU'RE STILL OUTSIDE, KYOICHI?
I HAD TO WORK LATE. I'M ON MY WAY HOME NOW.
THAT RAIN'S REALLY SOMETHING, HUH?
AND WE'RE LEAVING FOR OUR TRIP TOMORROW... I HOPE IT LETS UP SOON.
TOMORROW MORNING AT TEN AT SHINAGAWA STATION, OKAY?
RIGHT.
DON'T BE LATE.
RIGHT.
SNAP
TAXI

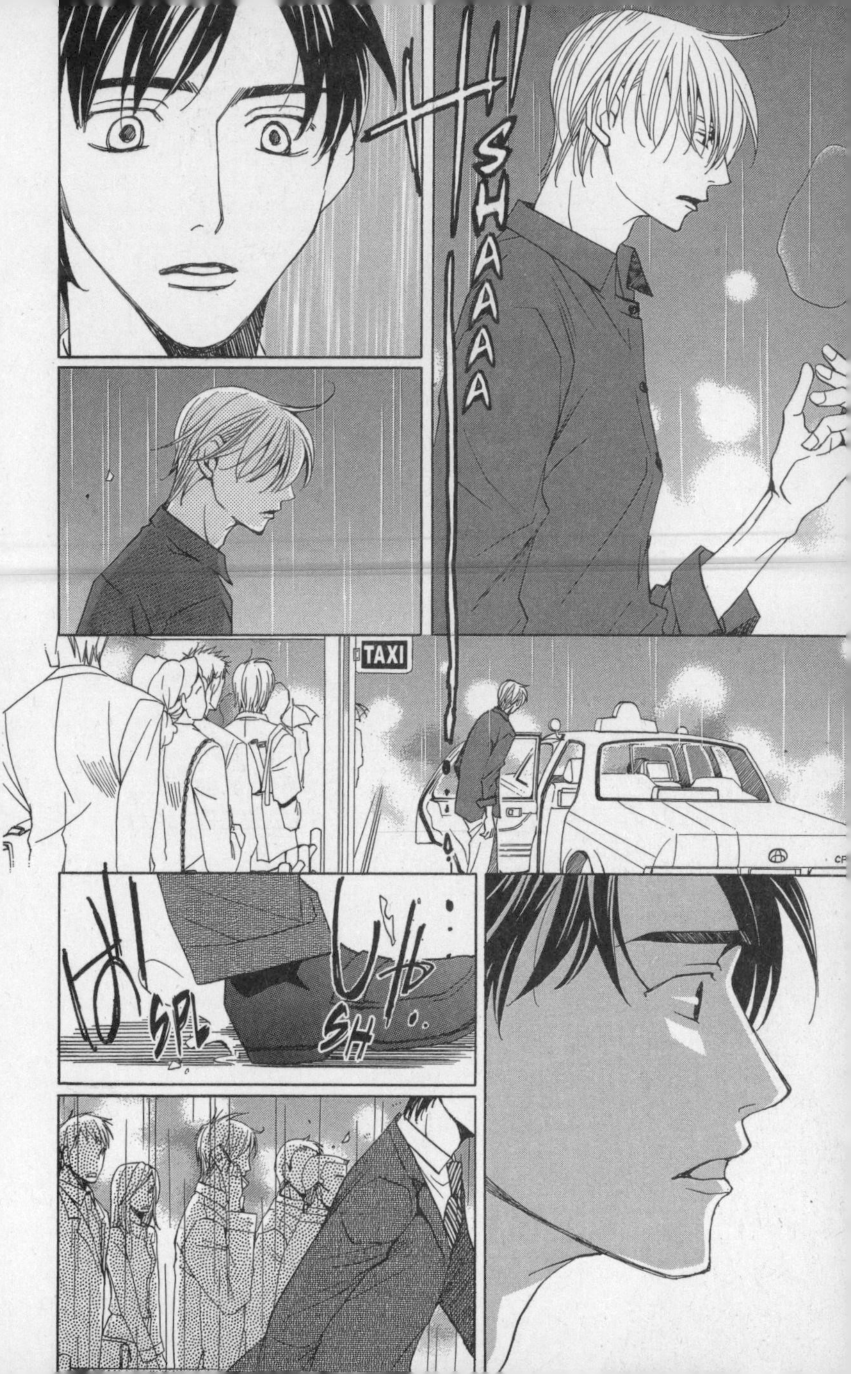
SHAAAAA
TAXI
SPL
SH

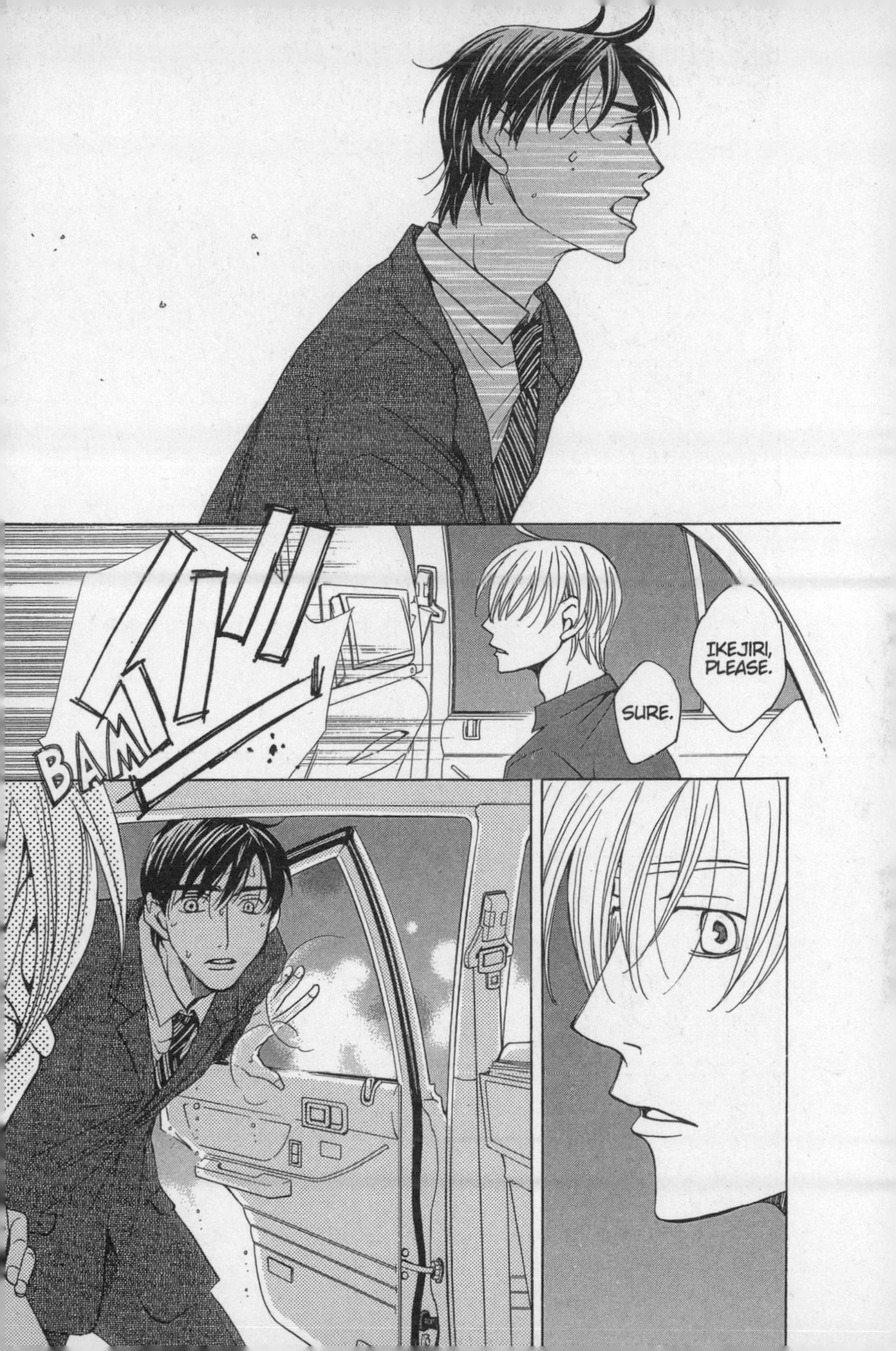
IKEJIRI, PLEASE.
SURE.
BAM

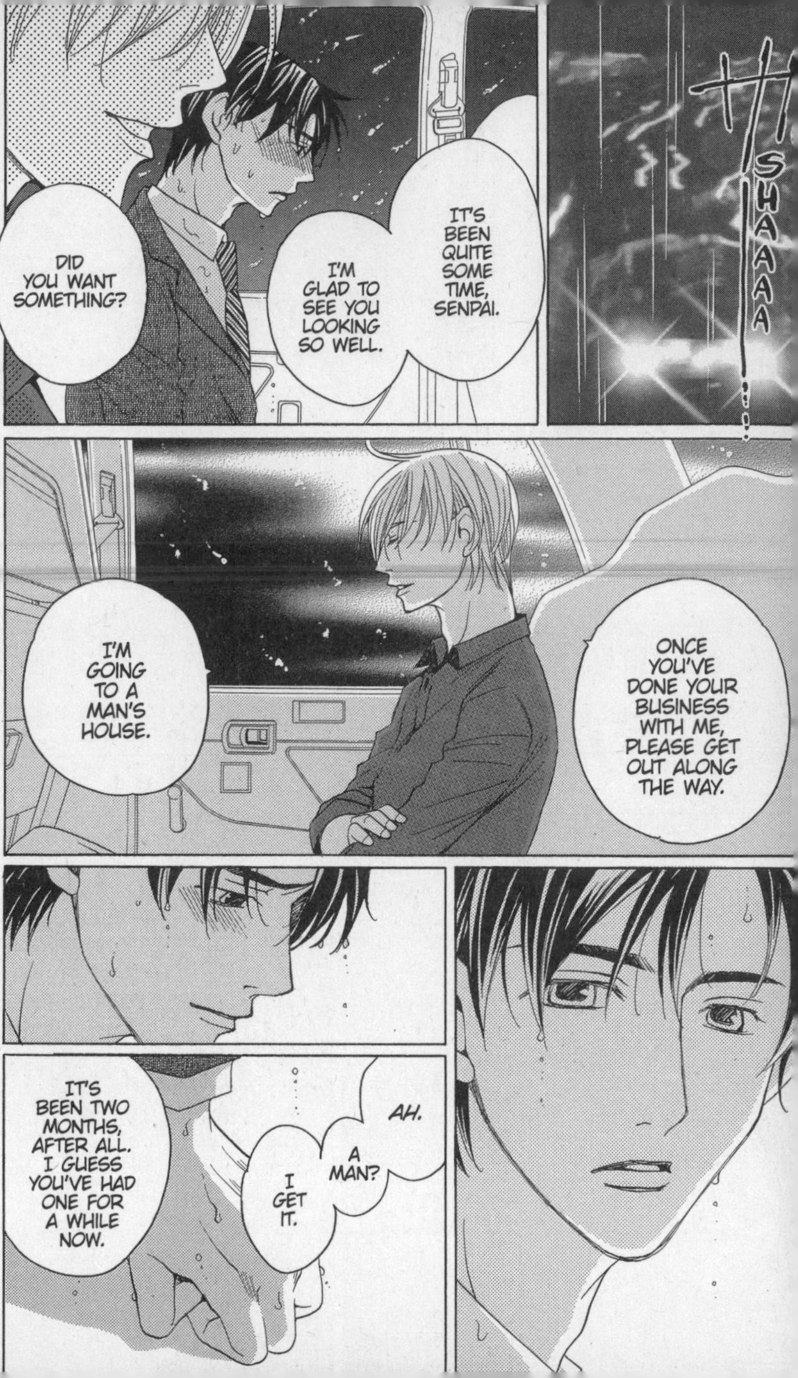
SHAAAA...!!
IT'S BEEN QUITE SOME TIME, SENPAI.
I'M GLAD TO SEE YOU LOOKING SO WELL.
DID YOU WANT SOMETHING?
ONCE YOU'VE DONE YOUR BUSINESS WITH ME, PLEASE GET OUT ALONG THE WAY.
I'M GOING TO A MAN'S HOUSE.
AH.
A MAN?
I GET IT.
IT'S BEEN TWO MONTHS, AFTER ALL. I GUESS YOU'VE HAD ONE FOR A WHILE NOW.

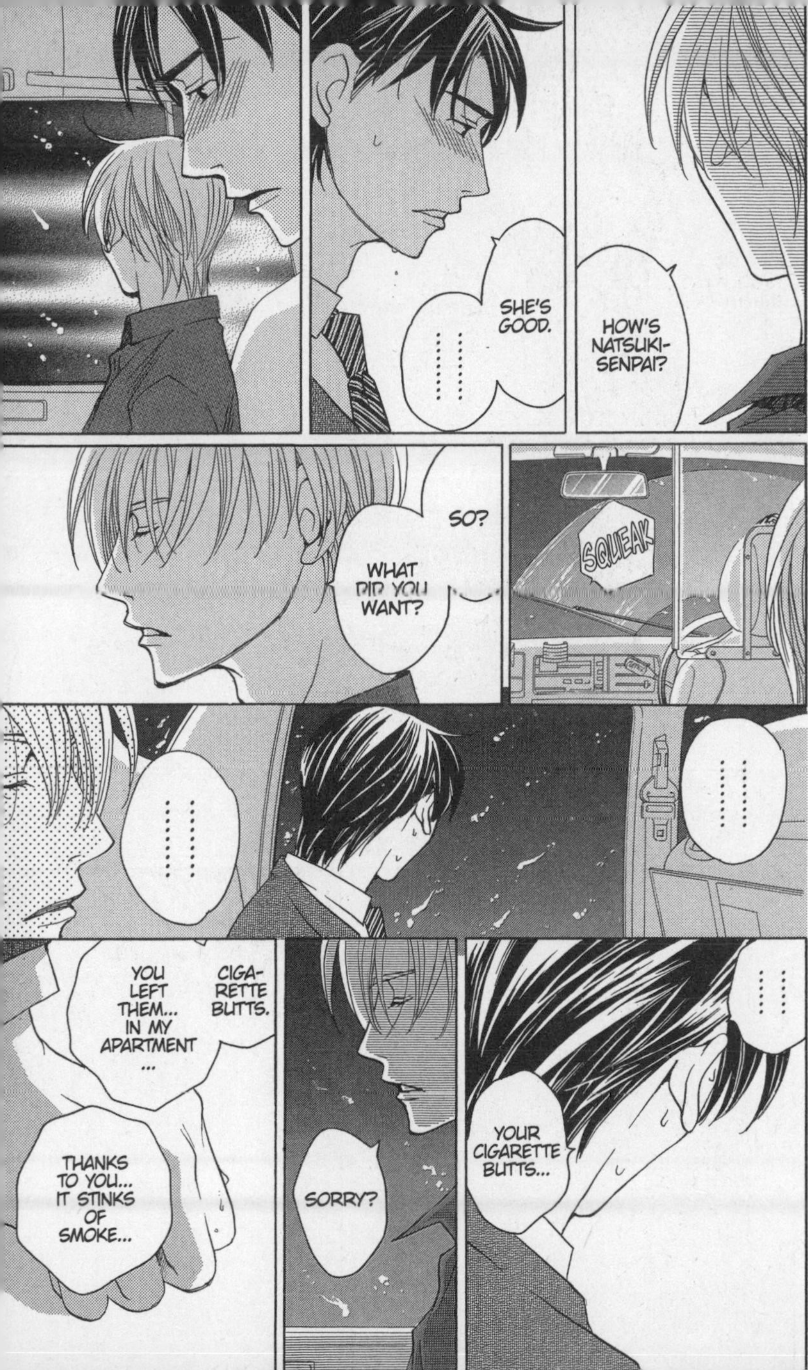
HOW'S NATSUKI-SENPAI?
SHE'S GOOD.
......
SQUEAK
SO?
WHAT DID YOU WANT?
......
......
......
YOUR CIGARETTE BUTTS...
SORRY?
CIGA-RETTE BUTTS.
YOU LEFT THEM... IN MY APARTMENT ...
THANKS TO YOU... IT STINKS OF SMOKE...

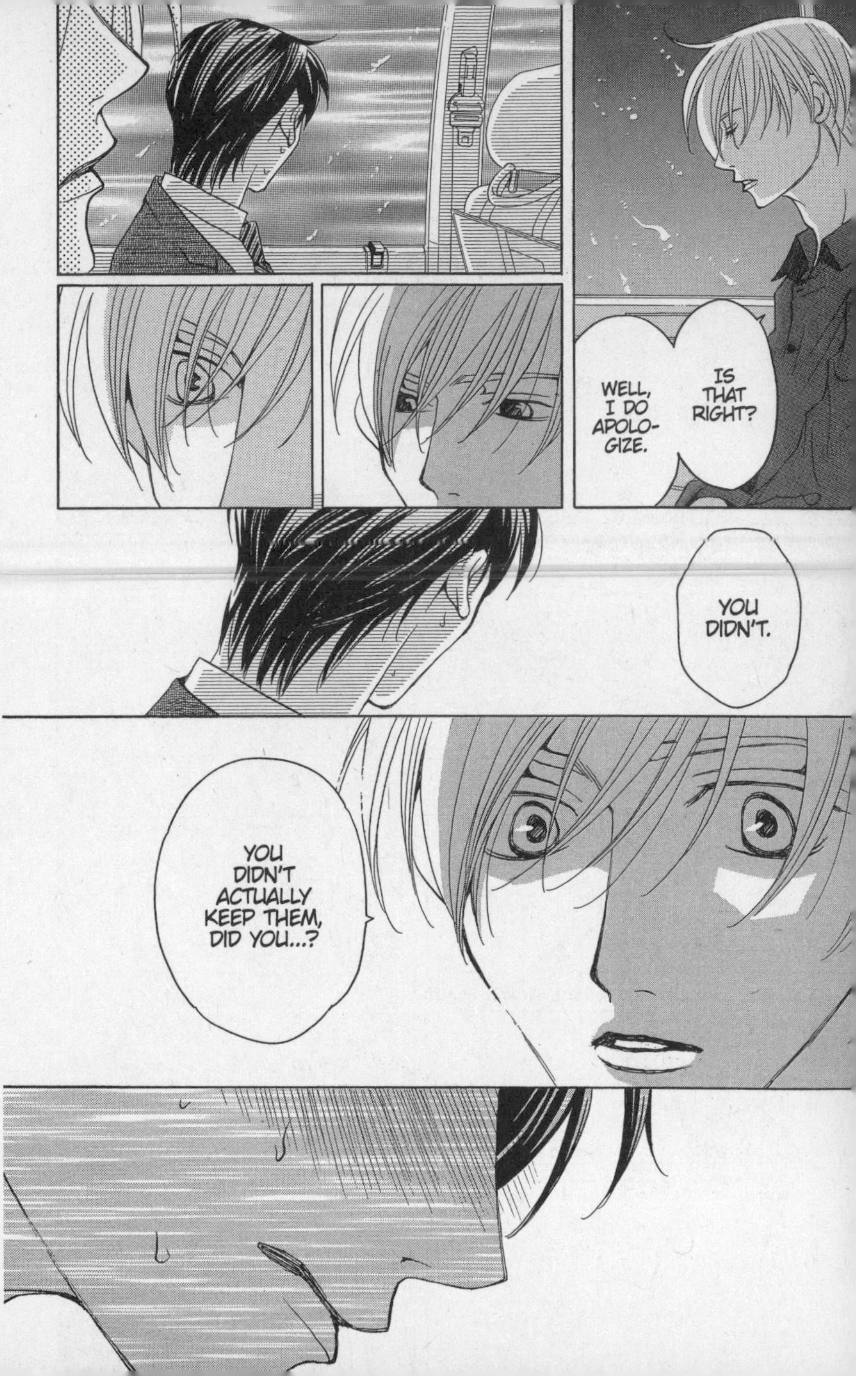
IS THAT RIGHT?
WELL, I DO APOLOGIZE.
YOU DIDN'T.
YOU DIDN'T ACTUALLY KEEP THEM, DID YOU...?

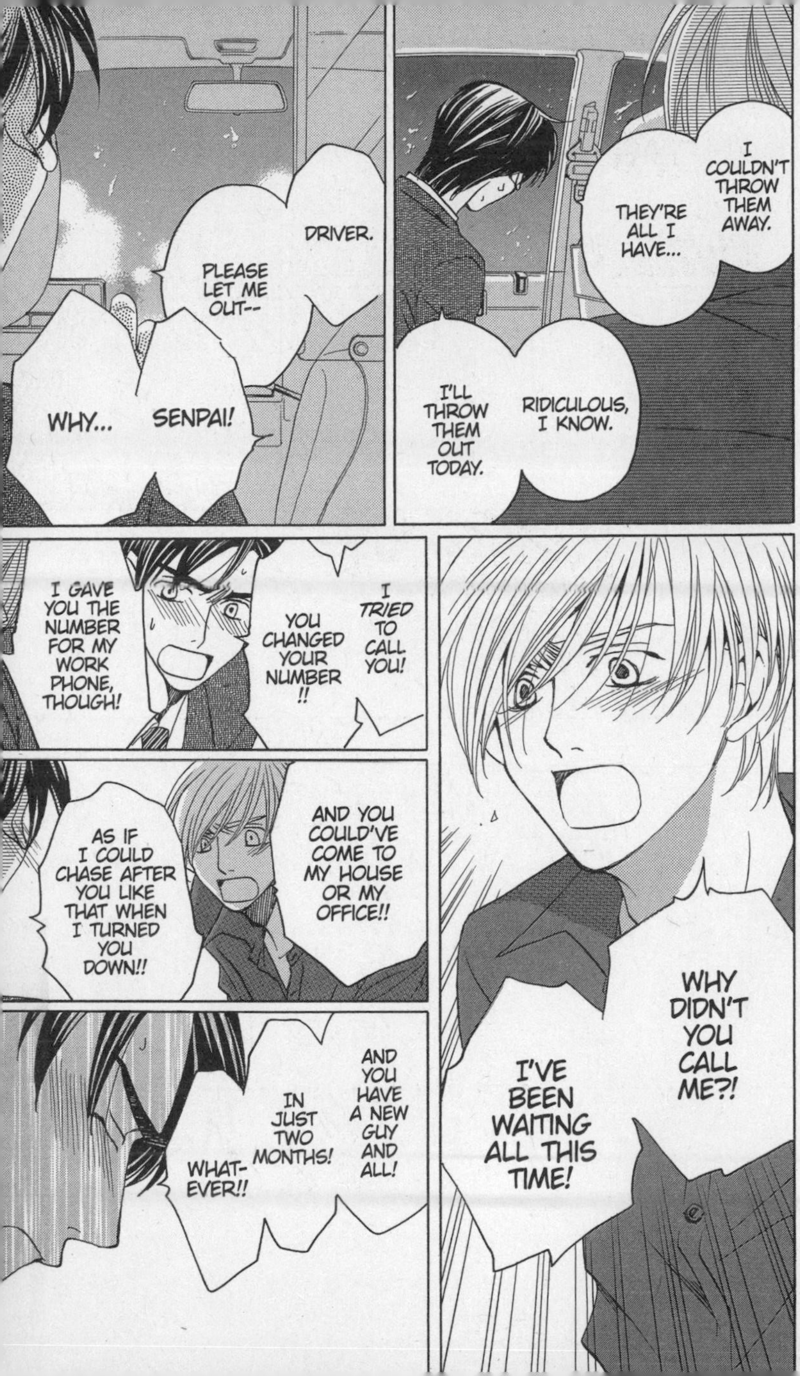
I COULDN'T THROW THEM AWAY.
THEY'RE ALL I HAVE...
RIDICULOUS, I KNOW.
I'LL THROW THEM OUT TODAY.
DRIVER.
PLEASE LET ME OUT--
SENPAI!
WHY...
WHY DIDN'T YOU CALL ME?!
I'VE BEEN WAITING ALL THIS TIME!
I *TRIED* TO CALL YOU!
YOU CHANGED YOUR NUMBER!!
I GAVE YOU THE NUMBER FOR MY WORK PHONE, THOUGH!
AND YOU COULD'VE COME TO MY HOUSE OR MY OFFICE!!
AS IF I COULD CHASE AFTER YOU LIKE THAT WHEN I TURNED YOU DOWN!!
AND YOU HAVE A NEW GUY AND ALL!
IN JUST TWO MONTHS!
WHAT-EVER!!

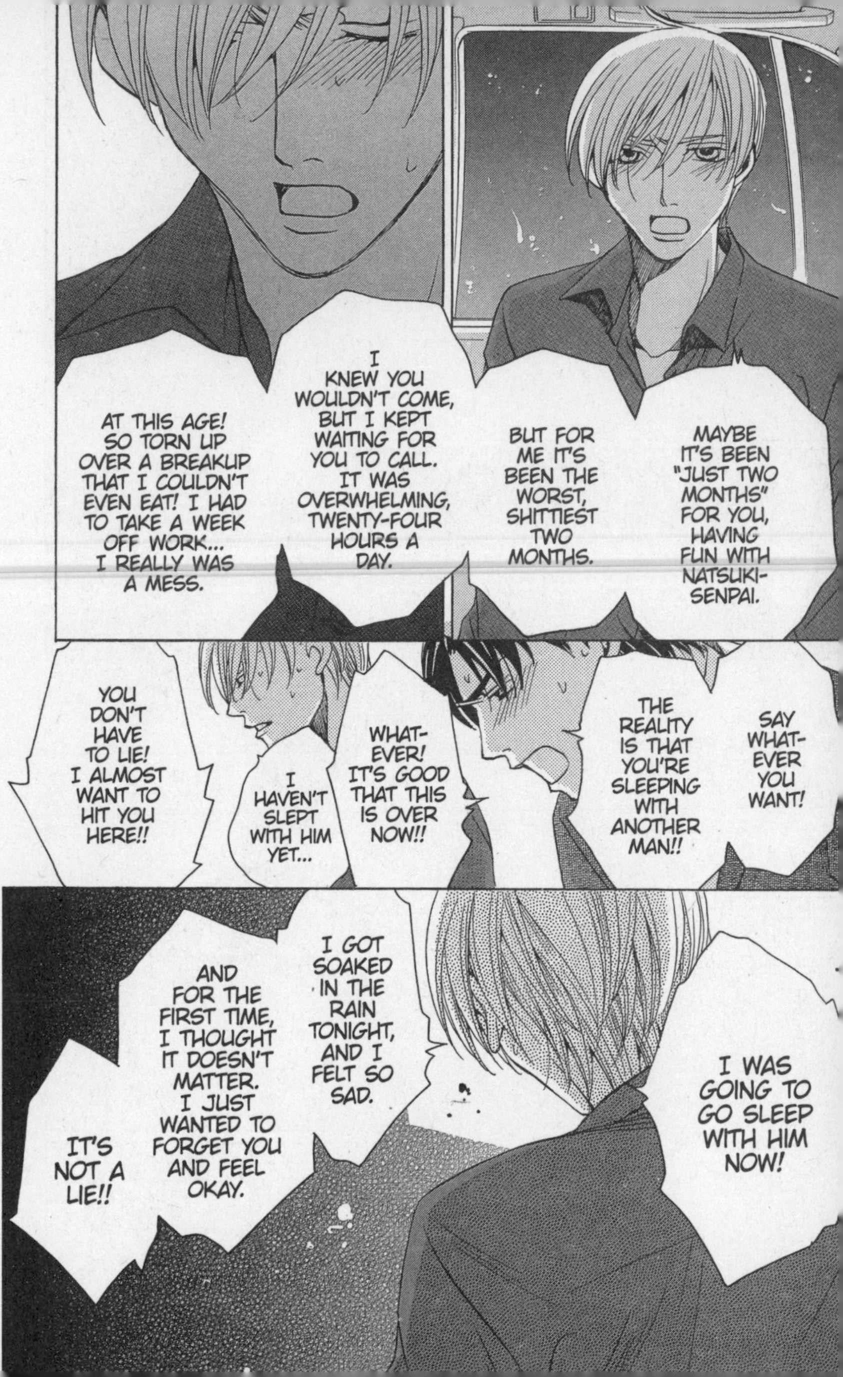
MAYBE IT'S BEEN "JUST TWO MONTHS" FOR YOU, HAVING FUN WITH NATSUKI-SENPAI.
BUT FOR ME IT'S BEEN THE WORST, SHITTIEST TWO MONTHS.
I KNEW YOU WOULDN'T COME, BUT I KEPT WAITING FOR YOU TO CALL. IT WAS OVERWHELMING, TWENTY-FOUR HOURS A DAY.
AT THIS AGE! SO TORN UP OVER A BREAKUP THAT I COULDN'T EVEN EAT! I HAD TO TAKE A WEEK OFF WORK... I REALLY WAS A MESS.
SAY WHATEVER YOU WANT!
THE REALITY IS THAT YOU'RE SLEEPING WITH ANOTHER MAN!!
WHATEVER! IT'S GOOD THAT THIS IS OVER NOW!!
I HAVEN'T SLEPT WITH HIM YET...
YOU DON'T HAVE TO LIE! I ALMOST WANT TO HIT YOU HERE!!
I WAS GOING TO GO SLEEP WITH HIM NOW!
I GOT SOAKED IN THE RAIN TONIGHT, AND I FELT SO SAD.
AND FOR THE FIRST TIME, I THOUGHT IT DOESN'T MATTER. I JUST WANTED TO FORGET YOU AND FEEL OKAY.
IT'S NOT A LIE!!

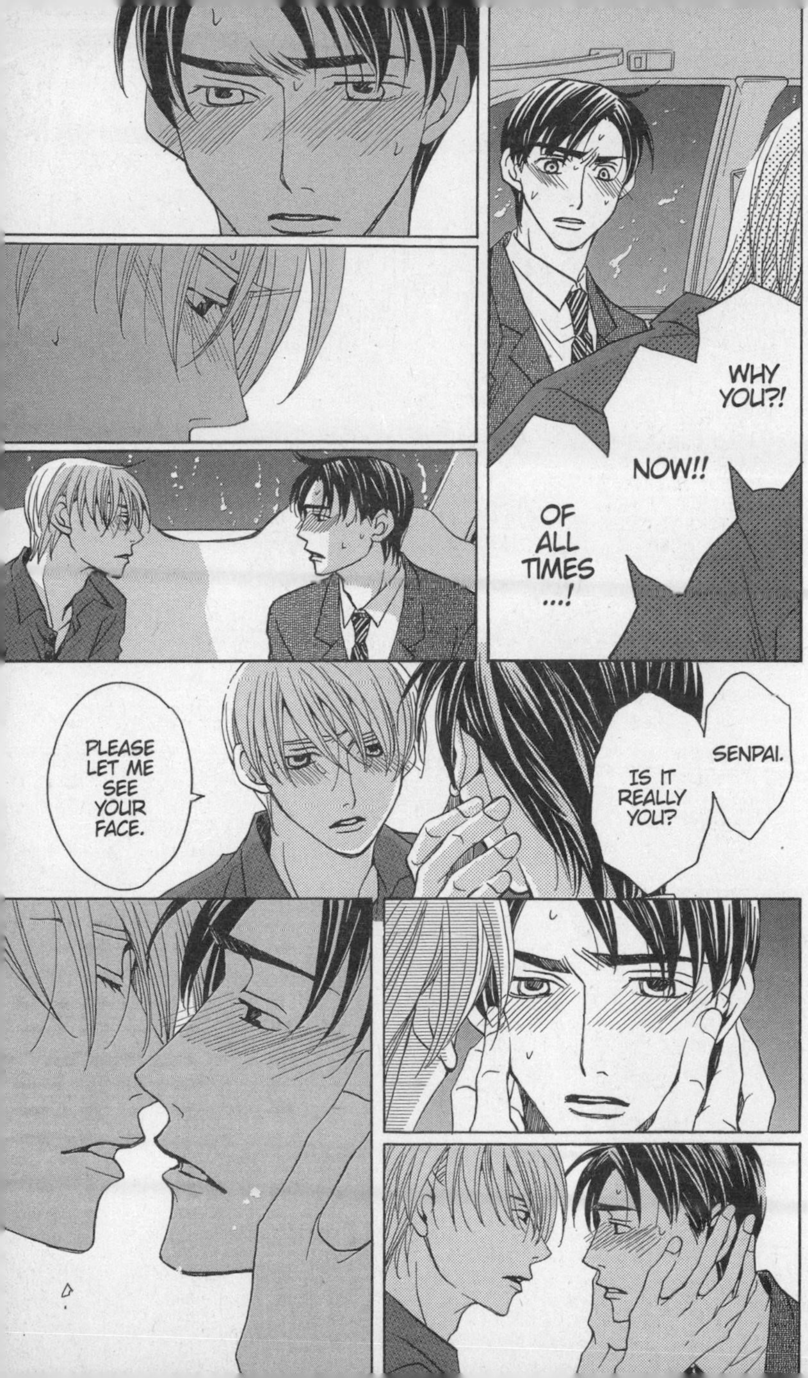
WHY YOU?!
NOW!!
OF ALL TIMES ...!
SENPAI.
IS IT REALLY YOU?
PLEASE LET ME SEE YOUR FACE.

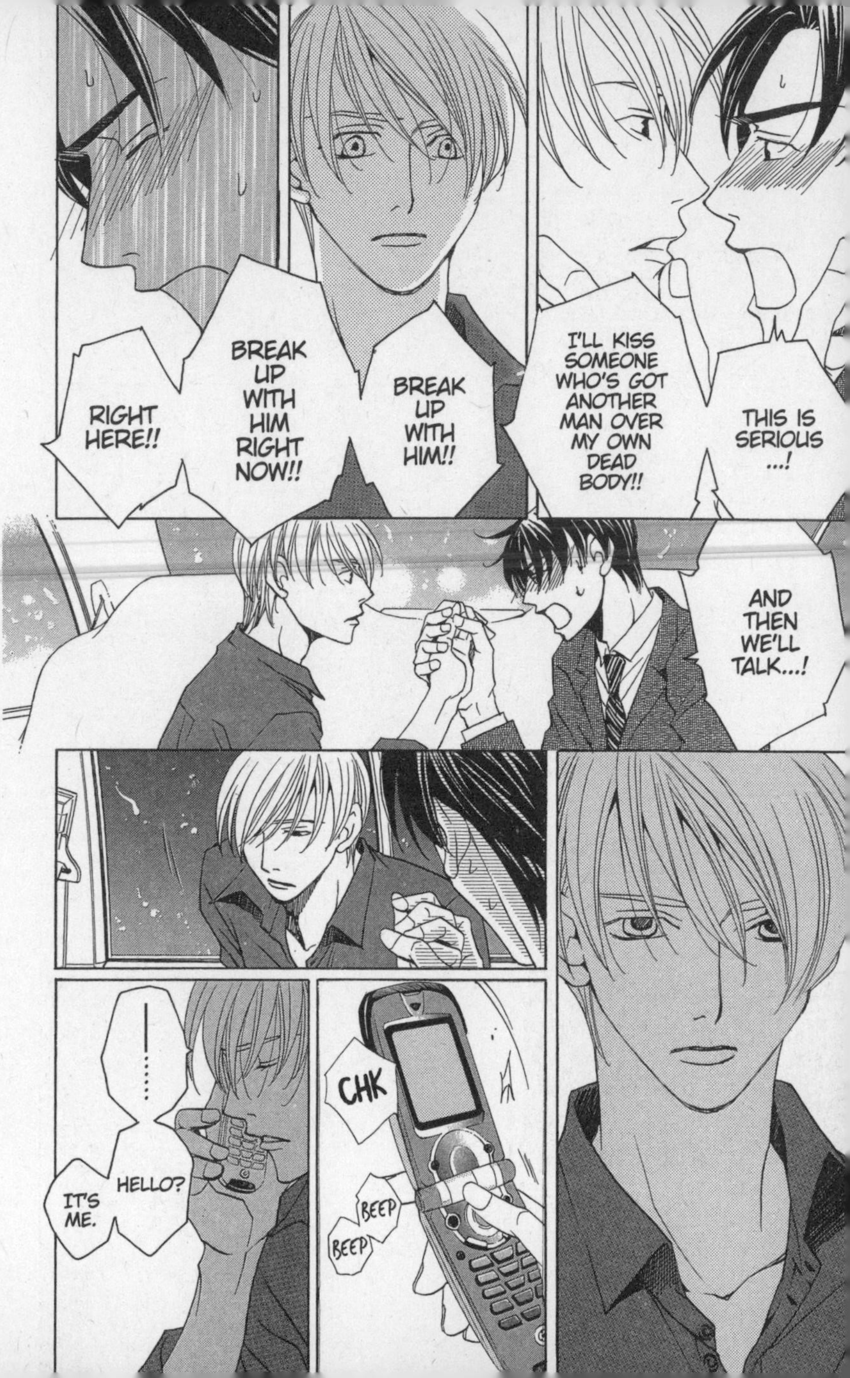
THIS IS SERIOUS ...!
I'LL KISS SOMEONE WHO'S GOT ANOTHER MAN OVER MY OWN DEAD BODY!!
BREAK UP WITH HIM!!
BREAK UP WITH HIM RIGHT NOW!!
RIGHT HERE!!
AND THEN WE'LL TALK...!
CHK
BEEP
BEEP
......
HELLO? IT'S ME.

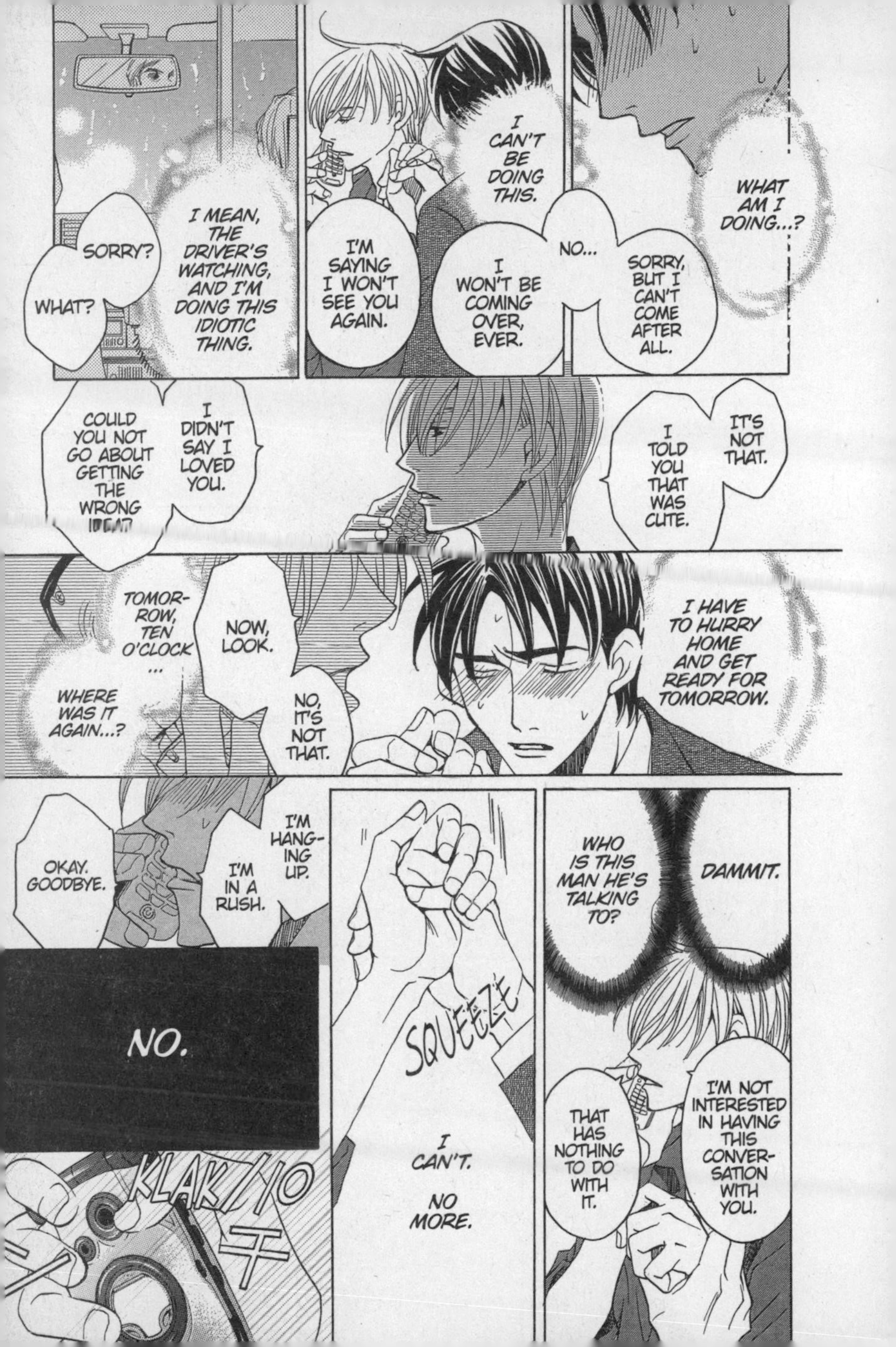
WHAT AM I DOING...?
SORRY, BUT I CAN'T COME AFTER ALL.
NO...
I WON'T BE COMING OVER, EVER.
I CAN'T BE DOING THIS.
I'M SAYING I WON'T SEE YOU AGAIN.
I MEAN, THE DRIVER'S WATCHING, AND I'M DOING THIS IDIOTIC THING.
SORRY?
WHAT?
IT'S NOT THAT.
I TOLD YOU THAT WAS CUTE.
I DIDN'T SAY I LOVED YOU.
COULD YOU NOT GO ABOUT GETTING THE WRONG IDEA?
I HAVE TO HURRY HOME AND GET READY FOR TOMORROW.
NOW, LOOK.
NO, IT'S NOT THAT.
TOMORROW, TEN O'CLOCK...
WHERE WAS IT AGAIN...?
DAMMIT.
WHO IS THIS MAN HE'S TALKING TO?
I'M NOT INTERESTED IN HAVING THIS CONVERSATION WITH YOU.
THAT HAS NOTHING TO DO WITH IT.
SQUEEZE
I CAN'T.
NO MORE.
I'M HANGING UP.
I'M IN A RUSH.
OKAY. GOODBYE.
NO.
KLAK

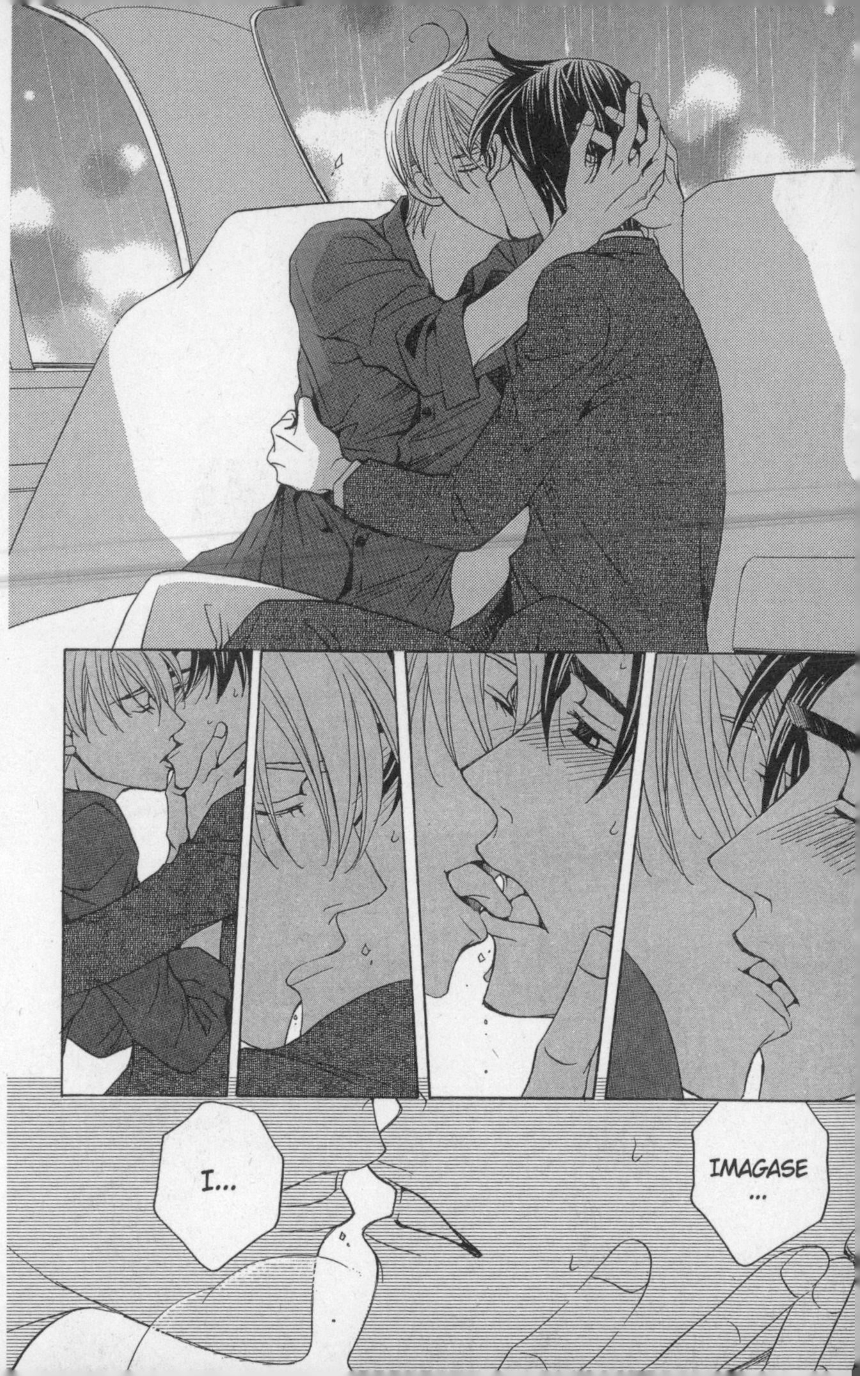
IMAGASE ...
I...

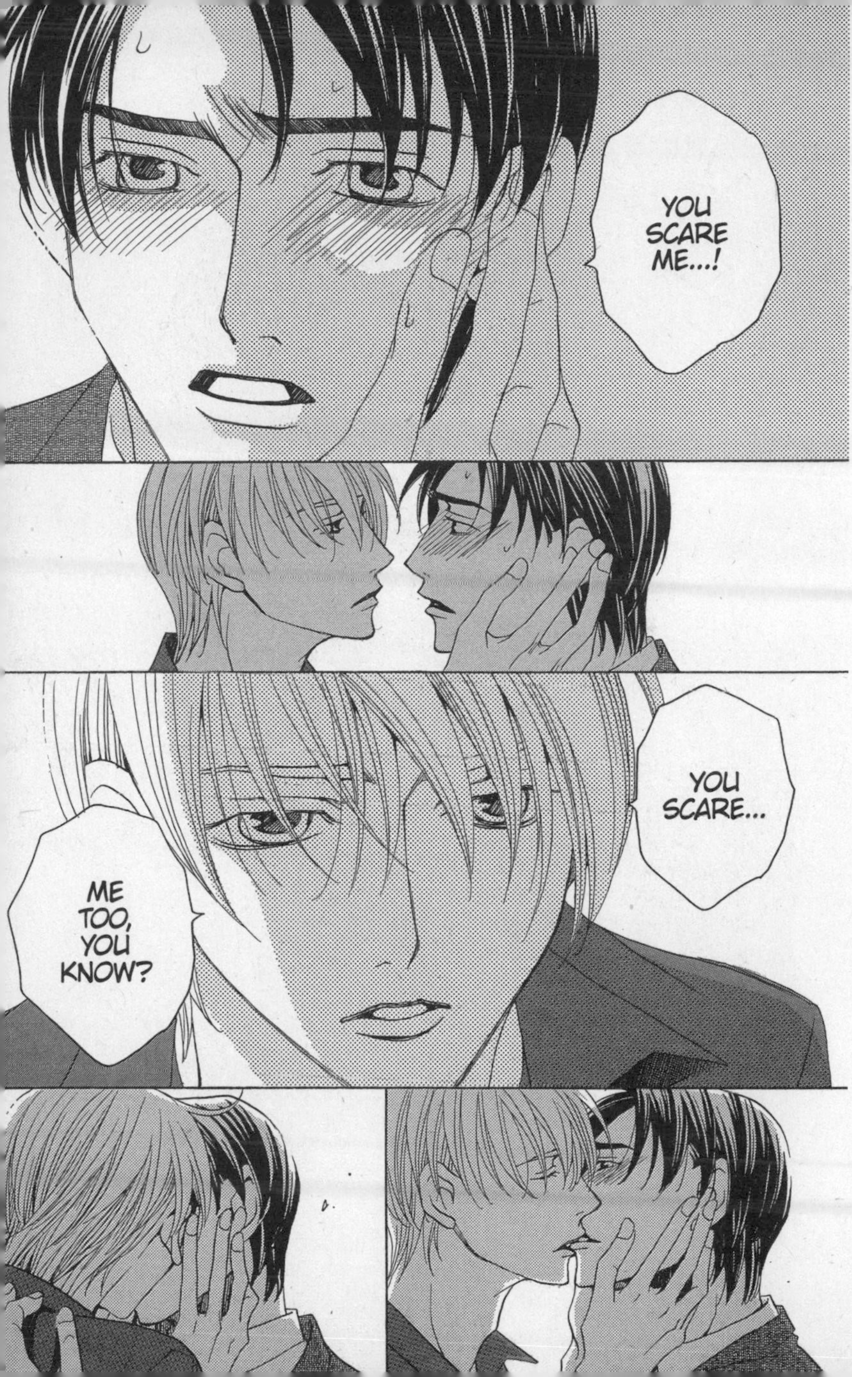
YOU SCARE ME...!
YOU SCARE...
ME TOO, YOU KNOW?

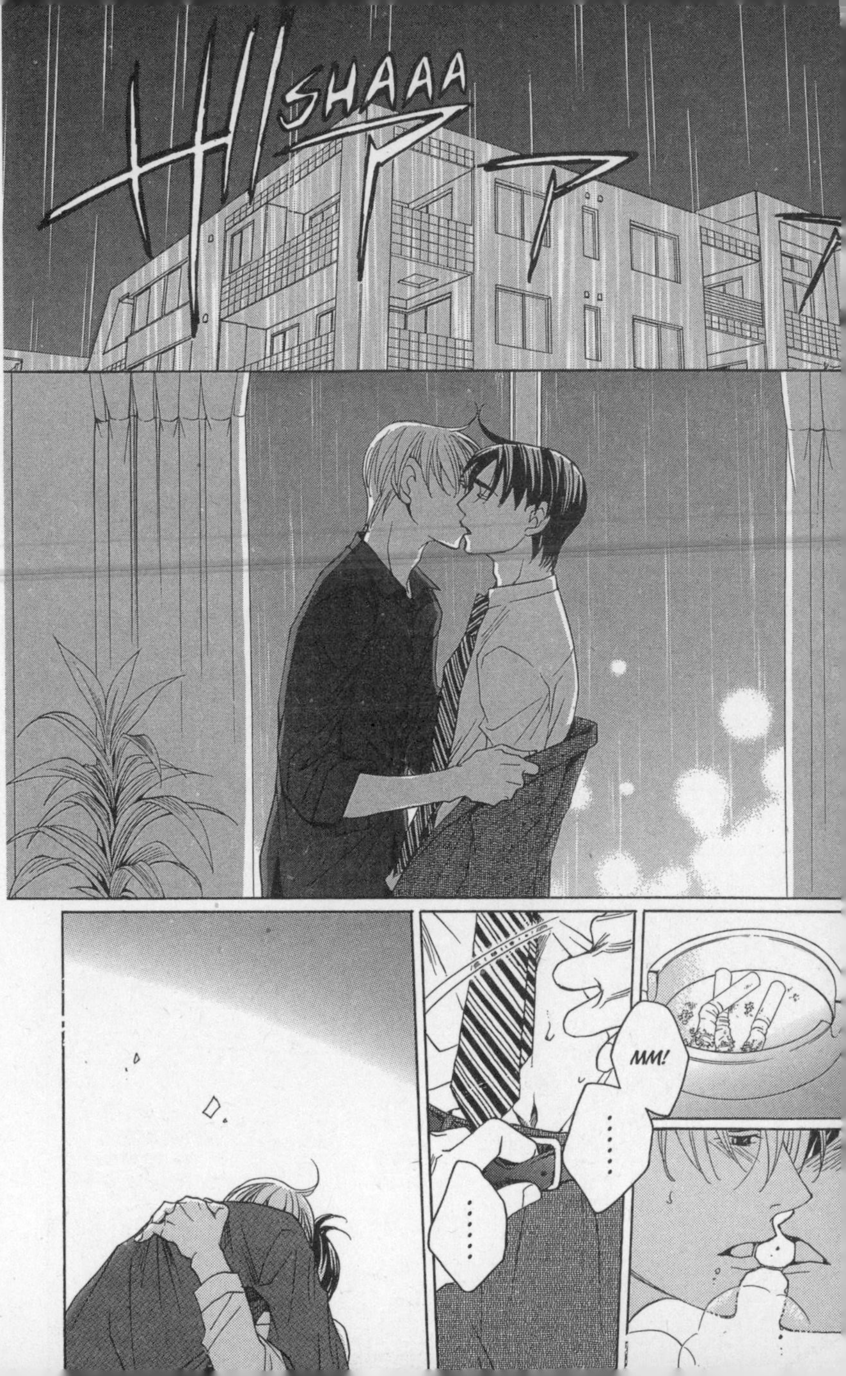
SHAAA
MM!
......
......

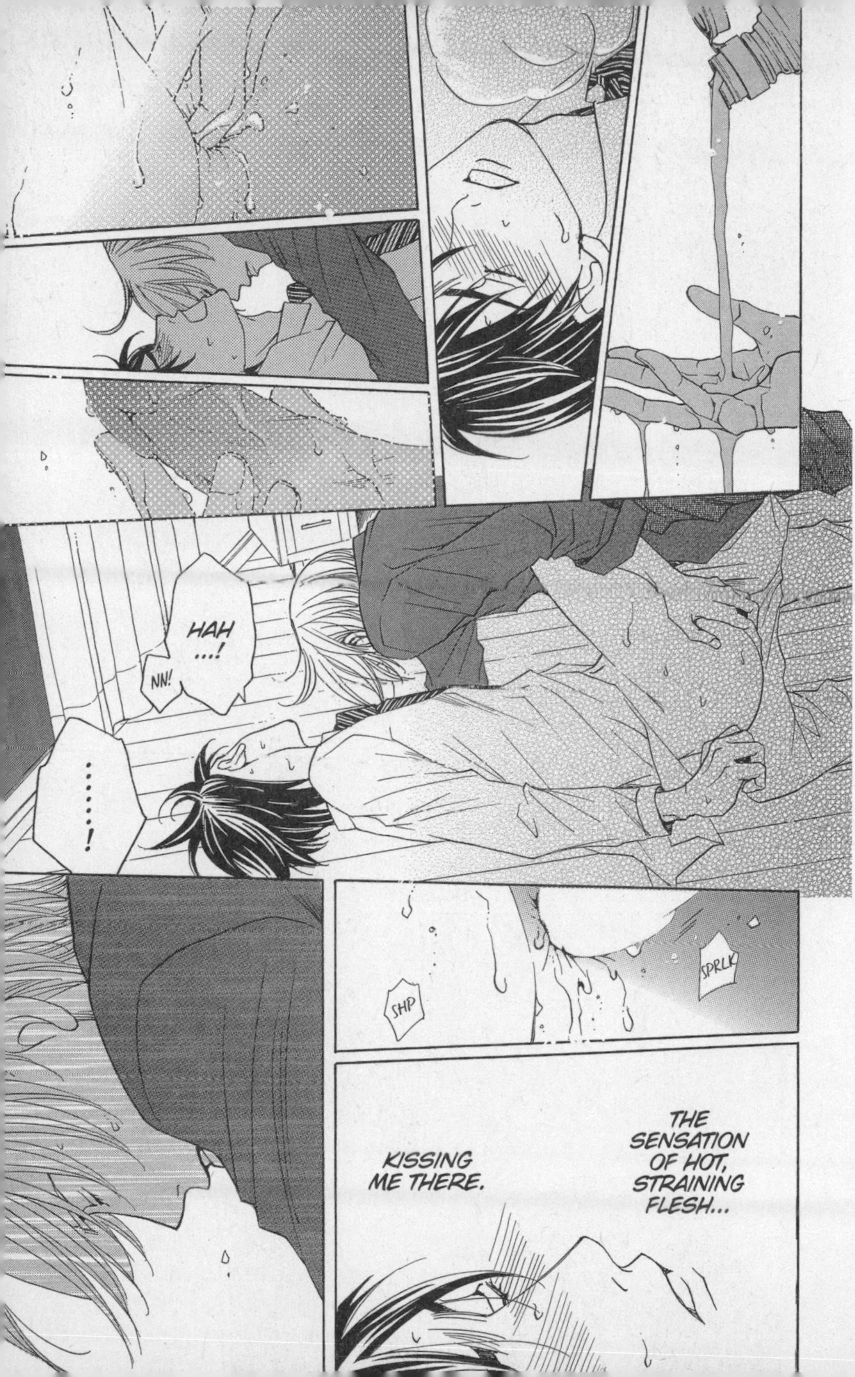
HAH ...!
NN!
......!
SPRLK
SHP
THE SENSATION OF HOT, STRAINING FLESH...
KISSING ME THERE.

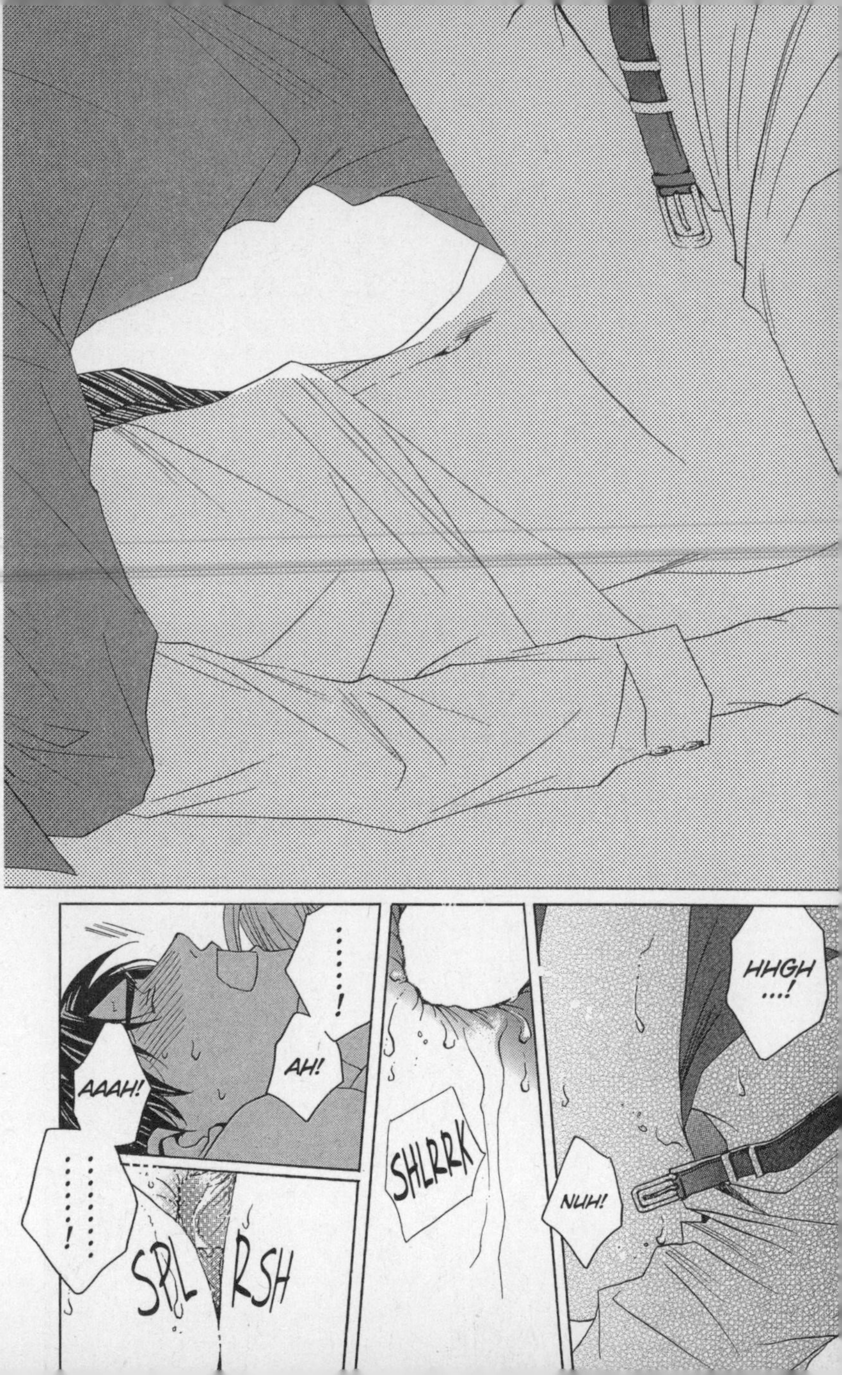
HHGH ...!
NUH!
SHLRRK
......!
AH!
AAAH!
......!
SPLRSH

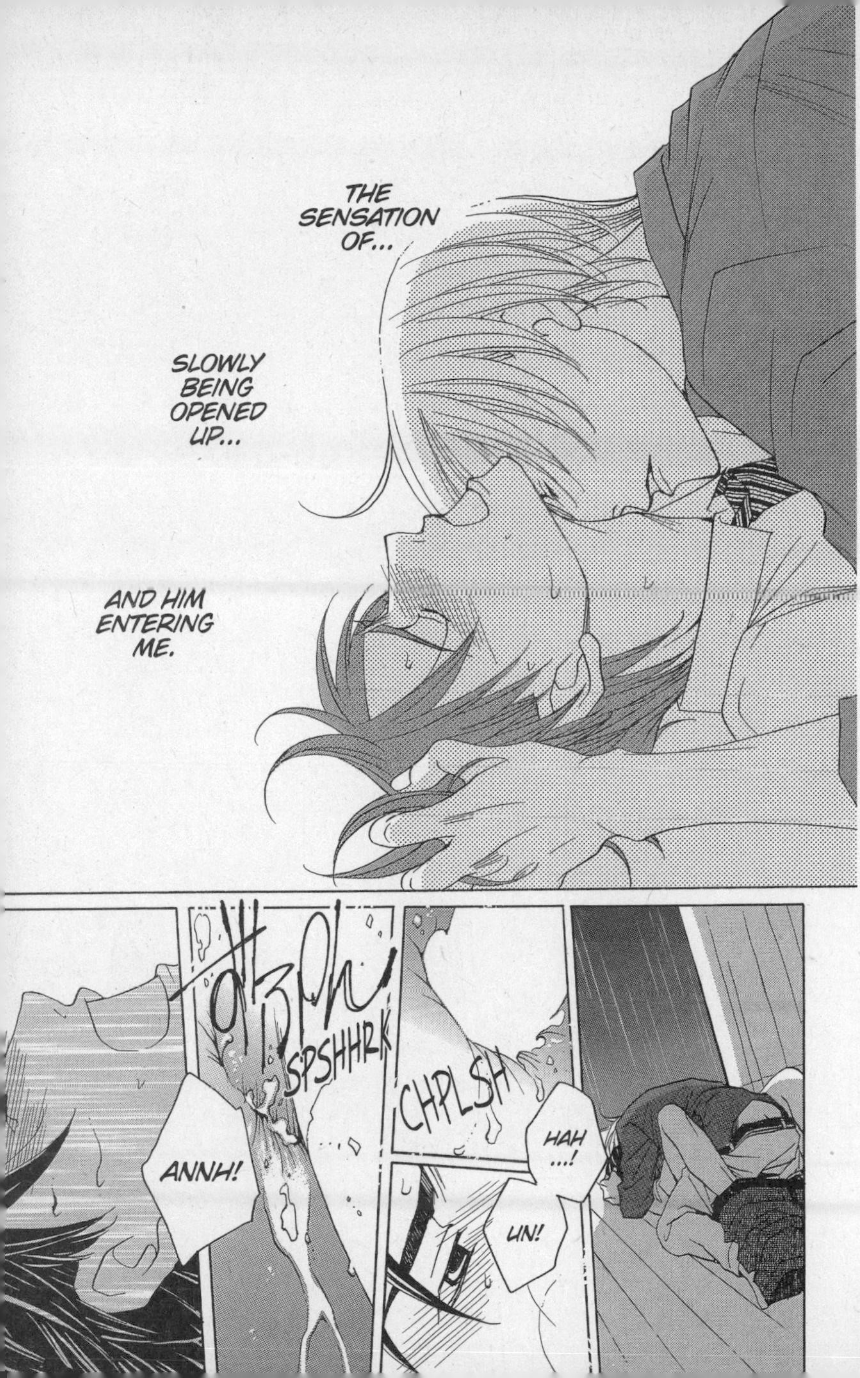
THE SENSATION OF...
SLOWLY BEING OPENED UP...
AND HIM ENTERING ME.
HAH ...!
CHPLSH
UN!
SPSHHRK
...
ANNH!

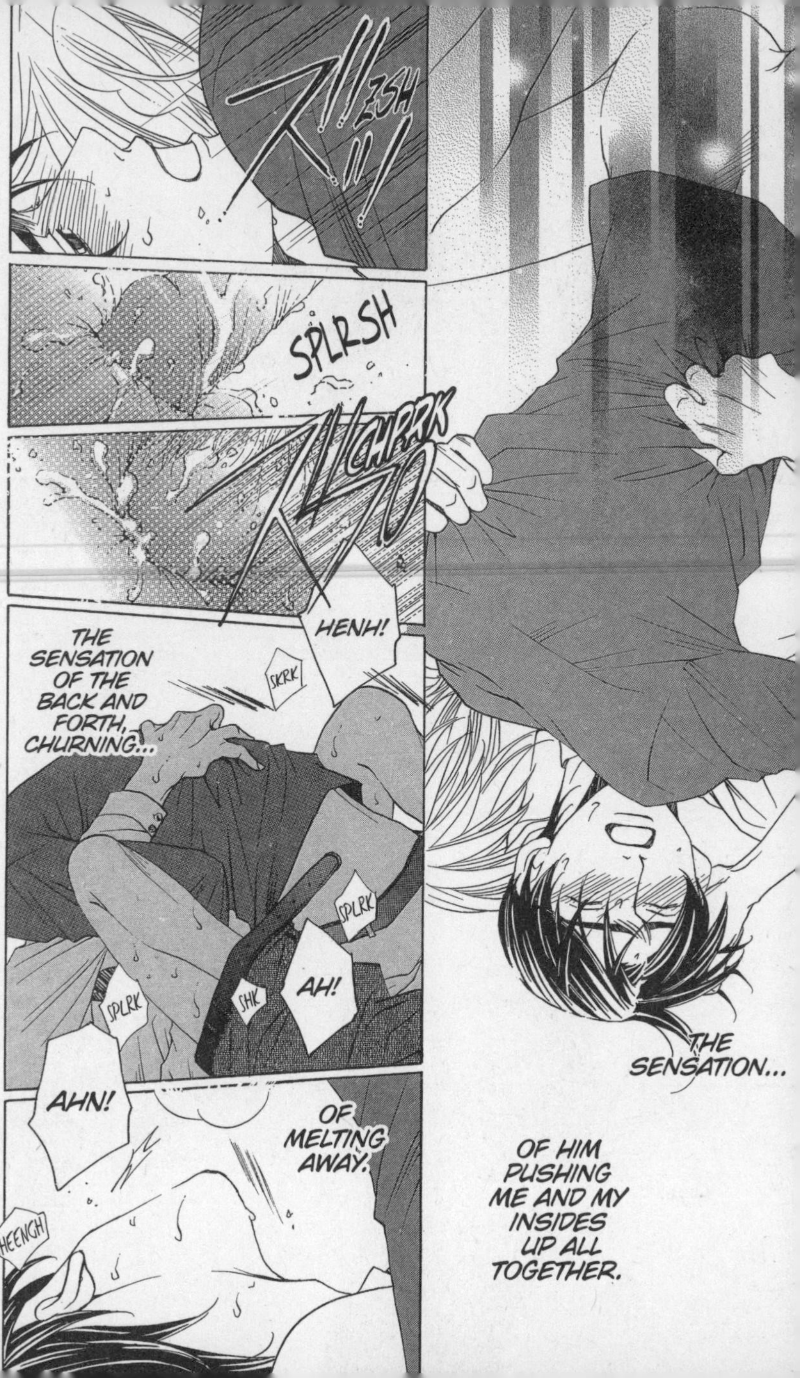
THE SENSATION...
OF HIM PUSHING ME AND MY INSIDES UP ALL TOGETHER.
SPLRSH
HENH!
THE SENSATION OF THE BACK AND FORTH, CHURNING...
SKRK
SPLRK
AH!
SHK
SPLRK
AHN!
OF MELTING AWAY.
HEENGH

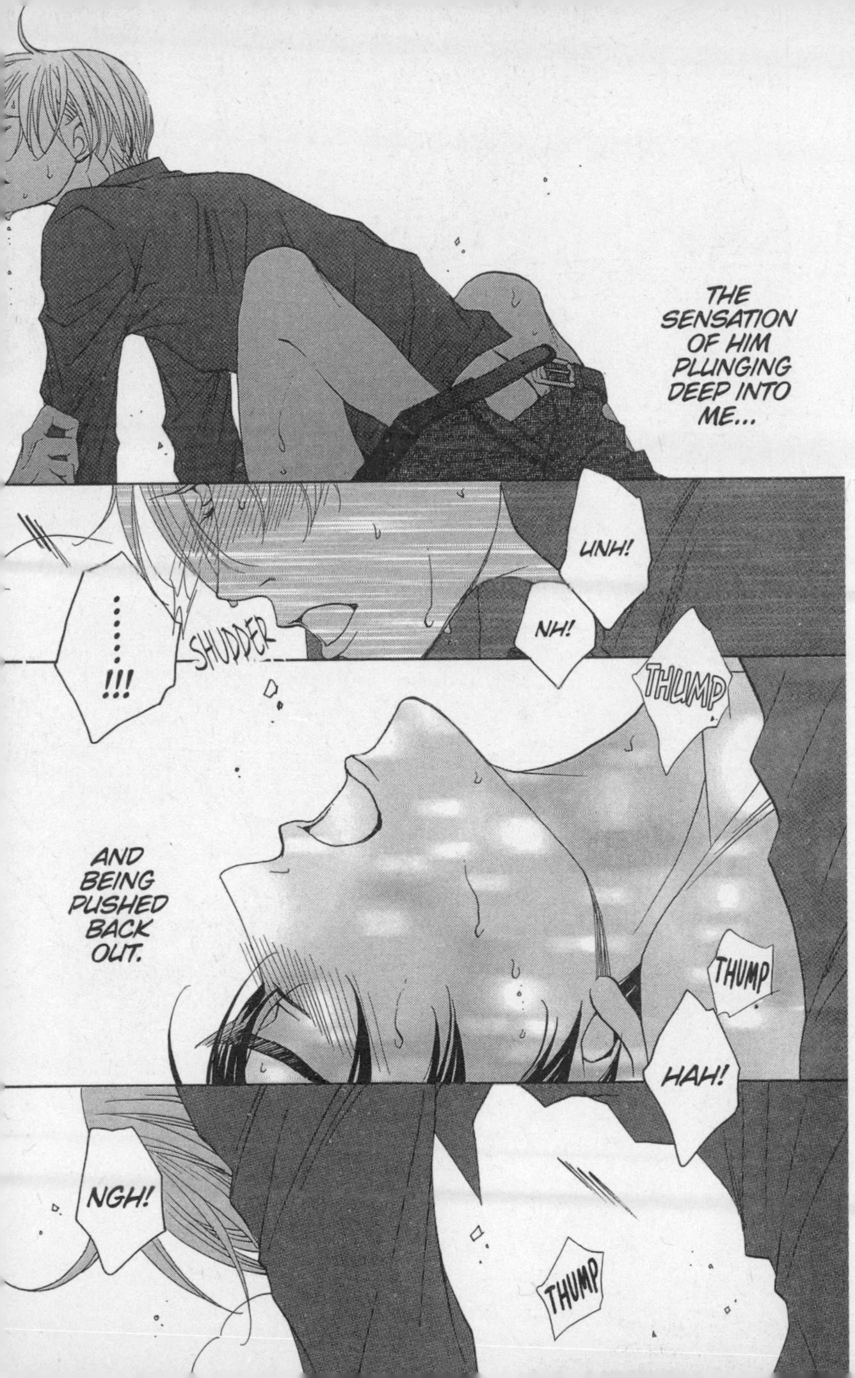
THE SENSATION OF HIM PLUNGING DEEP INTO ME...
UNH!
NH!
SHUDDER
......!!!
THUMP
AND BEING PUSHED BACK OUT.
THUMP
HAH!
THUMP
NGH!

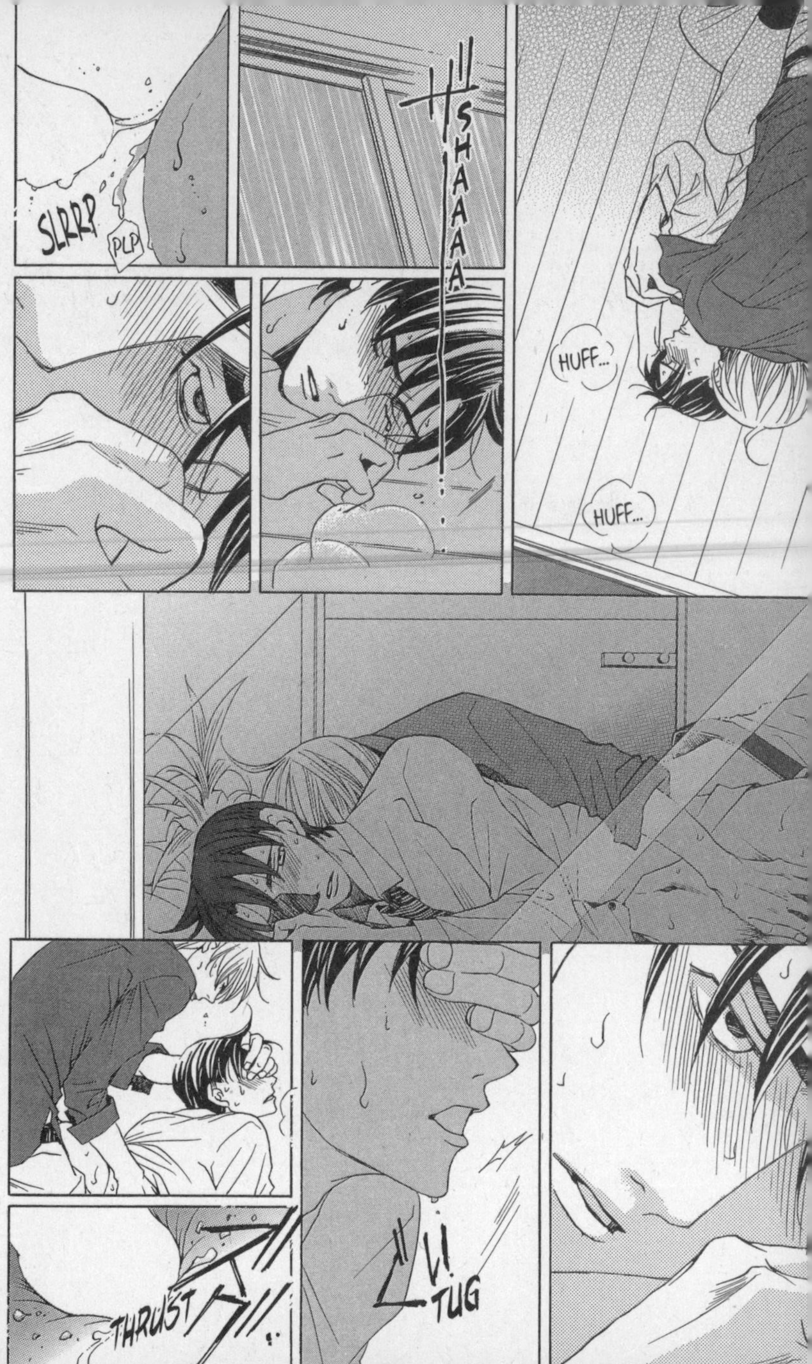
HUFF...
HUFF...
SHAAAAA
SLRRP
PLP
TUG
THRUST

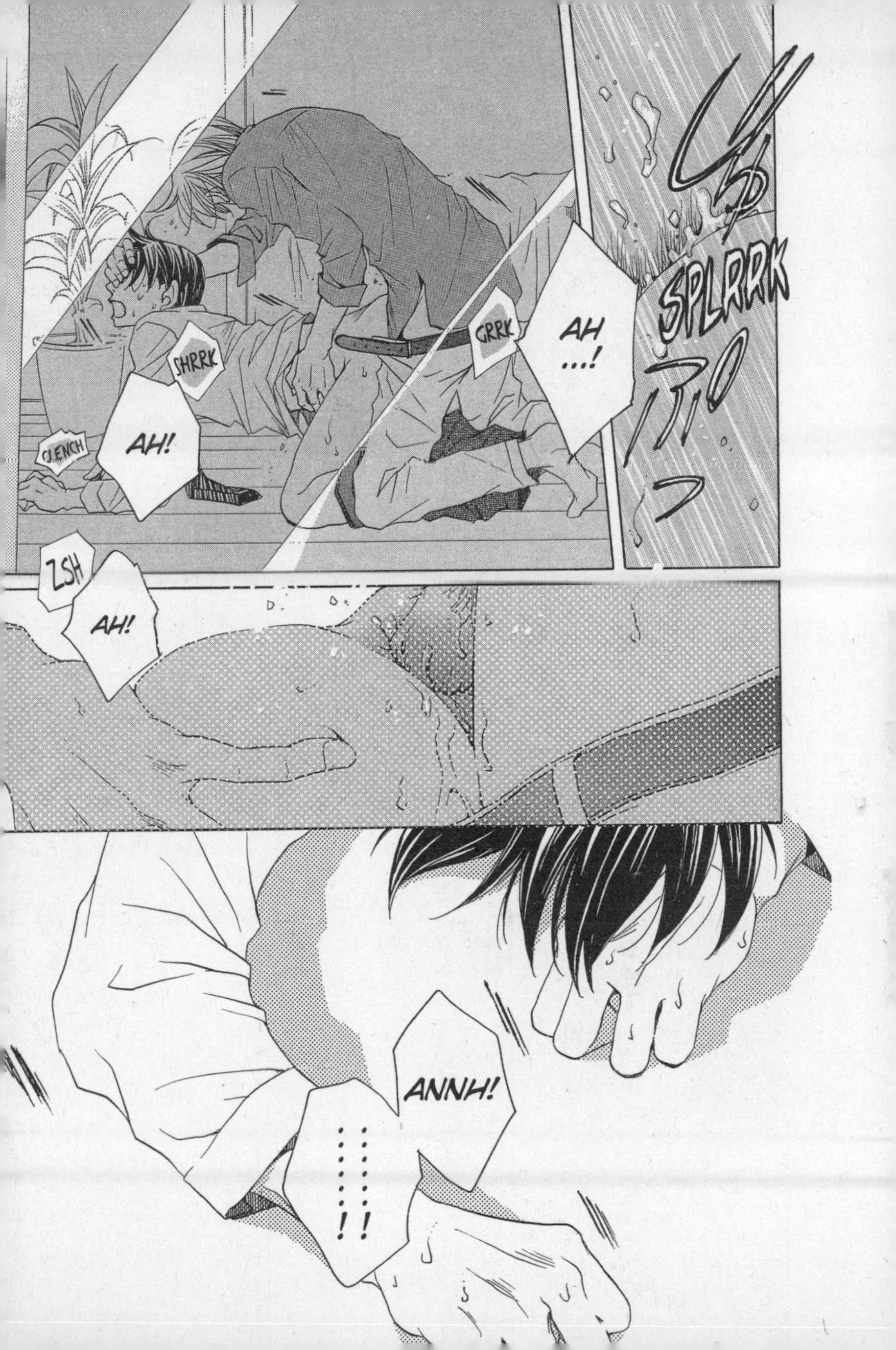
SPLRRK
AH ...!
GRRK
SHRRK
AH!
CLENCH
ZSH
AH!
ANNH!
......!!

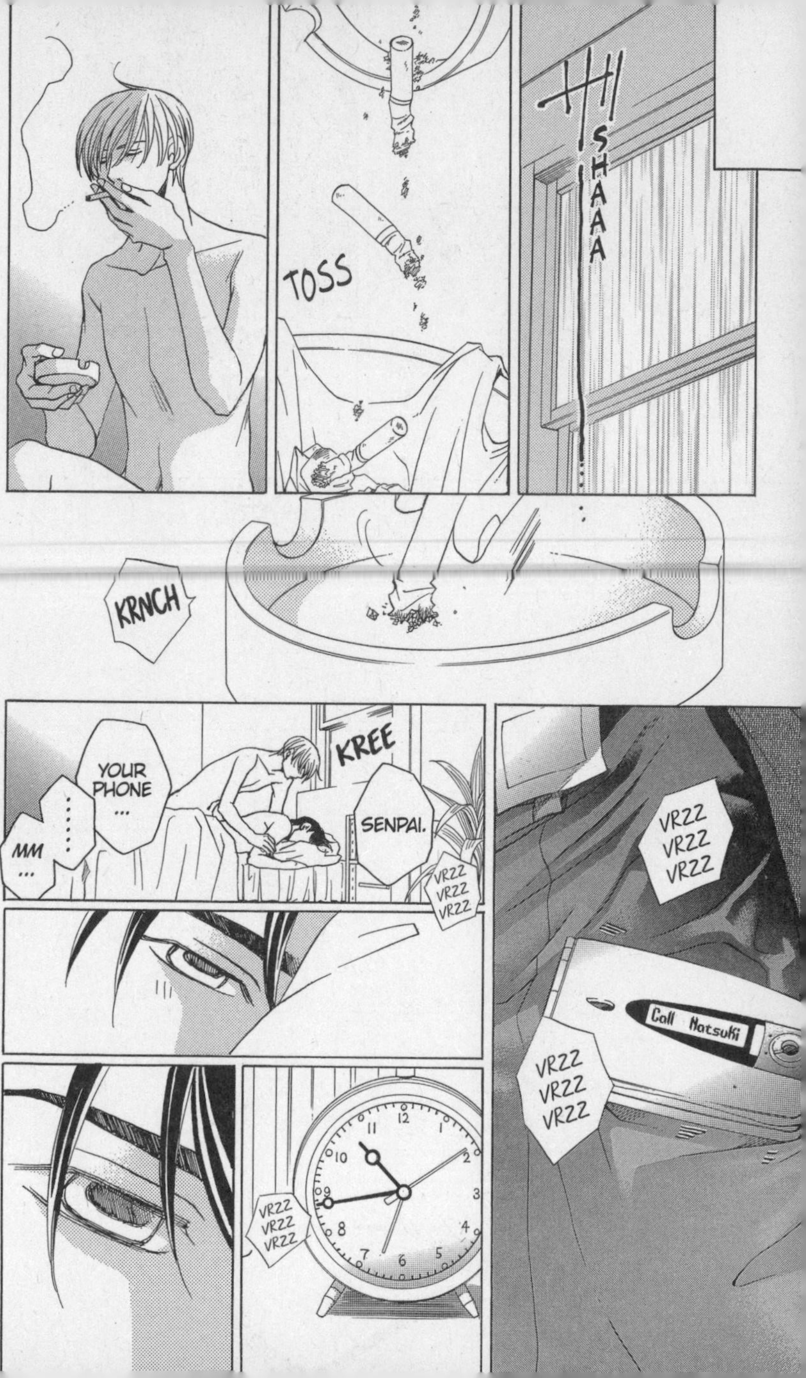
SHAAA
TOSS
KRNCH
VRZZ VRZZ VRZZ
Call Natsuki
VRZZ VRZZ VRZZ
KREE
SENPAI.
VRZZ VRZZ VRZZ
YOUR PHONE ...
......
MM ...
VRZZ VRZZ VRZZ

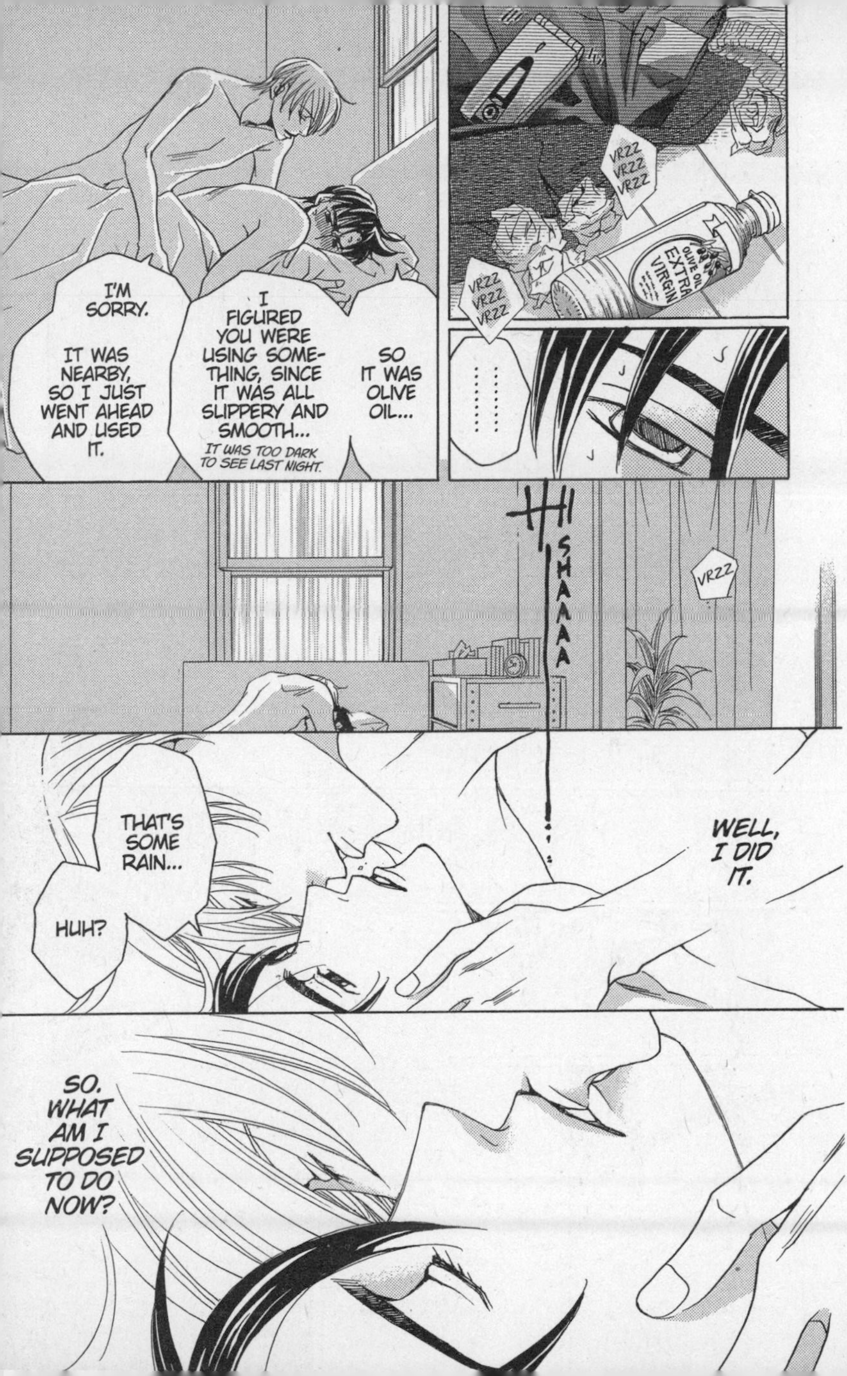
VRZZ VRZZ VRZZ
VRZZ VRZZ VRZZ
......
SO IT WAS OLIVE OIL...
I FIGURED YOU WERE USING SOME-THING, SINCE IT WAS ALL SLIPPERY AND SMOOTH...
IT WAS TOO DARK TO SEE LAST NIGHT.
I'M SORRY.
IT WAS NEARBY, SO I JUST WENT AHEAD AND USED IT.
SHAAAAA
VRZZ
WELL, I DID IT.
THAT'S SOME RAIN...
HUH?
SO. WHAT AM I SUPPOSED TO DO NOW?

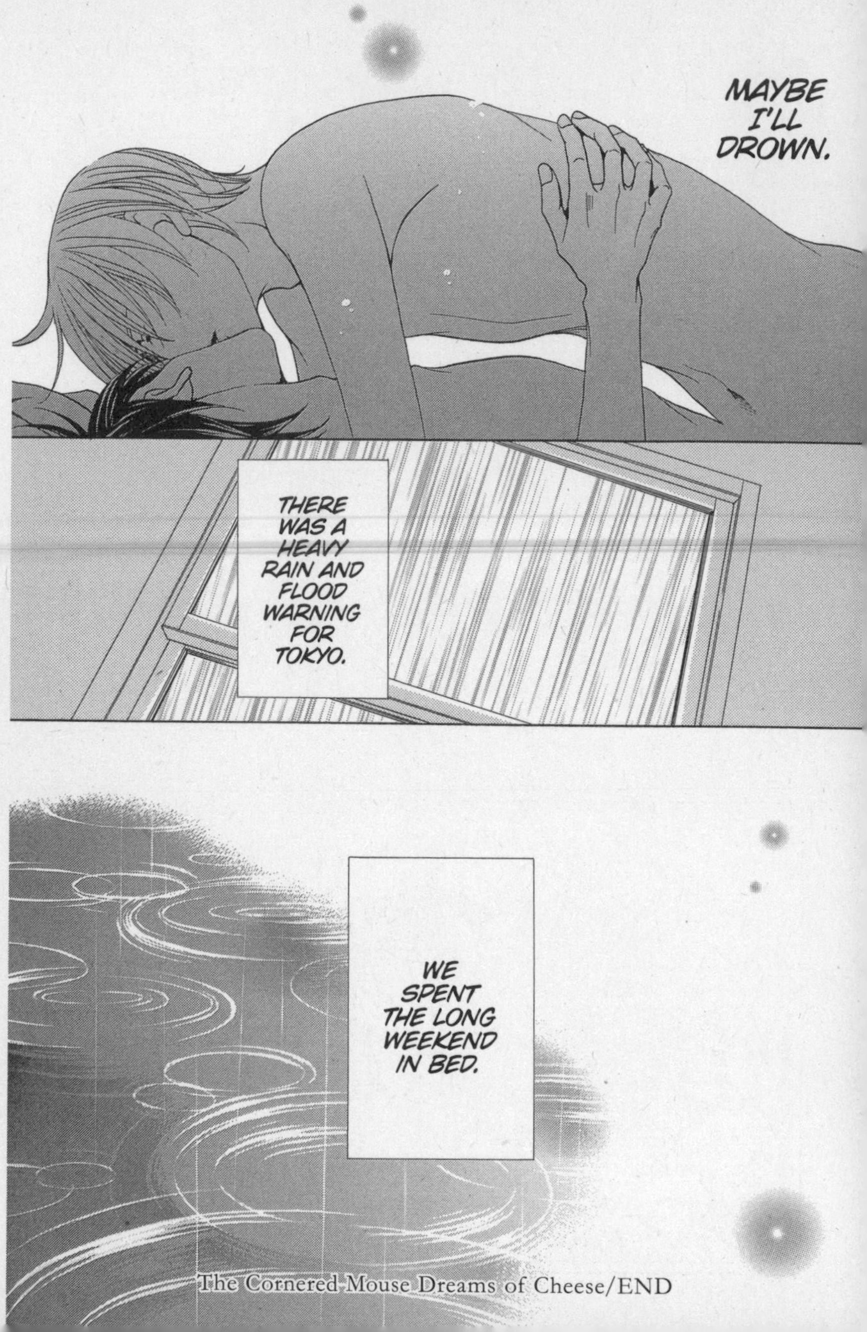
MAYBE I'LL DROWN.
THERE WAS A HEAVY RAIN AND FLOOD WARNING FOR TOKYO.
WE SPENT THE LONG WEEKEND IN BED.
The Cornered Mouse Dreams of Cheese/END

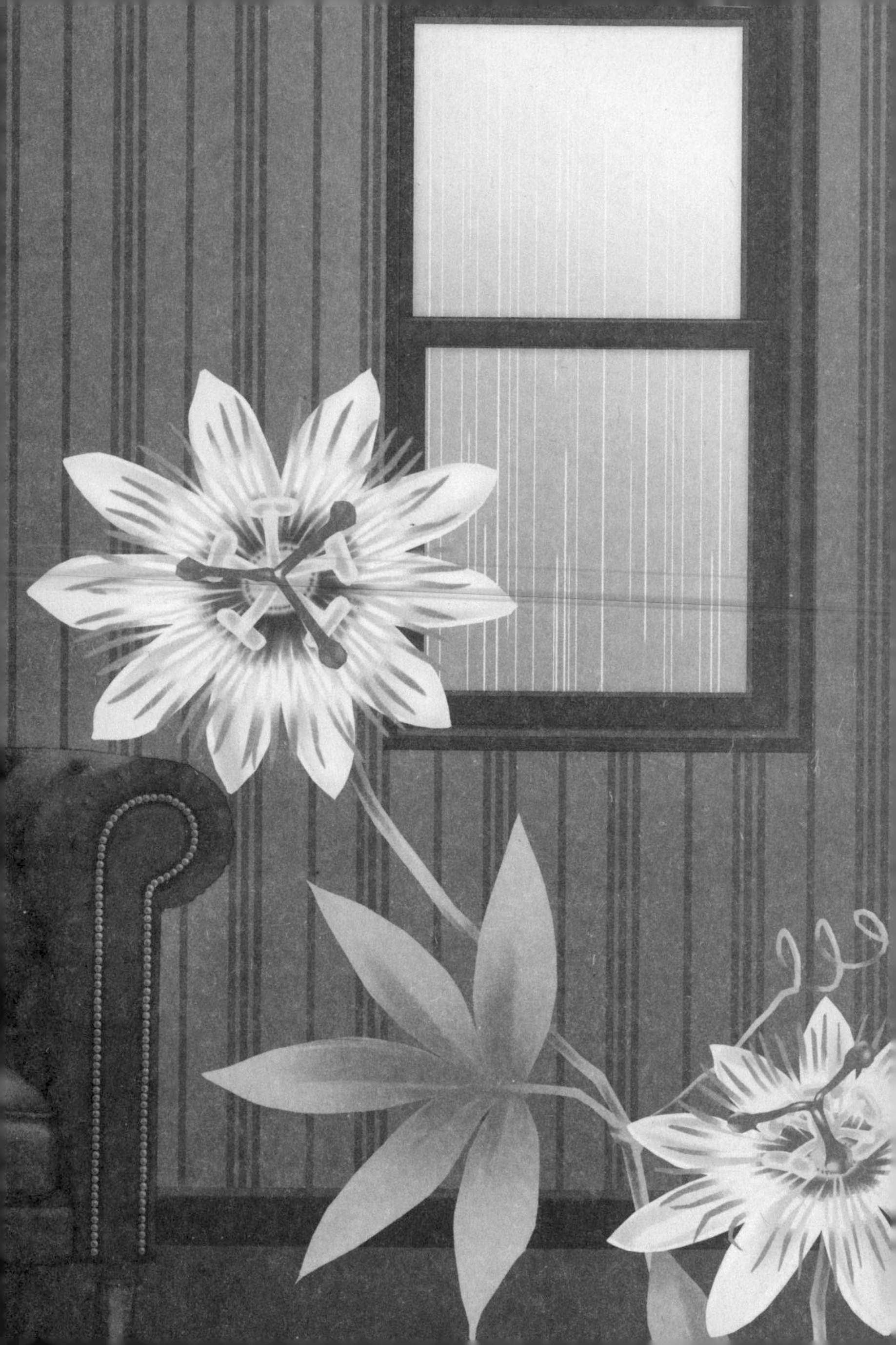

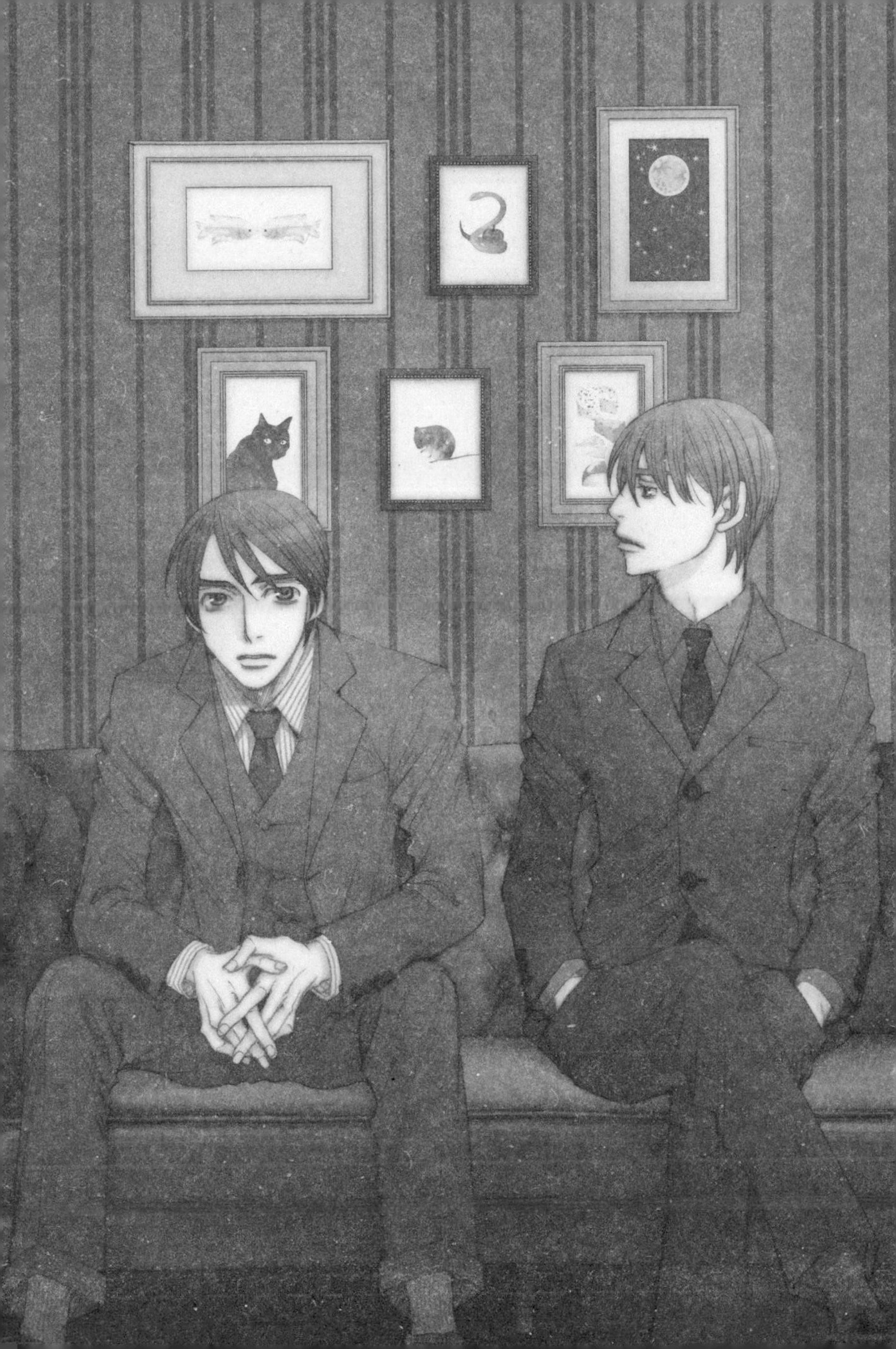